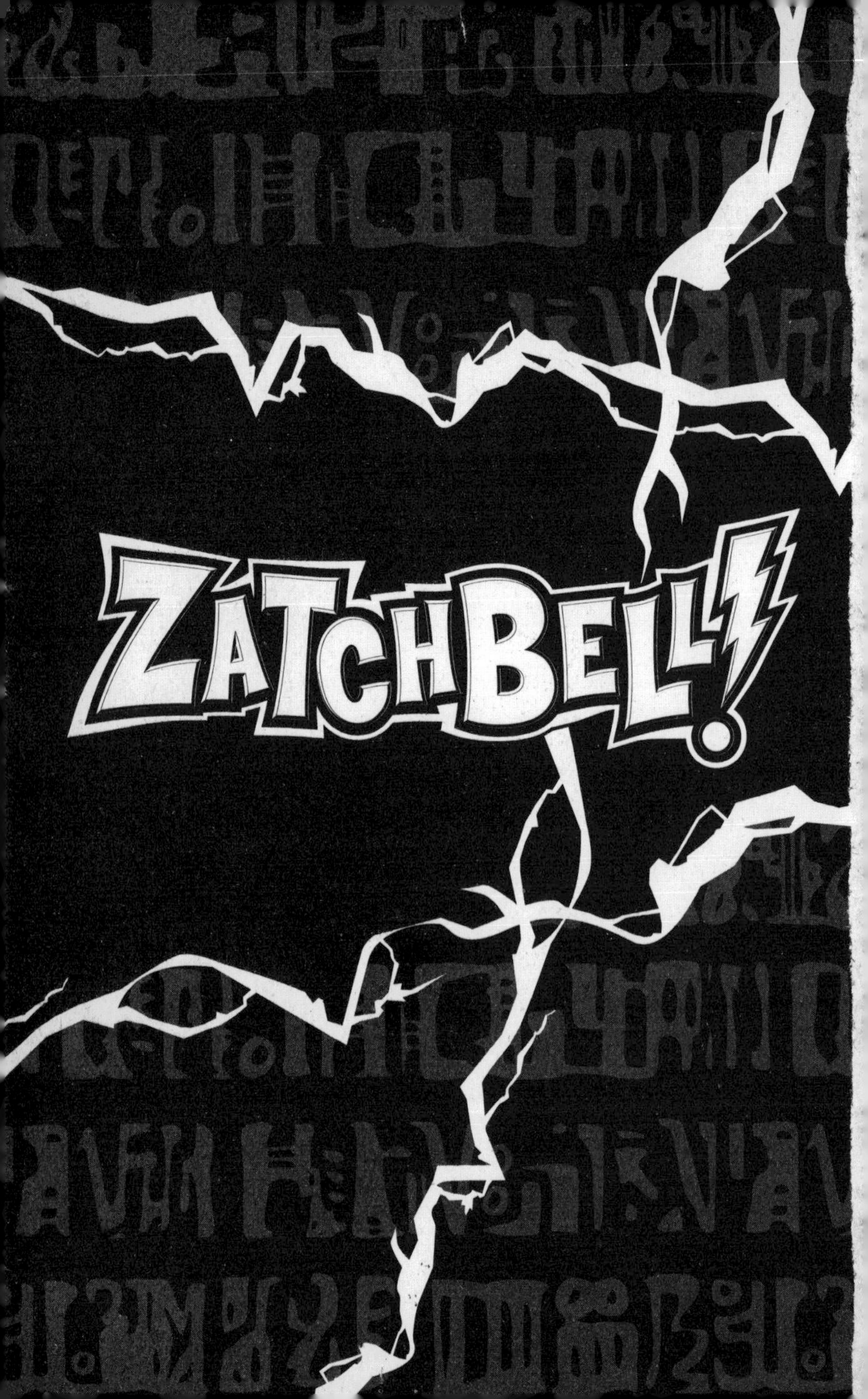
ZATCH BELL!

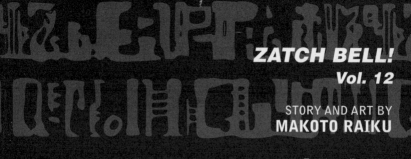

ZATCH BELL!
Vol. 12

STORY AND ART BY
MAKOTO RAIKU

Translation/David Ury
Touch-up Art & Lettering/Gabe Crate
Design/Izumi Hirayama
Special Thanks/Jessica Villat, Miki Macaluso,
Mitsuko Kitajima, and Akane Matsuo
Editor/Kit Fox

Managing Editor/Annette Roman
Editorial Director/Elizabeth Kawasaki
Editor in Chief/Alvin Lu
Sr. Director of Acquisitions/Rika Inouye
Sr. VP of Marketing/Liza Coppola
Exec. VP of Sales & Marketing/John Easum
Publisher/Hyoe Narita

Printed in the U.S.A.

Published by VIZ Media, LLC
P.O. Box 77010
San Francisco, CA 94107

10 9 8 7 6 5 4 3 2 1
First printing, April 2007

VIZ
MEDIA

www.viz.com

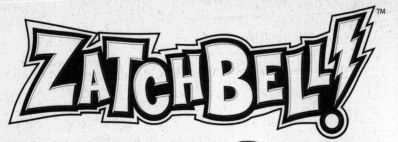

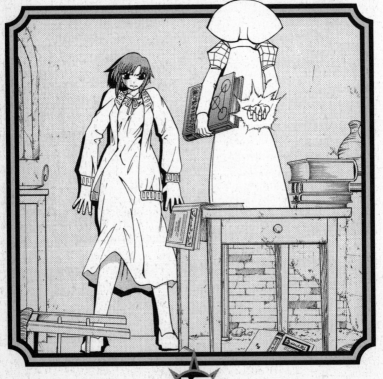

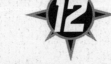

STORY AND ART BY
MAKOTO RAIKU

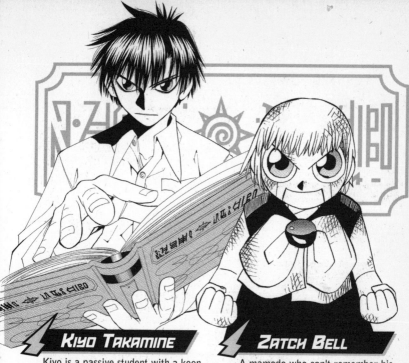

 KIYO TAKAMINE

Kiyo is a passive student with a keen intellect. When Kiyo meets Zatch he assumes ownership of the "Red Book" and starts to grow up.

 ZATCH BELL

A mamodo who can't remember his past. When Kiyo holds the "Red Book" and reads a spell, lightning bolts shoot from Zatch's mouth. He is fighting to be a "kind king."

✹ THE STORY THUS FAR ✹

The battle to determine who will be the next king of the mamodo world takes place every 1,000 years in the human world. Each mamodo owns a "book" which increases its unique powers, and they must team up with a human in order to fight for their own survival. Zatch is one of 100 mamodo chosen to fight in this battle, and his partner is Kiyo, a junior high school student. The bond between Zatch and Kiyo deepens as they continue to survive through many harsh battles. Zatch swears, "I will fight to become a kind king."

The battle continues, and now the numbers of the remaining mamodo are less than 40. Meanwhile, the evil Milordo-Z prepares for a super secret mission... with a scheme to manipulate mamodo from 1,000 years ago that were trapped in suspended animation. Milordo-Z plans to use them to get rid of the remaining mamodo all at once! Zatch and Kiyo must stand up against this fiend whose evil plan is to become king without even participating in battle!

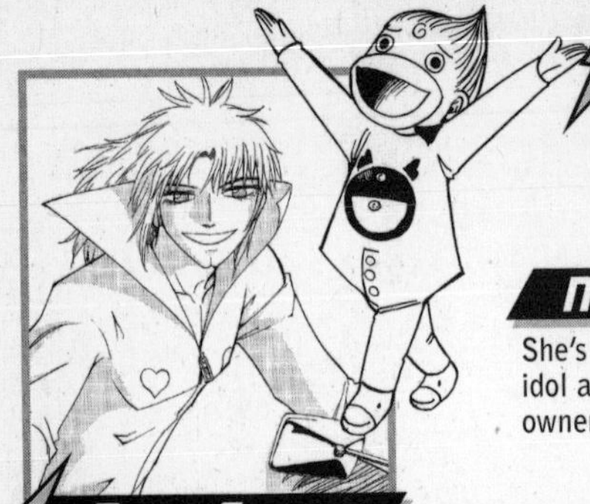

KANCHOMÉ

He was a failure in the mamodo world. He's a happy-go-lucky guy who makes mistakes all the time, but...

MEGUMI

She's a popular pop idol and Tia's book owner.

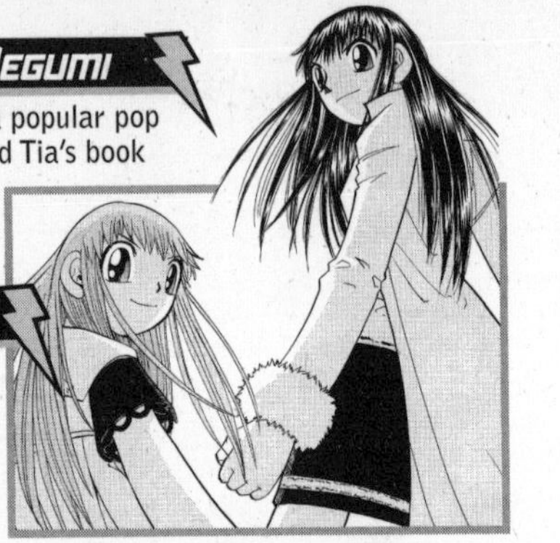

PARCO FOLGORE

He's an Italian super star and Kanchomé's book owner. He loves girls.

TIA

She's a mamodo who's friends with Zatch. She's a tough cookie..

KEDO

A mamodo who believes everything Doctor Riddles says.

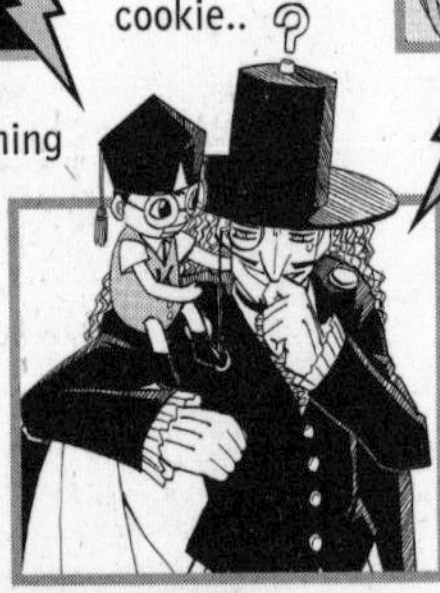

DOCTOR RIDDLES

He knows everything...or not. He's also Kedo's book owner.

SHERRY

Brago's book owner. She's searching for her best friend Koko.

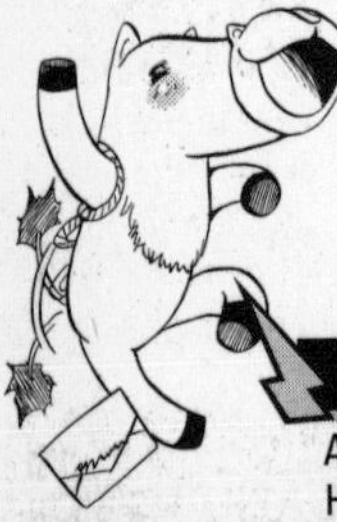

PONYGON

A mamodo who stays at Kiyo's house. He doesn't have a book owner yet.

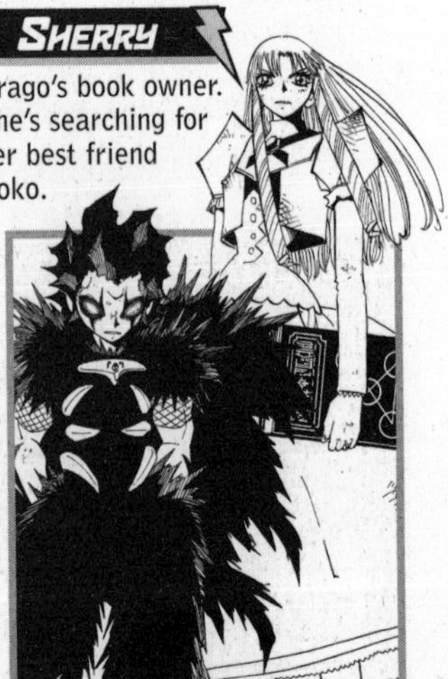

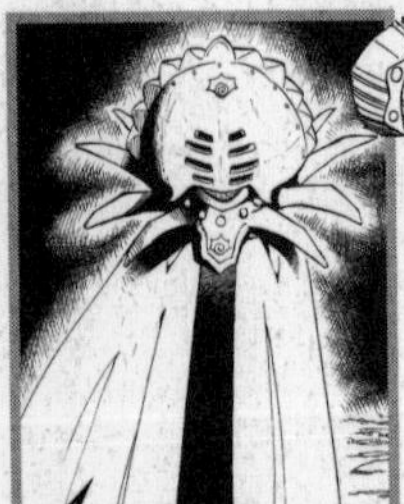

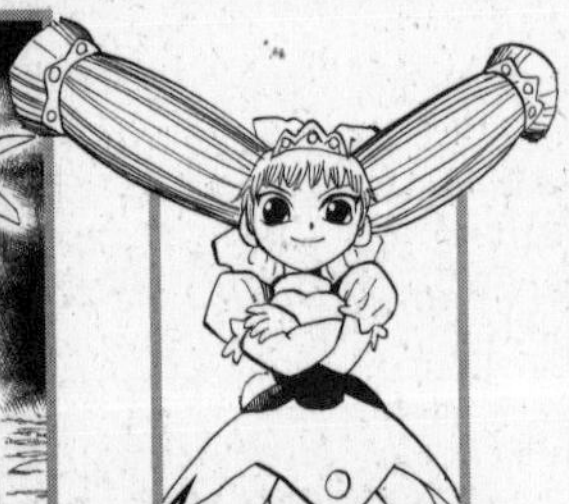

MILORDO-Z

A mysterious, evil mamodo who manipulates the mamodo from 1,000 years ago.

PENNY

She's a mamodo who was in love with Zatch in the mamodo world...and she's the jealous type.

BRAGO

A mamodo who has the power to control gravity. He's got a black book and is always tough and calm.

ZATCHBELL! 12

CONTENTS

LEVEL 104: The Rematch

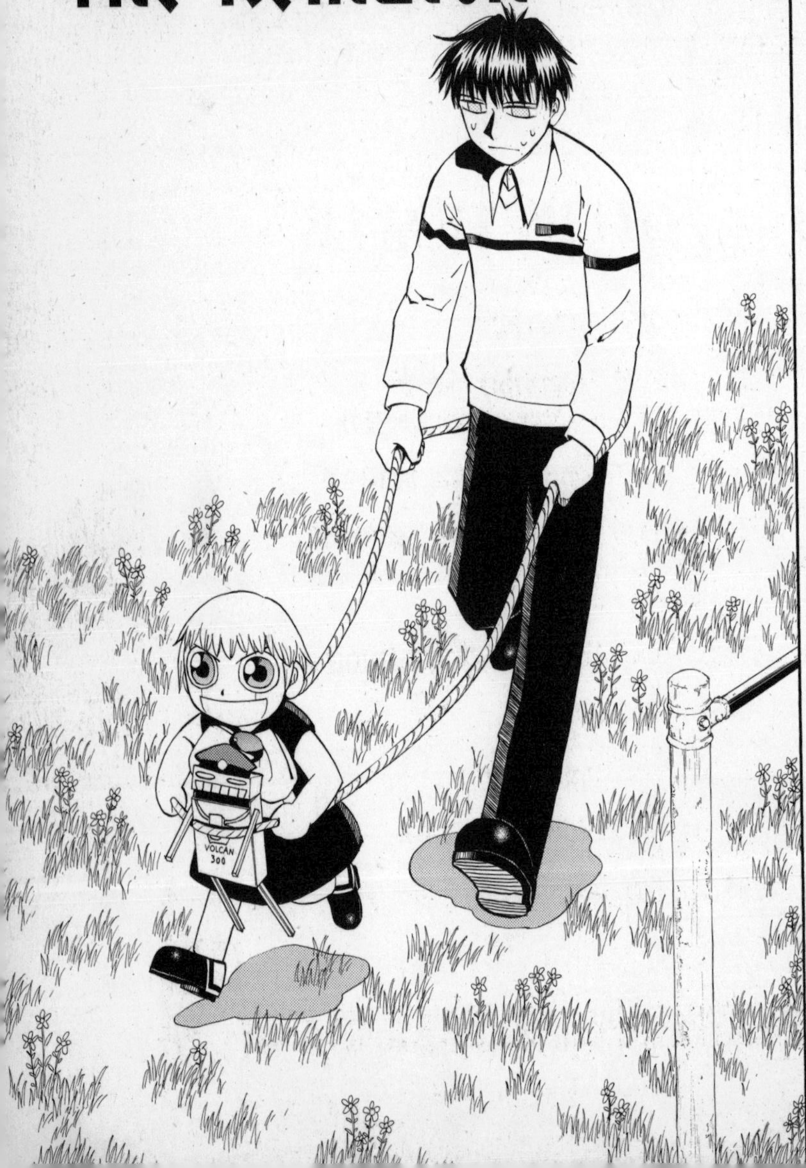
VOLCAN 300

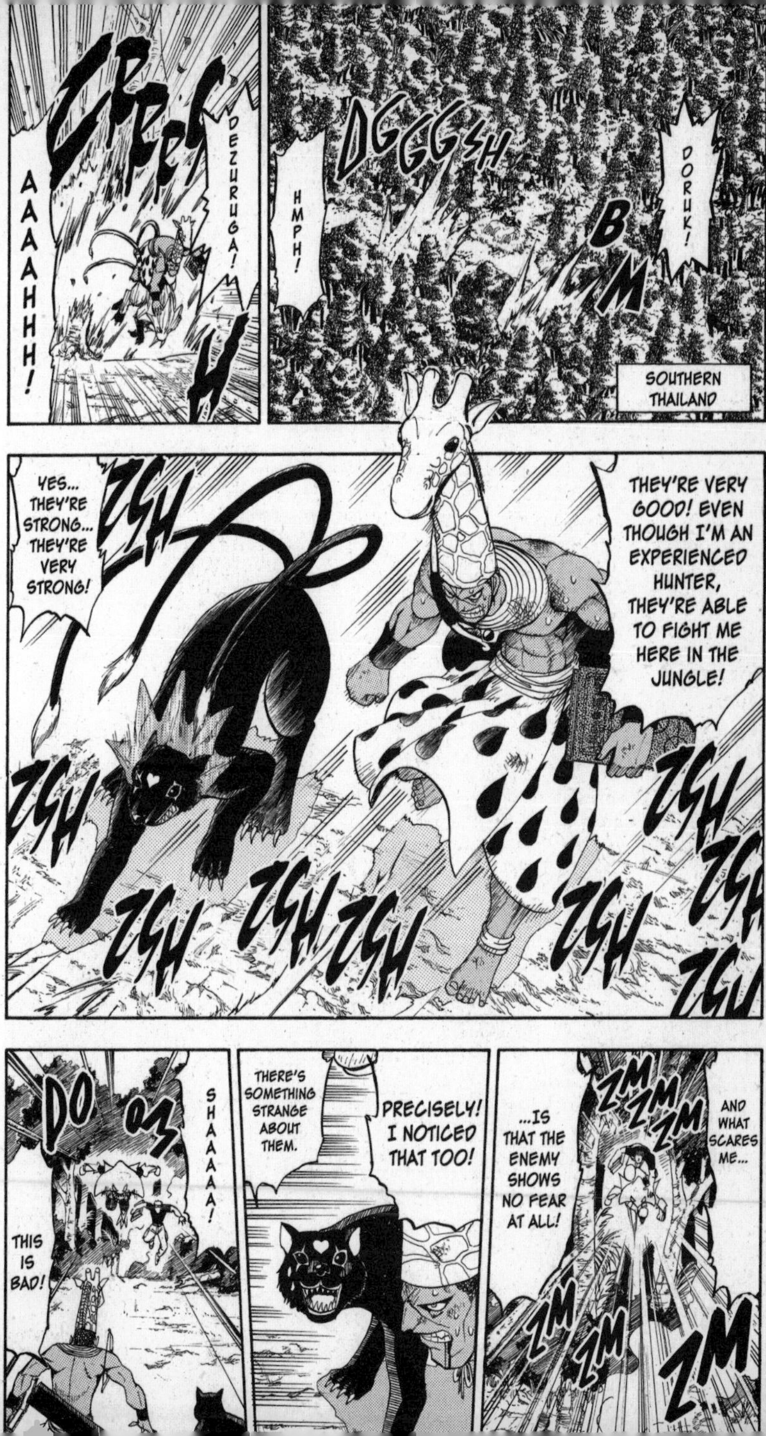
SOUTHERN THAILAND
DGGGSH
DORUK!
BMM
HMPH!
CRRRSH
DEZURUGA!
AAAAAHHH!
THEY'RE VERY GOOD! EVEN THOUGH I'M AN EXPERIENCED HUNTER, THEY'RE ABLE TO FIGHT ME HERE IN THE JUNGLE!
YES... THEY'RE STRONG... THEY'RE VERY STRONG!
ZSH ZSH ZSH ZSH ZSH ZSH ZSH ZSH
AND WHAT SCARES ME...
...IS THAT THE ENEMY SHOWS NO FEAR AT ALL!
ZM ZM ZM ZM ZM ZM
PRECISELY! I NOTICED THAT TOO!
THERE'S SOMETHING STRANGE ABOUT THEM.
SHAAAAAA!
DOOM
THIS IS BAD!

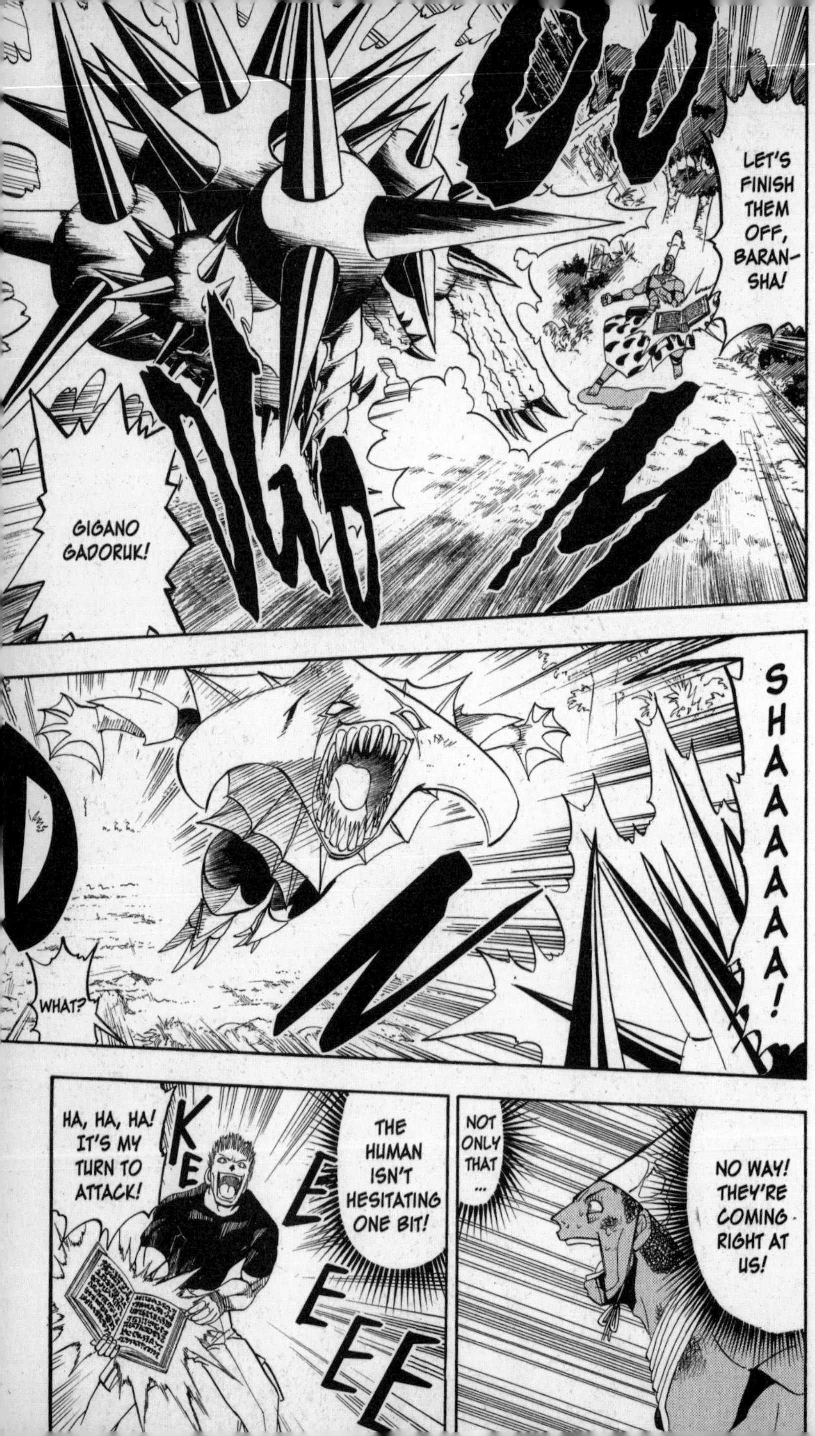
LET'S FINISH THEM OFF, BARAN-SHA!
GIGANO GADORUK!
SHAAAAAAA!
WHAT?
NO WAY! THEY'RE COMING RIGHT AT US!
NOT ONLY THAT ...
THE HUMAN ISN'T HESITATING ONE BIT!
HA, HA, HA! IT'S MY TURN TO ATTACK!

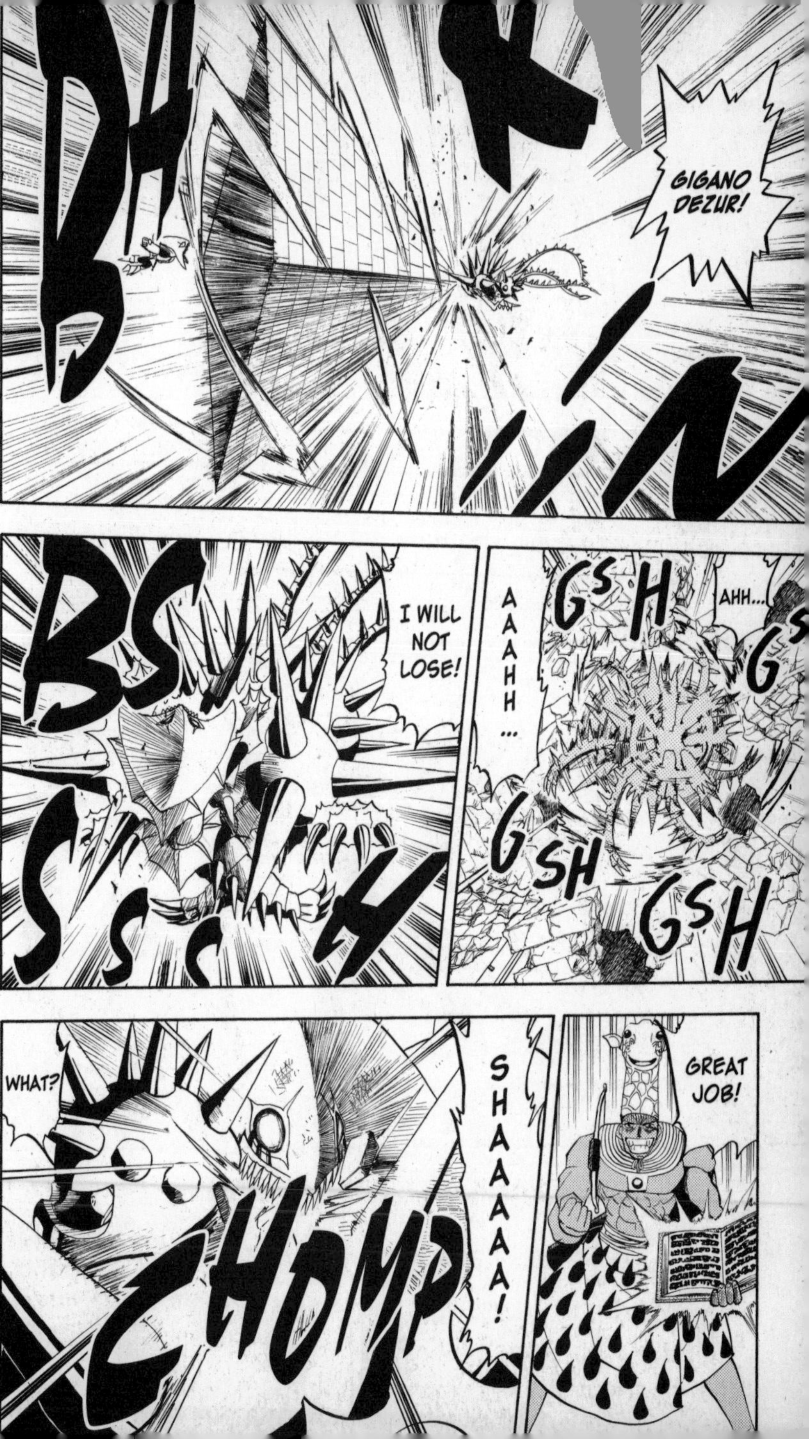
GIGANO DEZUR!
AHH...
GSH
GSH
GSH
GSH
AAAHH...
I WILL NOT LOSE!
BSSSCH
GREAT JOB!
SHAAAAAA!
WHAT?
CHOMP

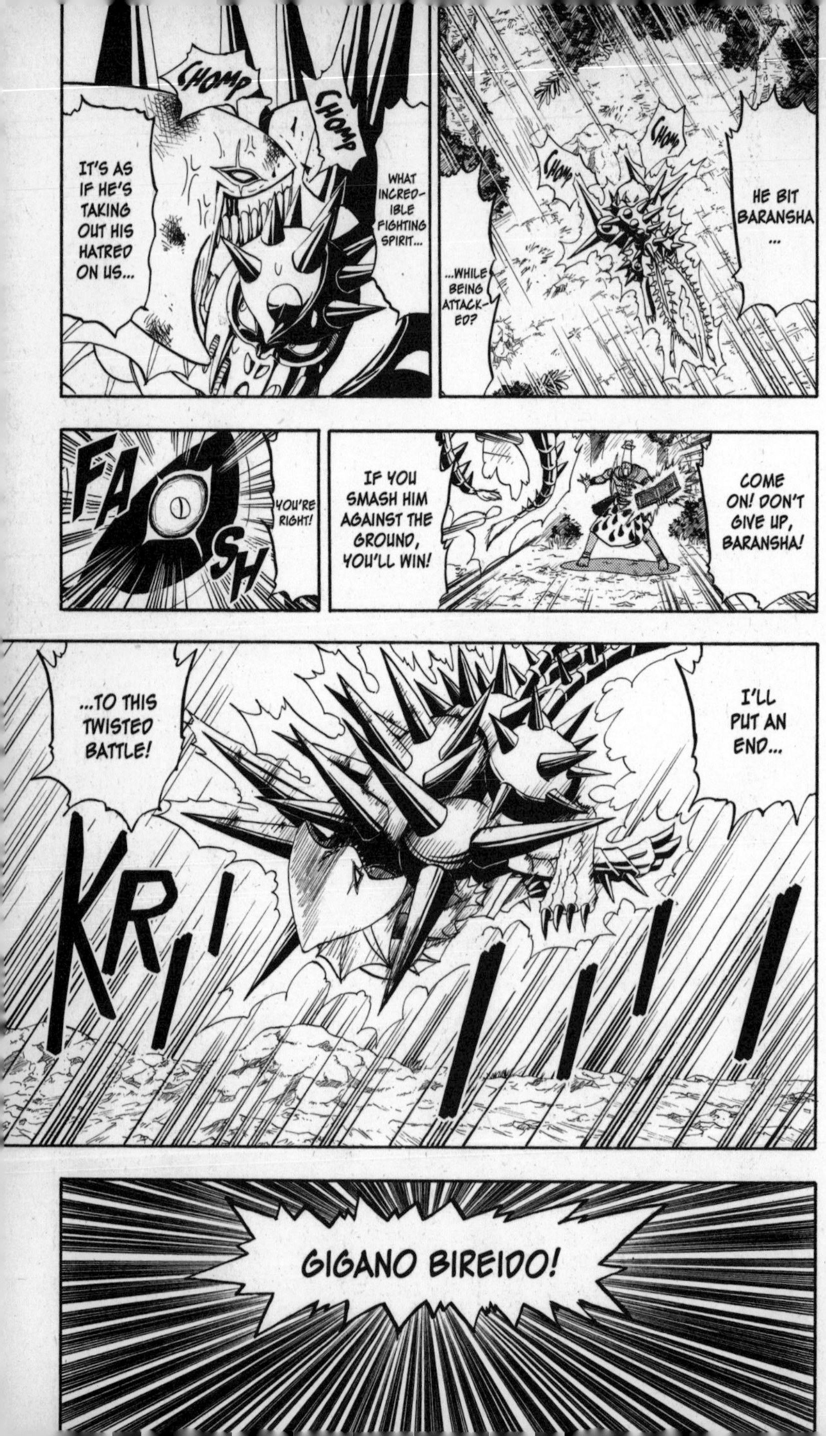
CHOMP
CHOMP
HE BIT BARANSHA...
...WHILE BEING ATTACKED?
CHOMP
CHOMP
WHAT INCREDIBLE FIGHTING SPIRIT...
IT'S AS IF HE'S TAKING OUT HIS HATRED ON US...
COME ON! DON'T GIVE UP, BARANSHA!
IF YOU SMASH HIM AGAINST THE GROUND, YOU'LL WIN!
YOU'RE RIGHT!
FASH
I'LL PUT AN END...
...TO THIS TWISTED BATTLE!
KRIIIII
GIGANO BIREIDO!

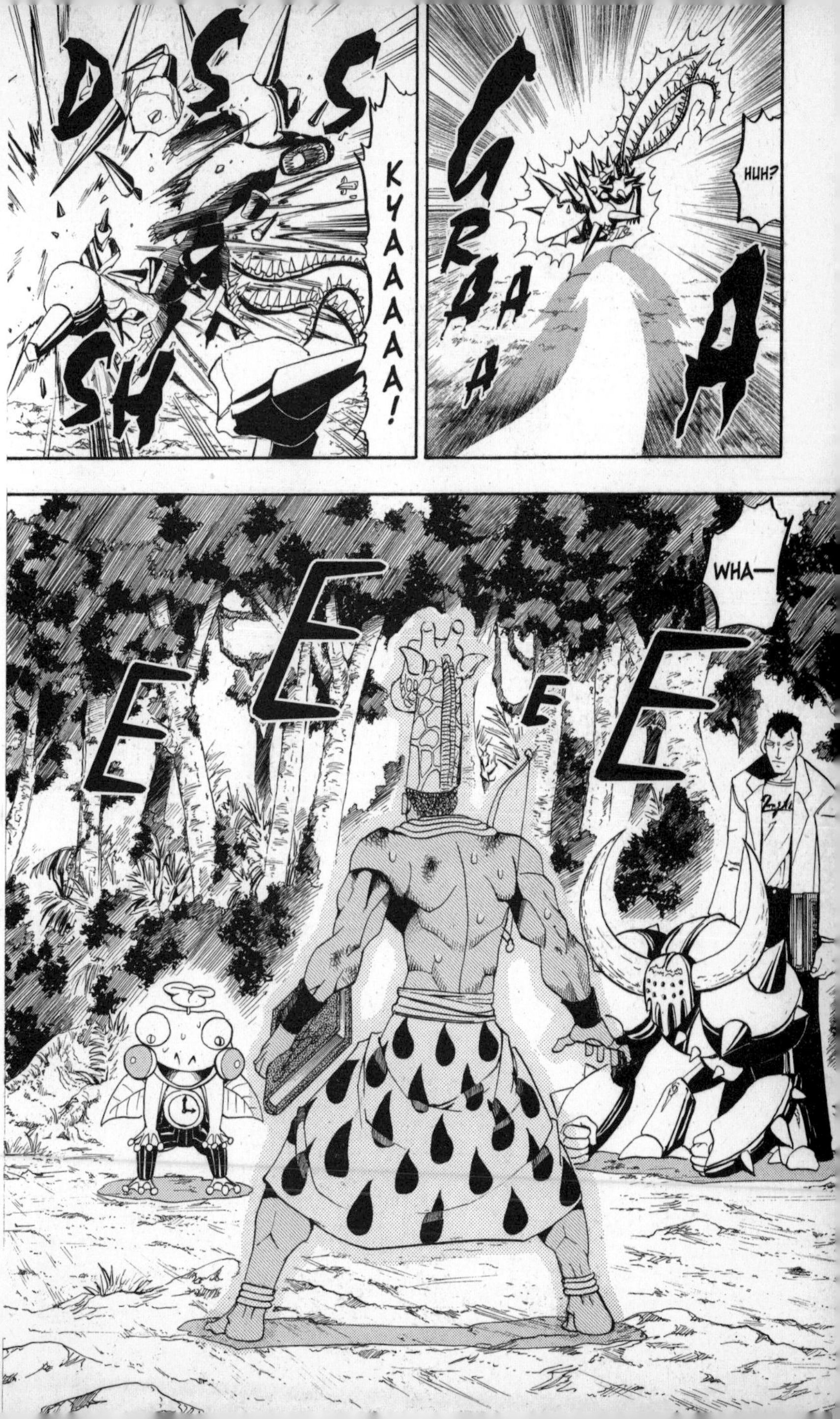
HUH?
GURAAAA
KYAAAAAA!
WHA—
EEeE

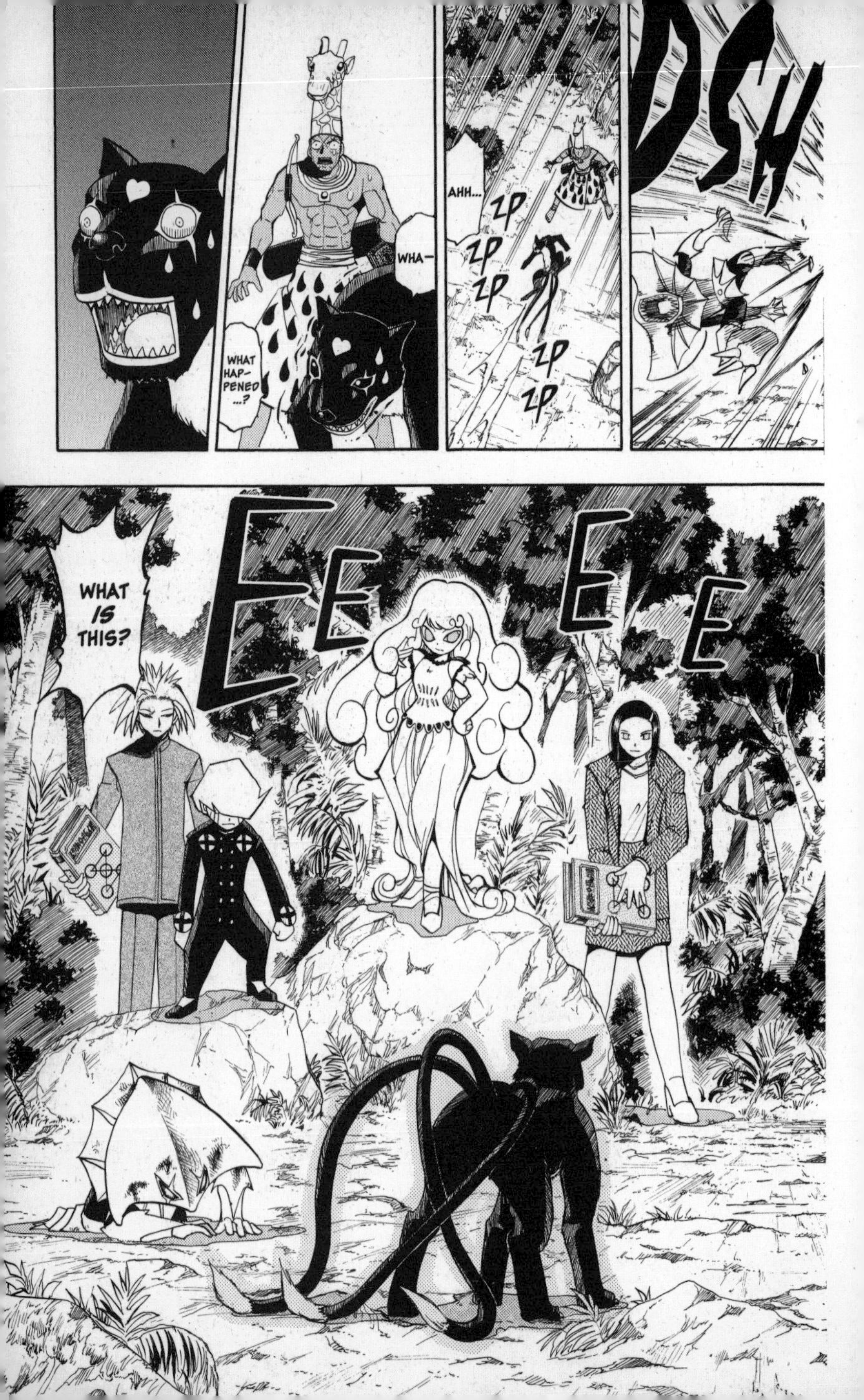
DSH
AHH...
ZP ZP ZP ZP ZP
WHA-
WHAT HAPPENED...?
EEEEE
WHAT IS THIS?

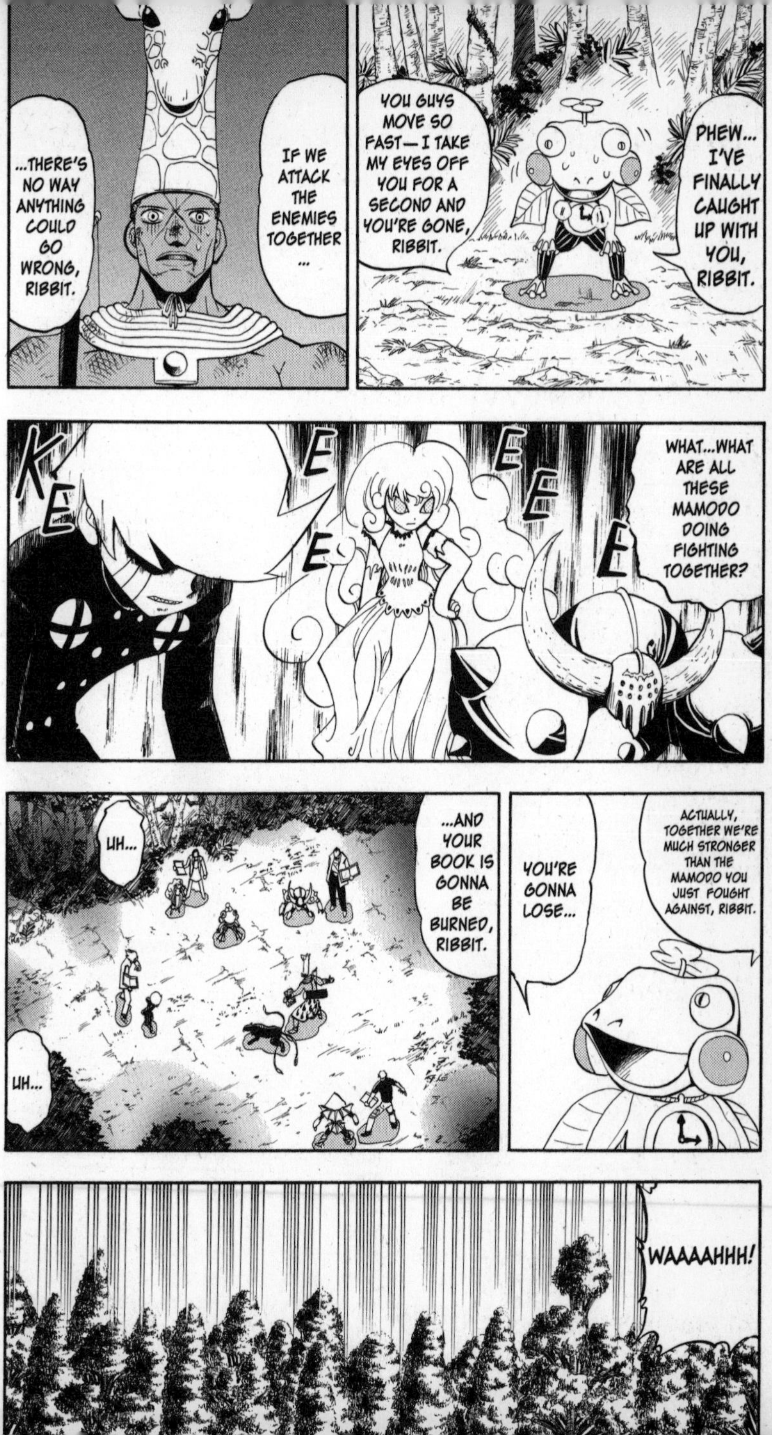
PHEW... I'VE FINALLY CAUGHT UP WITH YOU, RIBBIT.
YOU GUYS MOVE SO FAST—I TAKE MY EYES OFF YOU FOR A SECOND AND YOU'RE GONE, RIBBIT.
IF WE ATTACK THE ENEMIES TOGETHER...
...THERE'S NO WAY ANYTHING COULD GO WRONG, RIBBIT.
WHAT...WHAT ARE ALL THESE MAMODO DOING FIGHTING TOGETHER?
KEEEEEEE
ACTUALLY, TOGETHER WE'RE MUCH STRONGER THAN THE MAMODO YOU JUST FOUGHT AGAINST, RIBBIT.
YOU'RE GONNA LOSE...
...AND YOUR BOOK IS GONNA BE BURNED, RIBBIT.
UH...
UH...
WAAAAHHH!

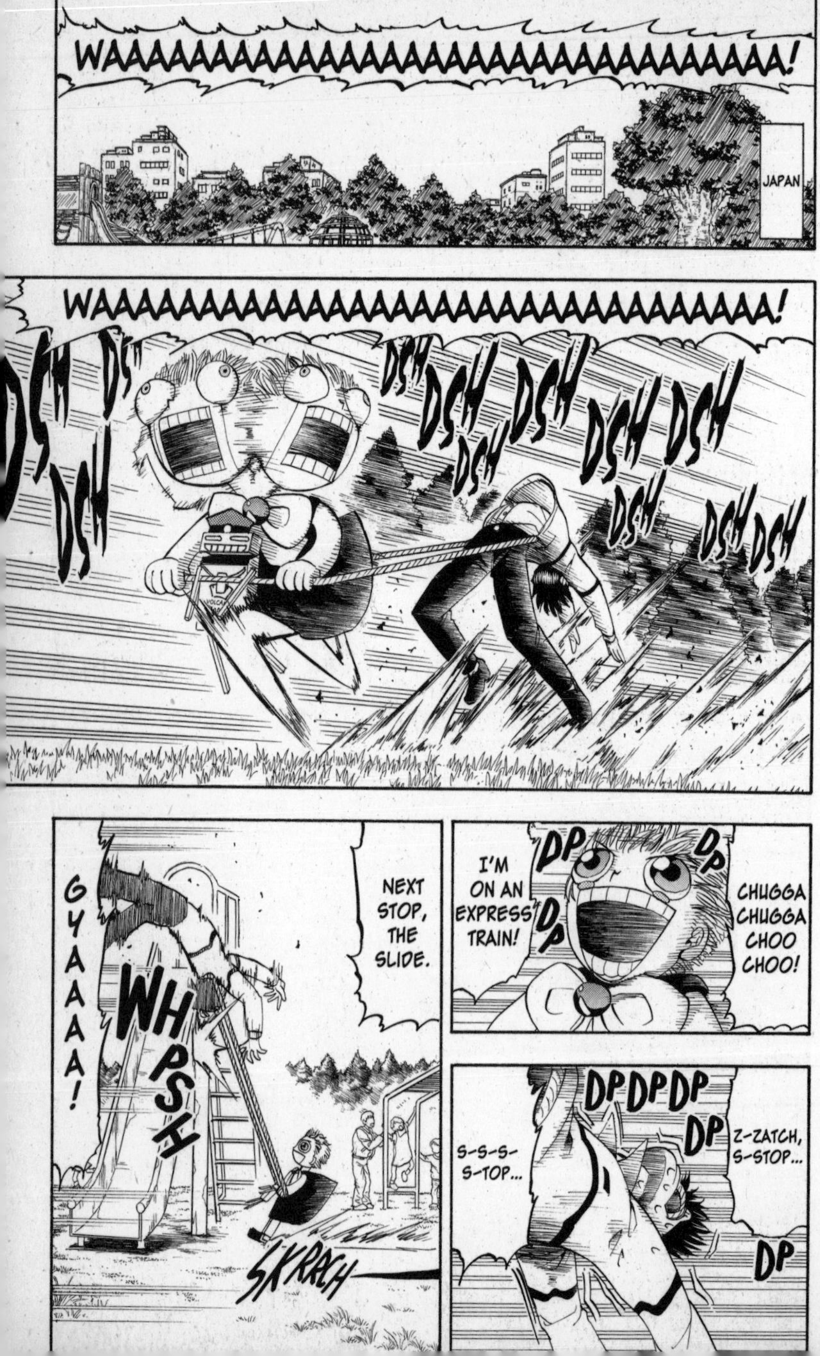
WAAAAAAAAAAAAAAAAAAAAAAAAAAAAAAAAAAA!
JAPAN
WAAAAAAAAAAAAAAAAAAAAAAAAAAAAAAAAAAAA!
DSH DSH DSH DSH DSH DSH DSH DSH DSH DSH DSH DSH DSH
CHUGGA CHUGGA CHOO CHOO!
DP DP DP
I'M ON AN EXPRESS TRAIN!
Z-ZATCH, S-STOP...
DP DP DP DP
S-S-S-S-TOP...
DP
NEXT STOP, THE SLIDE.
GYAAAAA!
WHPSH
SKRRCH

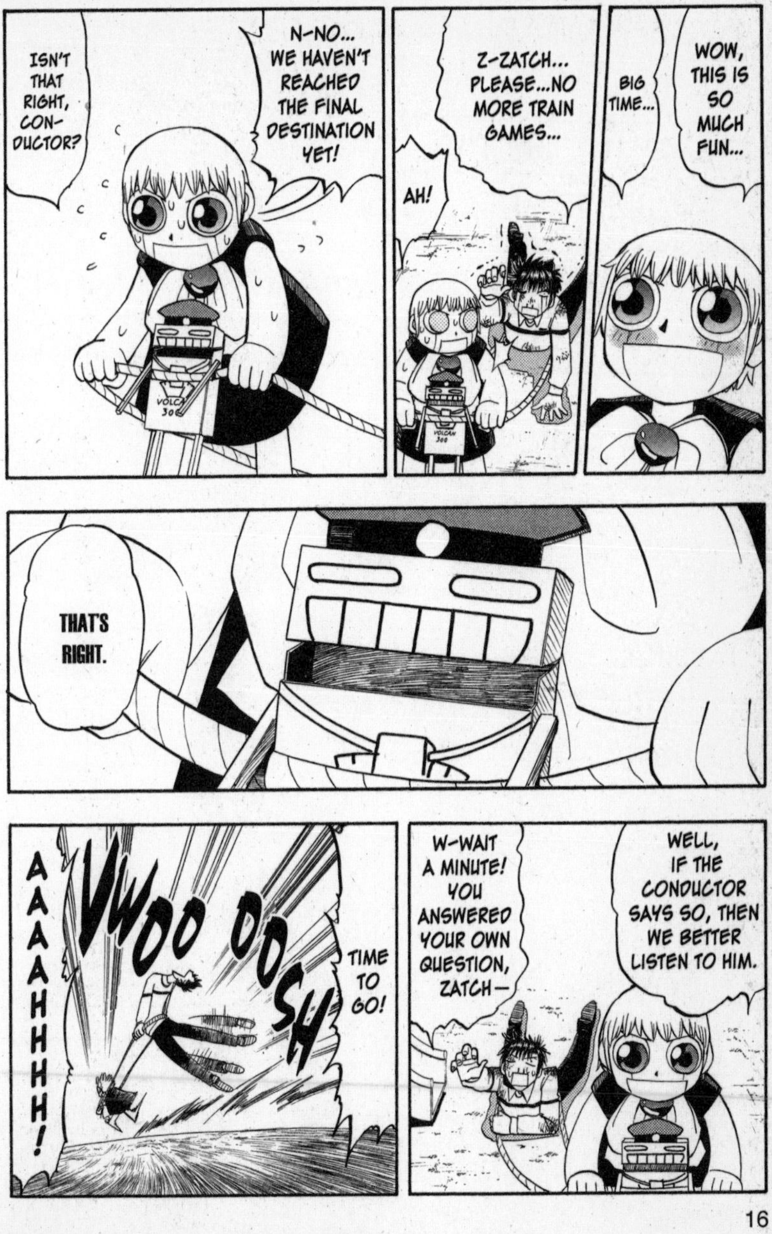
WOW, THIS IS SO MUCH FUN...
BIG TIME...
Z-ZATCH... PLEASE...NO MORE TRAIN GAMES...
AH!
N-NO... WE HAVEN'T REACHED THE FINAL DESTINATION YET!
ISN'T THAT RIGHT, CON-DUCTOR?
VOLCAN 300
VOLCAN 300
THAT'S RIGHT.
WELL, IF THE CONDUCTOR SAYS SO, THEN WE BETTER LISTEN TO HIM.
W-WAIT A MINUTE! YOU ANSWERED YOUR OWN QUESTION, ZATCH—
TIME TO GO!
VWOOOOSH
AAAAHHHHH!

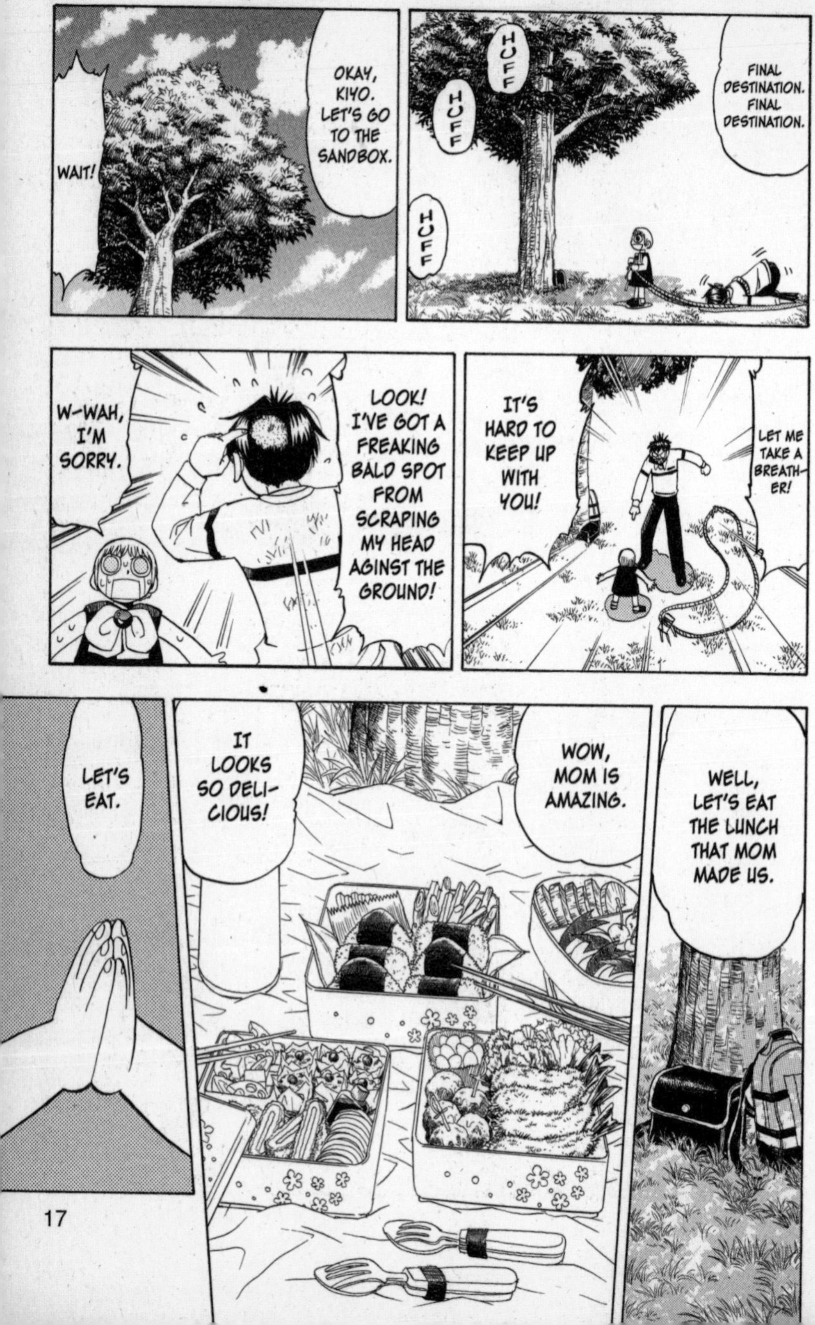
FINAL DESTINATION. FINAL DESTINATION.
HUFF
HUFF
HUFF
OKAY, KIYO. LET'S GO TO THE SANDBOX.
WAIT!
LET ME TAKE A BREATHER!
IT'S HARD TO KEEP UP WITH YOU!
LOOK! I'VE GOT A FREAKING BALD SPOT FROM SCRAPING MY HEAD AGINST THE GROUND!
W-WAH, I'M SORRY.
WELL, LET'S EAT THE LUNCH THAT MOM MADE US.
WOW, MOM IS AMAZING.
IT LOOKS SO DELI-CIOUS!
LET'S EAT.

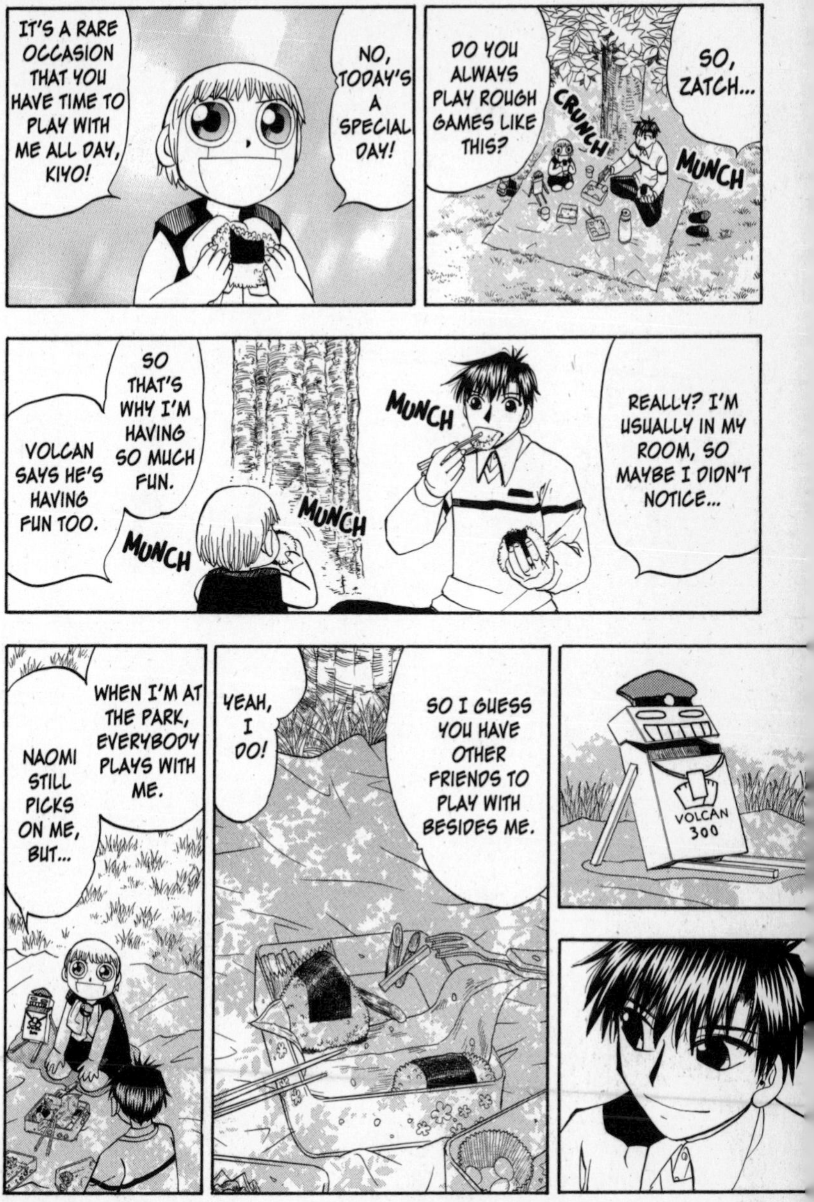
SO, ZATCH...
DO YOU ALWAYS PLAY ROUGH GAMES LIKE THIS?
CRUNCH
MUNCH
NO, TODAY'S A SPECIAL DAY!
IT'S A RARE OCCASION THAT YOU HAVE TIME TO PLAY WITH ME ALL DAY, KIYO!
REALLY? I'M USUALLY IN MY ROOM, SO MAYBE I DIDN'T NOTICE...
MUNCH
MUNCH
SO THAT'S WHY I'M HAVING SO MUCH FUN.
VOLCAN SAYS HE'S HAVING FUN TOO.
MUNCH
VOLCAN 300
SO I GUESS YOU HAVE OTHER FRIENDS TO PLAY WITH BESIDES ME.
YEAH, I DO!
WHEN I'M AT THE PARK, EVERYBODY PLAYS WITH ME.
NAOMI STILL PICKS ON ME, BUT...

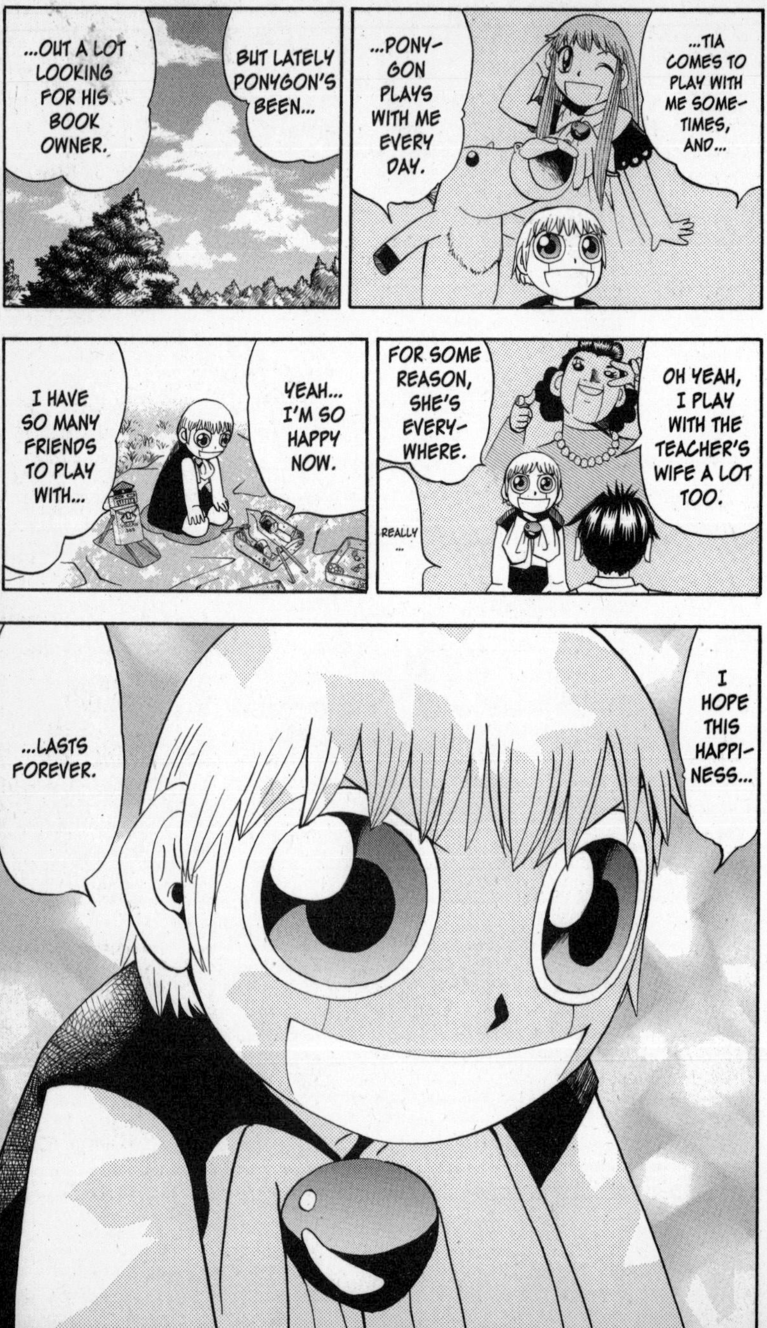
...TIA COMES TO PLAY WITH ME SOME-TIMES, AND...
...PONY-GON PLAYS WITH ME EVERY DAY.
BUT LATELY PONYGON'S BEEN...
...OUT A LOT LOOKING FOR HIS BOOK OWNER.
OH YEAH, I PLAY WITH THE TEACHER'S WIFE A LOT TOO.
FOR SOME REASON, SHE'S EVERY-WHERE.
REALLY...
YEAH... I'M SO HAPPY NOW.
I HAVE SO MANY FRIENDS TO PLAY WITH...
I HOPE THIS HAPPI-NESS...
...LASTS FOREVER.

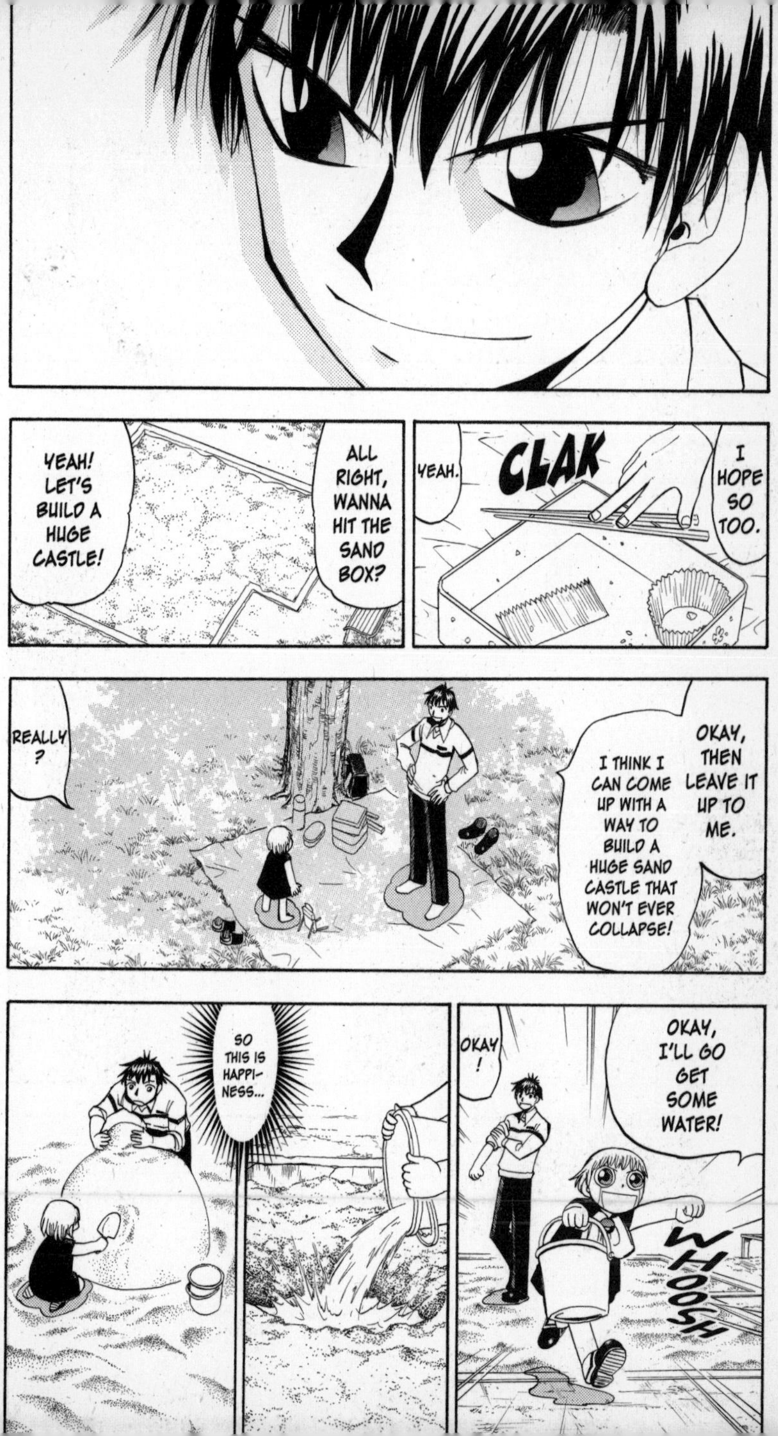
I HOPE SO TOO.
CLAK
YEAH.
ALL RIGHT, WANNA HIT THE SAND BOX?
YEAH! LET'S BUILD A HUGE CASTLE!
OKAY, THEN LEAVE IT UP TO ME.
I THINK I CAN COME UP WITH A WAY TO BUILD A HUGE SAND CASTLE THAT WON'T EVER COLLAPSE!
REALLY?
OKAY, I'LL GO GET SOME WATER!
OKAY!
WHOOSH
SO THIS IS HAPPI-NESS...

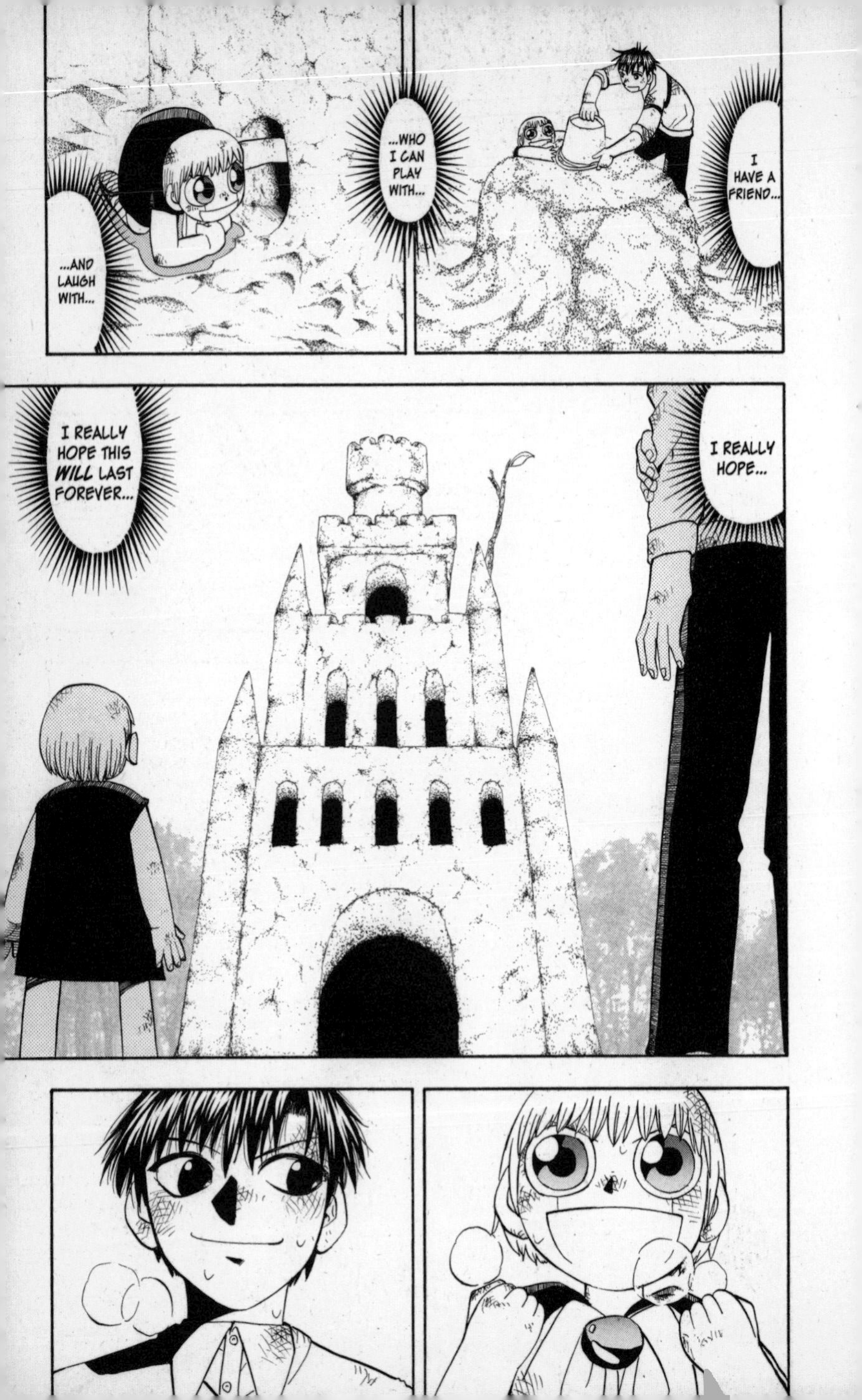
I HAVE A FRIEND...
...WHO I CAN PLAY WITH...
...AND LAUGH WITH...
I REALLY HOPE...
I REALLY HOPE THIS *WILL* LAST FOREVER...

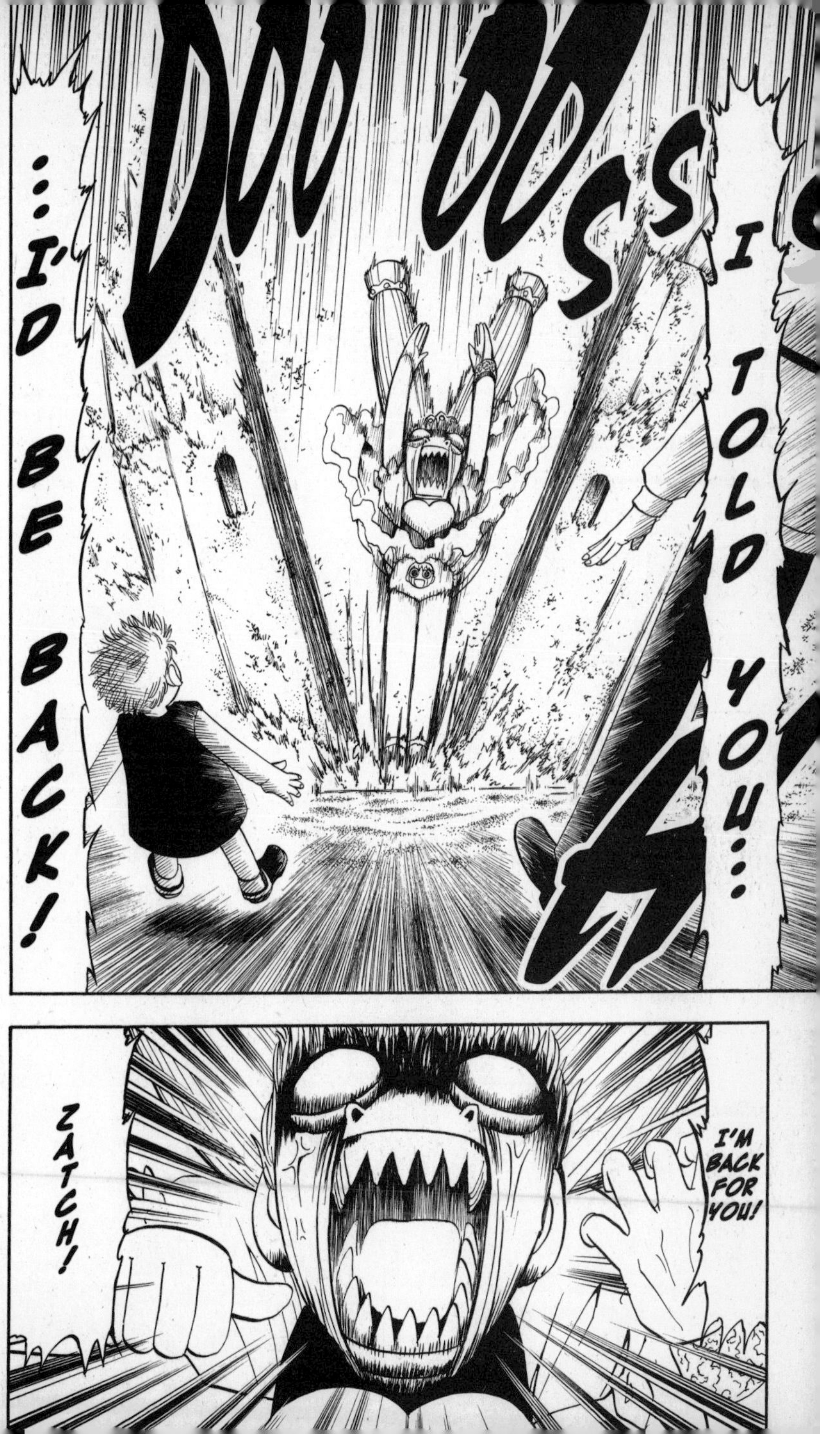
DOOOOSS
I TOLD YOU...
...I'D BE BACK!
I'M BACK FOR YOU!
ZATCH!

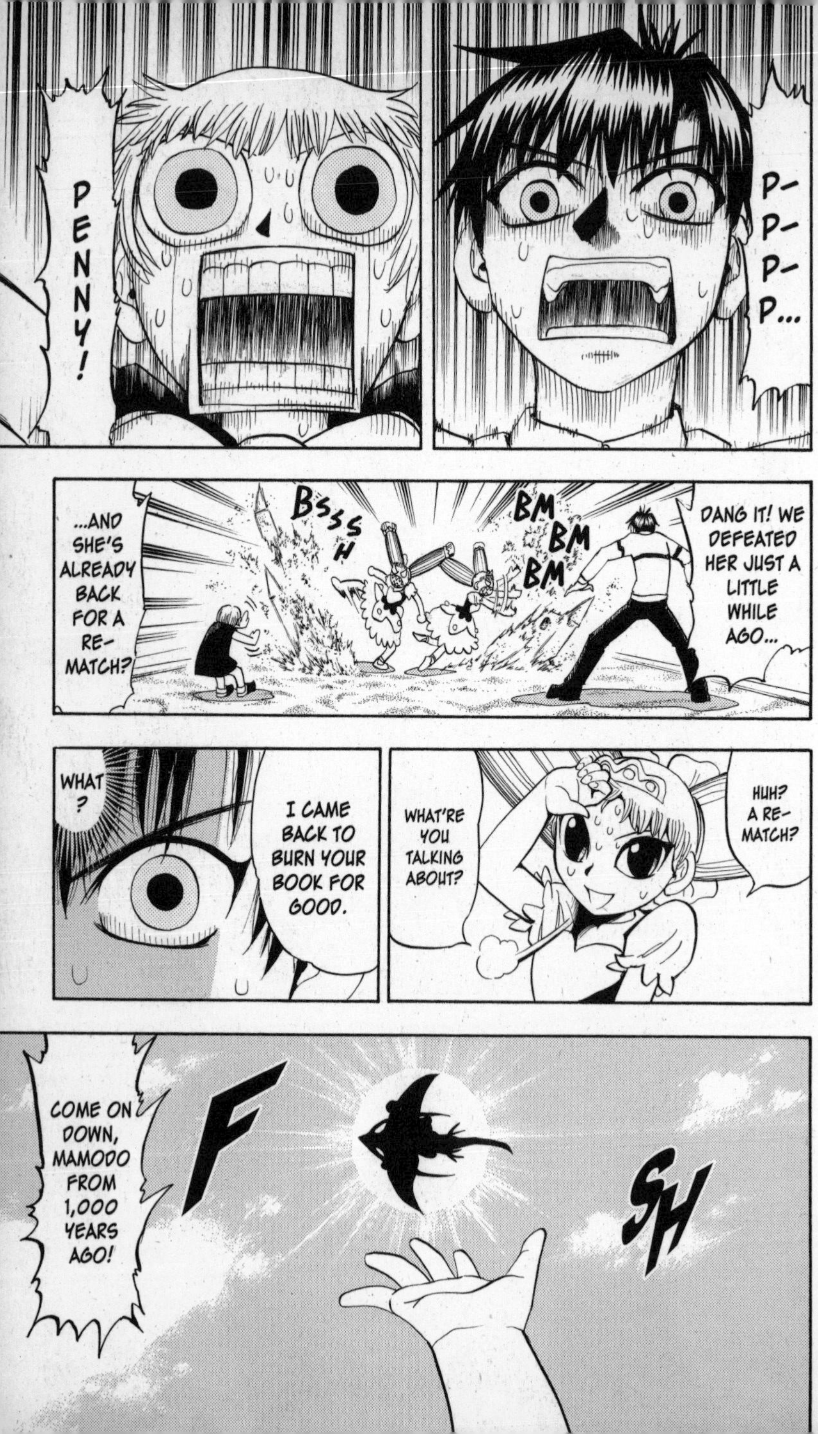
P- P- P- P...
PENNY!
DANG IT! WE DEFEATED HER JUST A LITTLE WHILE AGO...
BM BM BM
BSSSH
...AND SHE'S ALREADY BACK FOR A RE-MATCH?
HUH? A RE-MATCH?
WHAT'RE YOU TALKING ABOUT?
I CAME BACK TO BURN YOUR BOOK FOR GOOD.
WHAT?
SH
F
COME ON DOWN, MAMODO FROM 1,000 YEARS AGO!

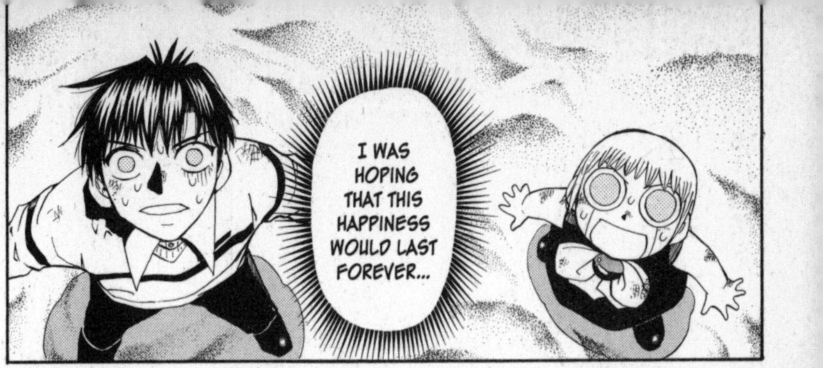
I WAS HOPING THAT THIS HAPPINESS WOULD LAST FOREVER...
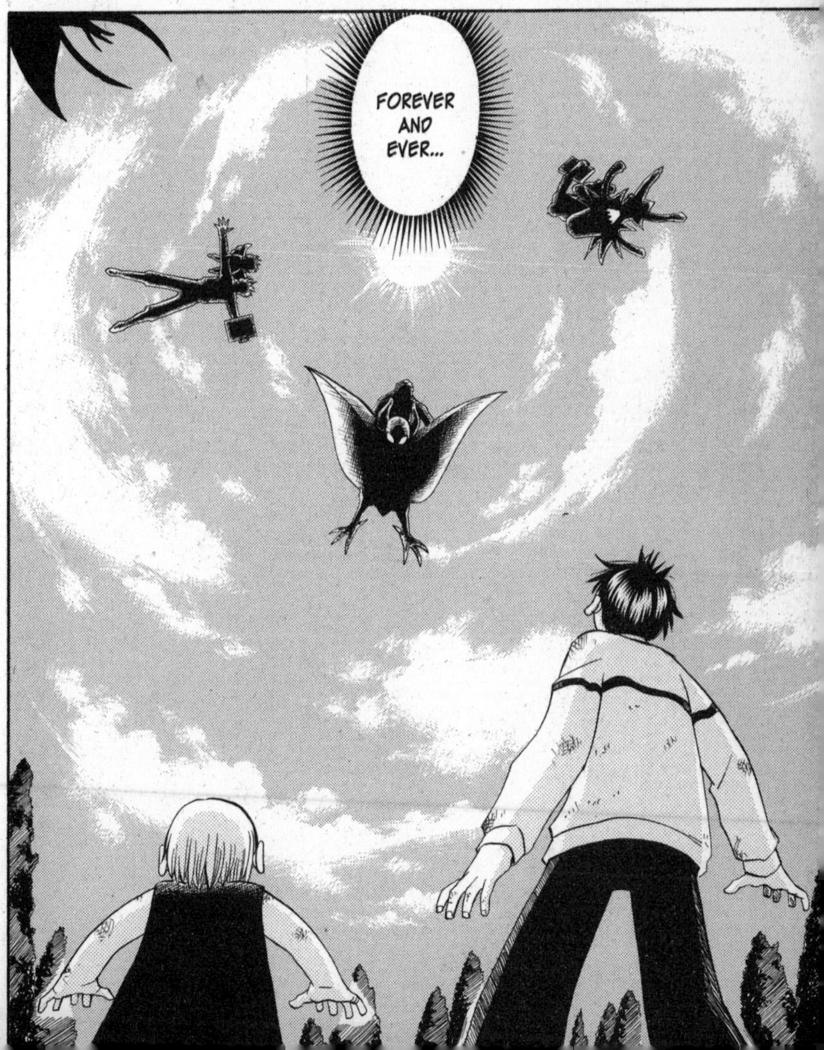
FOREVER AND EVER...

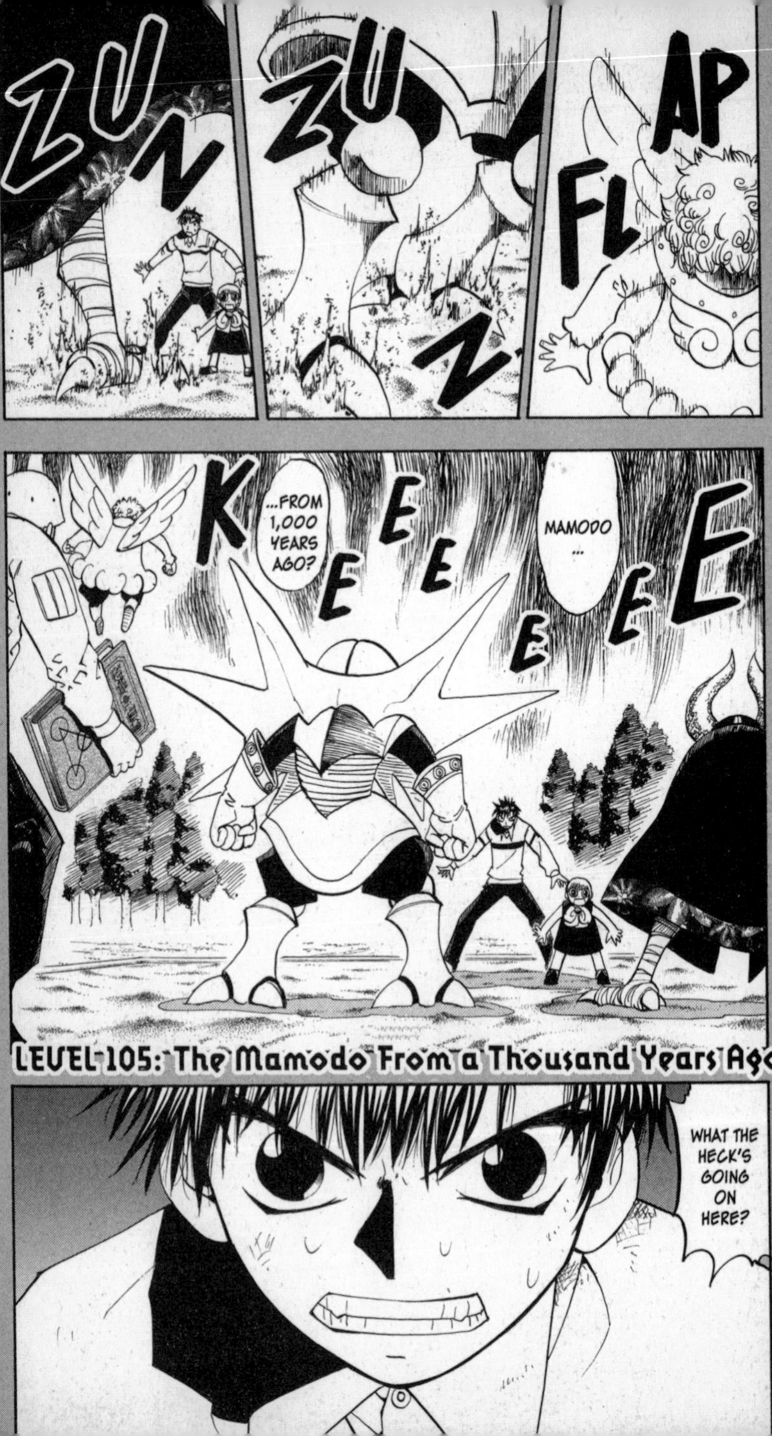
FLAP
ZUZUN
ZUN
MAMODO ...
...FROM 1,000 YEARS AGO?
KEEEEEEE
LEVEL 105: The Mamodo From a Thousand Years Ago
WHAT THE HECK'S GOING ON HERE?

LEVEL 105: The Mamodo From a Thousand Years Ago

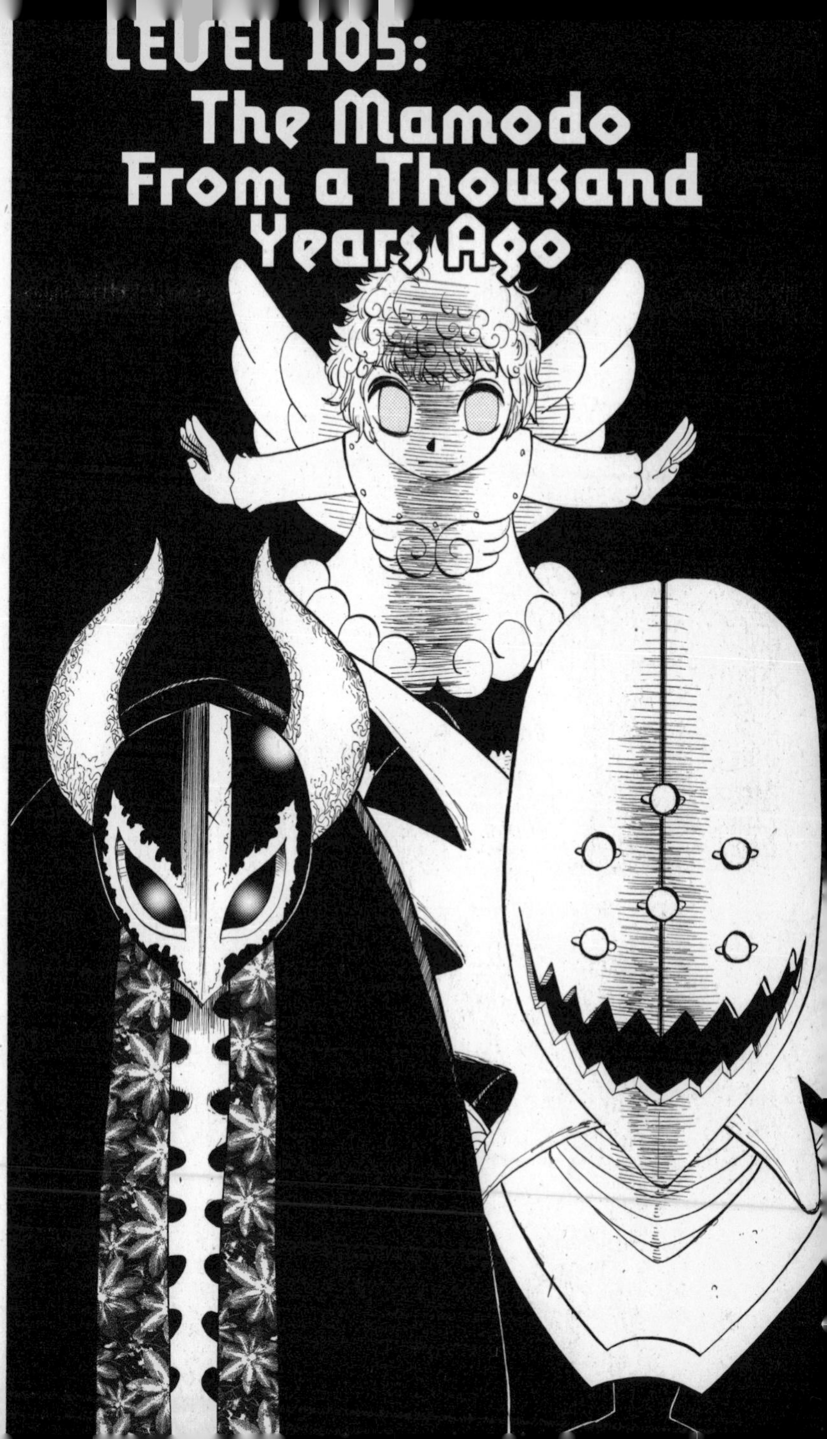

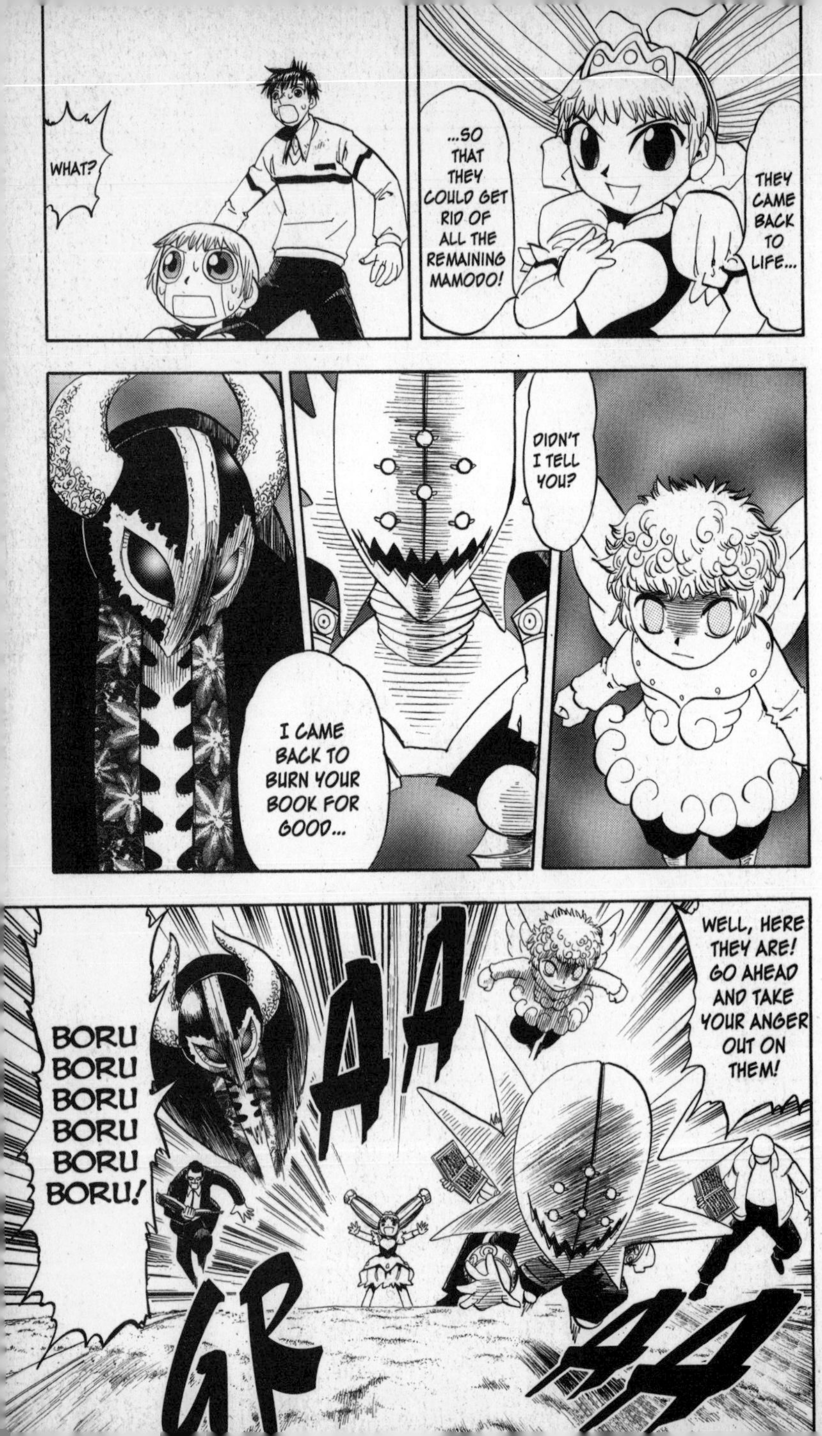
THEY CAME BACK TO LIFE...
...SO THAT THEY COULD GET RID OF ALL THE REMAINING MAMODO!
WHAT?
DIDN'T I TELL YOU?
I CAME BACK TO BURN YOUR BOOK FOR GOOD...
WELL, HERE THEY ARE! GO AHEAD AND TAKE YOUR ANGER OUT ON THEM!
AA
BORU BORU BORU BORU BORU BORU!
GR
AA

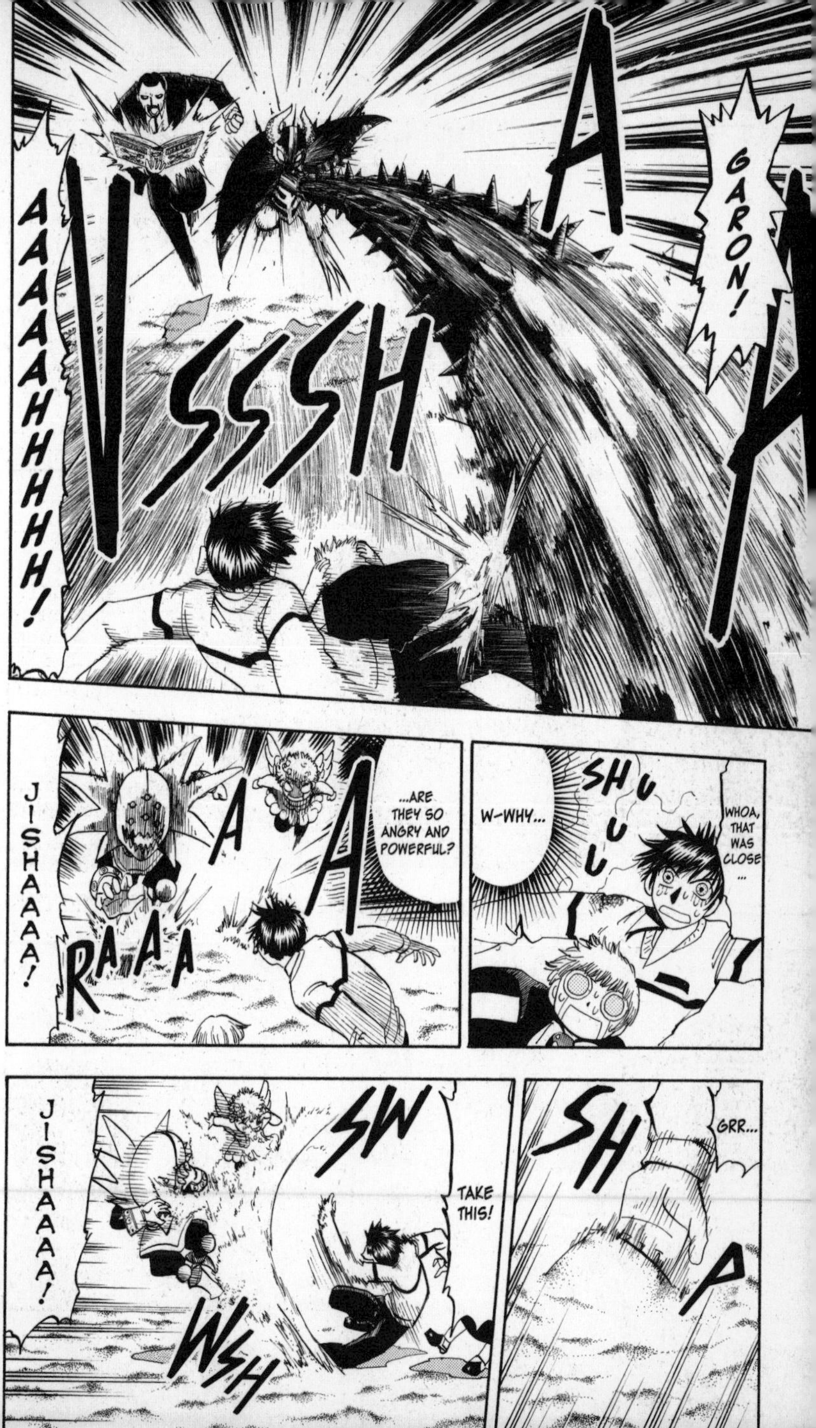
GARON!
VSSSH
AAAAAHHHHHH!
WHOA, THAT WAS CLOSE...
SHUUUU
W-WHY...
...ARE THEY SO ANGRY AND POWERFUL?
AA
JISHAAAAA!
RAAA
GRR...
SHP
TAKE THIS!
SW
WSH
JISHAAAAA!

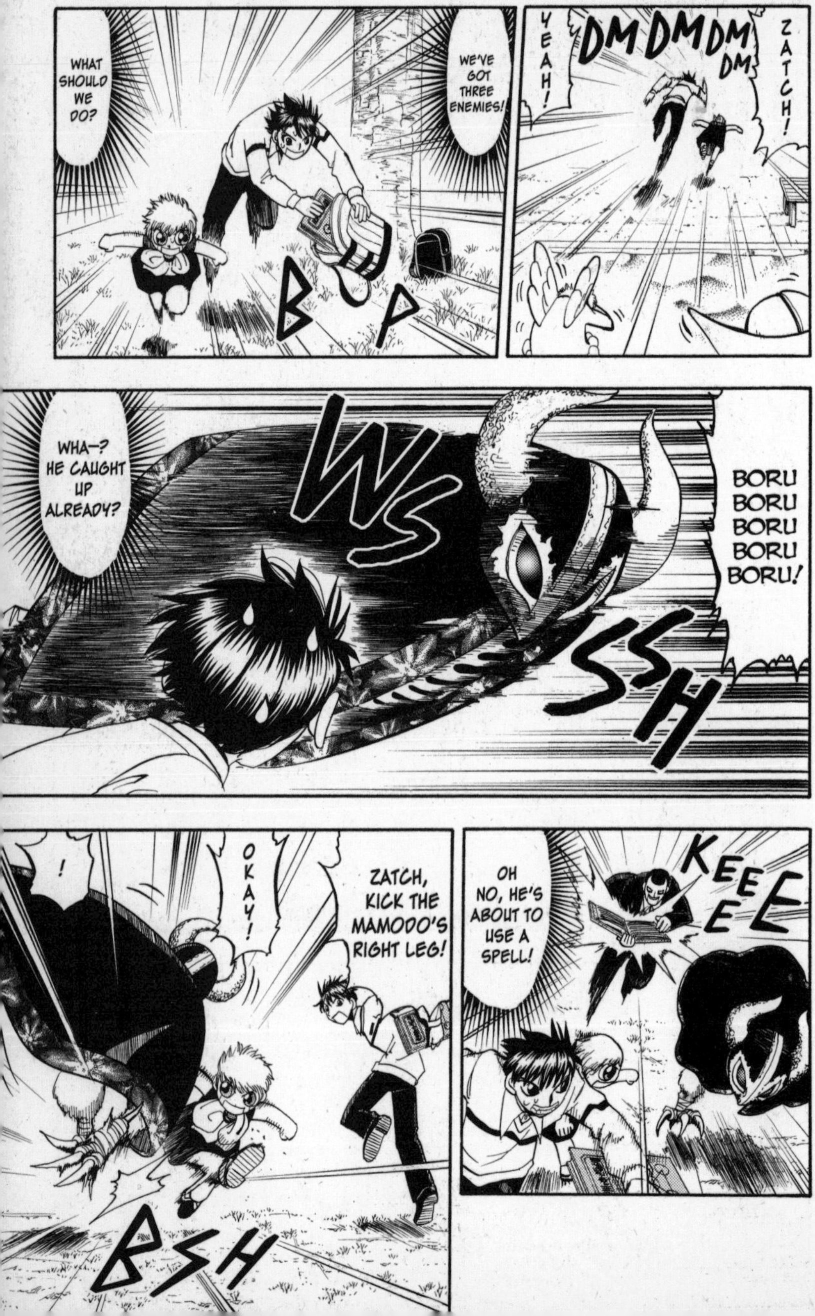
ZATCH!
DM DM DM DM DM
YEAH!
WE'VE GOT THREE ENEMIES!
WHAT SHOULD WE DO?
BP
BORU BORU BORU BORU BORU!
WS
SSH
WHA-? HE CAUGHT UP ALREADY?
KEEEE
OH NO, HE'S ABOUT TO USE A SPELL!
ZATCH, KICK THE MAMODO'S RIGHT LEG!
OKAY!
!
BSH

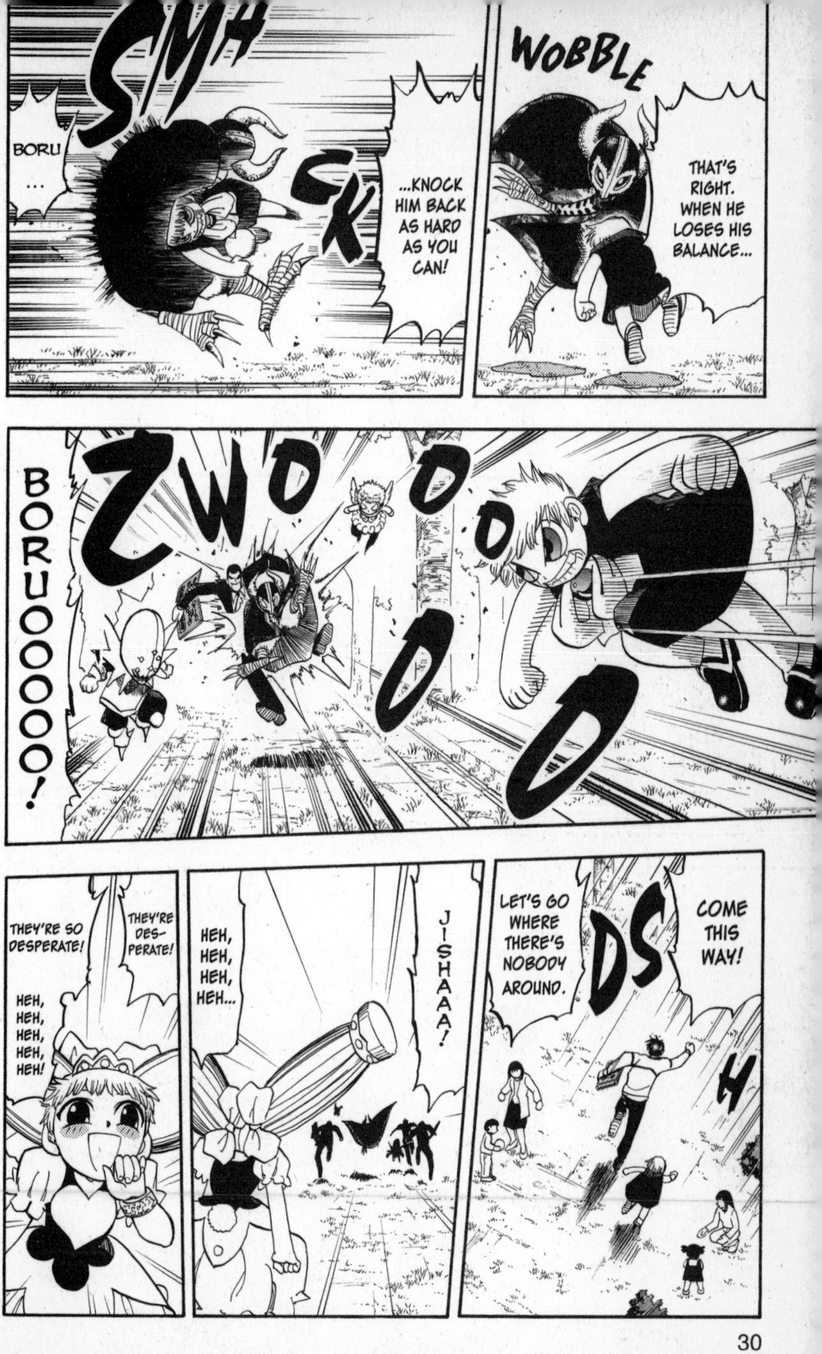
WOBBLE
THAT'S RIGHT. WHEN HE LOSES HIS BALANCE...
...KNOCK HIM BACK AS HARD AS YOU CAN!
SMACK
BORU ...
ZWOOOOOD
BORUOOOOOOO!
COME THIS WAY!
LET'S GO WHERE THERE'S NOBODY AROUND.
DSH
JISHAAA!
HEH, HEH, HEH, HEH...
THEY'RE DES-PERATE!
THEY'RE SO DESPERATE!
HEH, HEH, HEH, HEH, HEH!

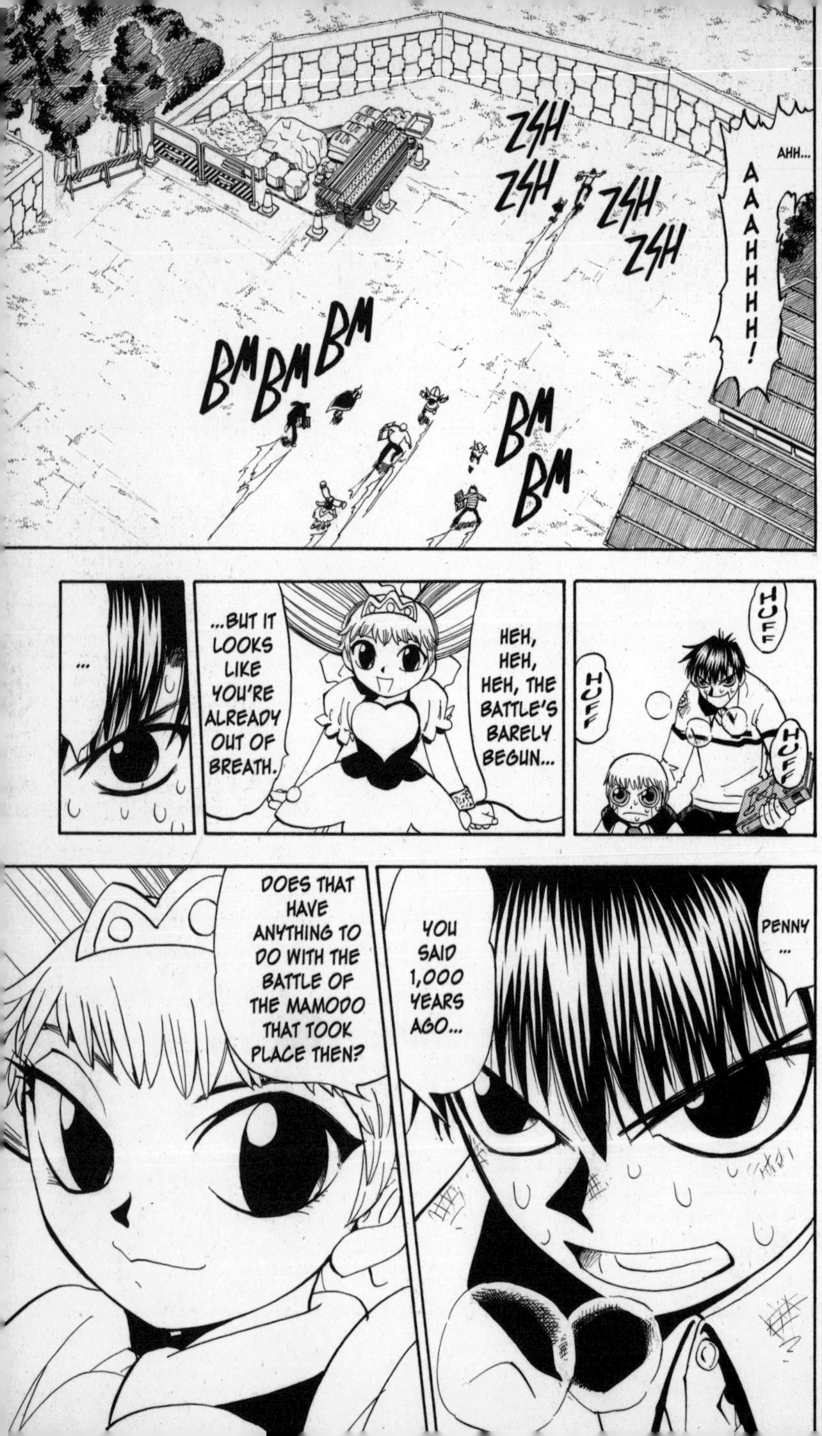
AHH... AAAAHHHHH!
ZSH ZSH ZSH ZSH
BM BM BM BM BM
HUFF
HUFF
HUFF
HEH, HEH, HEH, THE BATTLE'S BARELY BEGUN...
...BUT IT LOOKS LIKE YOU'RE ALREADY OUT OF BREATH.
...
PENNY...
YOU SAID 1,000 YEARS AGO...
DOES THAT HAVE ANYTHING TO DO WITH THE BATTLE OF THE MAMODO THAT TOOK PLACE THEN?

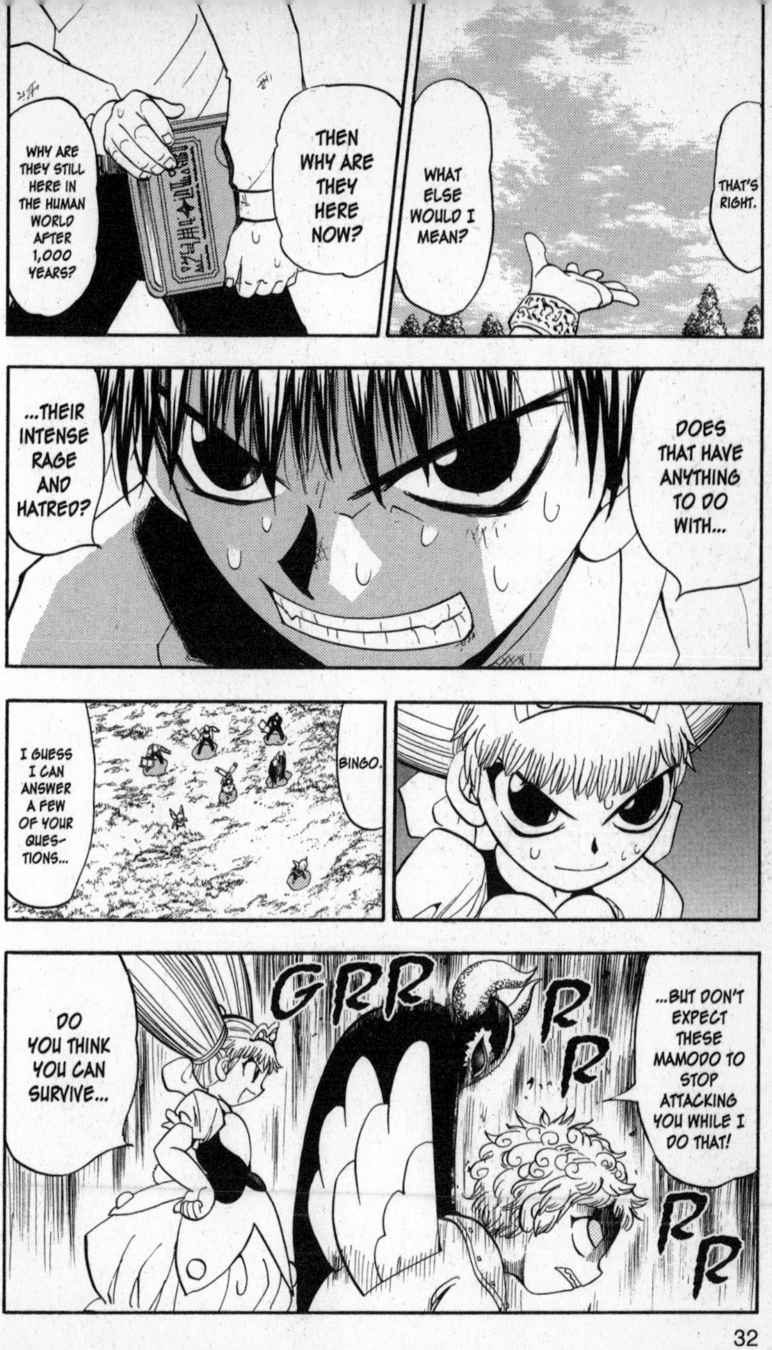
THAT'S RIGHT.
WHAT ELSE WOULD I MEAN?
THEN WHY ARE THEY HERE NOW?
WHY ARE THEY STILL HERE IN THE HUMAN WORLD AFTER 1,000 YEARS?
DOES THAT HAVE ANYTHING TO DO WITH...
...THEIR INTENSE RAGE AND HATRED?
BINGO.
I GUESS I CAN ANSWER A FEW OF YOUR QUES-TIONS...
...BUT DON'T EXPECT THESE MAMODO TO STOP ATTACKING YOU WHILE I DO THAT!
GRRRRRR
DO YOU THINK YOU CAN SURVIVE...

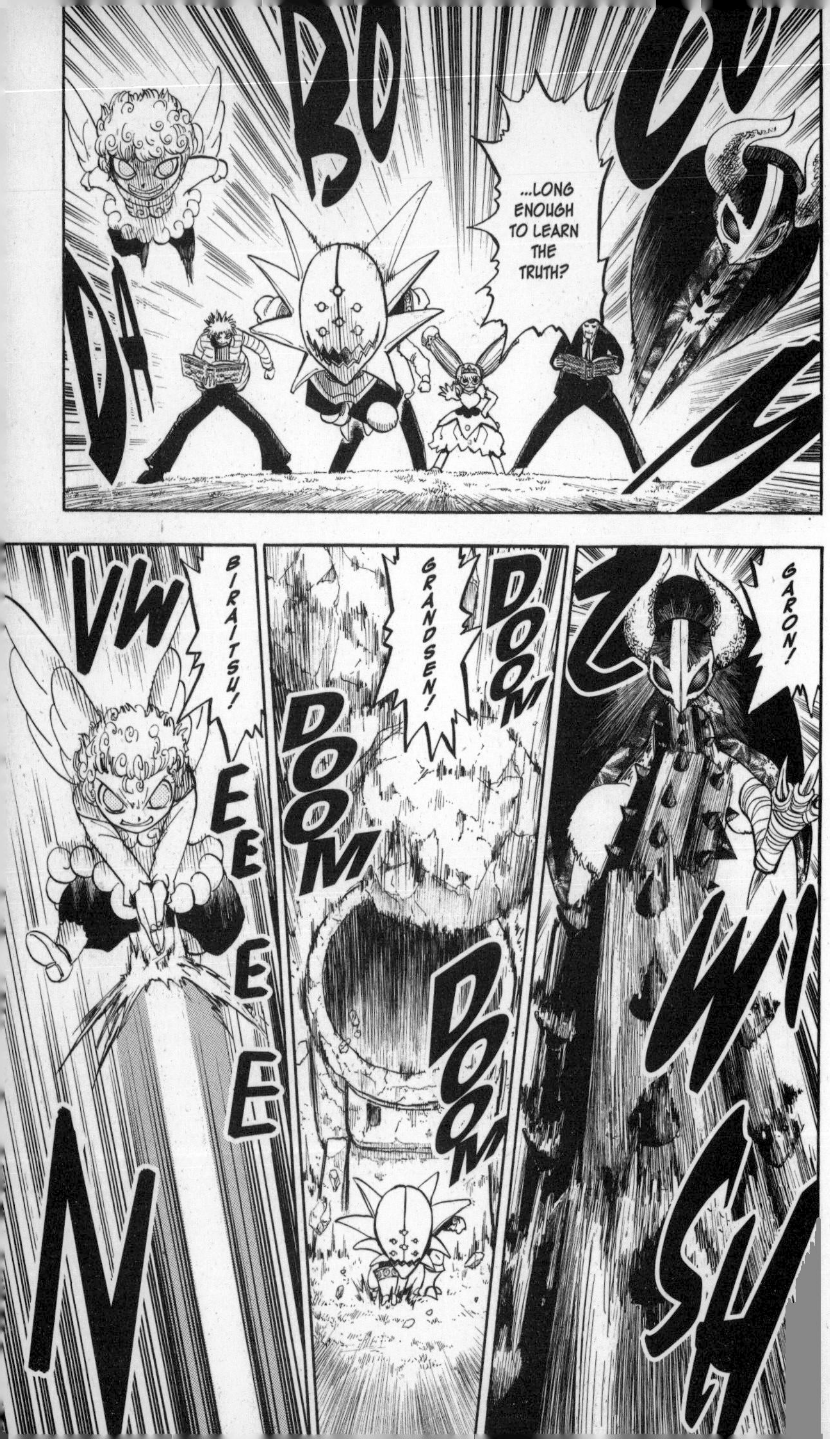
...LONG ENOUGH TO LEARN THE TRUTH?
GARON!
GRANDSEN!
DOOM
DOOM
DOOM
BIRAITSU!
VWEEEEN

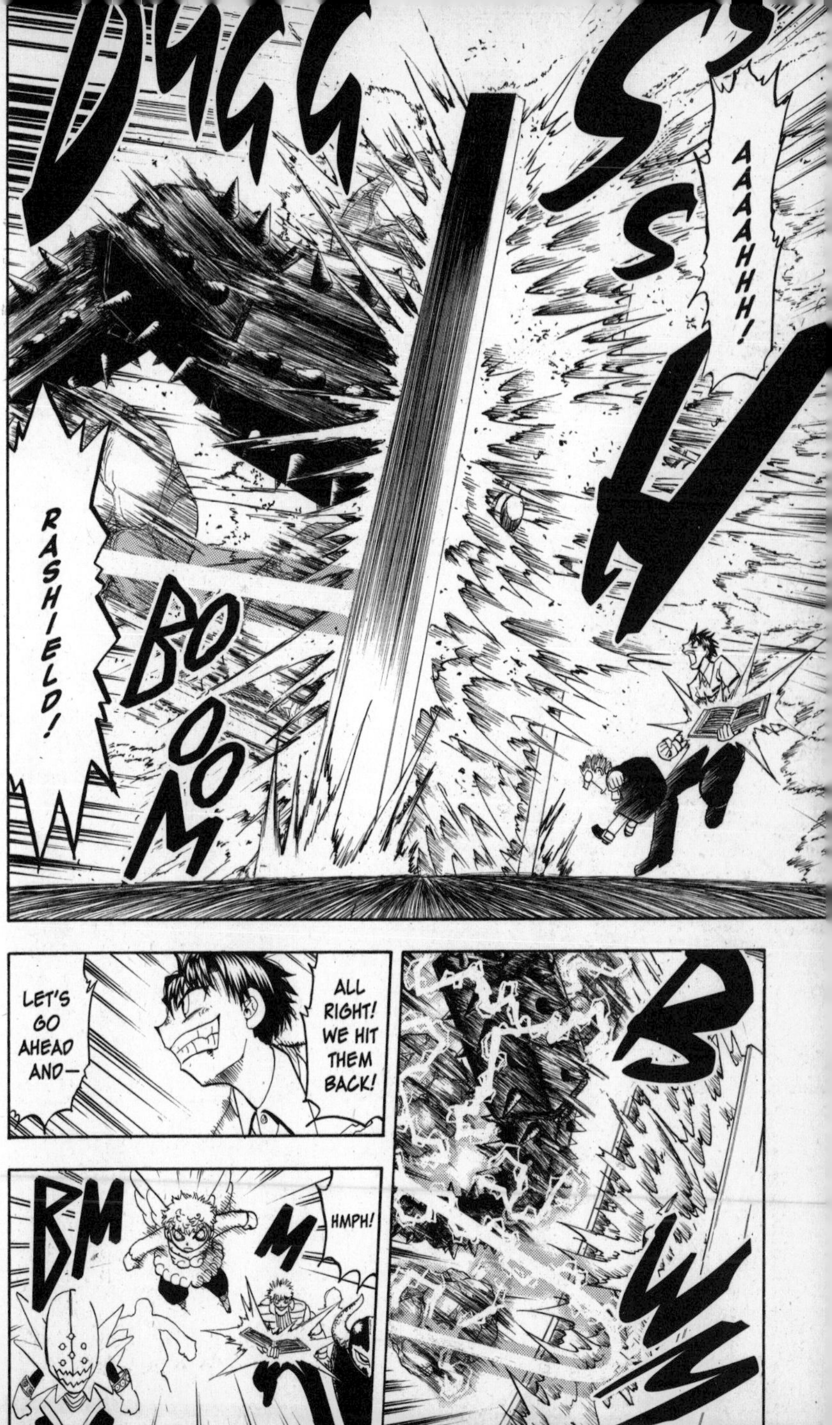
AAAAHHH!
SSH
DUGG
BOOOM
RASHIELD!
BWM
ALL RIGHT! WE HIT THEM BACK!
LET'S GO AHEAD AND—
HMPH!
M
BM

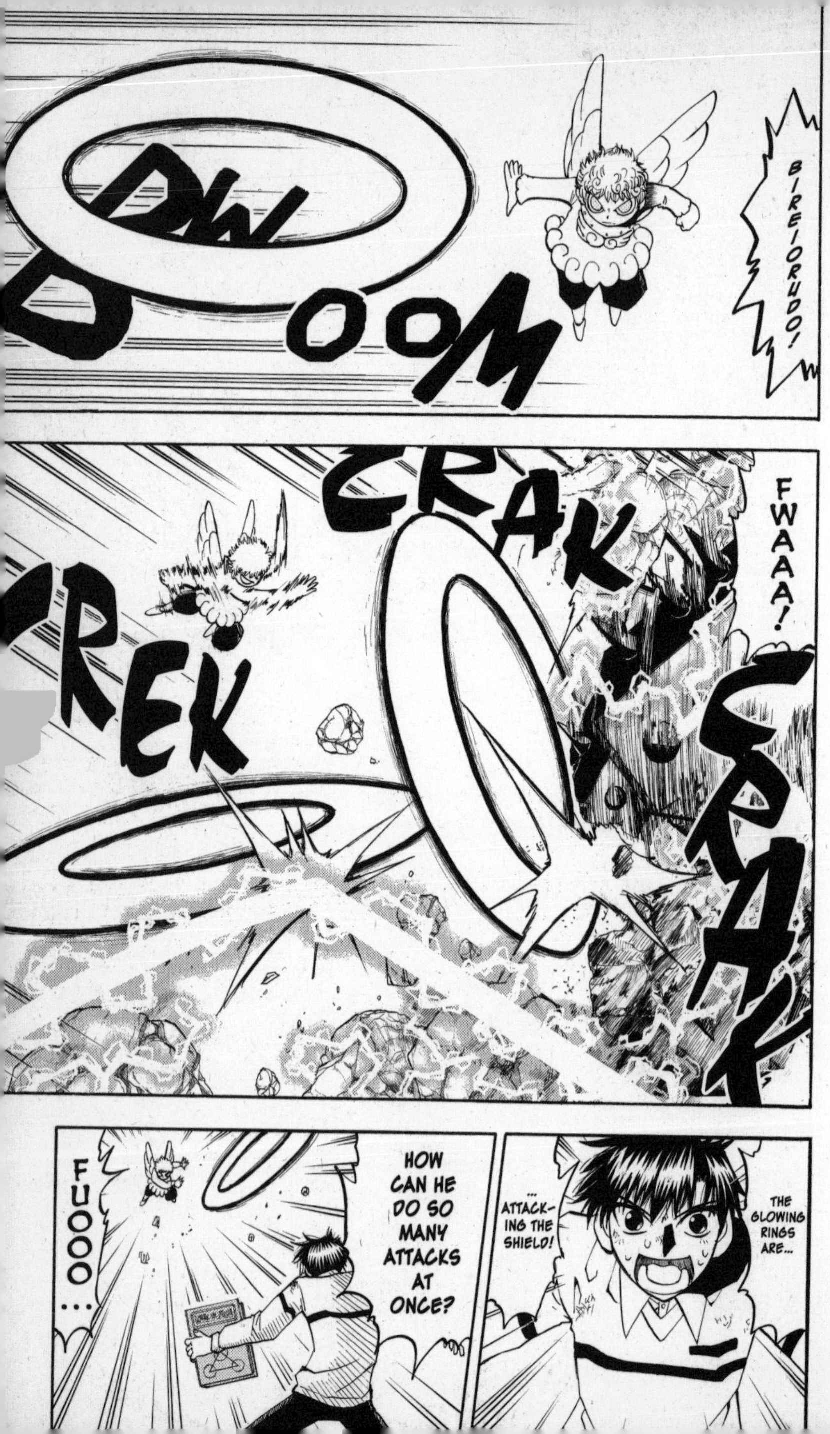
BIREIORUDO!
DW
DOOM
FWAAA!
CRAK
CRAK
REK
THE GLOWING RINGS ARE...
...ATTACKING THE SHIELD!
HOW CAN HE DO SO MANY ATTACKS AT ONCE?
FUOOO...

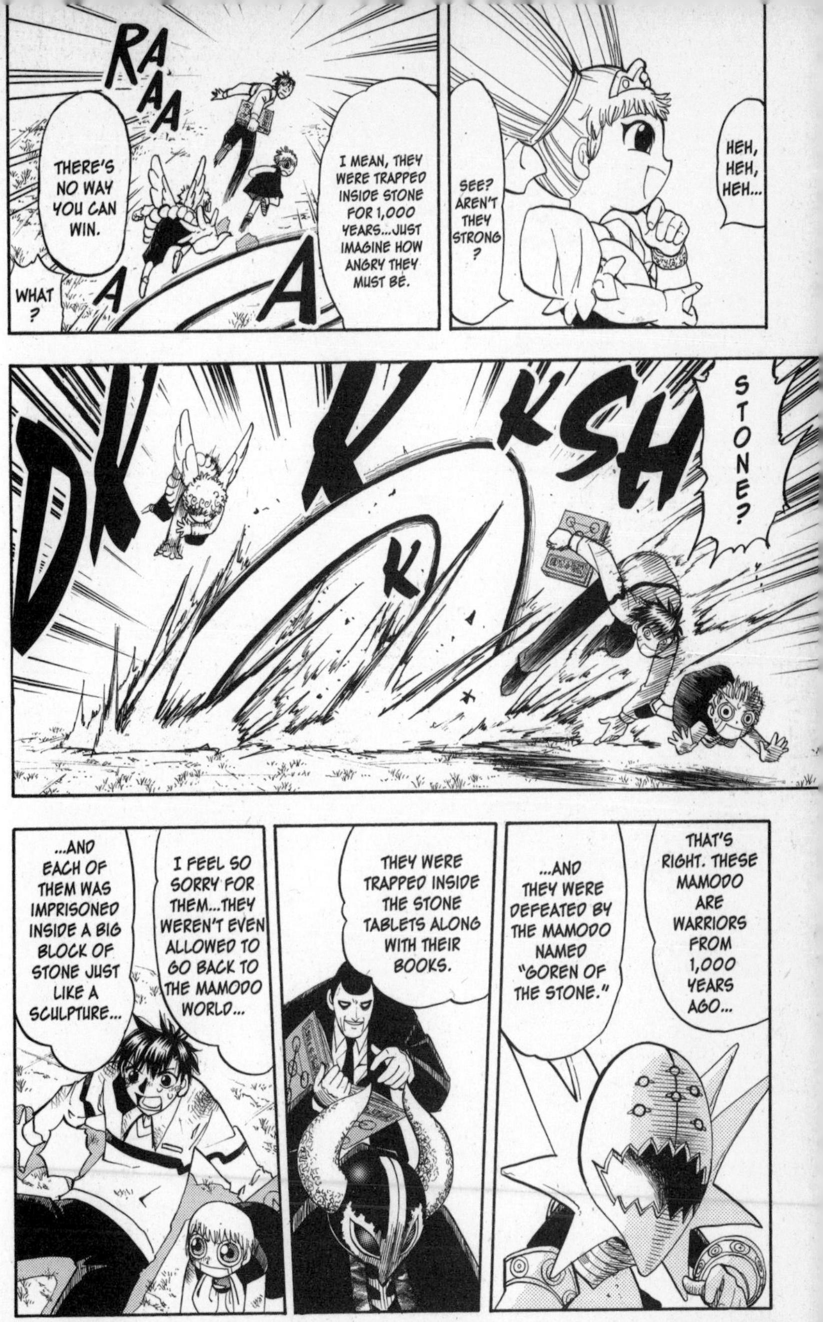
HEH, HEH, HEH...
SEE? AREN'T THEY STRONG?
I MEAN, THEY WERE TRAPPED INSIDE STONE FOR 1,000 YEARS...JUST IMAGINE HOW ANGRY THEY MUST BE.
RAAAAA
THERE'S NO WAY YOU CAN WIN.
WHAT?
STONE?
DKKKSH
THAT'S RIGHT. THESE MAMODO ARE WARRIORS FROM 1,000 YEARS AGO...
...AND THEY WERE DEFEATED BY THE MAMODO NAMED "GOREN OF THE STONE."
THEY WERE TRAPPED INSIDE THE STONE TABLETS ALONG WITH THEIR BOOKS.
I FEEL SO SORRY FOR THEM...THEY WEREN'T EVEN ALLOWED TO GO BACK TO THE MAMODO WORLD...
...AND EACH OF THEM WAS IMPRISONED INSIDE A BIG BLOCK OF STONE JUST LIKE A SCULPTURE...

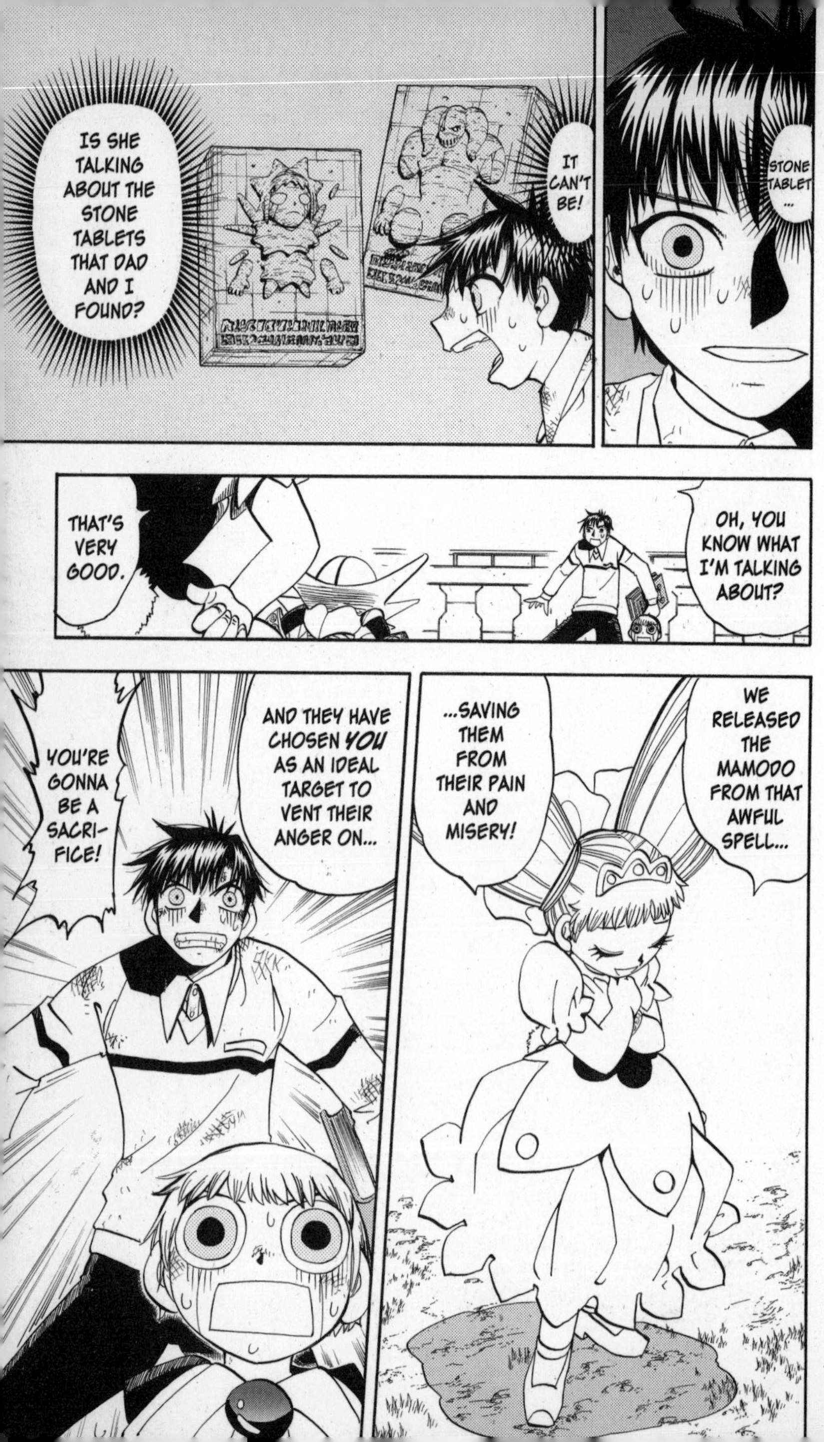
STONE TABLET...
IT CAN'T BE!
IS SHE TALKING ABOUT THE STONE TABLETS THAT DAD AND I FOUND?
OH, YOU KNOW WHAT I'M TALKING ABOUT?
THAT'S VERY GOOD.
WE RELEASED THE MAMODO FROM THAT AWFUL SPELL...
...SAVING THEM FROM THEIR PAIN AND MISERY!
AND THEY HAVE CHOSEN *YOU* AS AN IDEAL TARGET TO VENT THEIR ANGER ON...
YOU'RE GONNA BE A SACRI-FICE!

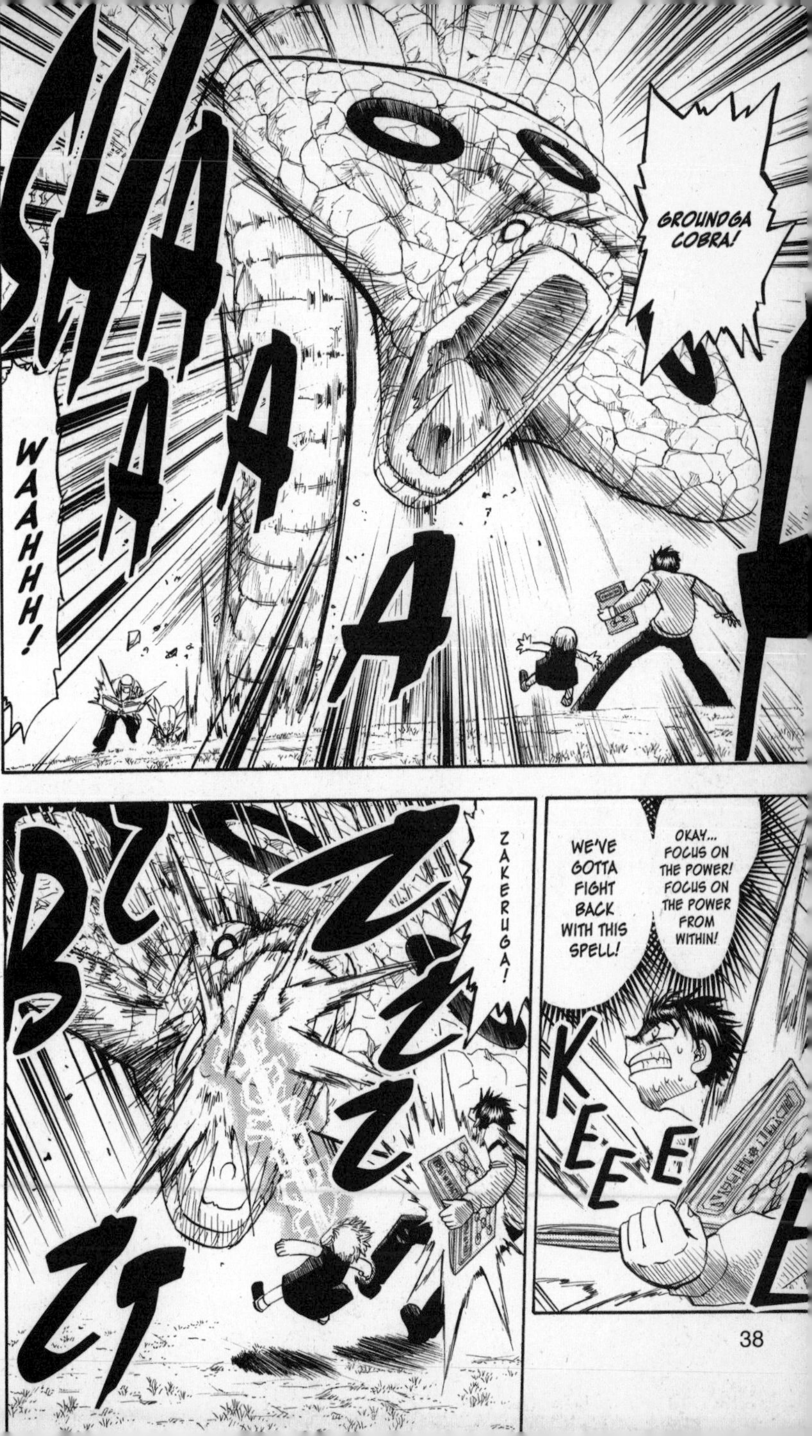
GROUNDGA COBRA!
WAAHHH!
OKAY... FOCUS ON THE POWER! FOCUS ON THE POWER FROM WITHIN!
WE'VE GOTTA FIGHT BACK WITH THIS SPELL!
KEEEE
ZAKERUGA!

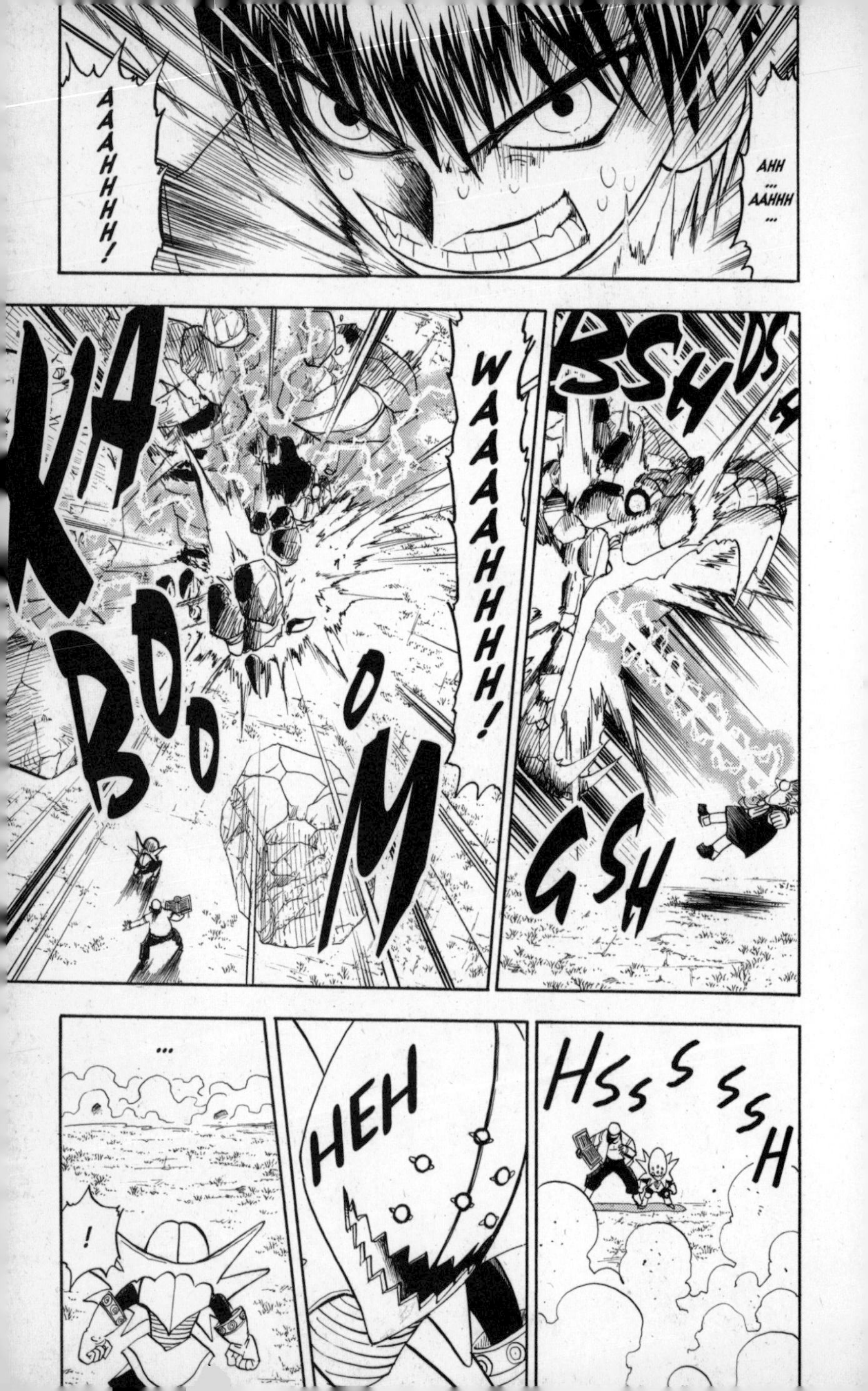
AHH... AAHHH...
AAAAHHHHH!
BSHDSH
GSH
WAAAAAAHHHHHH!
KA BOOOM
HSSSSSSH
HEH
...
!

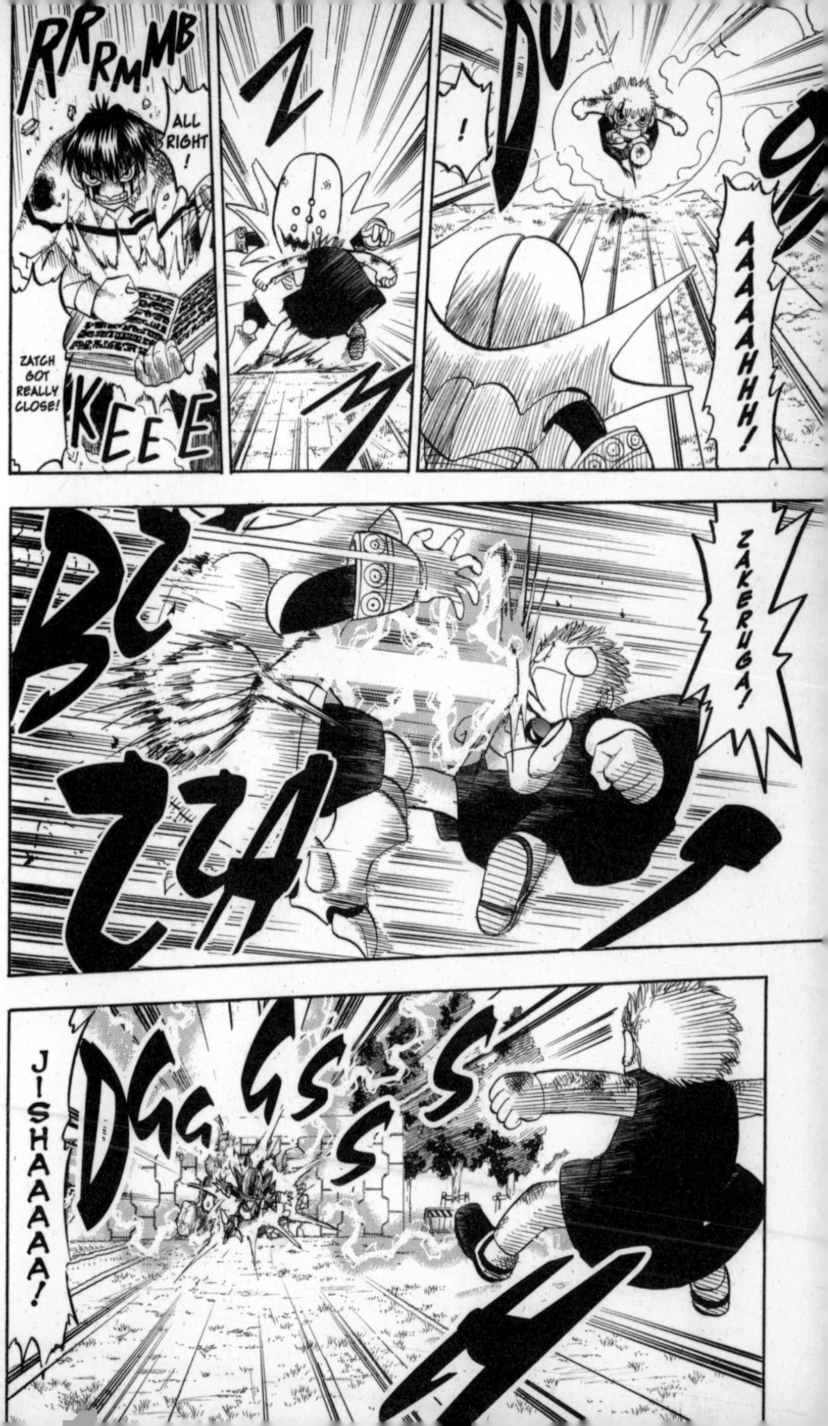
DOM
!
AAAAAHHH!
ZZM
RRRMMB
ALL RIGHT!
ZATCH GOT REALLY CLOSE!
KEEE
ZAKERUGA!
BZZZT
JISHAAAAAA!
DGGSSSSS

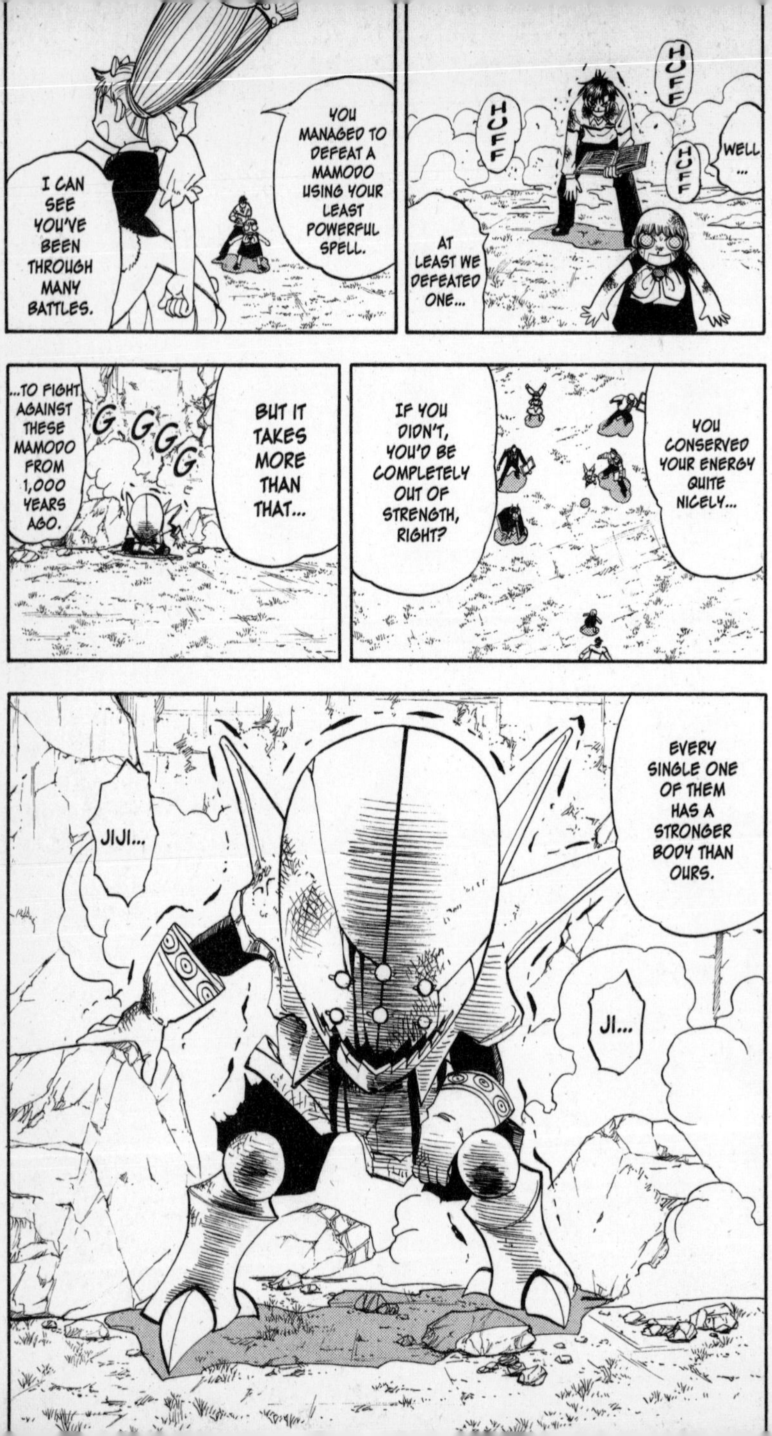
HUFF
HUFF
HUFF
WELL...
AT LEAST WE DEFEATED ONE...
YOU MANAGED TO DEFEAT A MAMODO USING YOUR LEAST POWERFUL SPELL.
I CAN SEE YOU'VE BEEN THROUGH MANY BATTLES.
YOU CONSERVED YOUR ENERGY QUITE NICELY...
IF YOU DIDN'T, YOU'D BE COMPLETELY OUT OF STRENGTH, RIGHT?
BUT IT TAKES MORE THAN THAT...
GGGG
...TO FIGHT AGAINST THESE MAMODO FROM 1,000 YEARS AGO.
EVERY SINGLE ONE OF THEM HAS A STRONGER BODY THAN OURS.
JI...
JIJI...

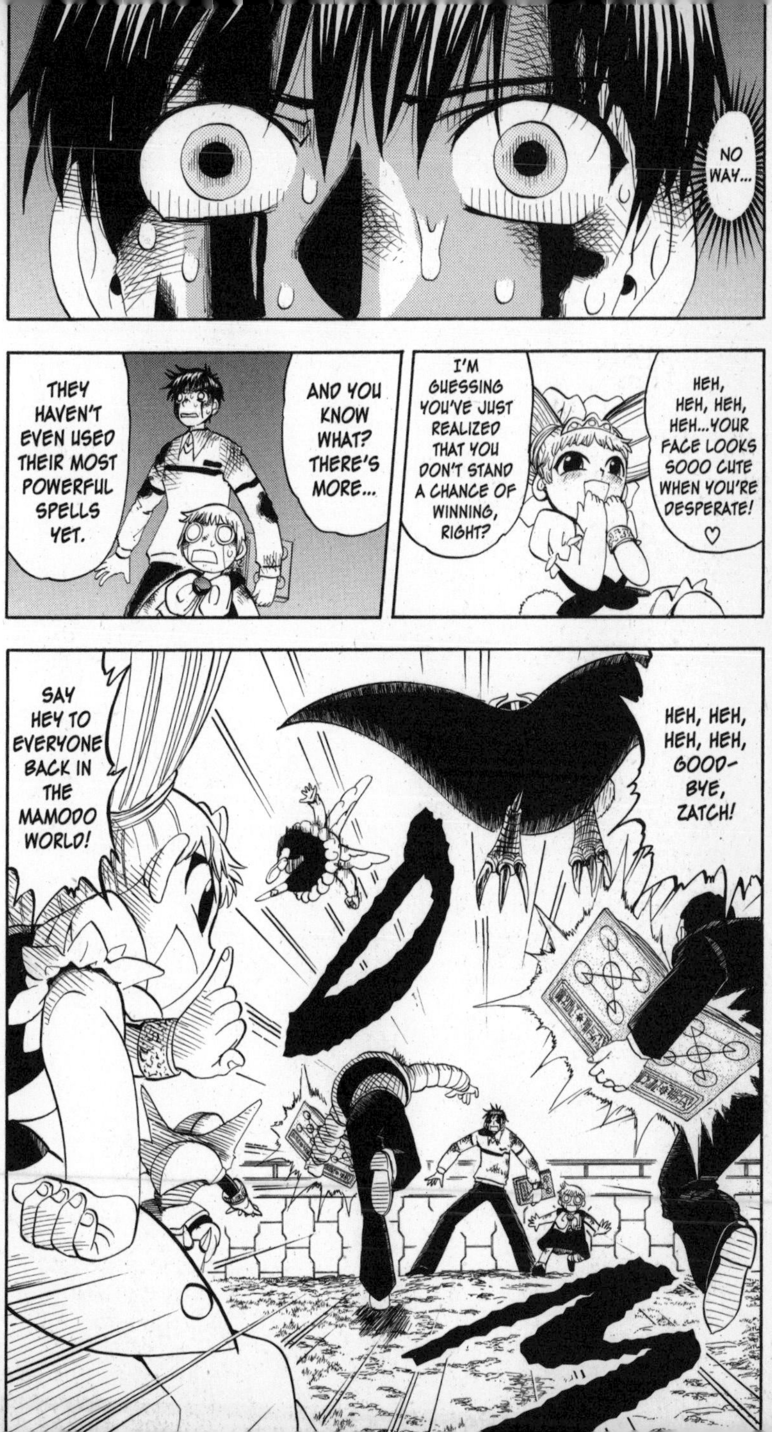
NO WAY...
HEH, HEH, HEH, HEH...YOUR FACE LOOKS SOOO CUTE WHEN YOU'RE DESPERATE! ♡
I'M GUESSING YOU'VE JUST REALIZED THAT YOU DON'T STAND A CHANCE OF WINNING, RIGHT?
AND YOU KNOW WHAT? THERE'S MORE...
THEY HAVEN'T EVEN USED THEIR MOST POWERFUL SPELLS YET.
HEH, HEH, HEH, HEH, GOOD-BYE, ZATCH!
SAY HEY TO EVERYONE BACK IN THE MAMODO WORLD!

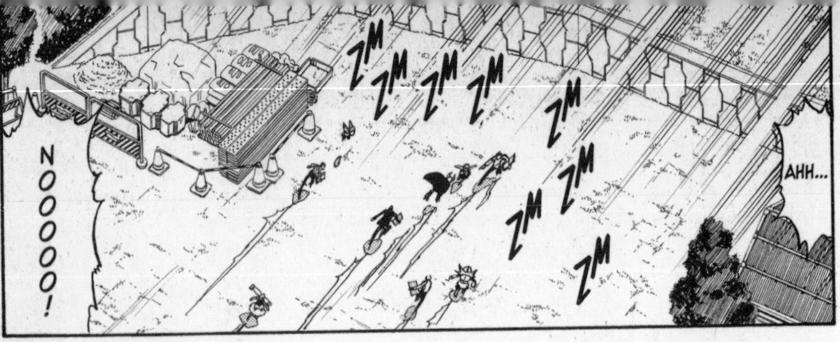
NOOOOOO!
ZM ZM ZM ZM ZM ZM ZM ZM
AHH...

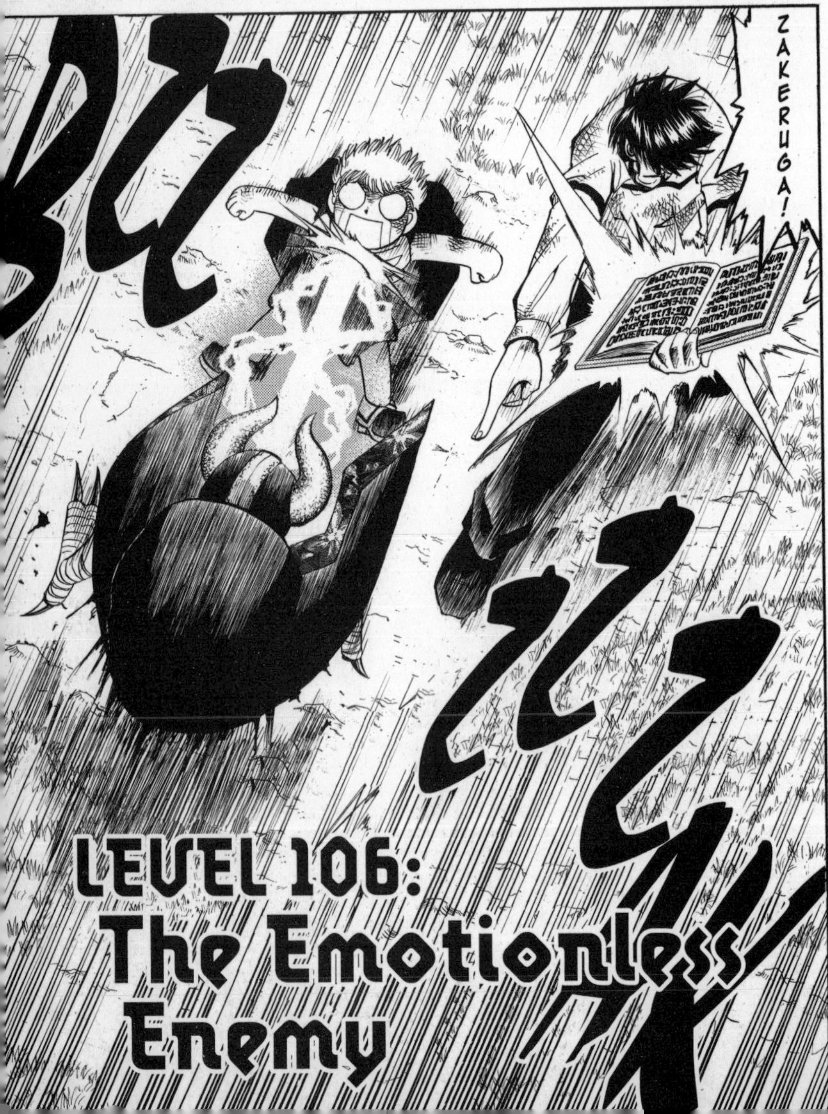
ZAKERUGA!

LEVEL 106: The Emotionless Enemy

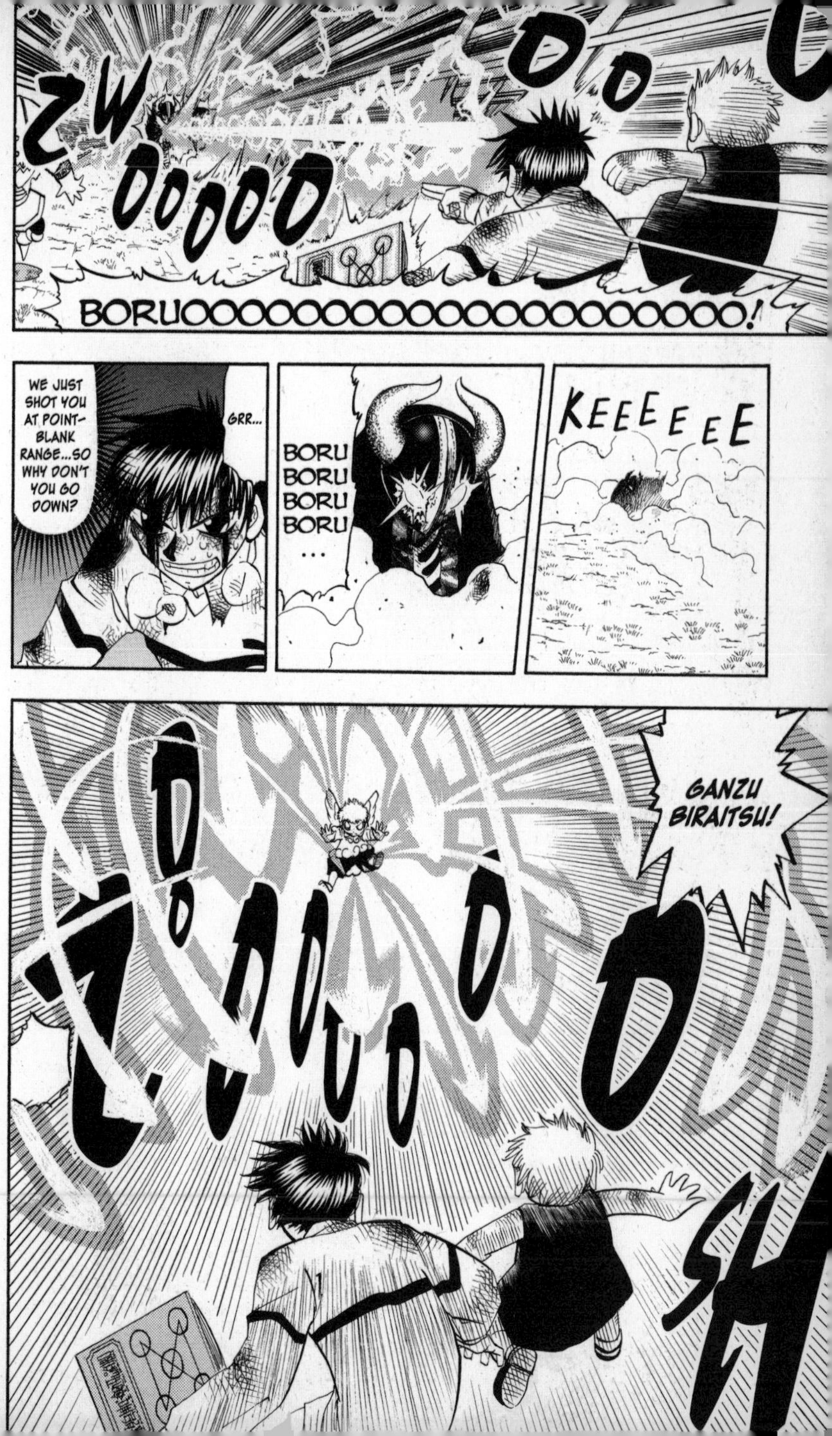

ZWOOOOOD
BORUOOOOOOOOOOOOOOOOOOOOOOOOO!
KEEEEEEE
BORU BORU BORU BORU ...
GRR...
WE JUST SHOT YOU AT POINT-BLANK RANGE...SO WHY DON'T YOU GO DOWN?
GANZU BIRAITSU!

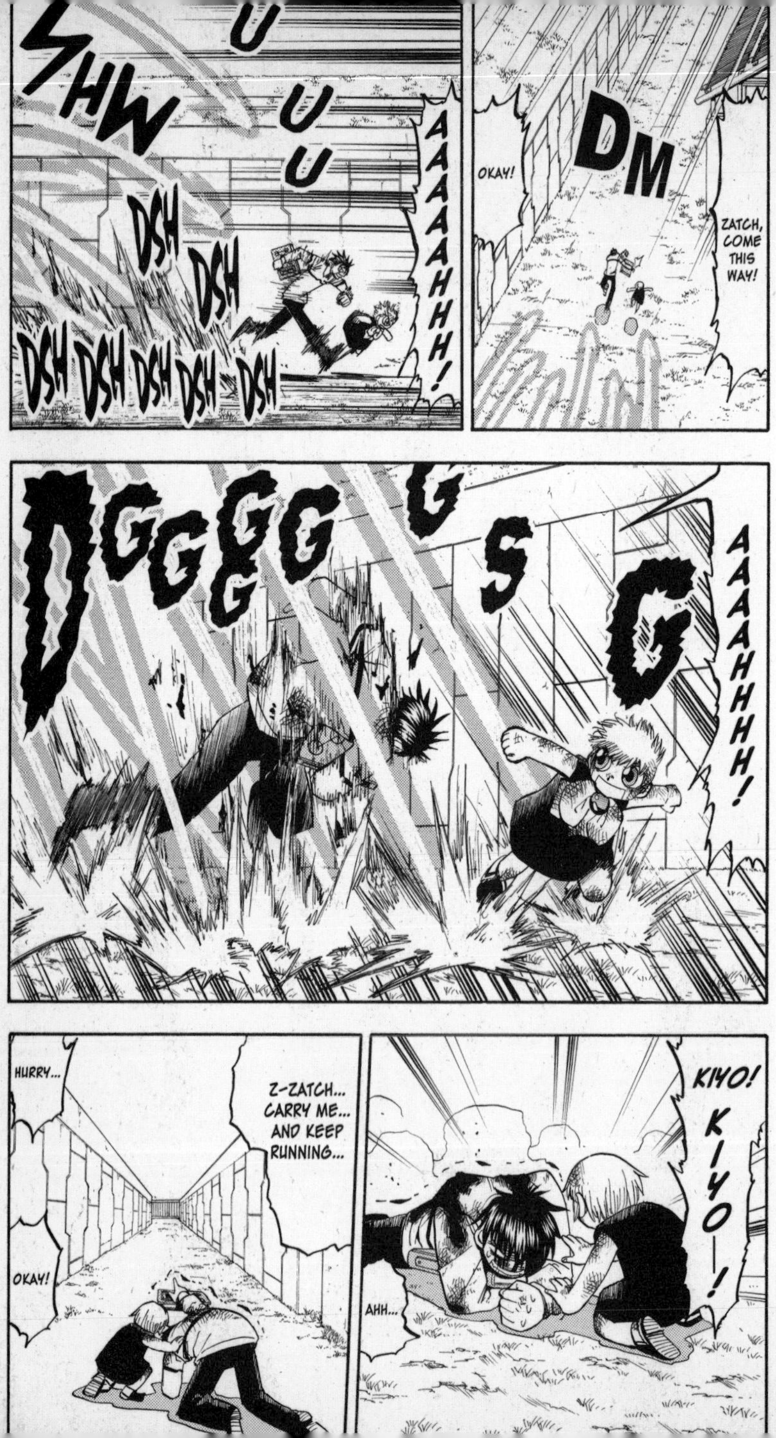
DM
ZATCH, COME THIS WAY!
OKAY!
SHWUUU
AAAAAAAHHHH!
DSH DSH DSH DSH DSH DSH DSH
DGGGGGG
S
G
AAAAAHHHHHH!
KIYO!
KIYO—!
AHH...
Z-ZATCH... CARRY ME... AND KEEP RUNNING...
HURRY...
OKAY!

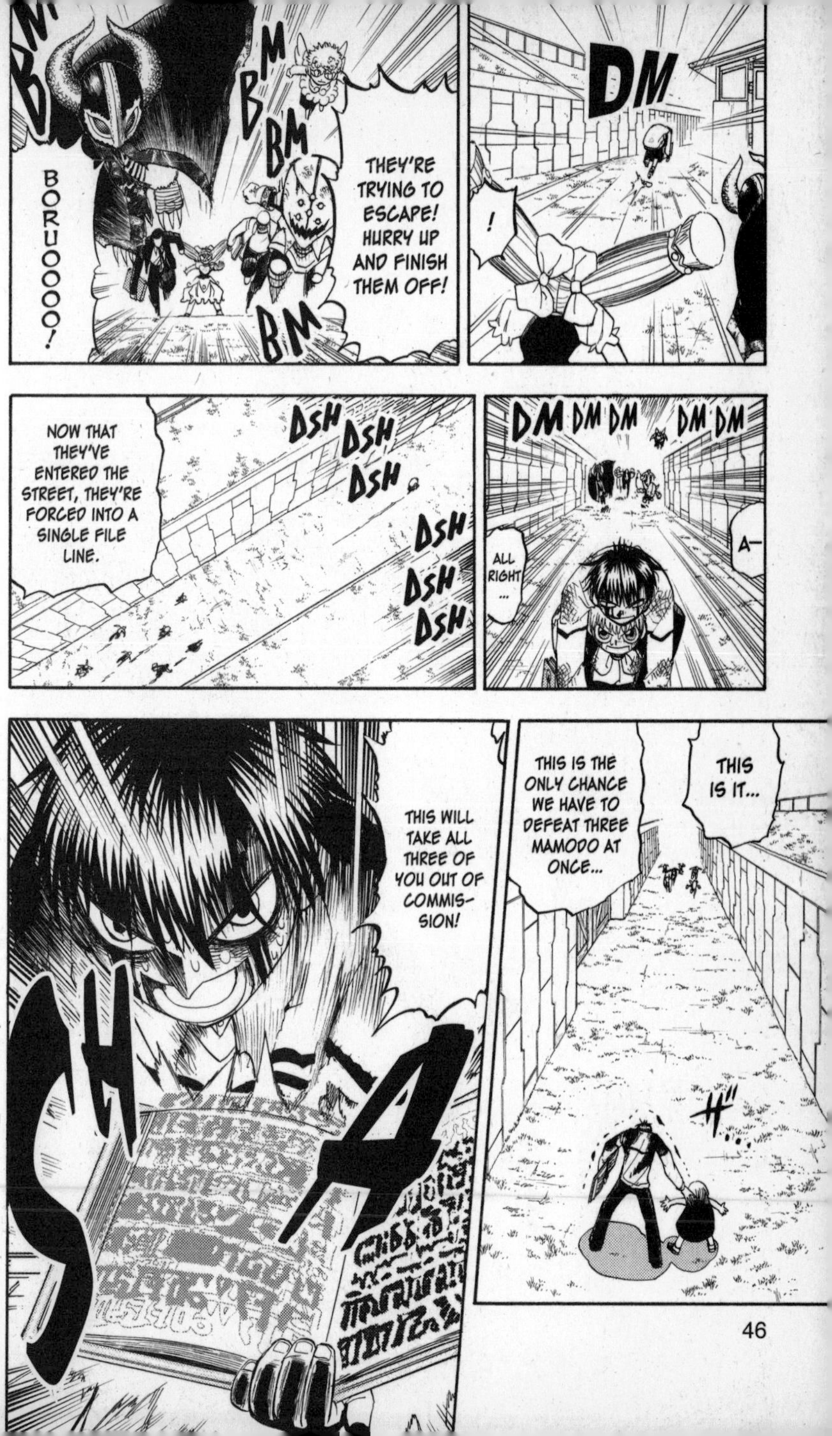

DM
!
BM BM BM
THEY'RE TRYING TO ESCAPE! HURRY UP AND FINISH THEM OFF!
BORUOOOO!
BM
DM DM DM DM DM
A—
ALL RIGHT...
DSH DSH DSH DSH DSH DSH
NOW THAT THEY'VE ENTERED THE STREET, THEY'RE FORCED INTO A SINGLE FILE LINE.
THIS IS IT...
THIS IS THE ONLY CHANCE WE HAVE TO DEFEAT THREE MAMODO AT ONCE...
THIS WILL TAKE ALL THREE OF YOU OUT OF COMMISSION!

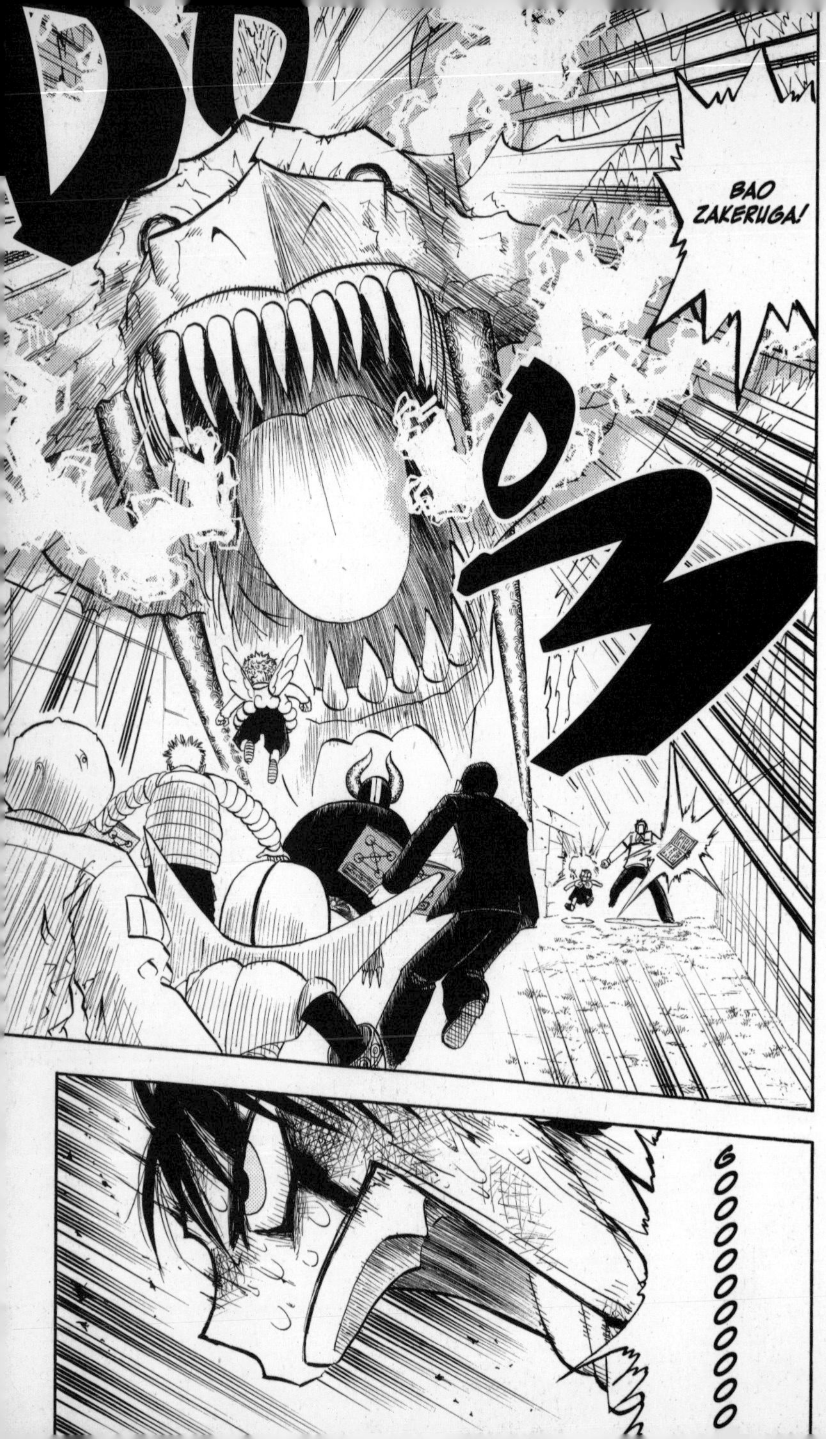
BAO ZAKERUGA!
GOOOOOOOOOOO

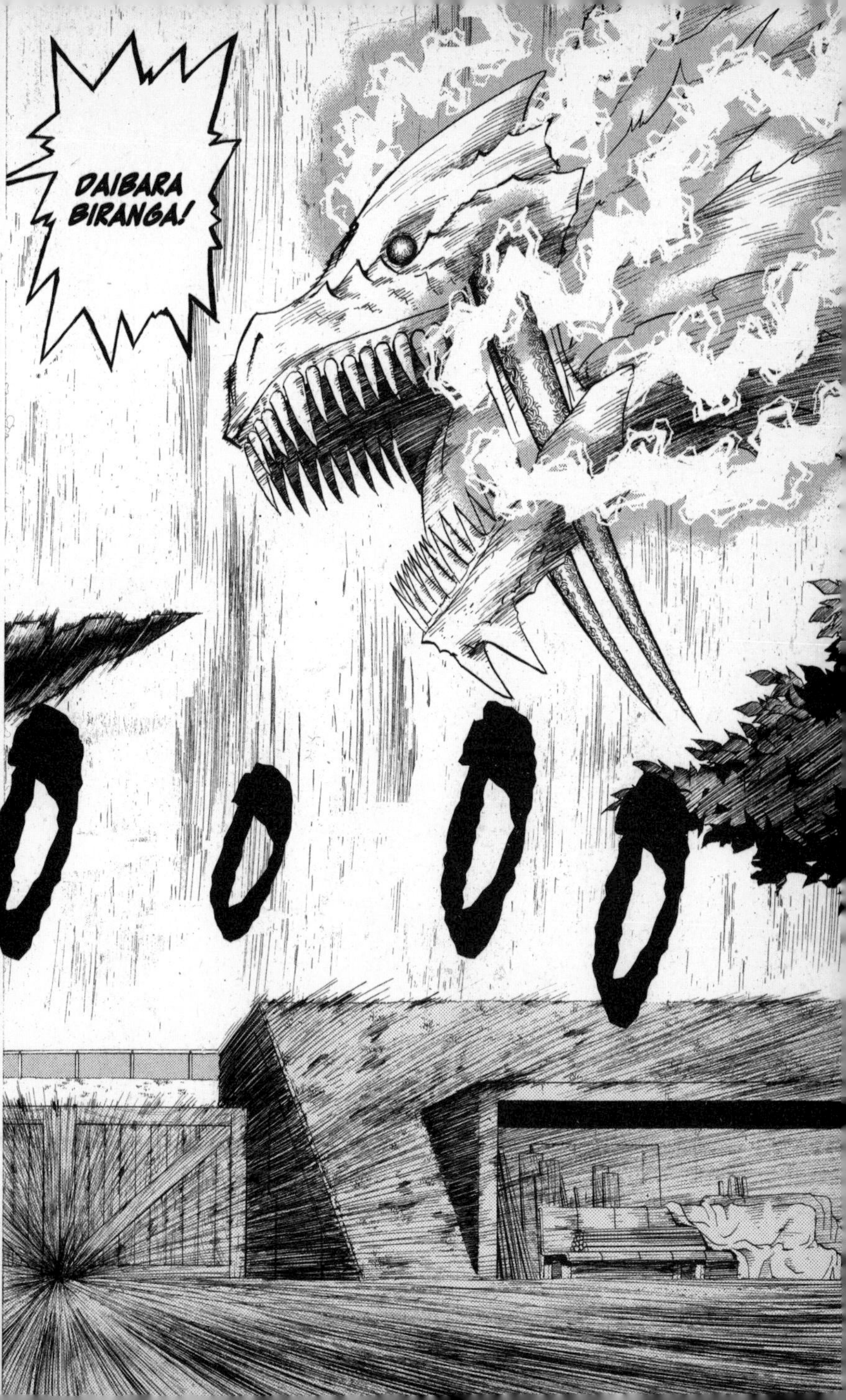
DAIBARA BIRANGA!

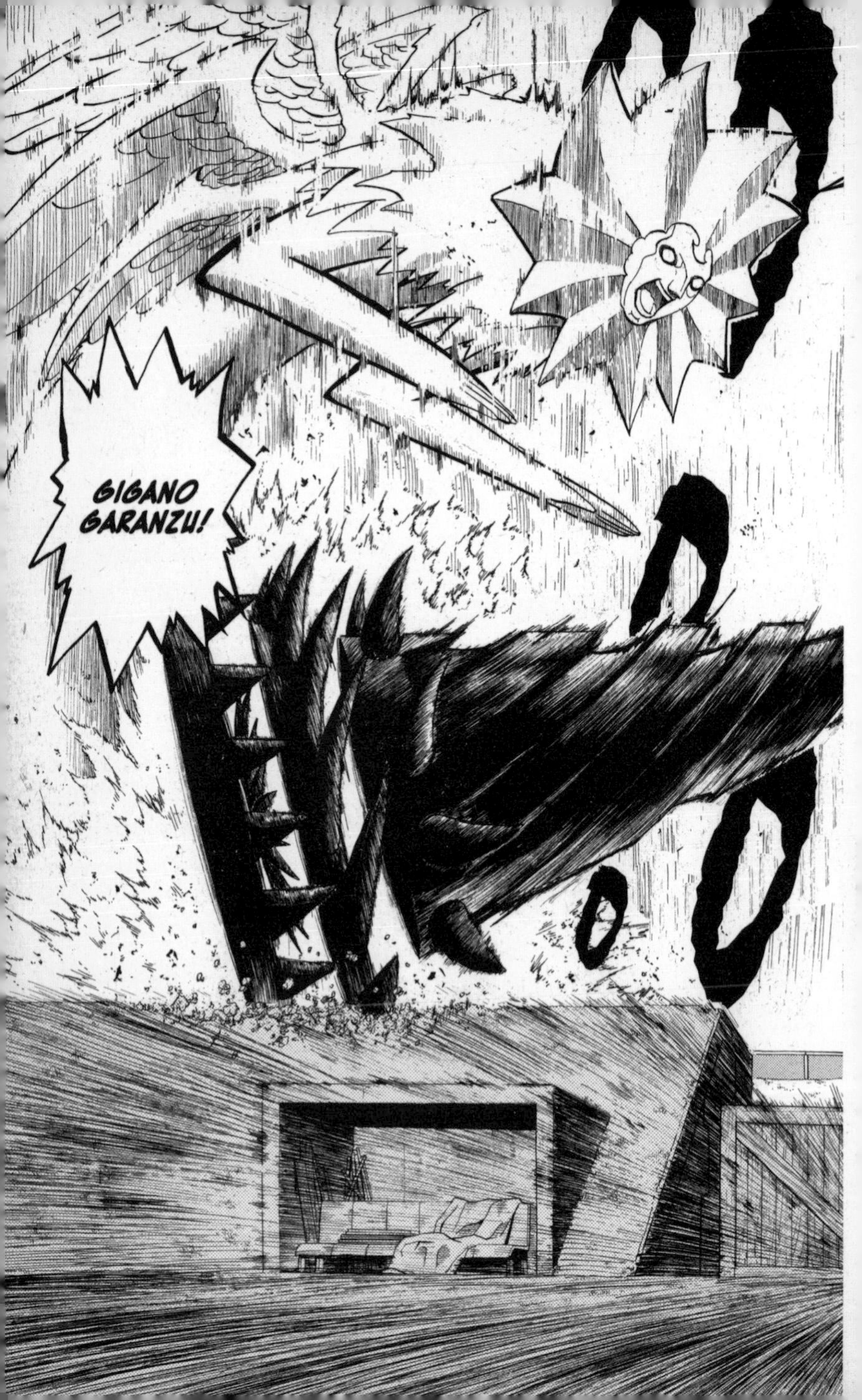
GIGANO GARANZU!

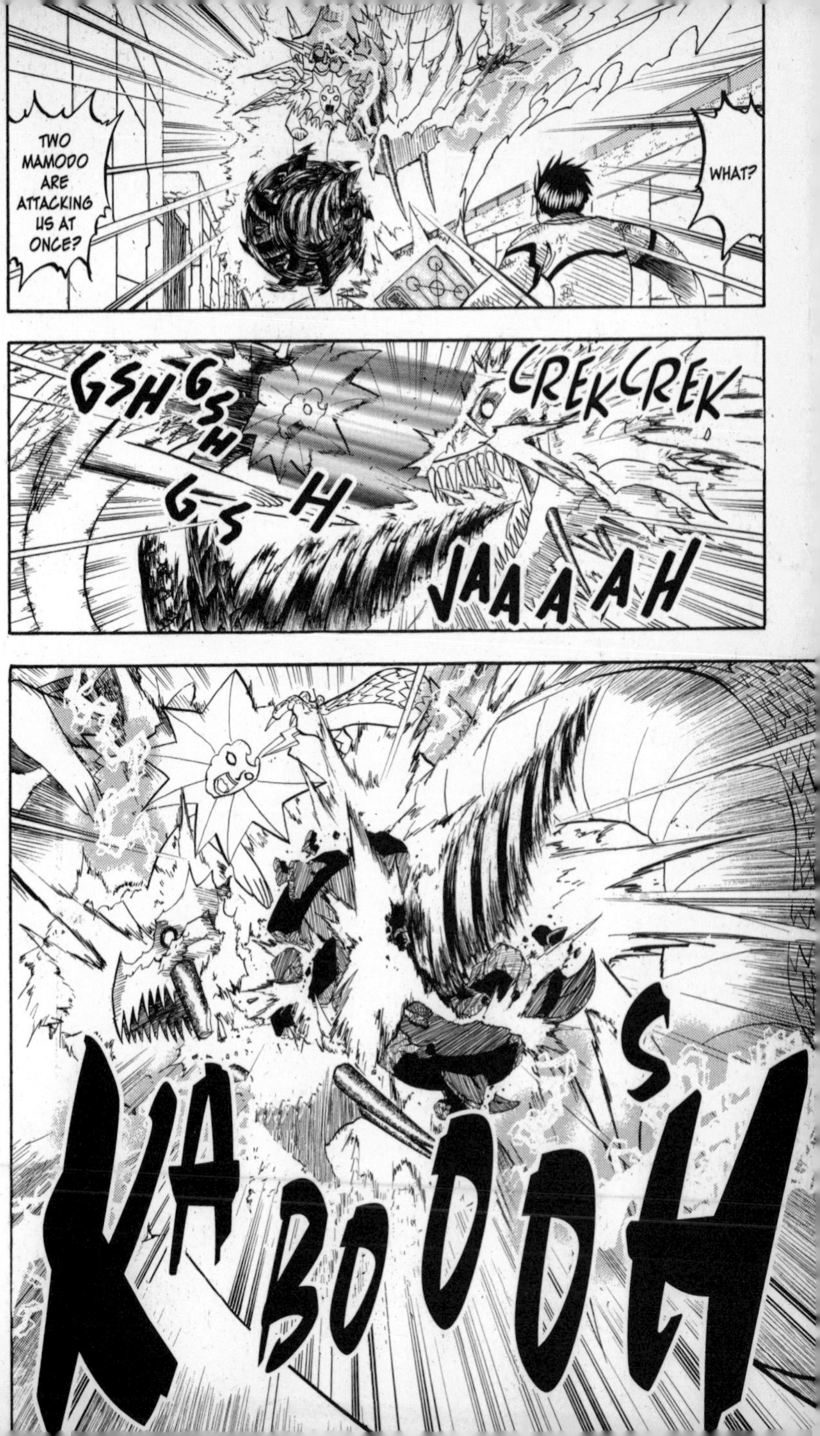
WHAT?
TWO MAMODO ARE ATTACKING US AT ONCE?
CREKCREK
GSHGSHGSH
JAAAAH
KABOOOSH

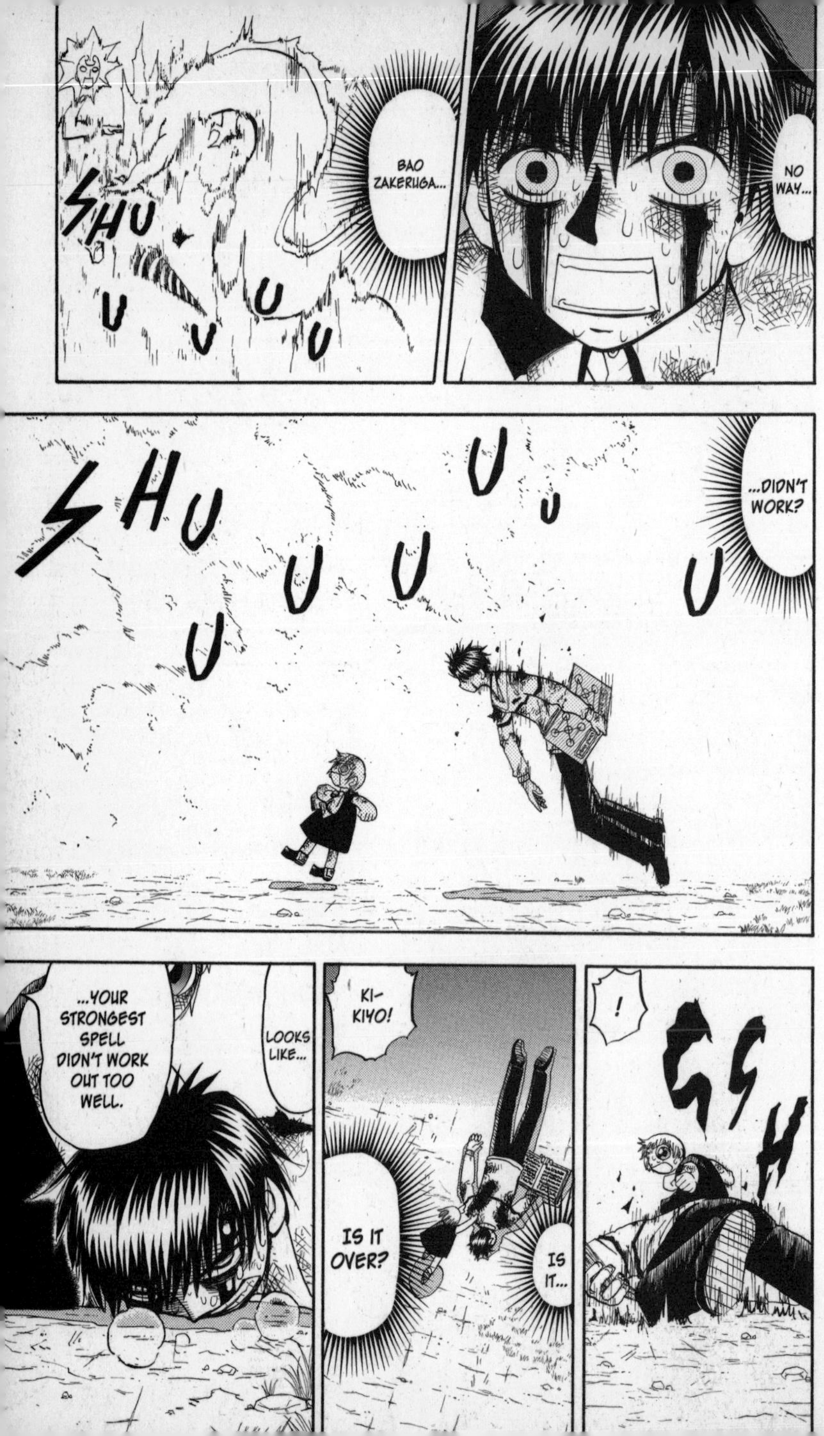
NO WAY...
BAO ZAKERUGA...
SHUUUUU
...DIDN'T WORK?
SHUUUUUUUU
!
GSH
IS IT...
IS IT OVER?
KI-KIYO!
LOOKS LIKE...
...YOUR STRONGEST SPELL DIDN'T WORK OUT TOO WELL.

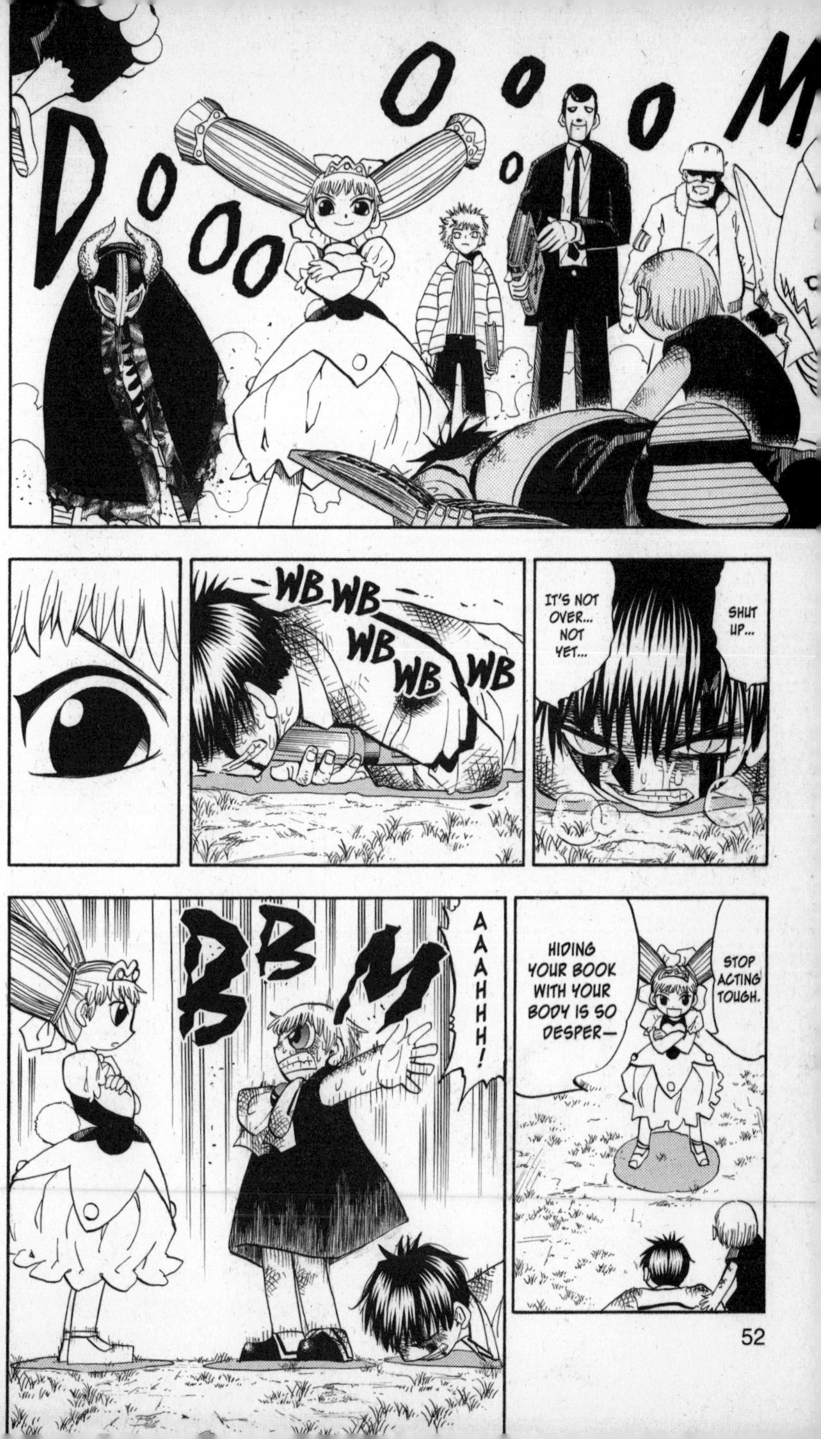
DOOOOOOOM
SHUT UP...
IT'S NOT OVER... NOT YET...
WB WB WB WB WB
STOP ACTING TOUGH.
HIDING YOUR BOOK WITH YOUR BODY IS SO DESPER—
AAAHHH!
DBM

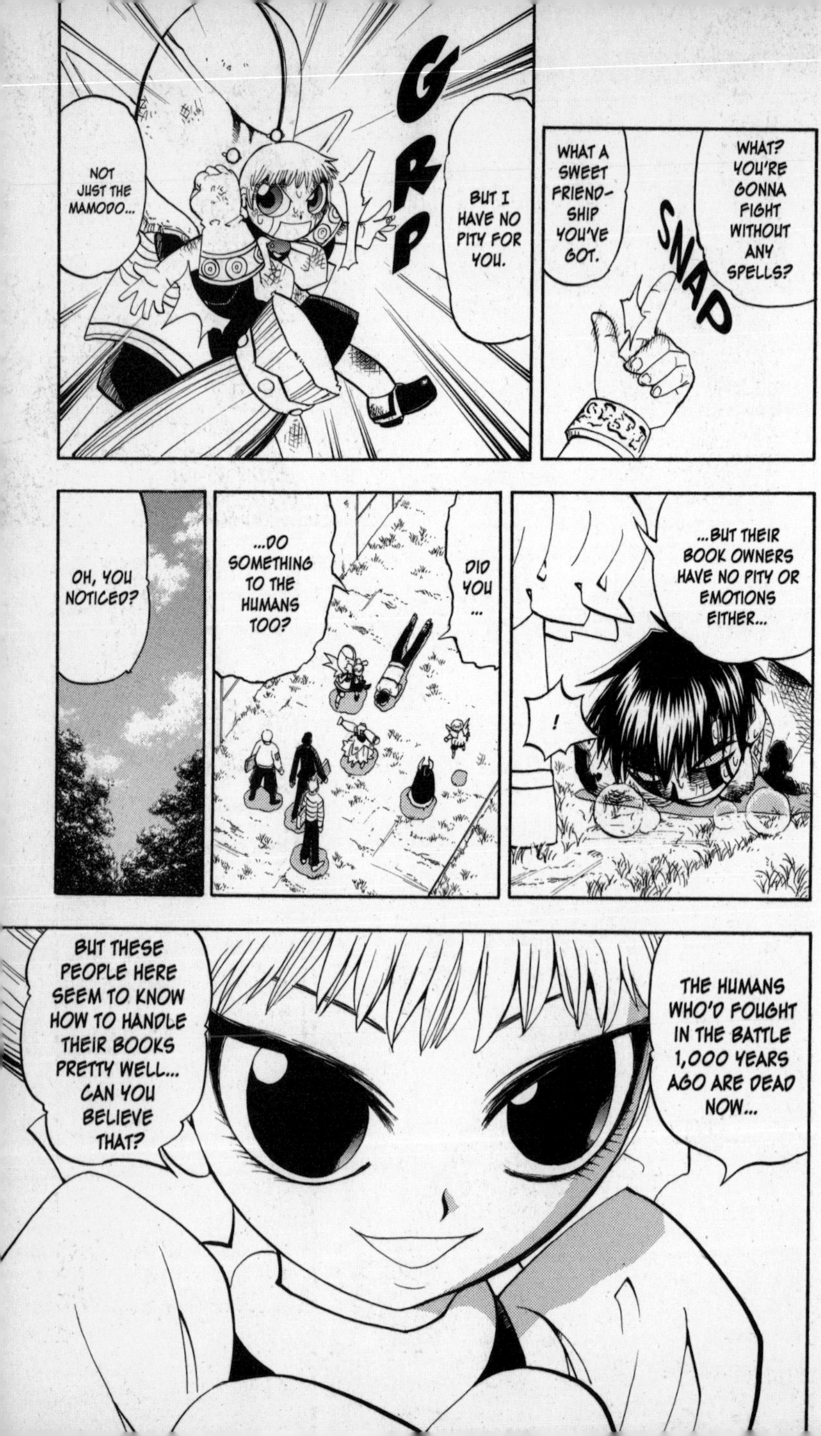
WHAT? YOU'RE GONNA FIGHT WITHOUT ANY SPELLS?
SNAP
WHAT A SWEET FRIEND-SHIP YOU'VE GOT.
GRP
BUT I HAVE NO PITY FOR YOU.
NOT JUST THE MAMODO...
...BUT THEIR BOOK OWNERS HAVE NO PITY OR EMOTIONS EITHER...
!
DID YOU ...
...DO SOMETHING TO THE HUMANS TOO?
OH, YOU NOTICED?
THE HUMANS WHO'D FOUGHT IN THE BATTLE 1,000 YEARS AGO ARE DEAD NOW...
BUT THESE PEOPLE HERE SEEM TO KNOW HOW TO HANDLE THEIR BOOKS PRETTY WELL... CAN YOU BELIEVE THAT?

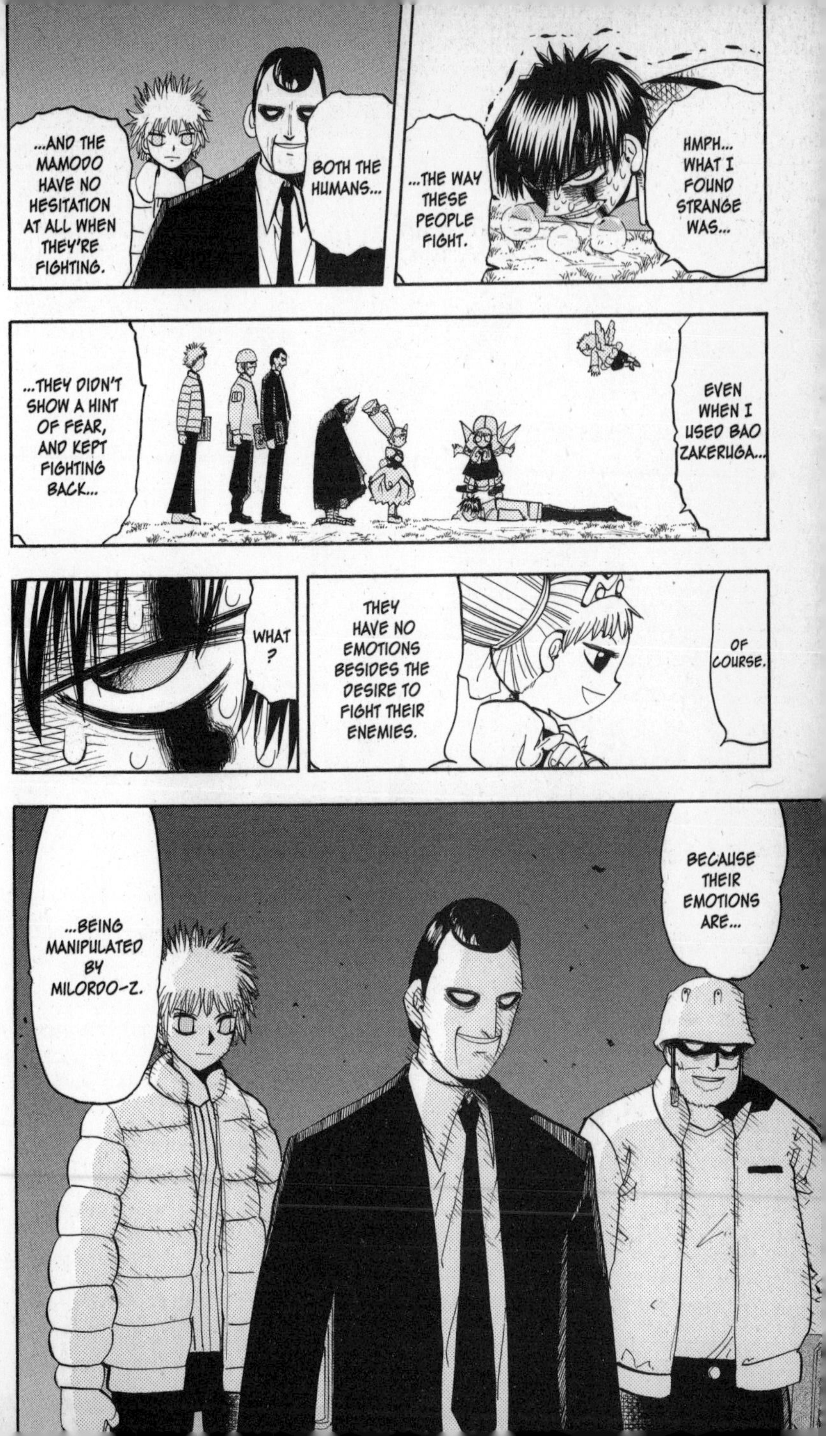
HMPH... WHAT I FOUND STRANGE WAS...
...THE WAY THESE PEOPLE FIGHT.
BOTH THE HUMANS...
...AND THE MAMODO HAVE NO HESITATION AT ALL WHEN THEY'RE FIGHTING.
EVEN WHEN I USED BAO ZAKERUGA...
...THEY DIDN'T SHOW A HINT OF FEAR, AND KEPT FIGHTING BACK...
OF COURSE.
THEY HAVE NO EMOTIONS BESIDES THE DESIRE TO FIGHT THEIR ENEMIES.
WHAT?
BECAUSE THEIR EMOTIONS ARE...
...BEING MANIPULATED BY MILORDO-Z.

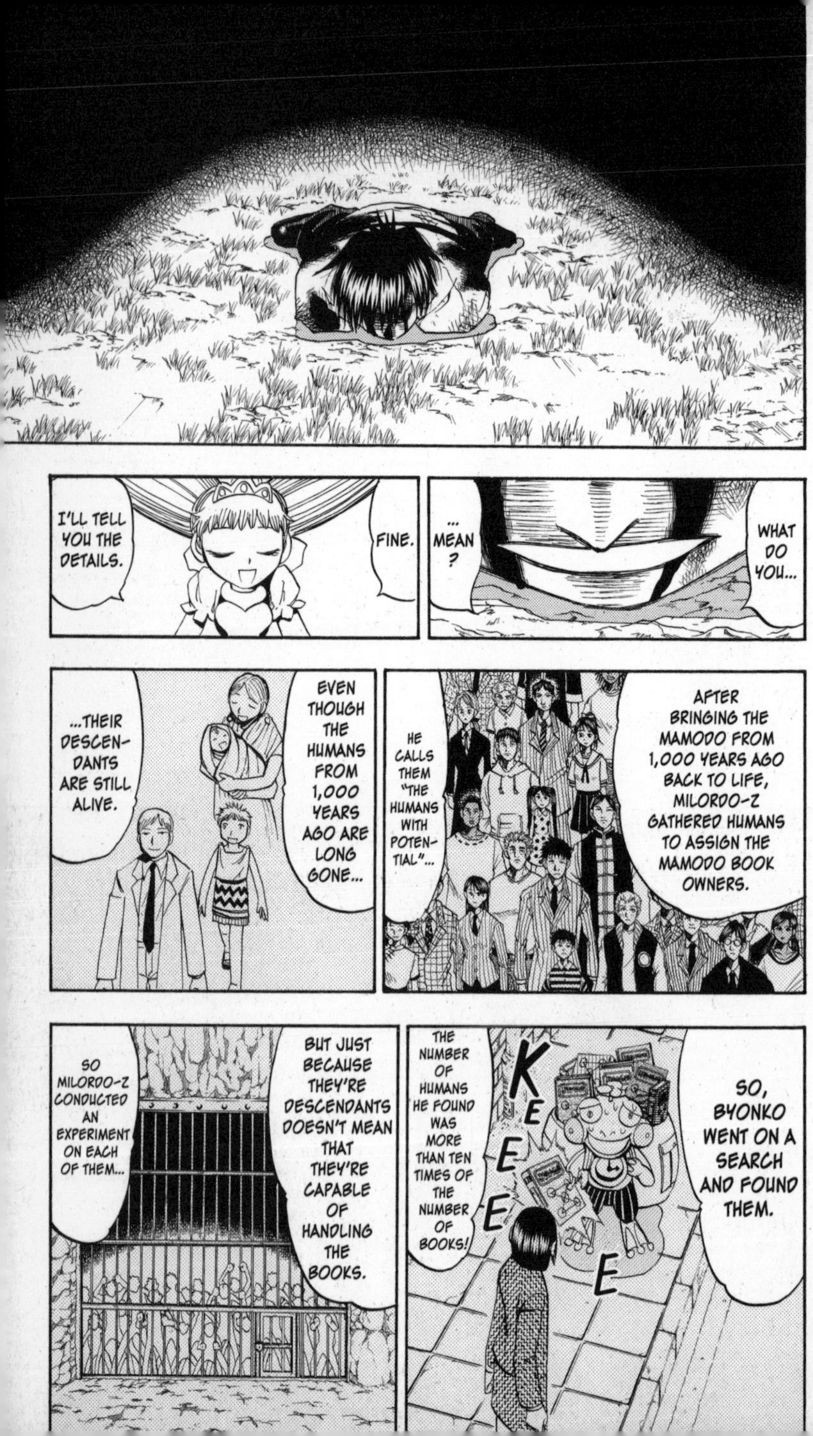
WHAT DO YOU...
...MEAN?
FINE.
I'LL TELL YOU THE DETAILS.
AFTER BRINGING THE MAMODO FROM 1,000 YEARS AGO BACK TO LIFE, MILORDO-Z GATHERED HUMANS TO ASSIGN THE MAMODO BOOK OWNERS.
HE CALLS THEM "THE HUMANS WITH POTENTIAL"...
EVEN THOUGH THE HUMANS FROM 1,000 YEARS AGO ARE LONG GONE...
...THEIR DESCENDANTS ARE STILL ALIVE.
SO, BYONKO WENT ON A SEARCH AND FOUND THEM.
KEEEEE
THE NUMBER OF HUMANS HE FOUND WAS MORE THAN TEN TIMES OF THE NUMBER OF BOOKS!
BUT JUST BECAUSE THEY'RE DESCENDANTS DOESN'T MEAN THAT THEY'RE CAPABLE OF HANDLING THE BOOKS.
SO MILORDO-Z CONDUCTED AN EXPERIMENT ON EACH OF THEM...

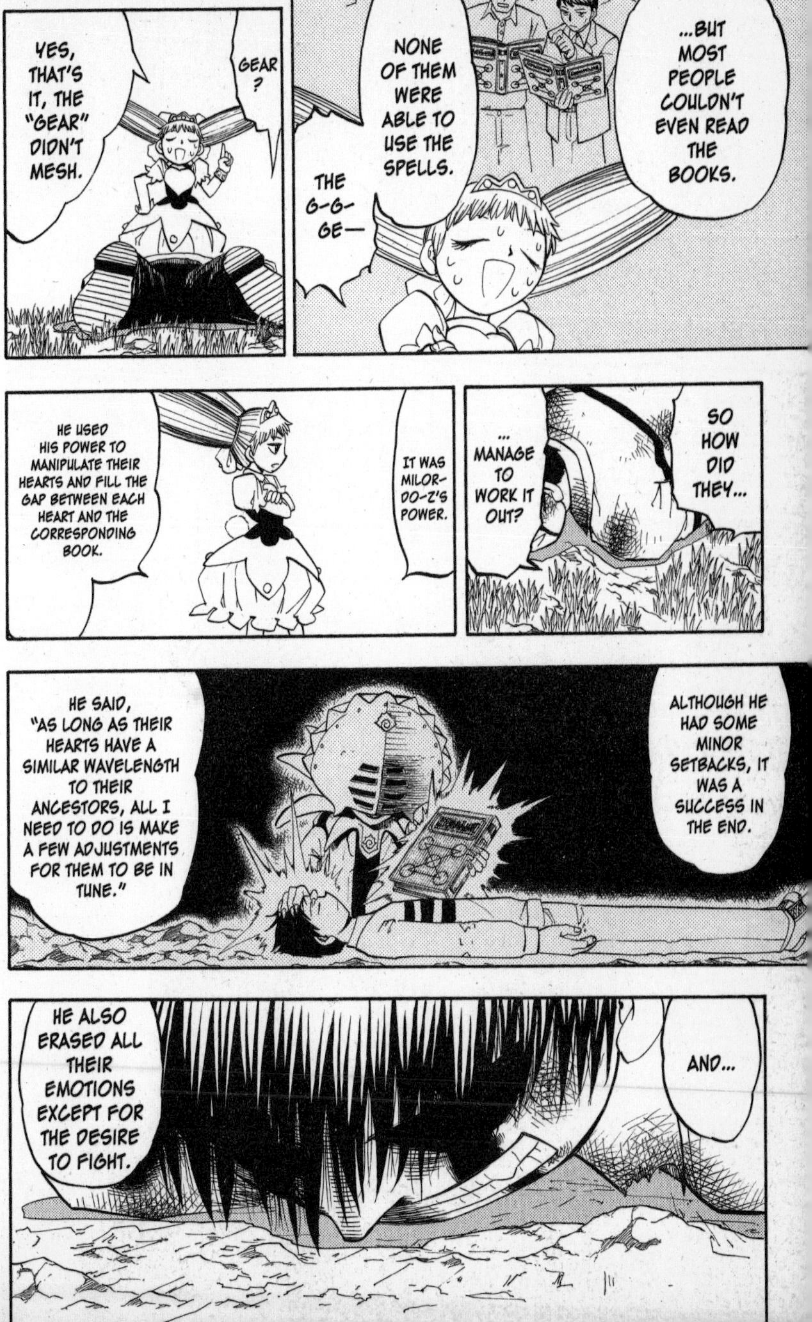
...BUT MOST PEOPLE COULDN'T EVEN READ THE BOOKS.
NONE OF THEM WERE ABLE TO USE THE SPELLS.
THE G-G-GE—
GEAR?
YES, THAT'S IT, THE "GEAR" DIDN'T MESH.
SO HOW DID THEY...
... MANAGE TO WORK IT OUT?
IT WAS MILOR-DO-Z'S POWER.
HE USED HIS POWER TO MANIPULATE THEIR HEARTS AND FILL THE GAP BETWEEN EACH HEART AND THE CORRESPONDING BOOK.
ALTHOUGH HE HAD SOME MINOR SETBACKS, IT WAS A SUCCESS IN THE END.
HE SAID, "AS LONG AS THEIR HEARTS HAVE A SIMILAR WAVELENGTH TO THEIR ANCESTORS, ALL I NEED TO DO IS MAKE A FEW ADJUSTMENTS FOR THEM TO BE IN TUNE."
AND...
HE ALSO ERASED ALL THEIR EMOTIONS EXCEPT FOR THE DESIRE TO FIGHT.

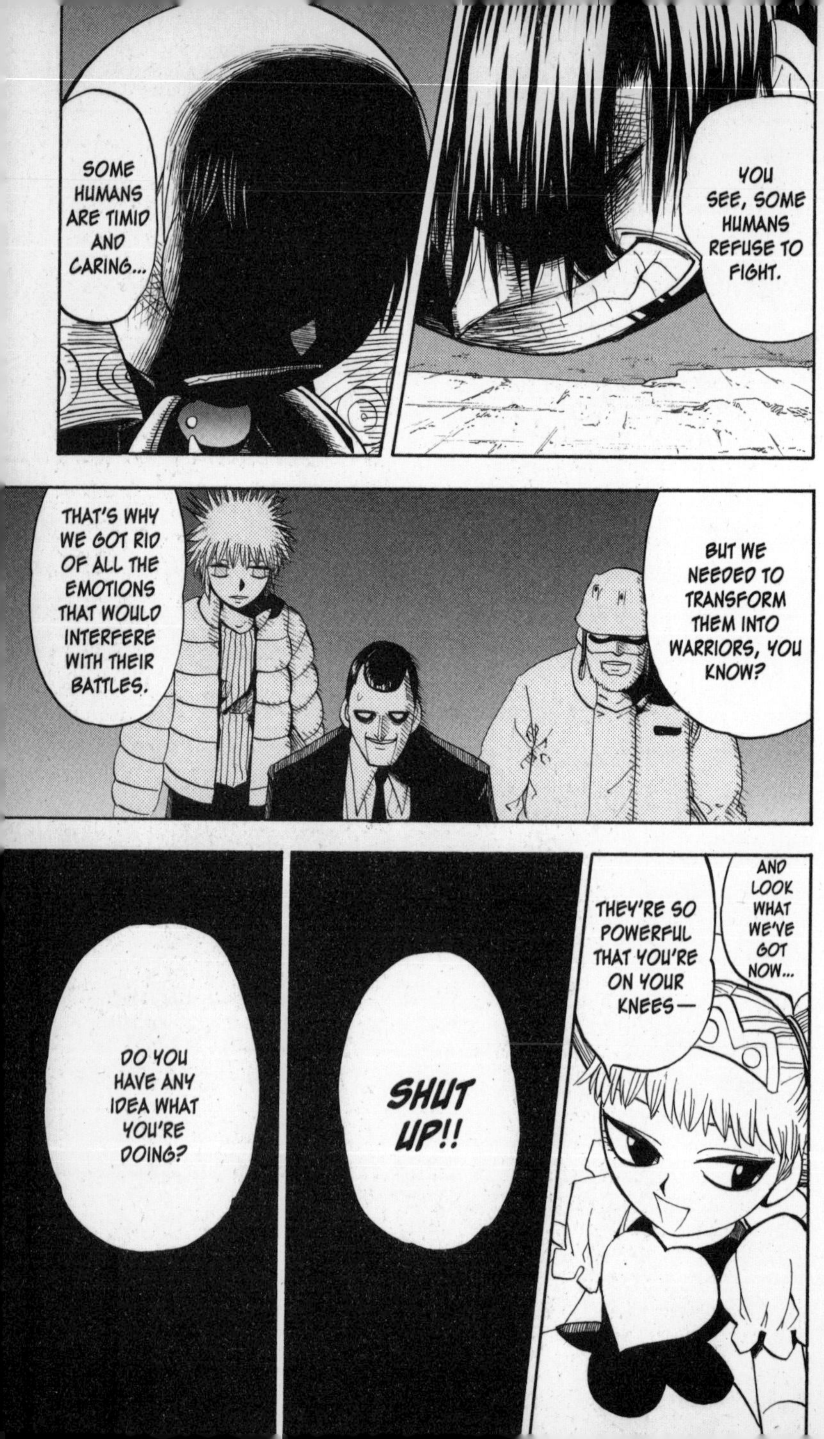
YOU SEE, SOME HUMANS REFUSE TO FIGHT.
SOME HUMANS ARE TIMID AND CARING...
BUT WE NEEDED TO TRANSFORM THEM INTO WARRIORS, YOU KNOW?
THAT'S WHY WE GOT RID OF ALL THE EMOTIONS THAT WOULD INTERFERE WITH THEIR BATTLES.
AND LOOK WHAT WE'VE GOT NOW...
THEY'RE SO POWERFUL THAT YOU'RE ON YOUR KNEES—
SHUT UP!!
DO YOU HAVE ANY IDEA WHAT YOU'RE DOING?

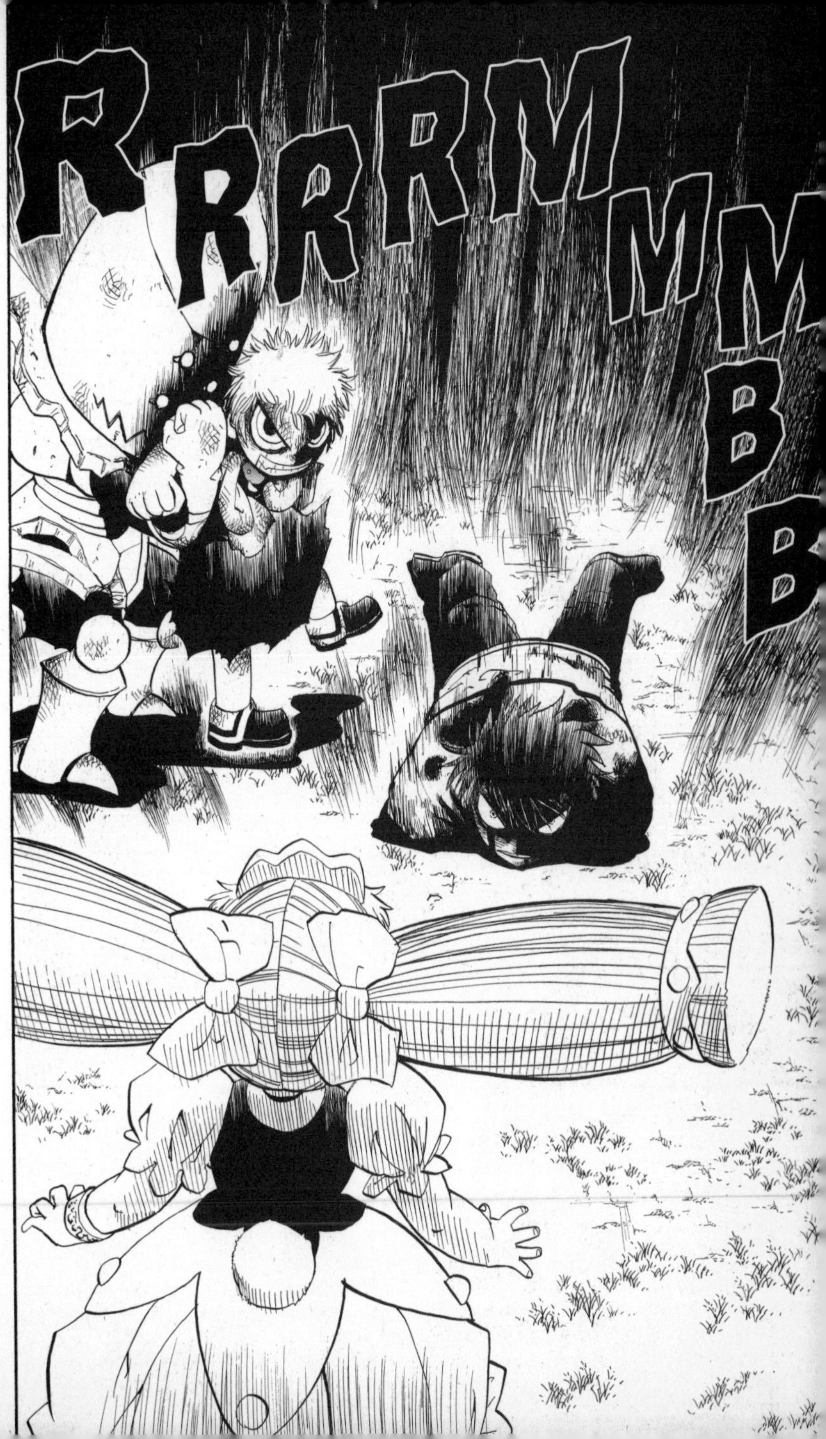
RRRRMMMMBB

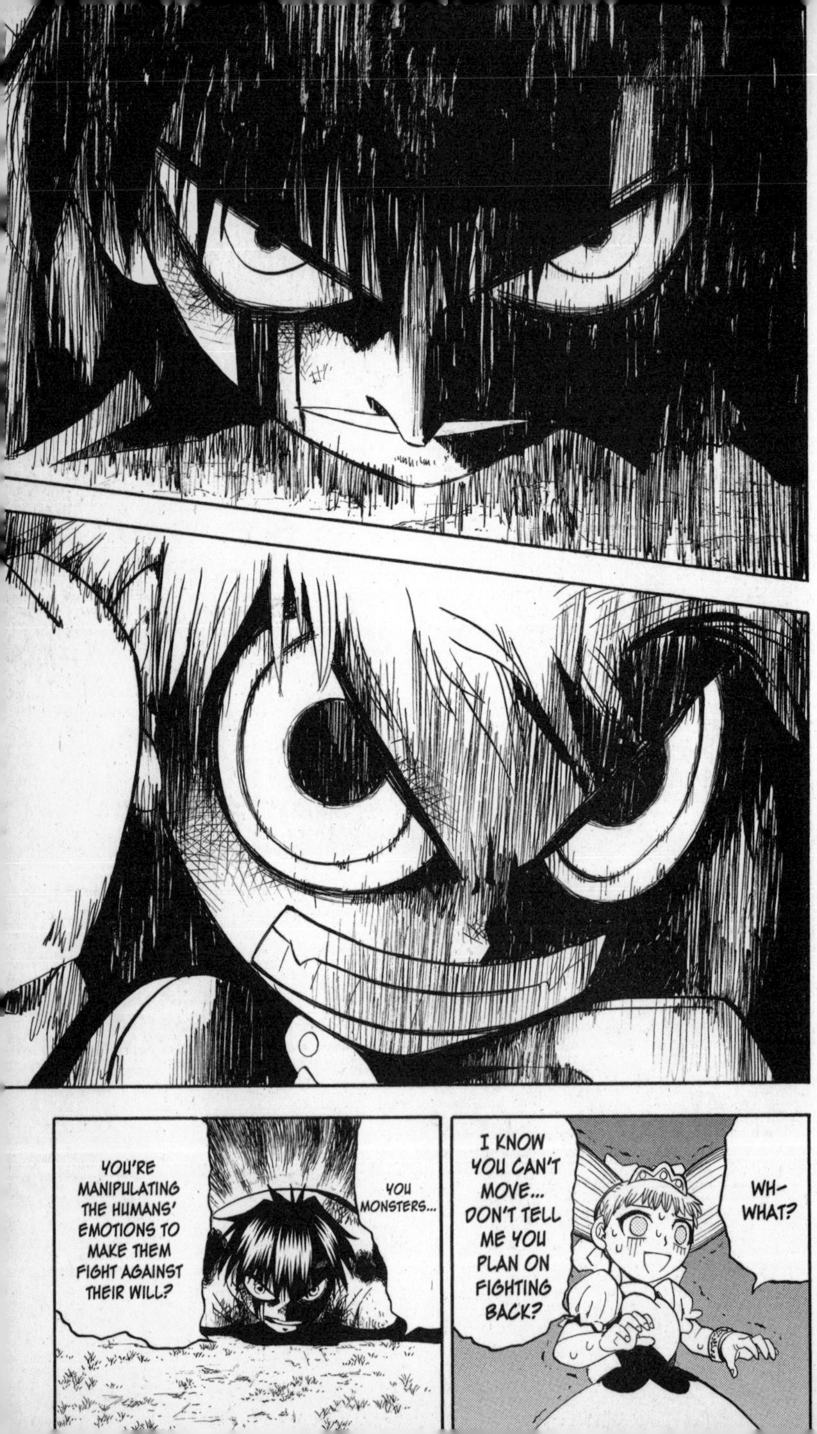

I KNOW YOU CAN'T MOVE... DON'T TELL ME YOU PLAN ON FIGHTING BACK?
WH-WHAT?
YOU MONSTERS...
YOU'RE MANIPULATING THE HUMANS' EMOTIONS TO MAKE THEM FIGHT AGAINST THEIR WILL?

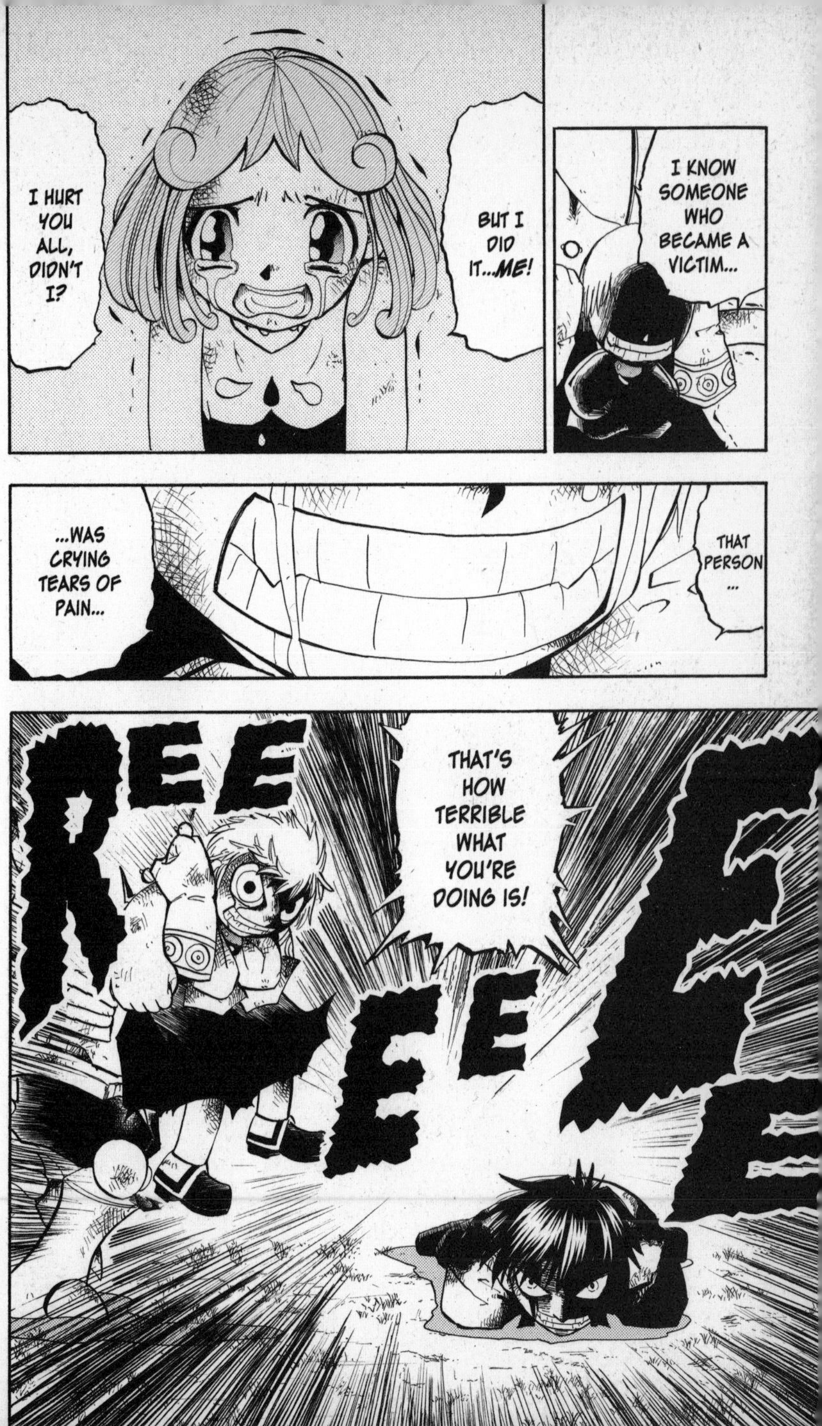
I KNOW SOMEONE WHO BECAME A VICTIM...
BUT I DID IT...**ME!**
I HURT YOU ALL, DIDN'T I?
THAT PERSON...
...WAS CRYING TEARS OF PAIN...
THAT'S HOW TERRIBLE WHAT YOU'RE DOING IS!

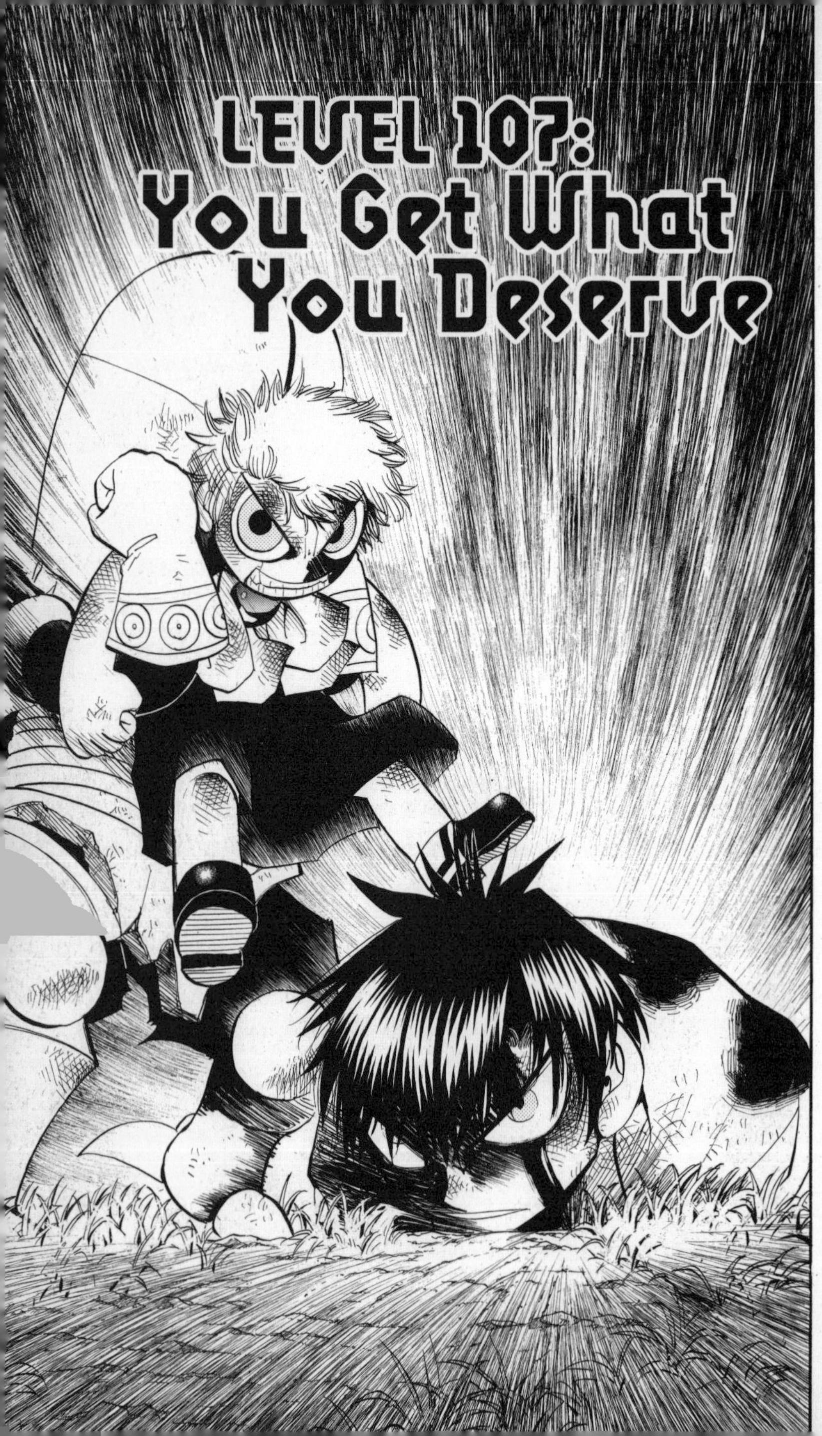
LEVEL 107:
You Get What You Deserve

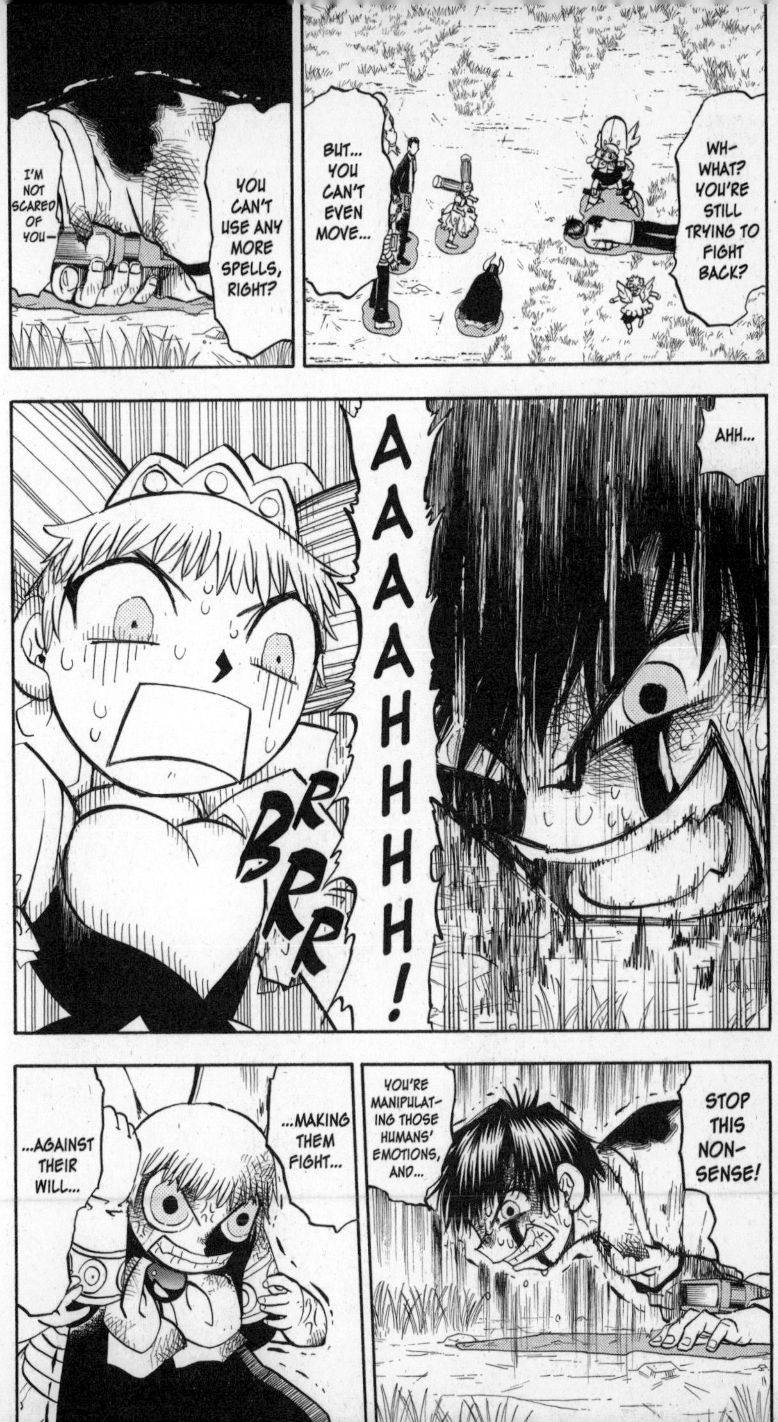
WH-WHAT? YOU'RE STILL TRYING TO FIGHT BACK?
BUT... YOU CAN'T EVEN MOVE...
YOU CAN'T USE ANY MORE SPELLS, RIGHT?
I'M NOT SCARED OF YOU—
AHH...
AAAAHHHH!
BRRRR
STOP THIS NON-SENSE!
YOU'RE MANIPULAT-ING THOSE HUMANS' EMOTIONS, AND...
...MAKING THEM FIGHT...
...AGAINST THEIR WILL...

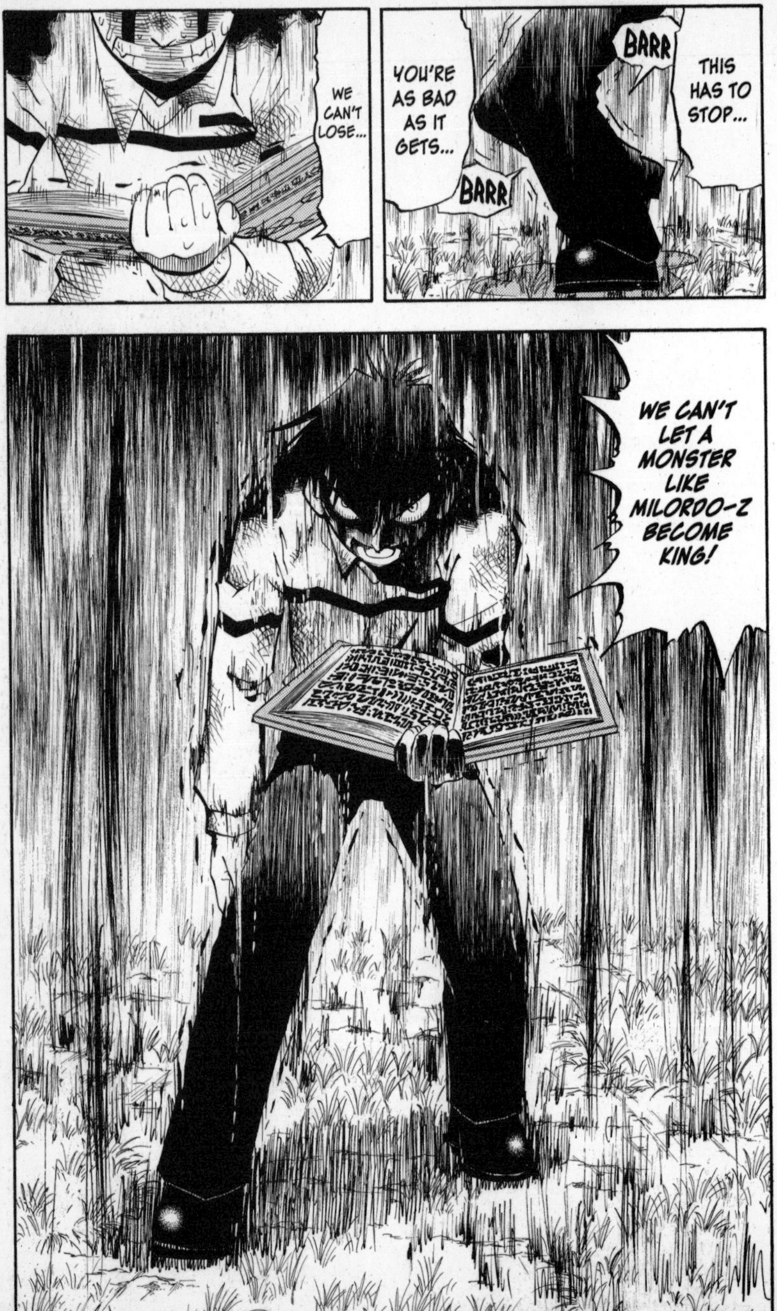
THIS HAS TO STOP...
BRRR
YOU'RE AS BAD AS IT GETS...
BRRR
WE CAN'T LOSE...
WE CAN'T LET A MONSTER LIKE MILORDO-Z BECOME KING!

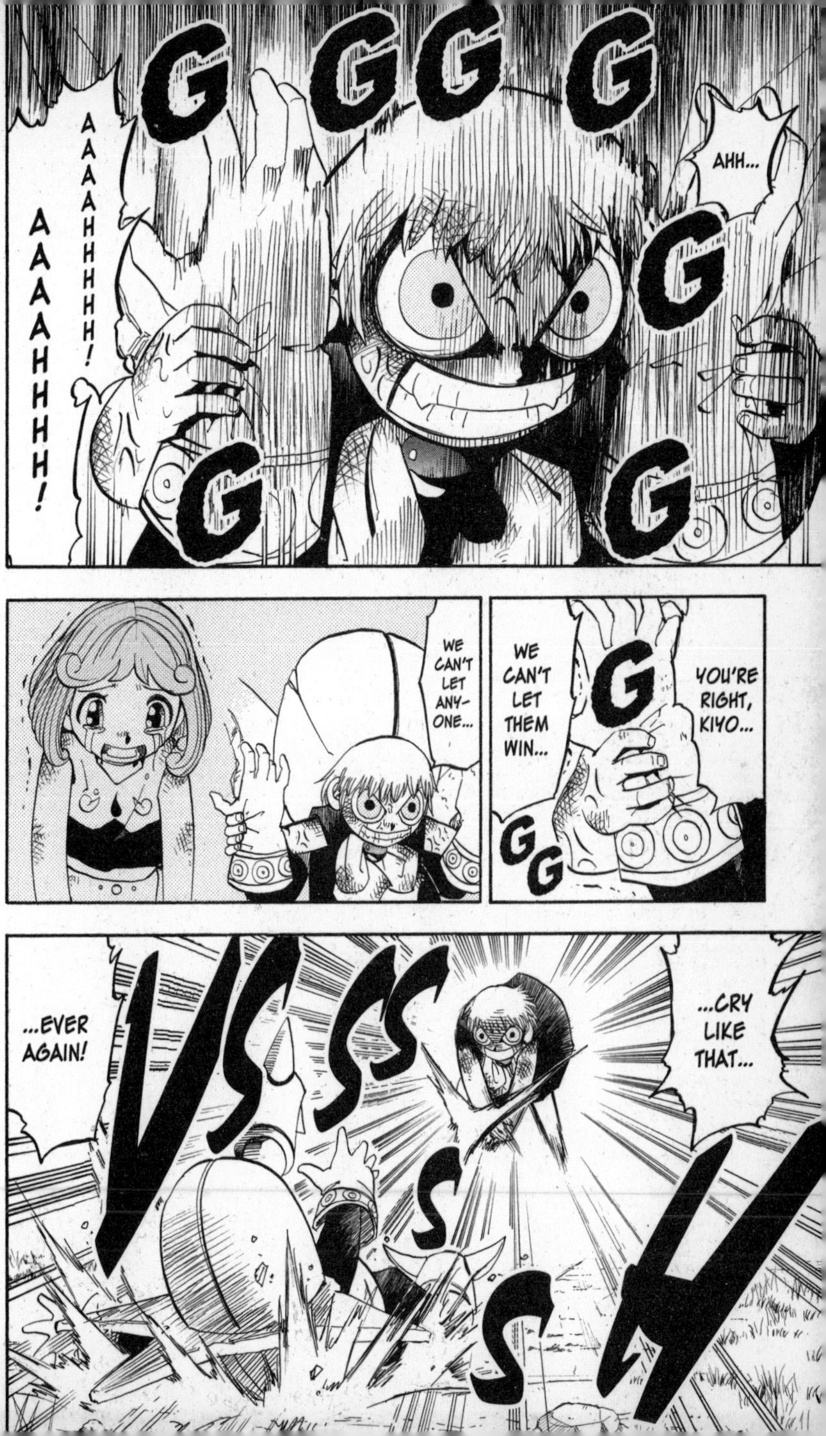
GGGGGGG
AHH...
AAAAHHHHHHH!
AAAAAHHHHHH!
YOU'RE RIGHT, KIYO...
G
WE CAN'T LET THEM WIN...
GG
WE CAN'T LET ANY-ONE...
...CRY LIKE THAT...
...EVER AGAIN!
VSSSSSH

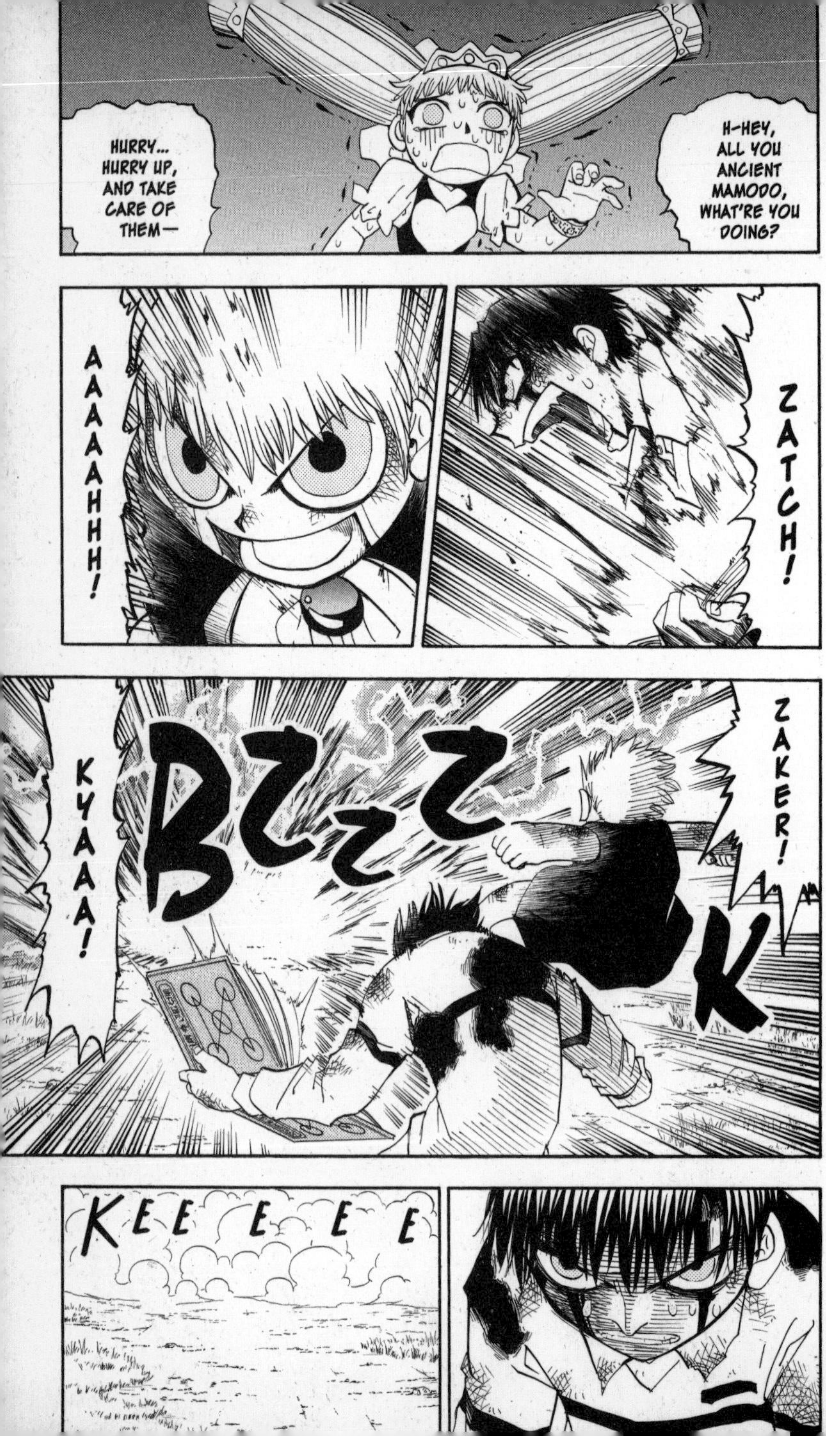
H-HEY, ALL YOU ANCIENT MAMODO, WHAT'RE YOU DOING?
HURRY... HURRY UP, AND TAKE CARE OF THEM—
ZATCH!
AAAAAAHHH!
ZAKER!
BZZZK
KYAAAA!
KEEEEE

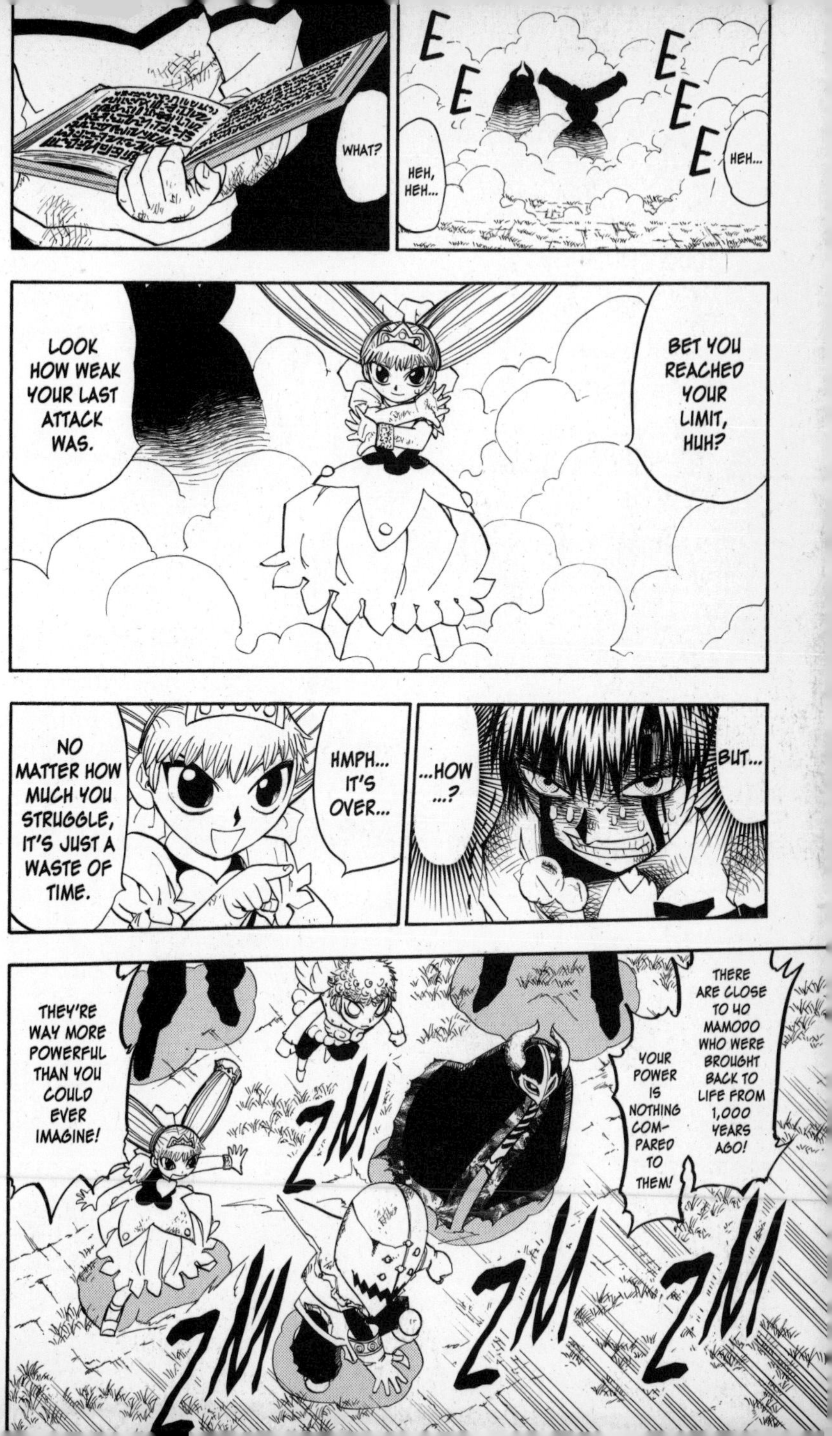
HEH...
EEEEEE
HEH, HEH...
WHAT?
BET YOU REACHED YOUR LIMIT, HUH?
LOOK HOW WEAK YOUR LAST ATTACK WAS.
BUT...
...HOW ...?
HMPH... IT'S OVER...
NO MATTER HOW MUCH YOU STRUGGLE, IT'S JUST A WASTE OF TIME.
THERE ARE CLOSE TO 40 MAMODO WHO WERE BROUGHT BACK TO LIFE FROM 1,000 YEARS AGO!
YOUR POWER IS NOTHING COM-PARED TO THEM!
THEY'RE WAY MORE POWERFUL THAN YOU COULD EVER IMAGINE!
ZM ZM ZM ZM ZM

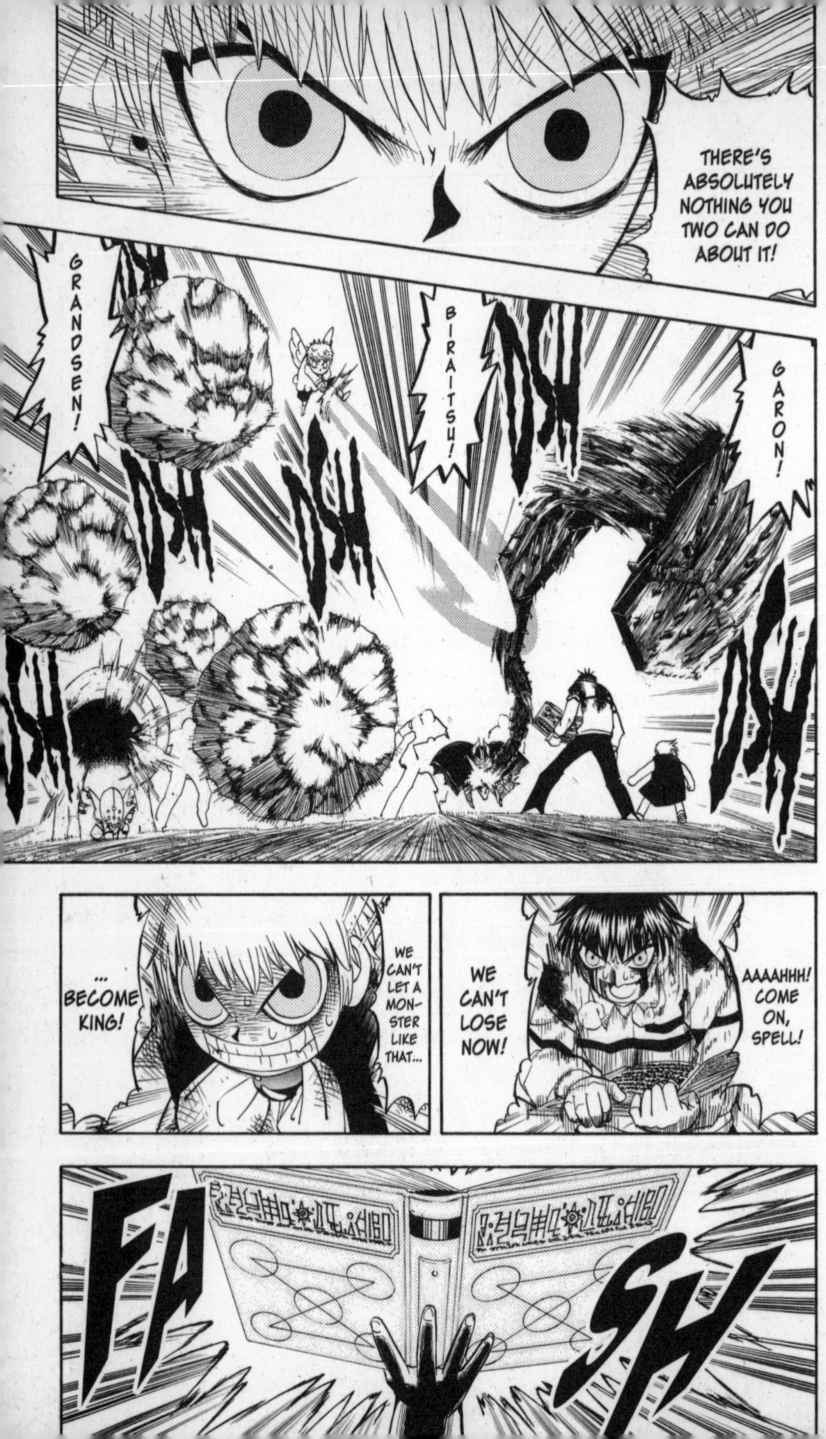
THERE'S ABSOLUTELY NOTHING YOU TWO CAN DO ABOUT IT!
GARON!
DSH
DSH
BIRAITSU!
DSH
GRANDSEN!
DSH
DSH
AAAAHHH! COME ON, SPELL!
WE CAN'T LOSE NOW!
WE CAN'T LET A MON-STER LIKE THAT...
... BECOME KING!
FASH

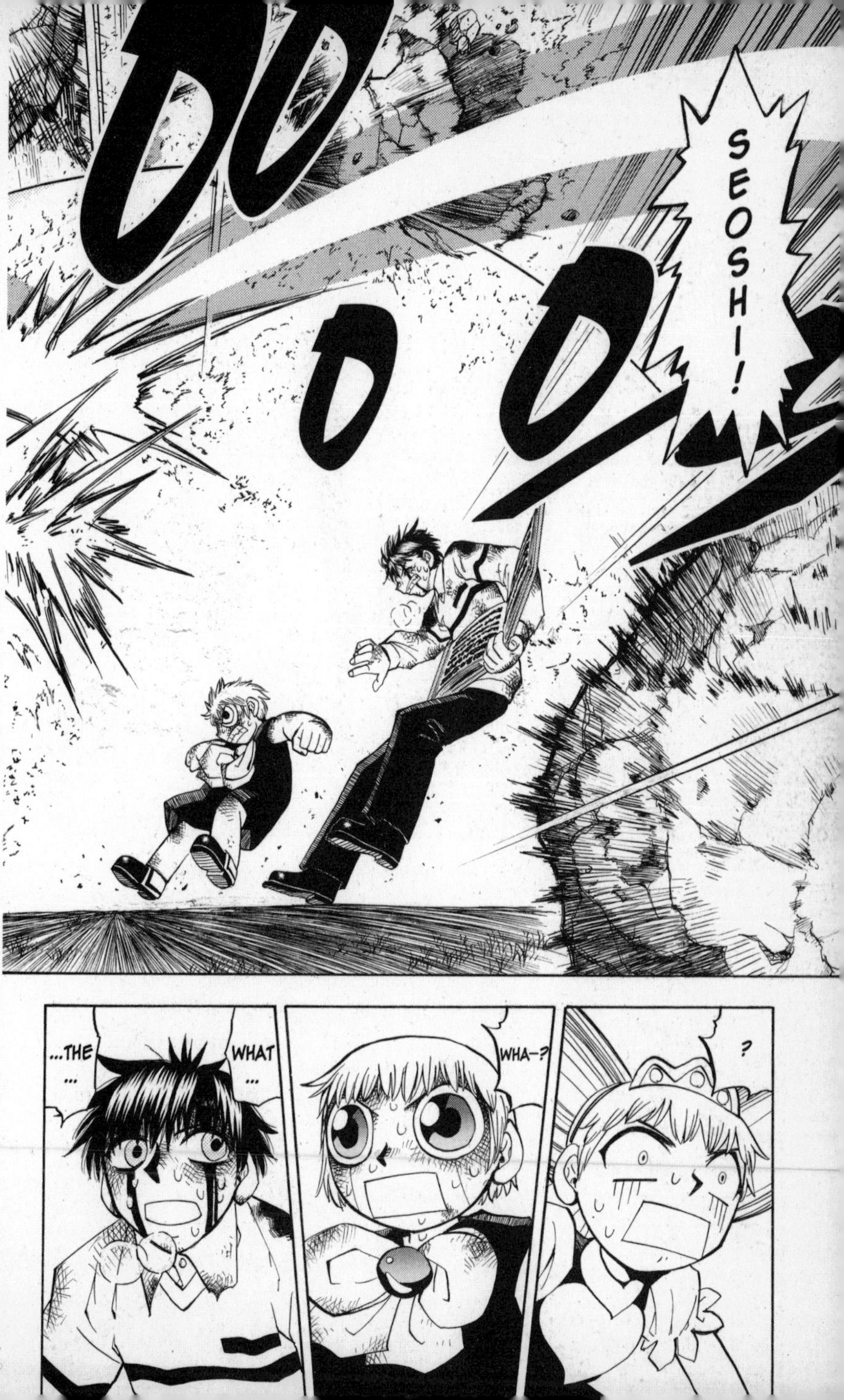
SEOSHI!!
DO DO DO
?
WHA-?
WHAT ...
...THE ...

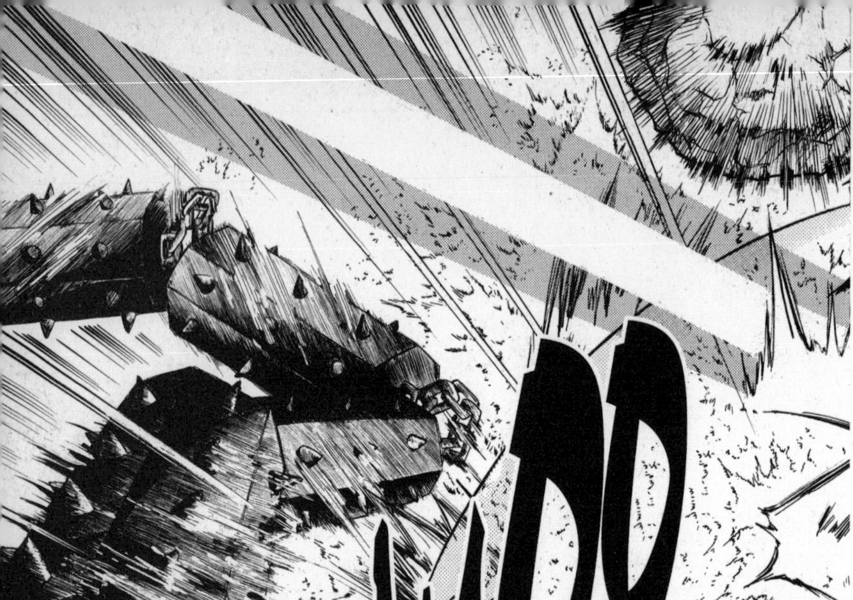
VWOO
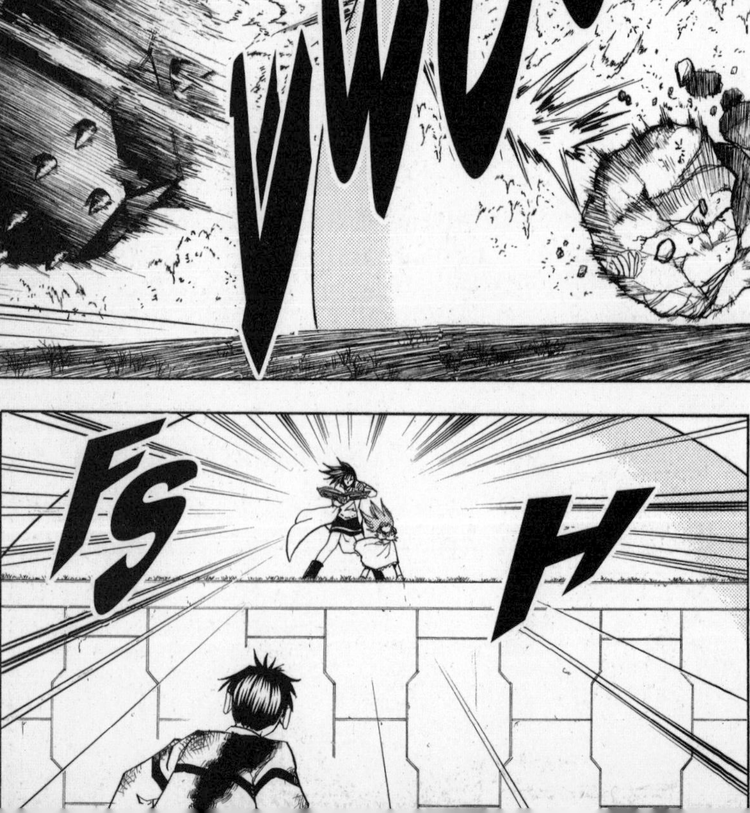
FSH

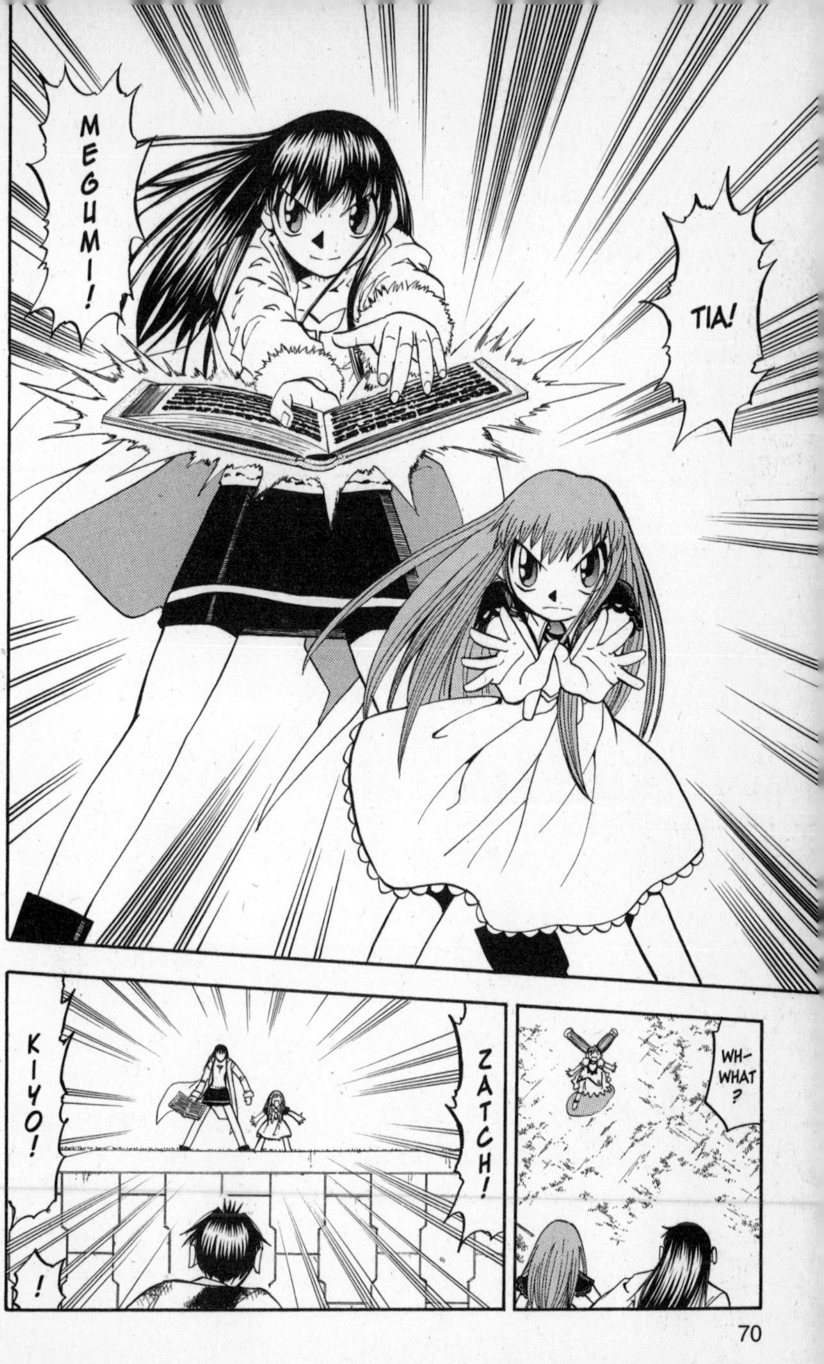
TIA!
MEGUMI!
WH-WHAT?
ZATCH!
KIYO!
!

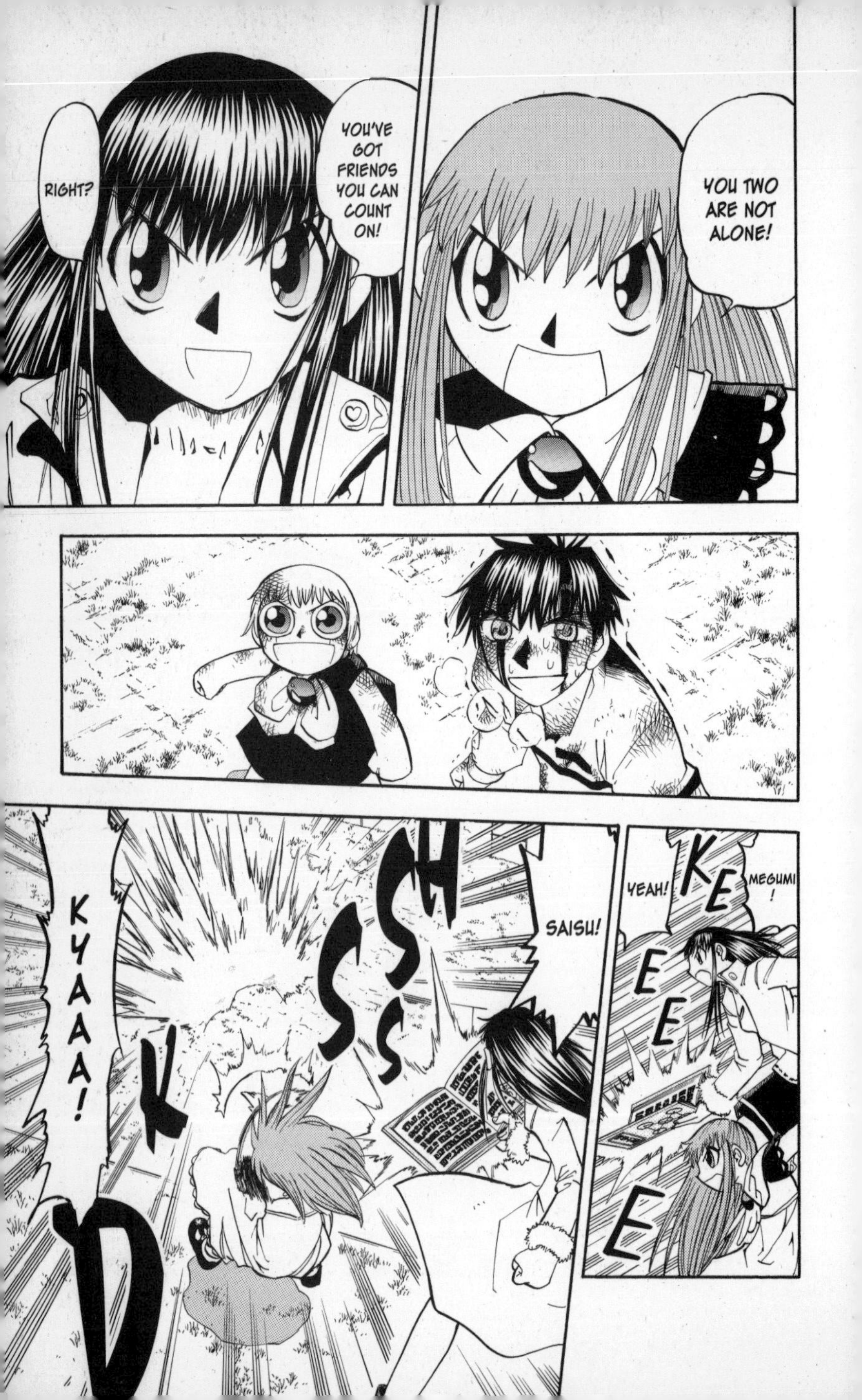
YOU TWO ARE NOT ALONE!
YOU'VE GOT FRIENDS YOU CAN COUNT ON!
RIGHT?
MEGUMI!
KEEEE
YEAH!
SAISU!
SHSS
KYAAAA!
DK

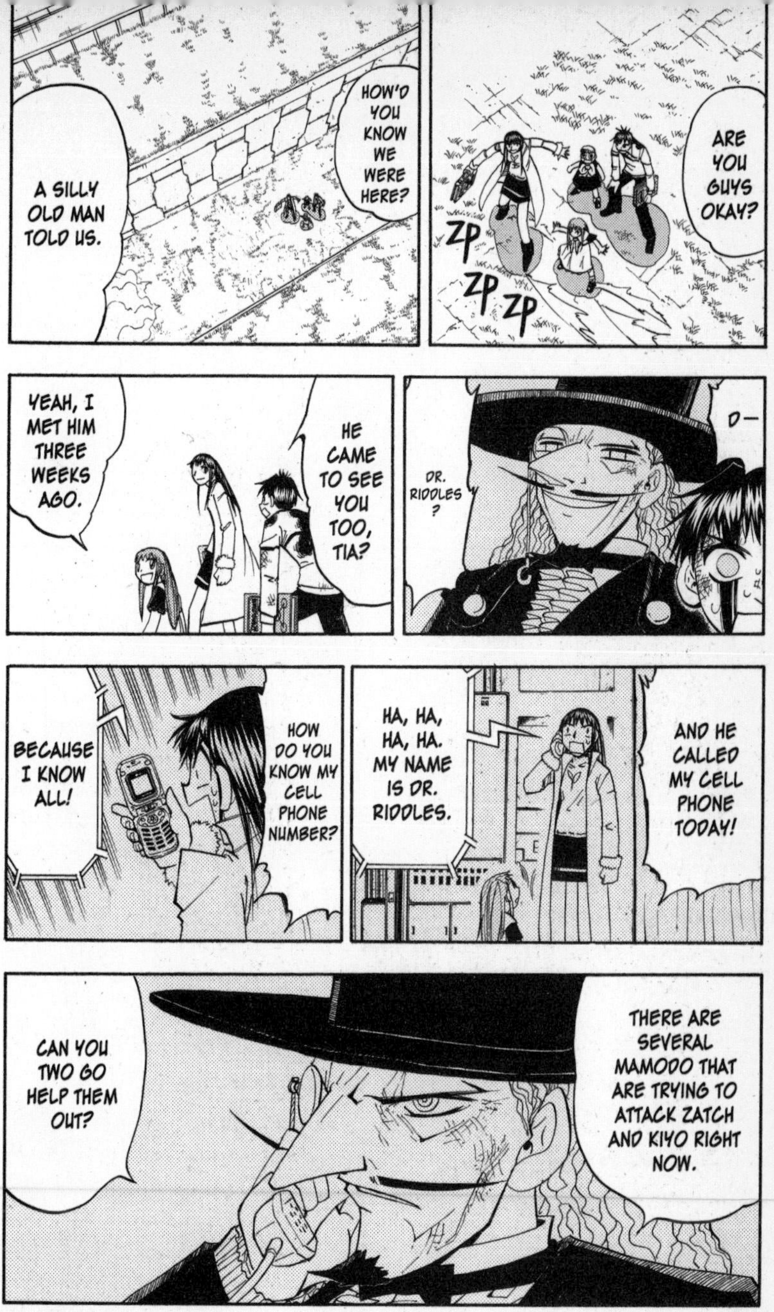
ARE YOU GUYS OKAY?
ZP
ZP
ZP
HOW'D YOU KNOW WE WERE HERE?
A SILLY OLD MAN TOLD US.
D—
DR. RIDDLES?
HE CAME TO SEE YOU TOO, TIA?
YEAH, I MET HIM THREE WEEKS AGO.
AND HE CALLED MY CELL PHONE TODAY!
HA, HA, HA, HA. MY NAME IS DR. RIDDLES.
HOW DO YOU KNOW MY CELL PHONE NUMBER?
BECAUSE I KNOW ALL!
THERE ARE SEVERAL MAMODO THAT ARE TRYING TO ATTACK ZATCH AND KIYO RIGHT NOW.
CAN YOU TWO GO HELP THEM OUT?

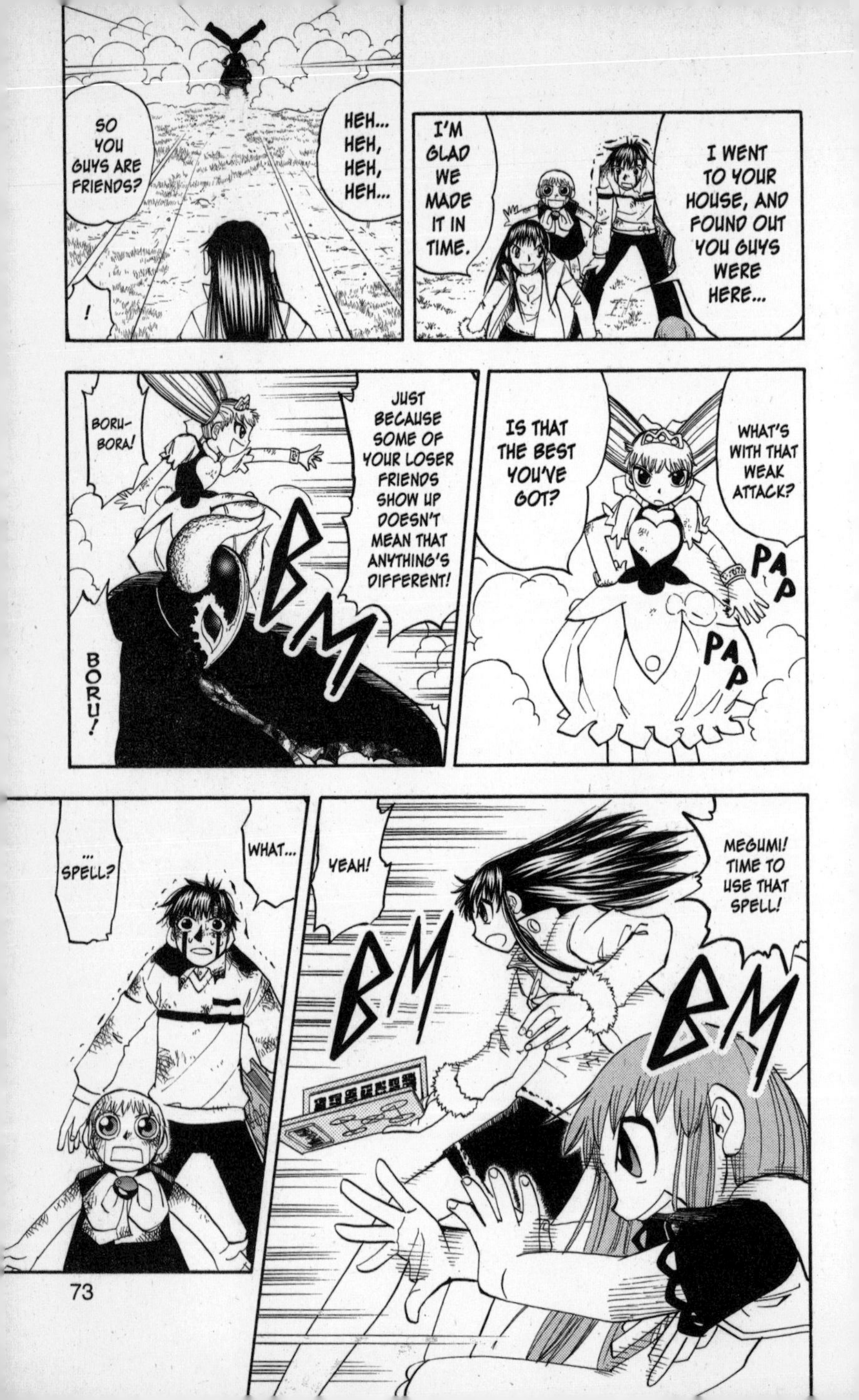
I WENT TO YOUR HOUSE, AND FOUND OUT YOU GUYS WERE HERE...
I'M GLAD WE MADE IT IN TIME.
HEH... HEH, HEH, HEH...
SO YOU GUYS ARE FRIENDS?
!
WHAT'S WITH THAT WEAK ATTACK?
IS THAT THE BEST YOU'VE GOT?
PAP PAP
PAP PAP
JUST BECAUSE SOME OF YOUR LOSER FRIENDS SHOW UP DOESN'T MEAN THAT ANYTHING'S DIFFERENT!
BORU-BORA!
BM
BORU!
MEGUMI! TIME TO USE THAT SPELL!
YEAH!
BM
BM
WHAT...
... SPELL?

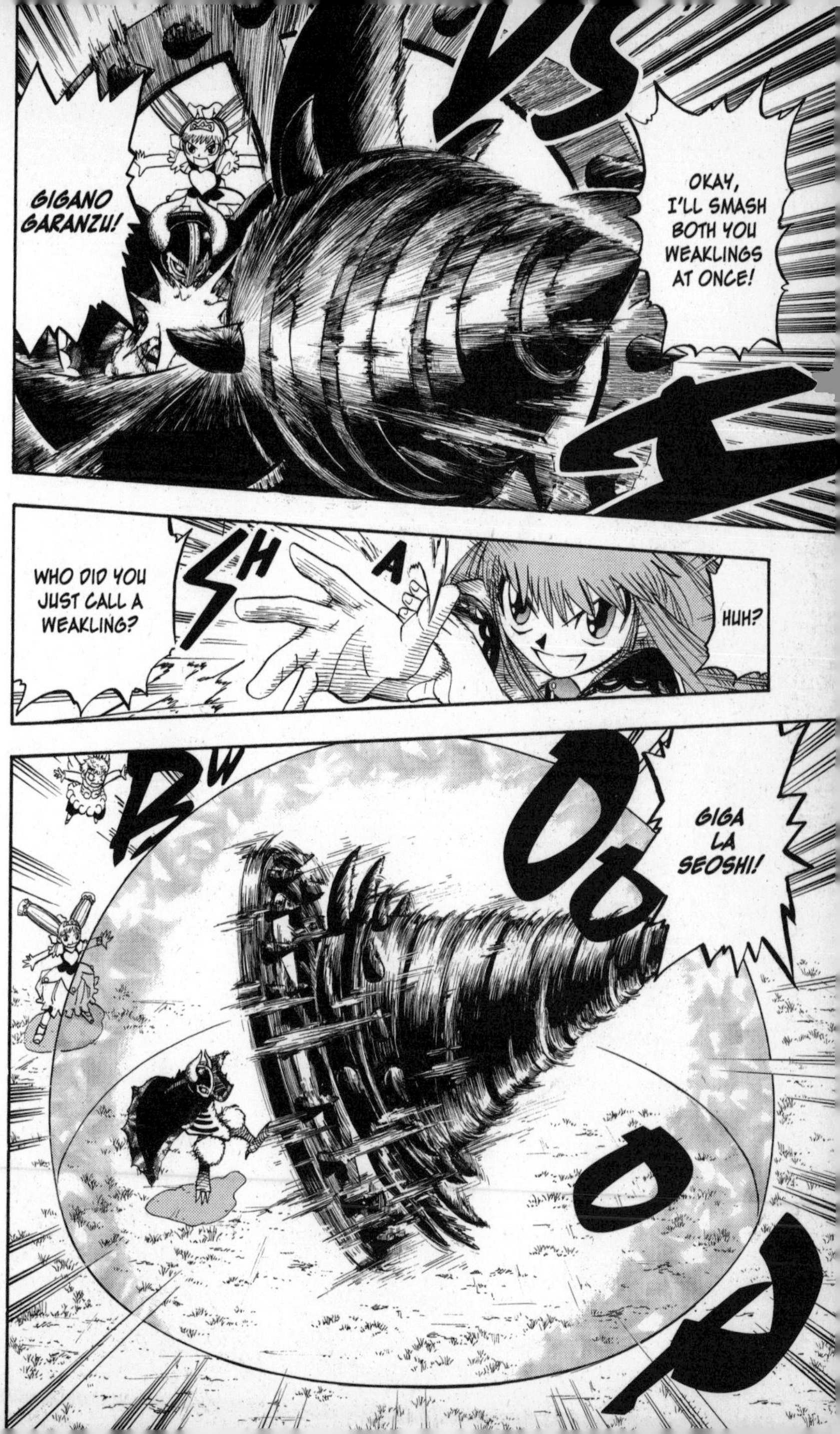
OKAY, I'LL SMASH BOTH YOU WEAKLINGS AT ONCE!
GIGANO GARANZU!
HUH?
WHO DID YOU JUST CALL A WEAKLING?
GIGA LA SEOSHI!

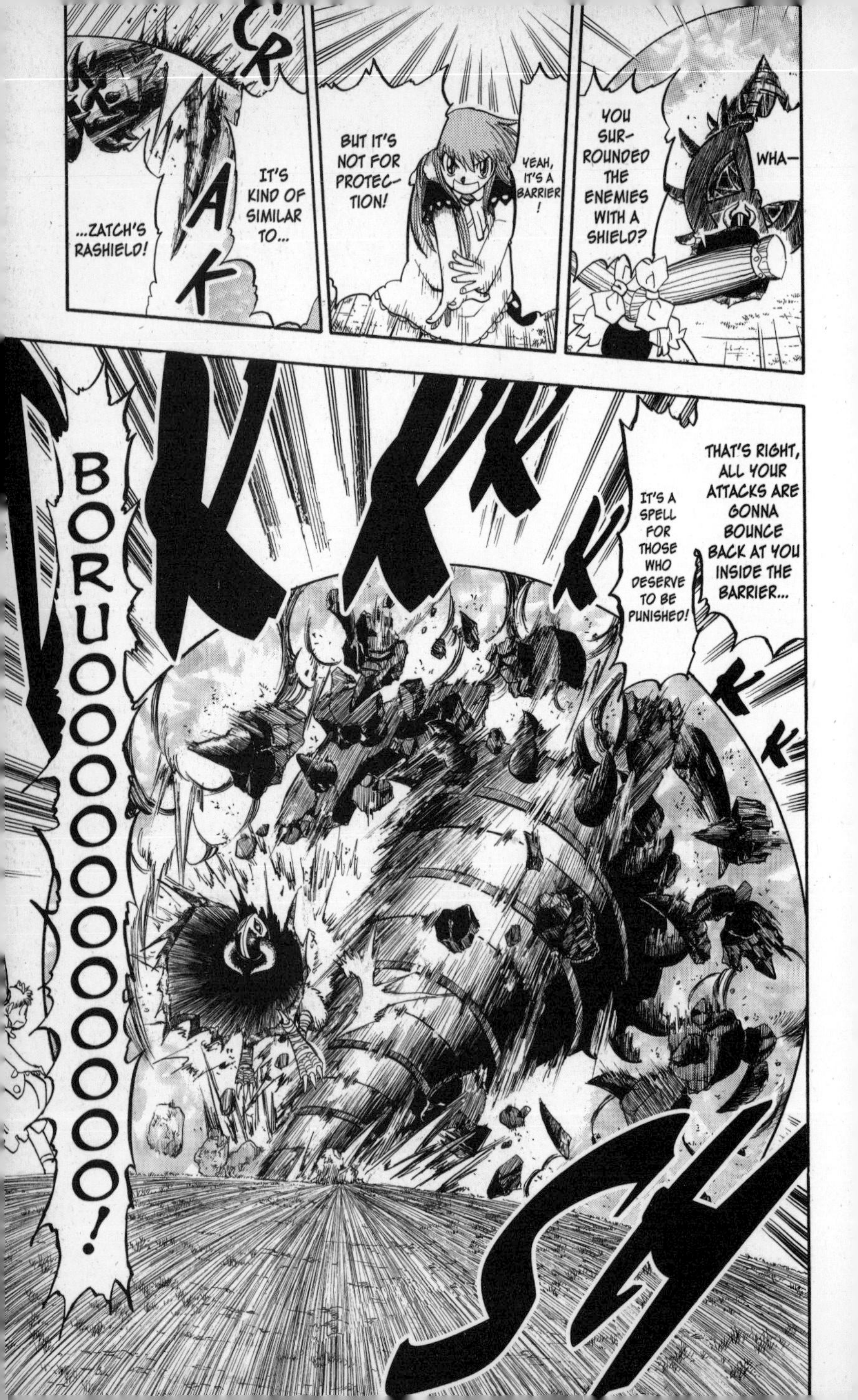
WHA-
YOU SURROUNDED THE ENEMIES WITH A SHIELD?
YEAH, IT'S A BARRIER!
BUT IT'S NOT FOR PROTECTION!
IT'S KIND OF SIMILAR TO...
...ZATCH'S RASHIELD!
CRAK
THAT'S RIGHT, ALL YOUR ATTACKS ARE GONNA BOUNCE BACK AT YOU INSIDE THE BARRIER...
IT'S A SPELL FOR THOSE WHO DESERVE TO BE PUNISHED!
BORUOOOOOOOOOOOOOO!

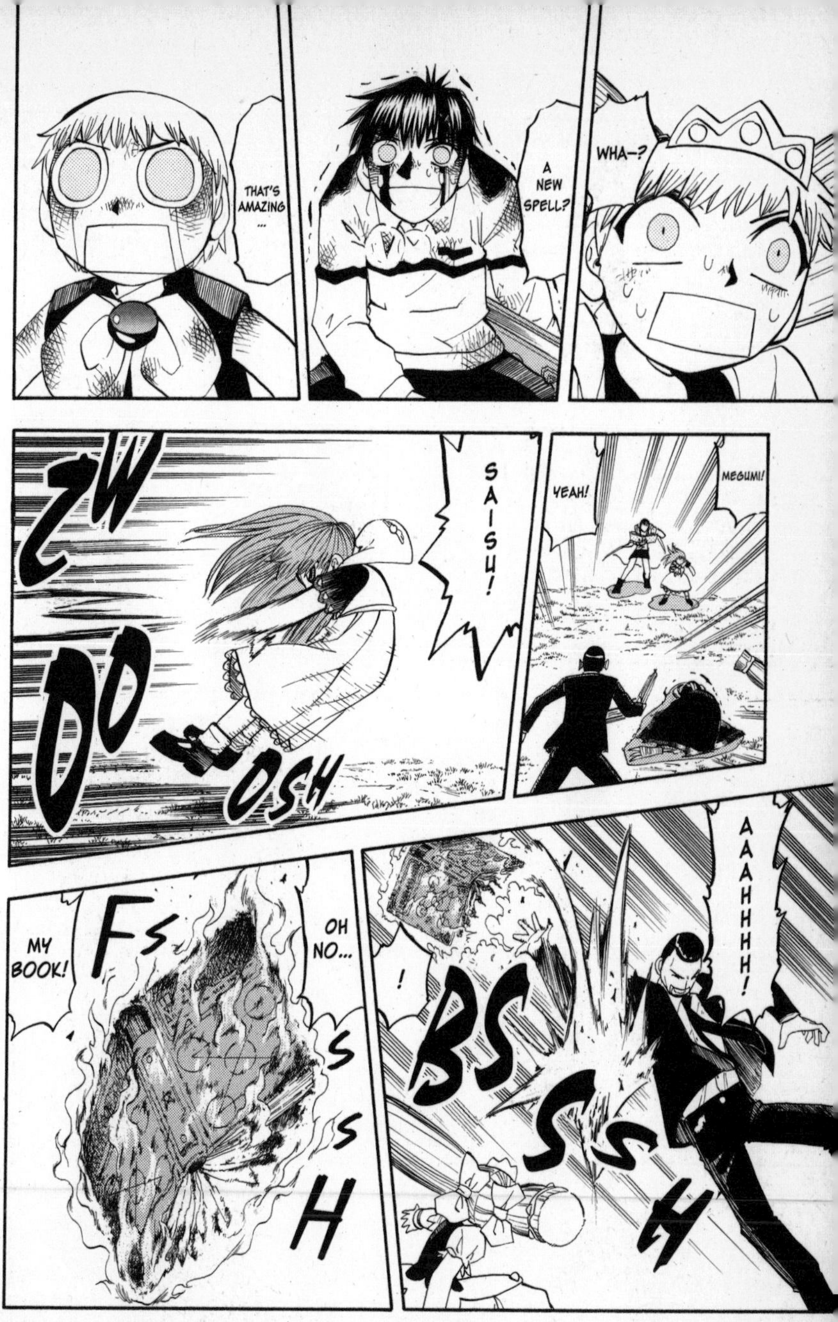
WHA–?
A NEW SPELL?
THAT'S AMAZING ...
MEGUMI!
YEAH!
SAISU!
ZWOOOSH
AAAHHHH!
!
BSSSH
OH NO...
MY BOOK!
FSSSH

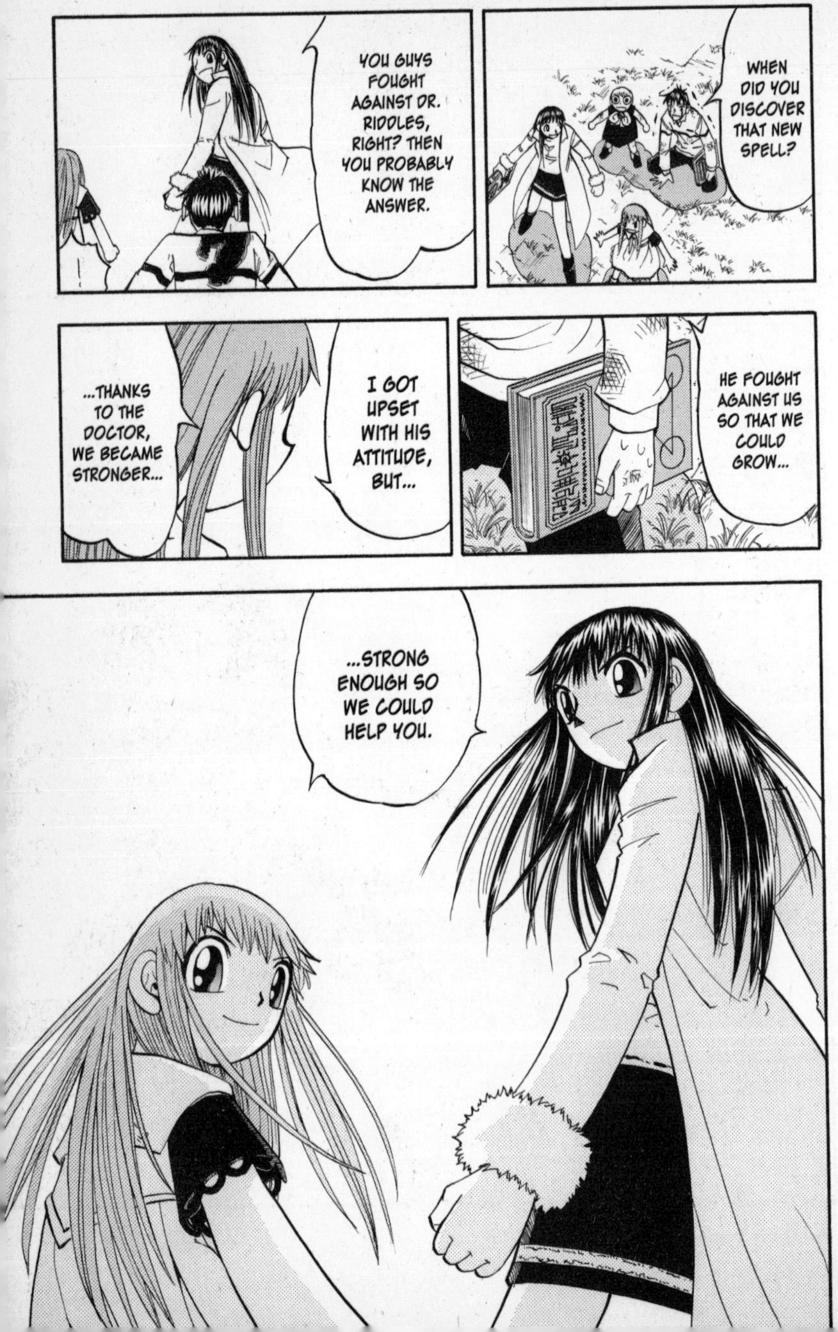
WHEN DID YOU DISCOVER THAT NEW SPELL?
YOU GUYS FOUGHT AGAINST DR. RIDDLES, RIGHT? THEN YOU PROBABLY KNOW THE ANSWER.
HE FOUGHT AGAINST US SO THAT WE COULD GROW...
I GOT UPSET WITH HIS ATTITUDE, BUT...
...THANKS TO THE DOCTOR, WE BECAME STRONGER...
...STRONG ENOUGH SO WE COULD HELP YOU.

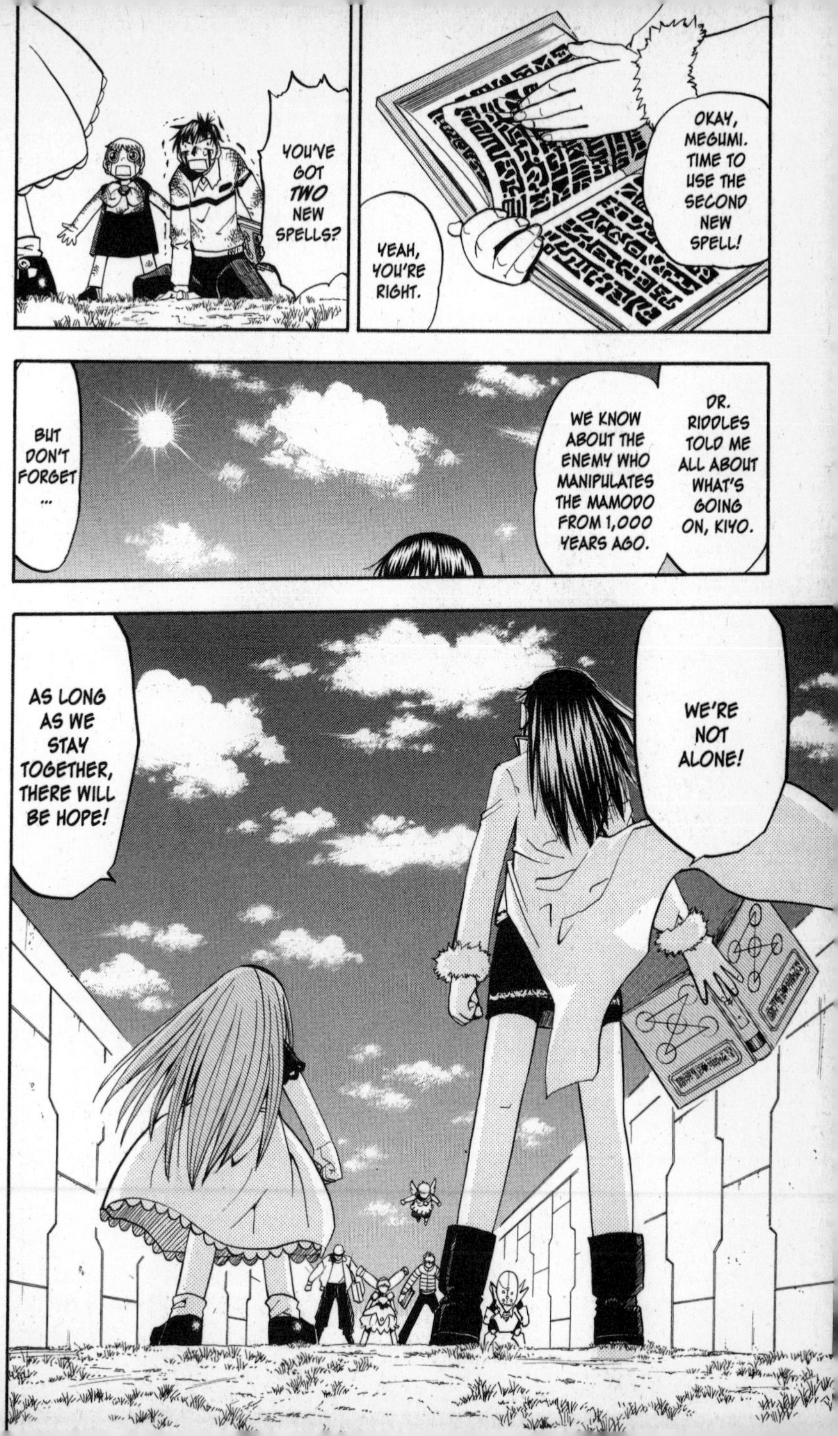
OKAY, MEGUMI. TIME TO USE THE SECOND NEW SPELL!
YEAH, YOU'RE RIGHT.
YOU'VE GOT TWO NEW SPELLS?
DR. RIDDLES TOLD ME ALL ABOUT WHAT'S GOING ON, KIYO.
WE KNOW ABOUT THE ENEMY WHO MANIPULATES THE MAMODO FROM 1,000 YEARS AGO.
BUT DON'T FORGET...
WE'RE NOT ALONE!
AS LONG AS WE STAY TOGETHER, THERE WILL BE HOPE!

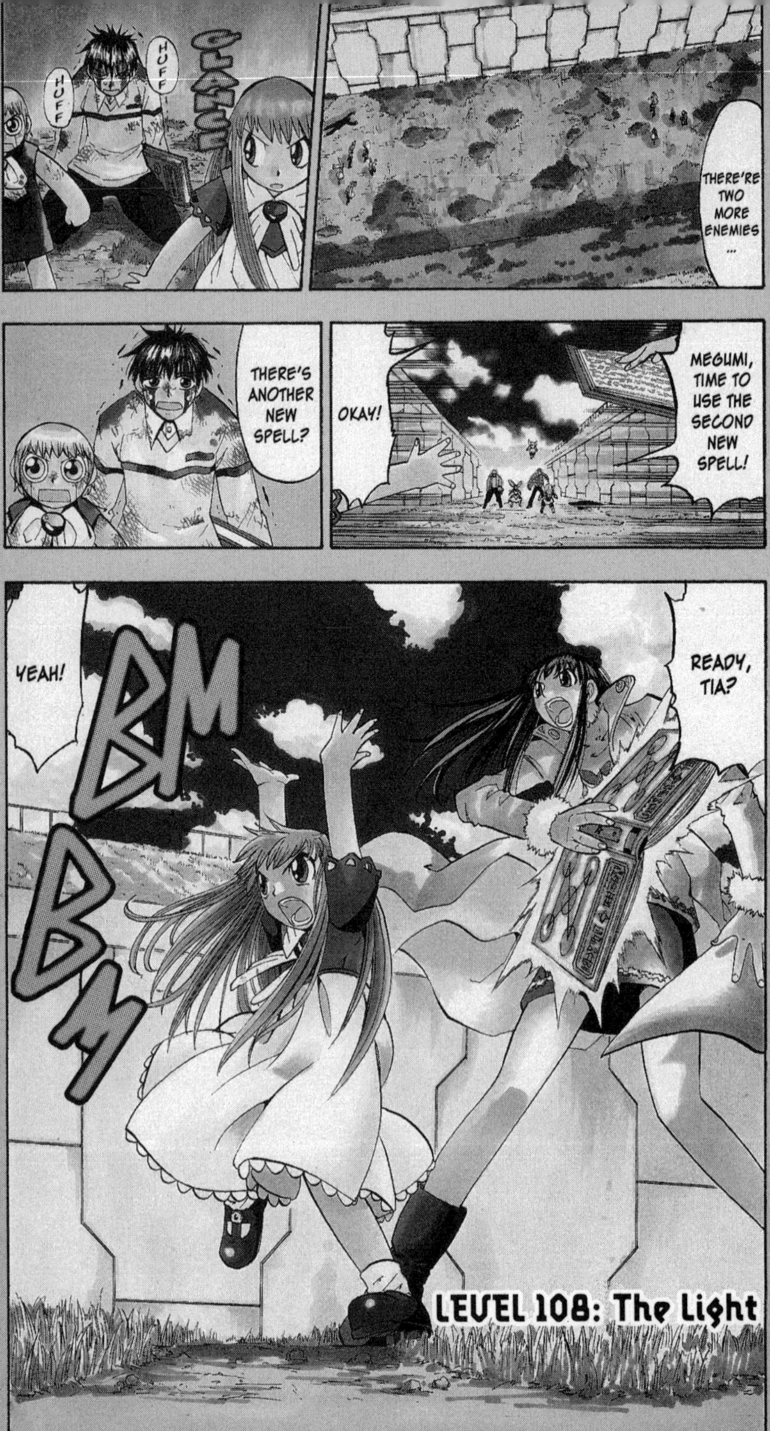
THERE'RE TWO MORE ENEMIES ...
HUFF
HUFF
MEGUMI, TIME TO USE THE SECOND NEW SPELL!
OKAY!
THERE'S ANOTHER NEW SPELL?
READY, TIA?
YEAH!
BMM
BMM
LEVEL 108: The Light

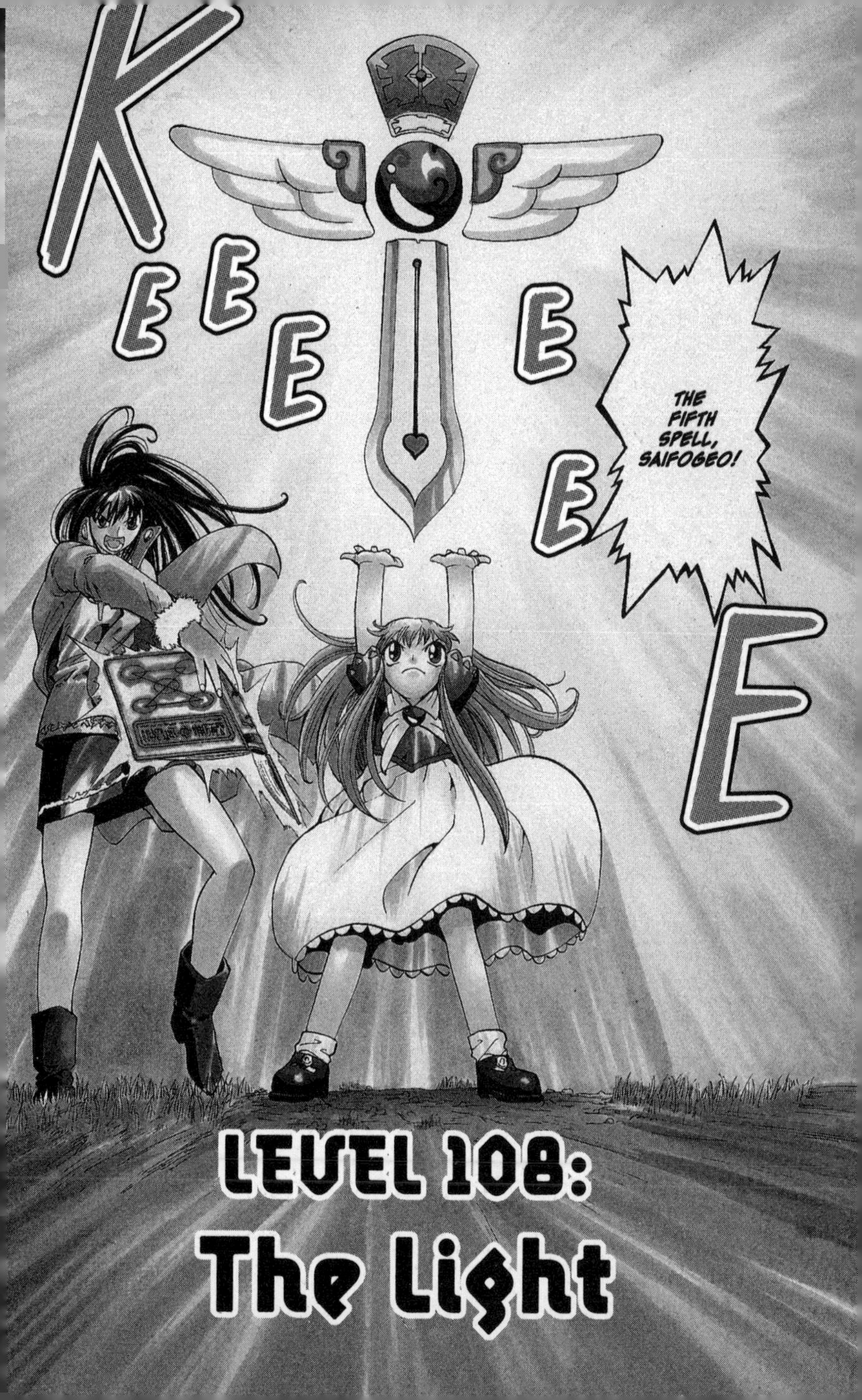
KEEEEEEE
THE FIFTH SPELL, SAIFOGEO!
LEVEL 108:
The Light

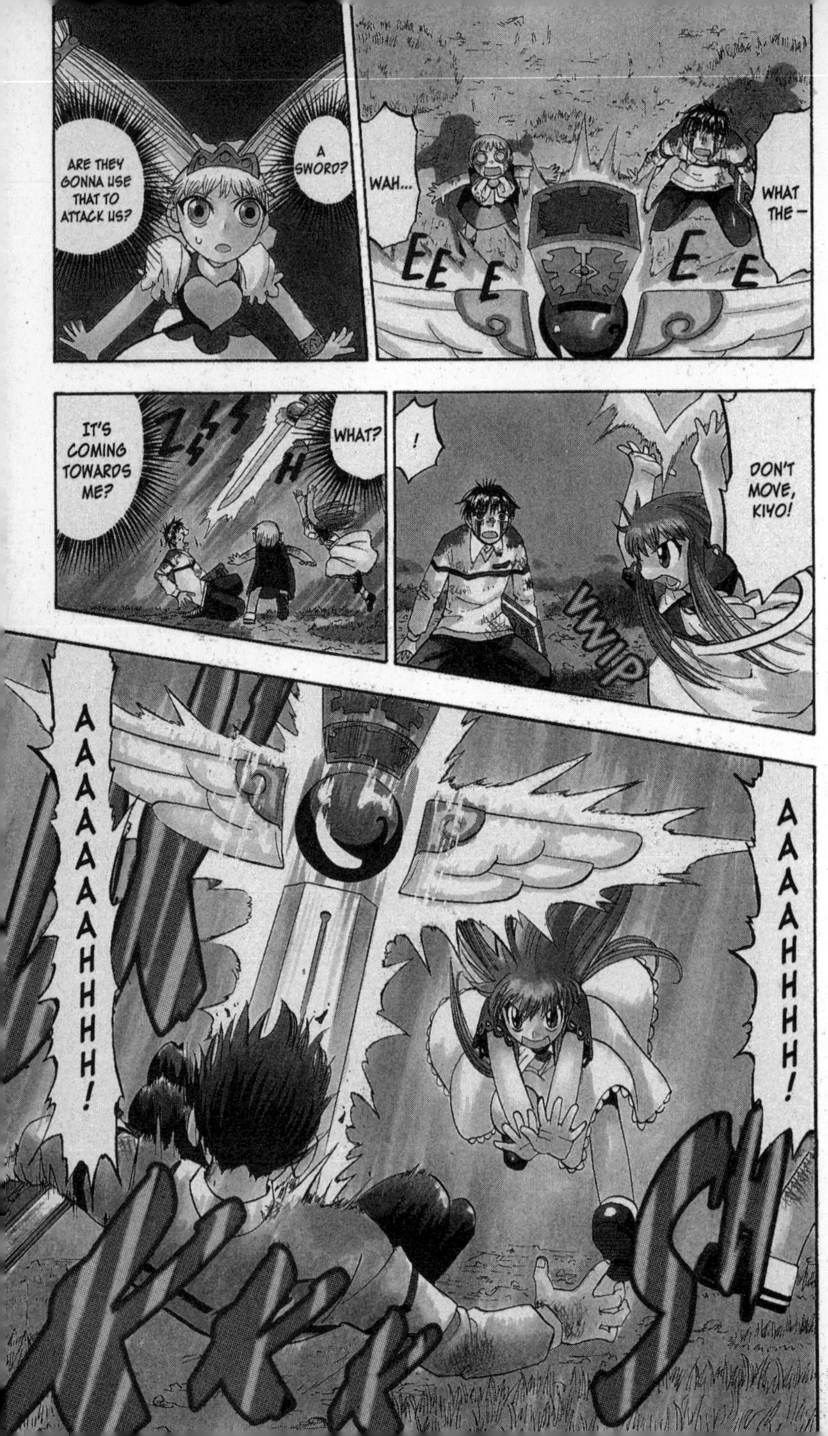
WHAT THE—
WAH...
A SWORD?
ARE THEY GONNA USE THAT TO ATTACK US?
DON'T MOVE, KIYO!
!
VWIP
WHAT?
IT'S COMING TOWARDS ME?
AAAAHHHH!
AAAAAAAHHHH!

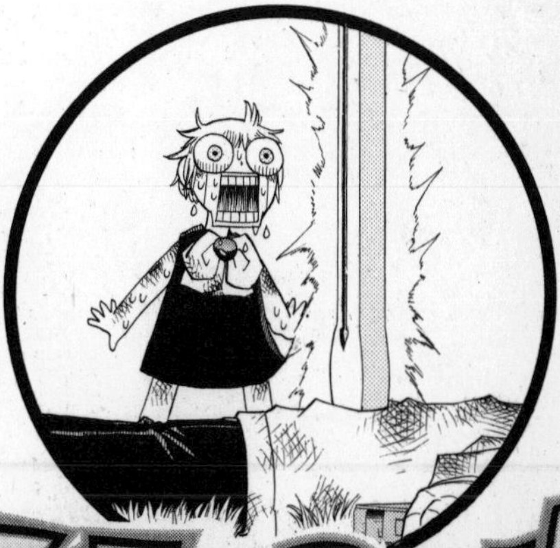

ZATCH BELL!

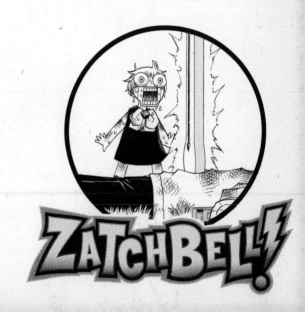

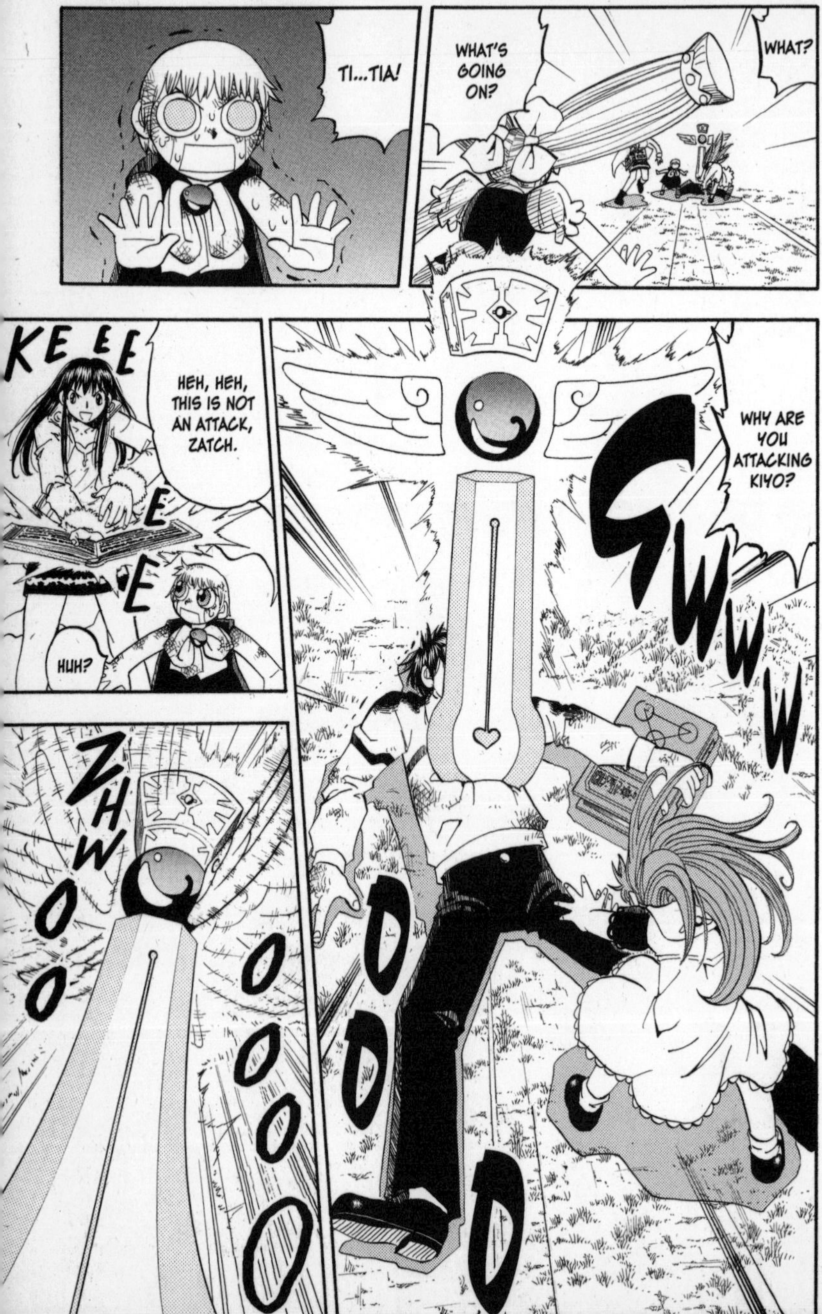
WHAT?
WHAT'S GOING ON?
TI...TIA!
WHY ARE YOU ATTACKING KIYO?
GWWWW
DOOOO
KEEEEE
HEH, HEH, THIS IS NOT AN ATTACK, ZATCH.
HUH?
ZHWOOOO
OOOOOO

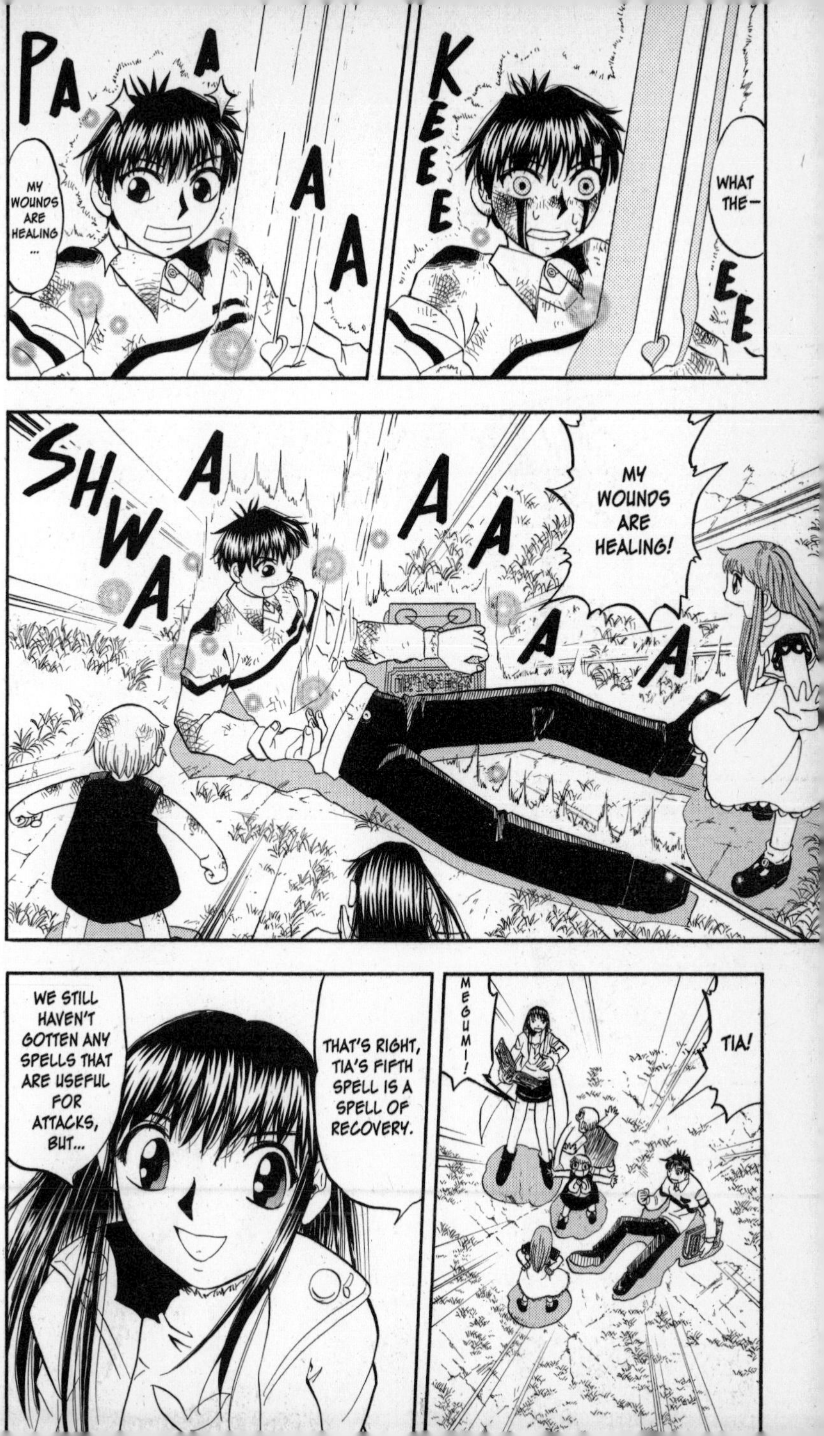
KEEEE
WHAT THE—
EE
PAAAA
MY WOUNDS ARE HEALING ...
SHWAAAAAAA
MY WOUNDS ARE HEALING!
TIA!
MEGUMI!
THAT'S RIGHT, TIA'S FIFTH SPELL IS A SPELL OF RECOVERY.
WE STILL HAVEN'T GOTTEN ANY SPELLS THAT ARE USEFUL FOR ATTACKS, BUT...

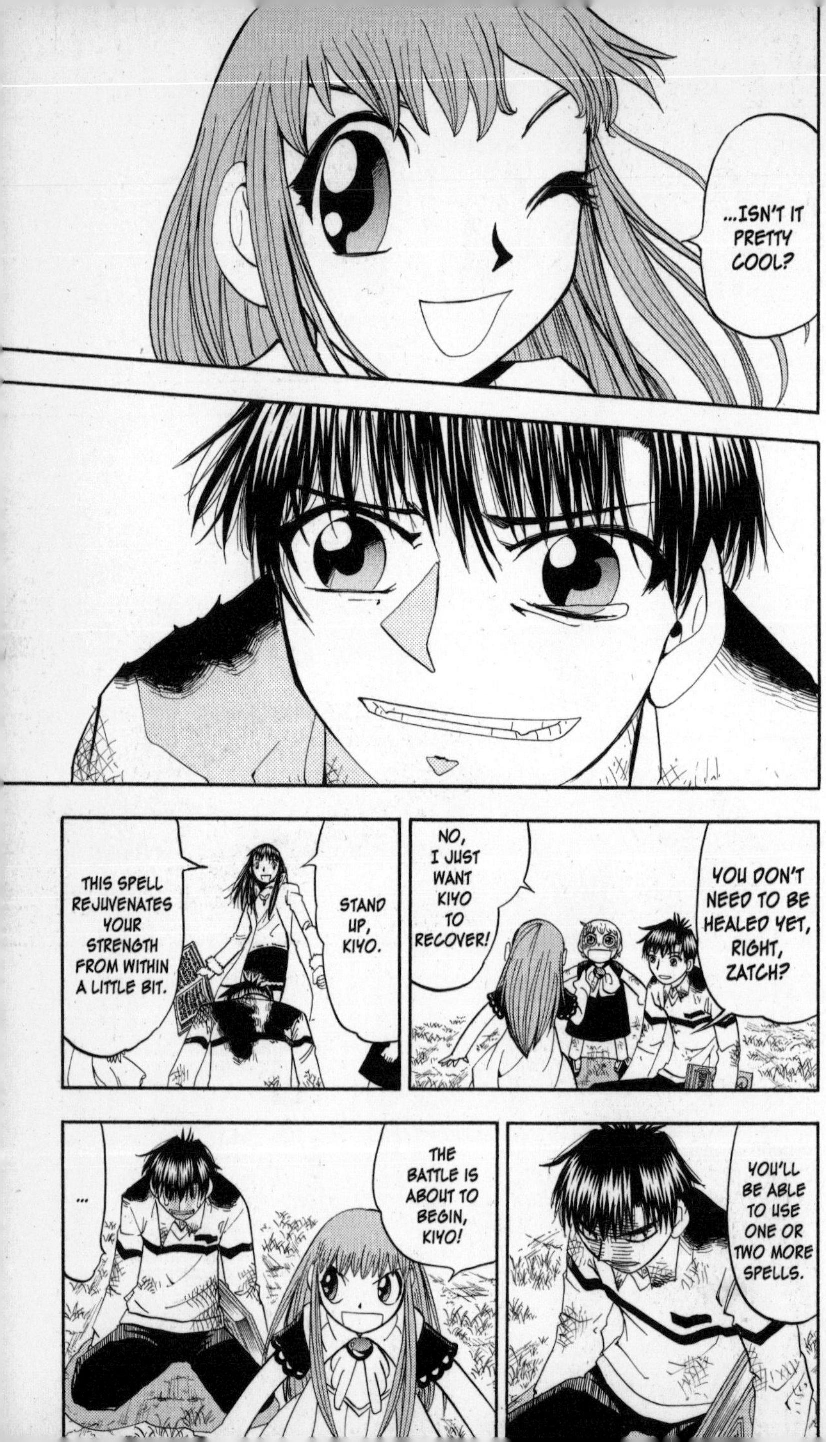
...ISN'T IT PRETTY COOL?
YOU DON'T NEED TO BE HEALED YET, RIGHT, ZATCH?
NO, I JUST WANT KIYO TO RECOVER!
STAND UP, KIYO.
THIS SPELL REJUVENATES YOUR STRENGTH FROM WITHIN A LITTLE BIT.
YOU'LL BE ABLE TO USE ONE OR TWO MORE SPELLS.
THE BATTLE IS ABOUT TO BEGIN, KIYO!
...

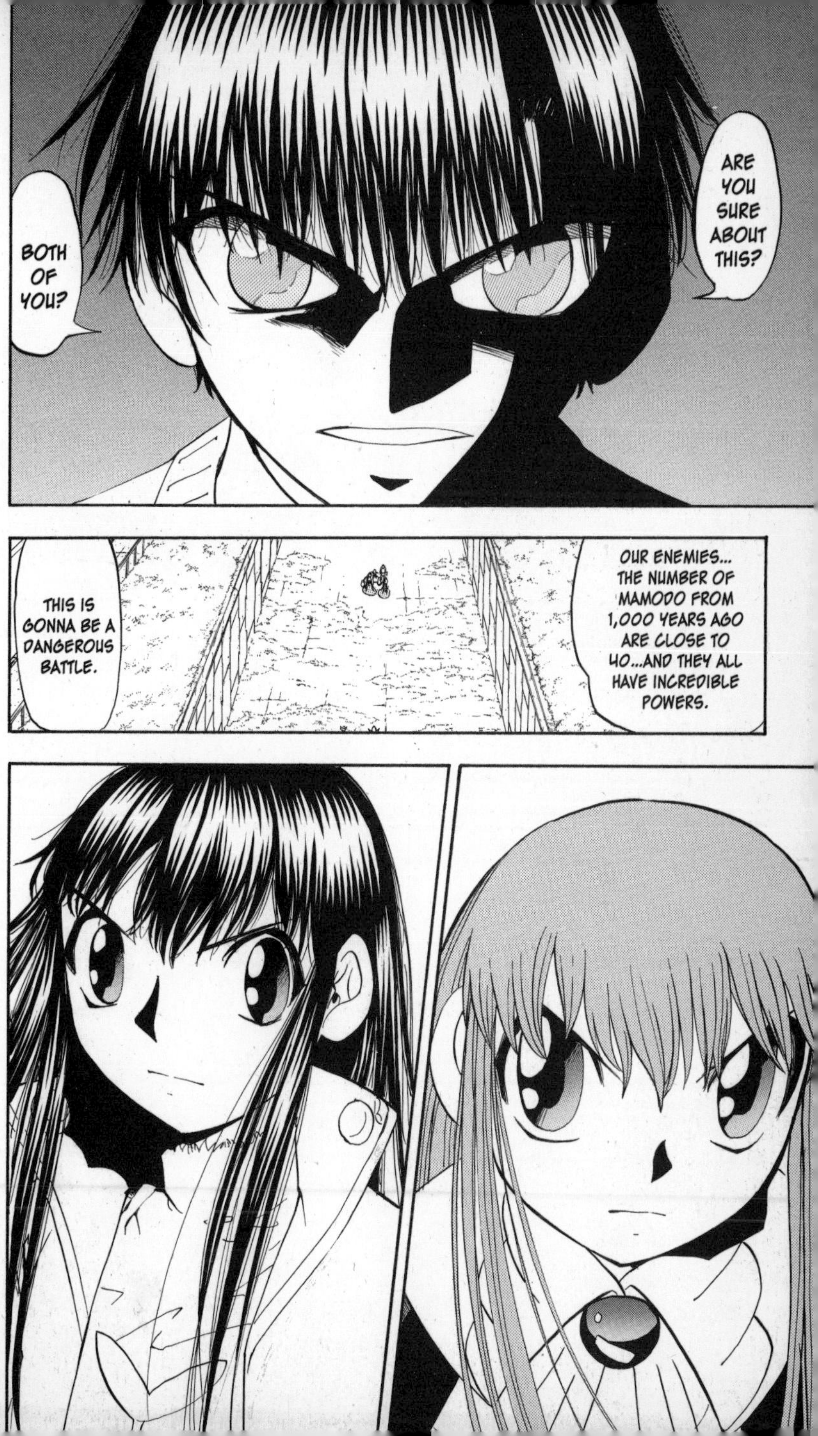
ARE YOU SURE ABOUT THIS?
BOTH OF YOU?
OUR ENEMIES... THE NUMBER OF MAMODO FROM 1,000 YEARS AGO ARE CLOSE TO 40...AND THEY ALL HAVE INCREDIBLE POWERS.
THIS IS GONNA BE A DANGEROUS BATTLE.

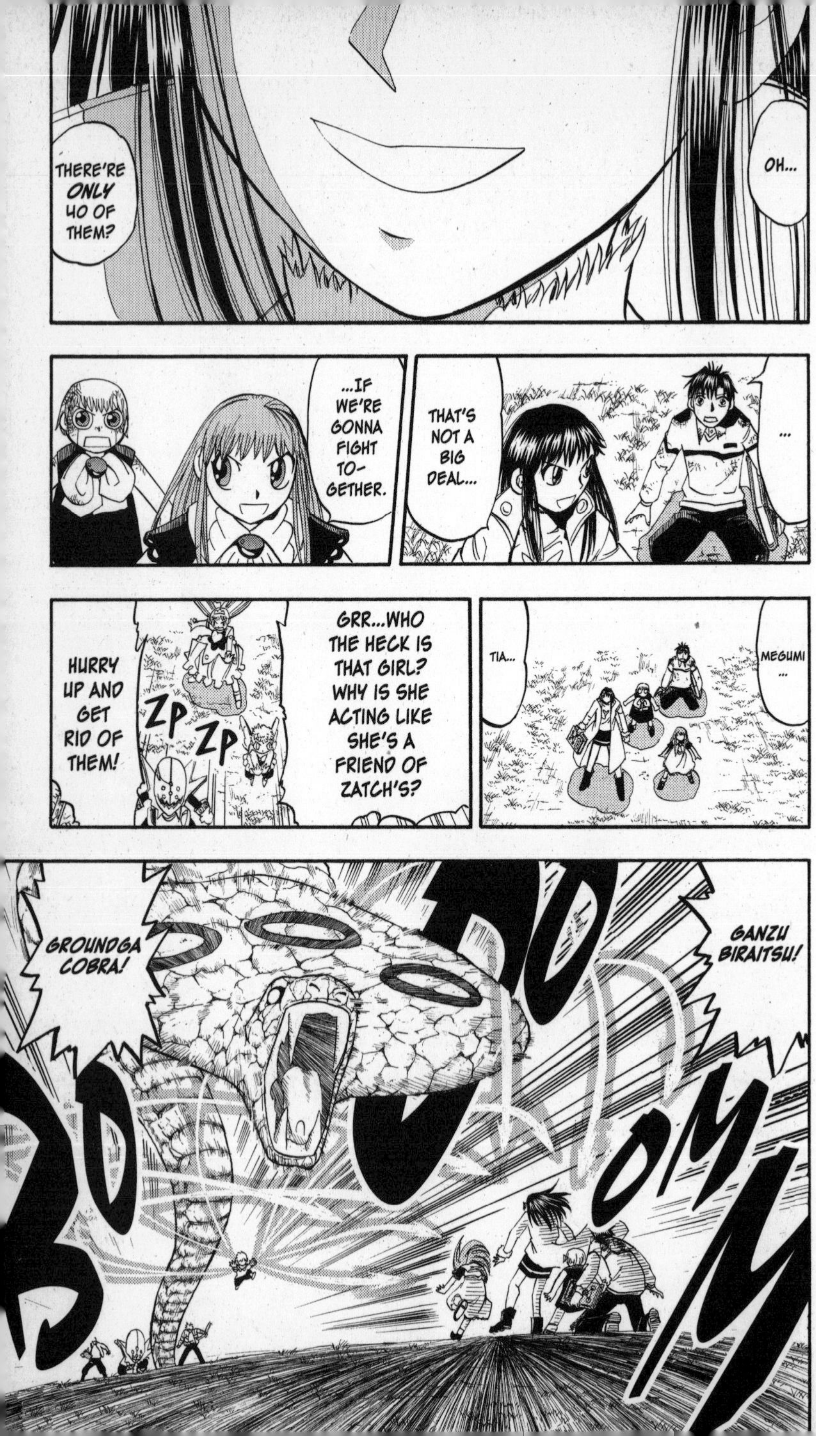
OH...
THERE'RE ONLY 40 OF THEM?
...
THAT'S NOT A BIG DEAL...
...IF WE'RE GONNA FIGHT TO-GETHER.
MEGUMI ...
TIA...
GRR...WHO THE HECK IS THAT GIRL? WHY IS SHE ACTING LIKE SHE'S A FRIEND OF ZATCH'S?
ZP ZP
HURRY UP AND GET RID OF THEM!
GANZU BIRAITSU!
GROUNDGA COBRA!
BOOM

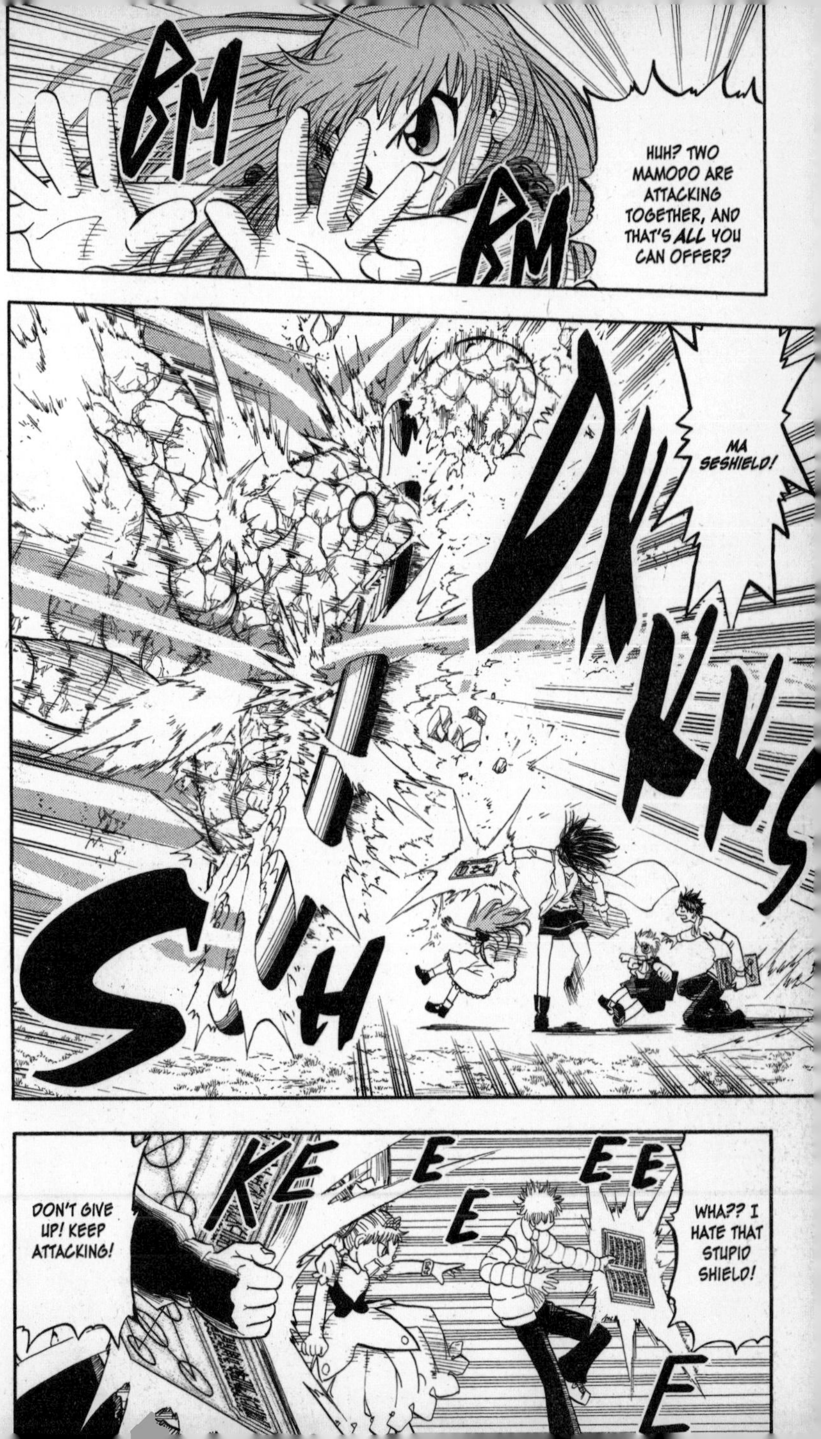
HUH? TWO MAMODO ARE ATTACKING TOGETHER, AND THAT'S ALL YOU CAN OFFER?
BM
BM
MA SESHIELD!
DKKKS
SHH
WHA?? I HATE THAT STUPID SHIELD!
KEEEEEE
DON'T GIVE UP! KEEP ATTACKING!

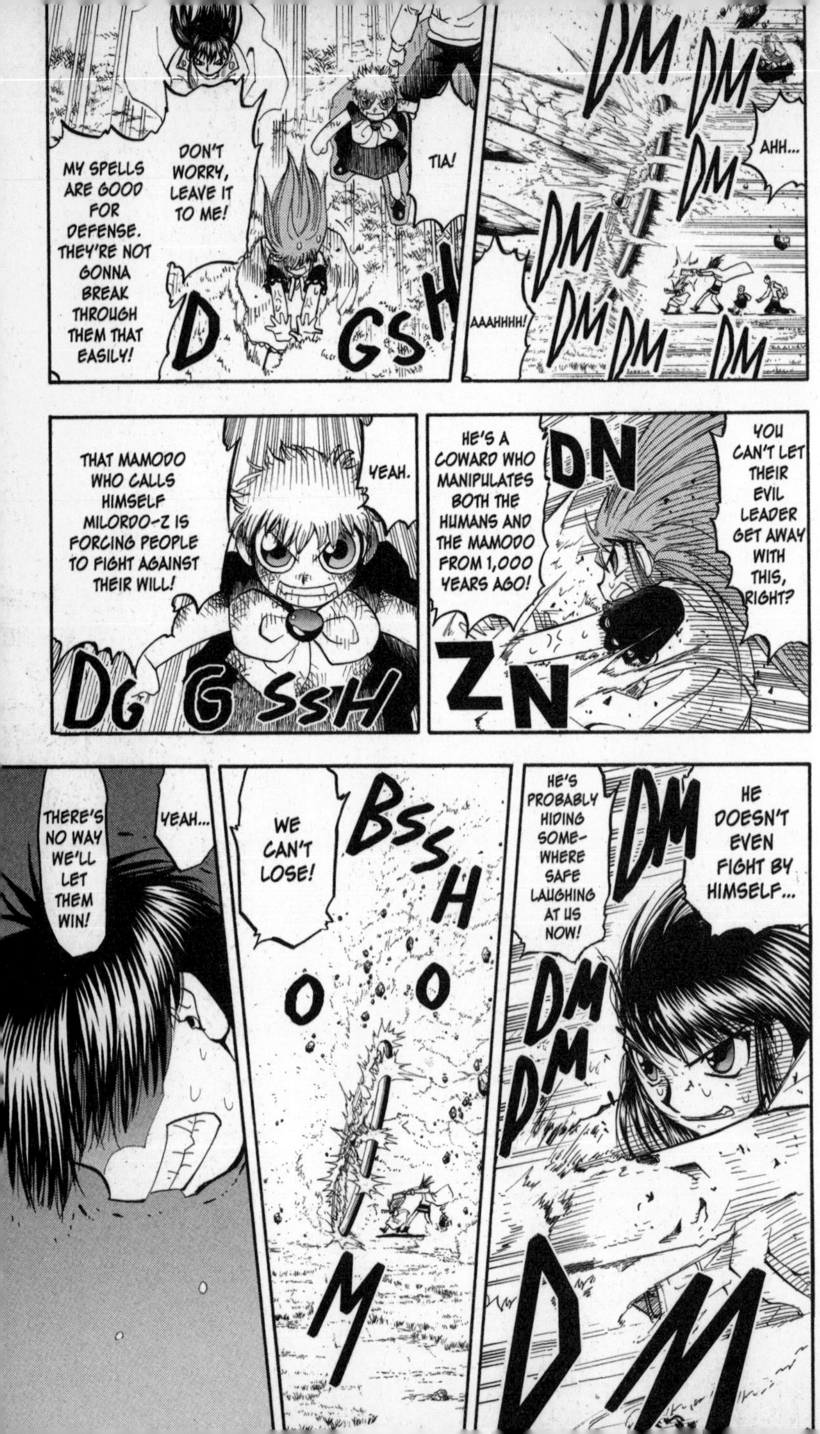
DM DM DM DM DM DM DM DM DM
AHH...
AAAHHHH!
TIA!
DON'T WORRY, LEAVE IT TO ME!
MY SPELLS ARE GOOD FOR DEFENSE. THEY'RE NOT GONNA BREAK THROUGH THEM THAT EASILY!
DGSH
YOU CAN'T LET THEIR EVIL LEADER GET AWAY WITH THIS, RIGHT?
DN
HE'S A COWARD WHO MANIPULATES BOTH THE HUMANS AND THE MAMODO FROM 1,000 YEARS AGO!
ZN
YEAH.
THAT MAMODO WHO CALLS HIMSELF MILORDO-Z IS FORCING PEOPLE TO FIGHT AGAINST THEIR WILL!
DGGSSH
HE DOESN'T EVEN FIGHT BY HIMSELF...
DM
HE'S PROBABLY HIDING SOME-WHERE SAFE LAUGHING AT US NOW!
DM DM DM
DM
BSSH
WE CAN'T LOSE!
OOM
YEAH...
THERE'S NO WAY WE'LL LET THEM WIN!

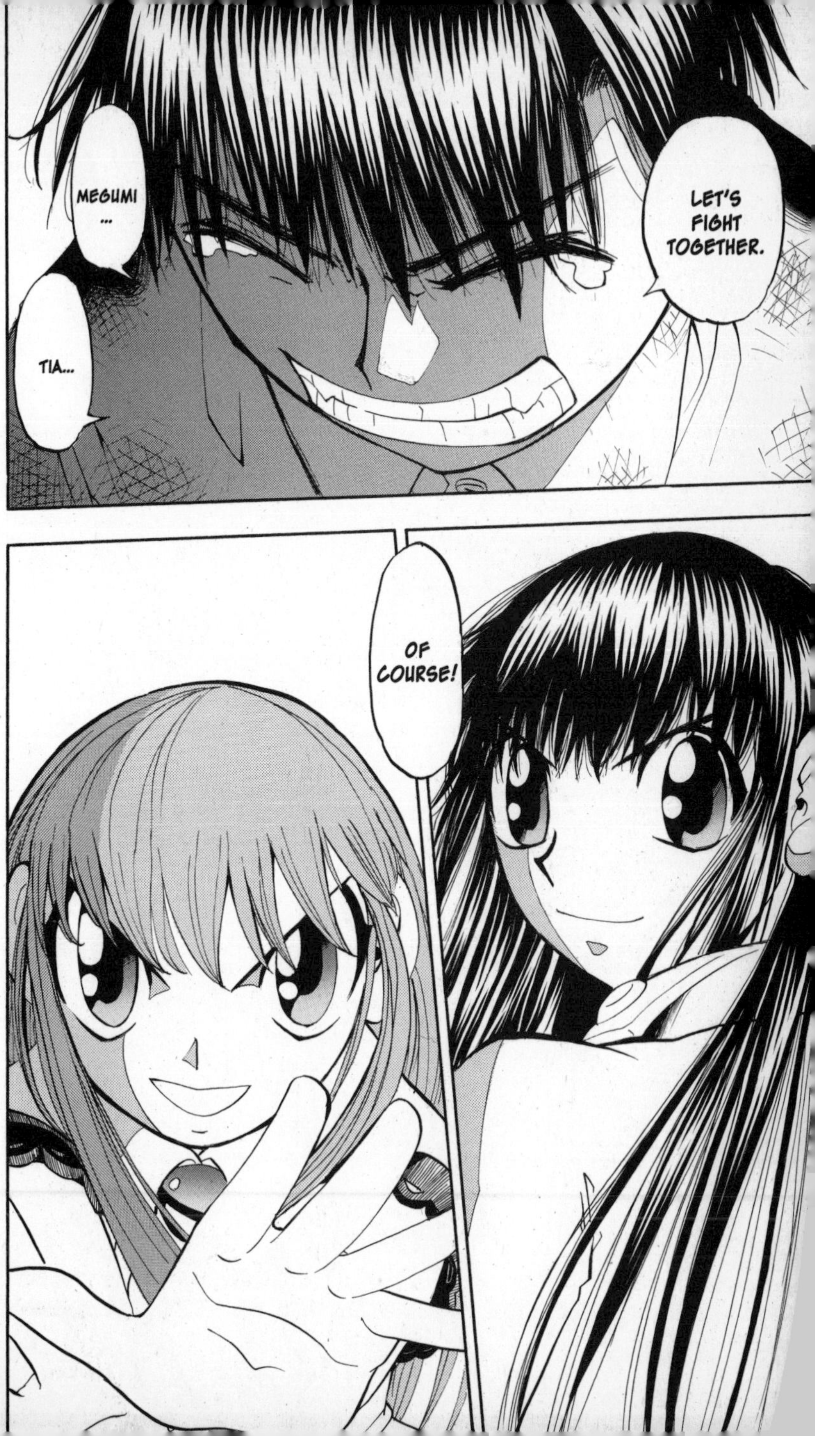
LET'S FIGHT TOGETHER.
MEGUMI...
TIA...
OF COURSE!

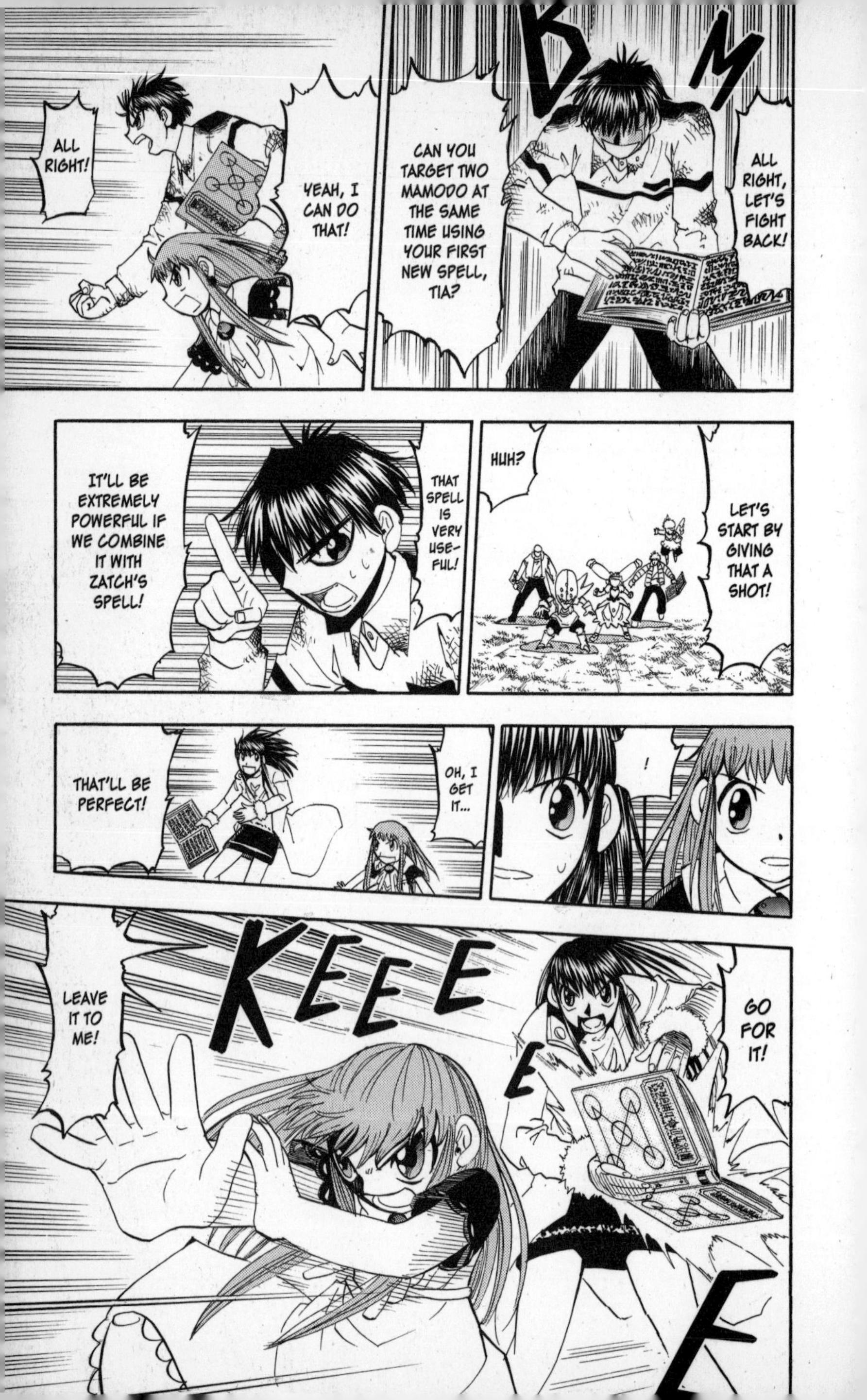
ALL RIGHT, LET'S FIGHT BACK!
CAN YOU TARGET TWO MAMODO AT THE SAME TIME USING YOUR FIRST NEW SPELL, TIA?
YEAH, I CAN DO THAT!
ALL RIGHT!
LET'S START BY GIVING THAT A SHOT!
HUH?
THAT SPELL IS VERY USE-FUL!
IT'LL BE EXTREMELY POWERFUL IF WE COMBINE IT WITH ZATCH'S SPELL!
!
OH, I GET IT...
THAT'LL BE PERFECT!
GO FOR IT!
LEAVE IT TO ME!

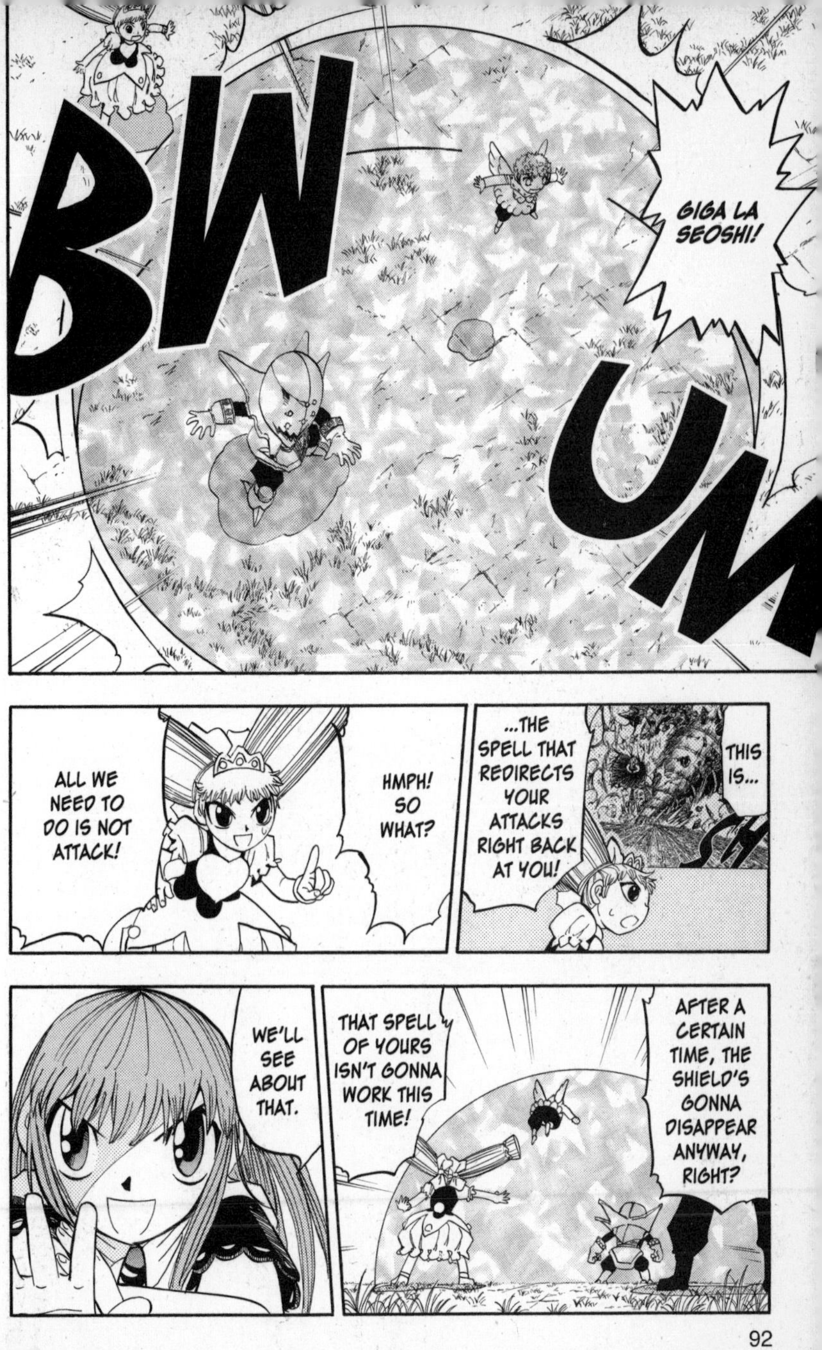
GIGA LA SEOSHI!
BWUM
THIS IS...
...THE SPELL THAT REDIRECTS YOUR ATTACKS RIGHT BACK AT YOU!
HMPH! SO WHAT?
ALL WE NEED TO DO IS NOT ATTACK!
AFTER A CERTAIN TIME, THE SHIELD'S GONNA DISAPPEAR ANYWAY, RIGHT?
THAT SPELL OF YOURS ISN'T GONNA WORK THIS TIME!
WE'LL SEE ABOUT THAT.

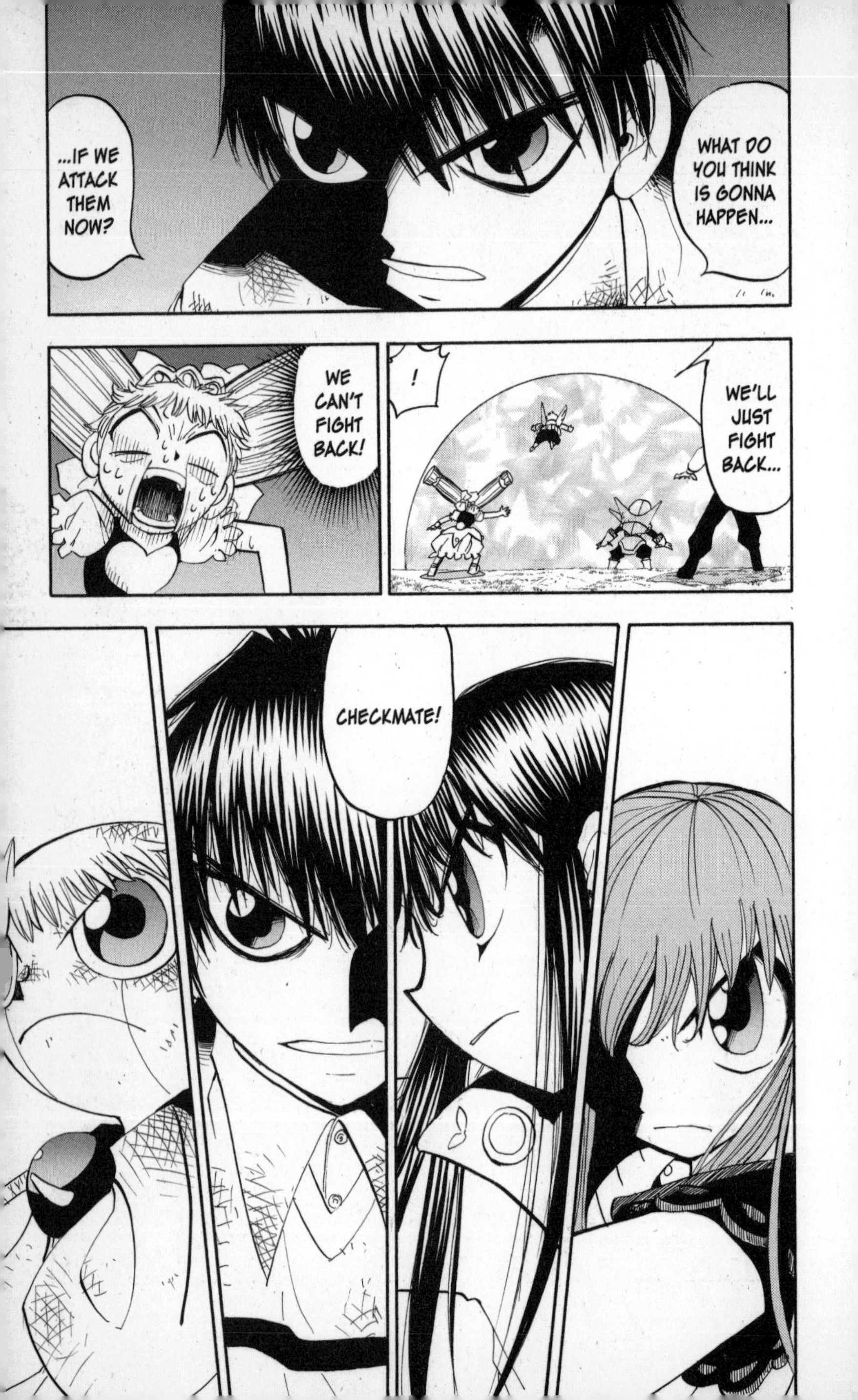
WHAT DO YOU THINK IS GONNA HAPPEN...
...IF WE ATTACK THEM NOW?
WE'LL JUST FIGHT BACK...
!
WE CAN'T FIGHT BACK!
CHECKMATE!

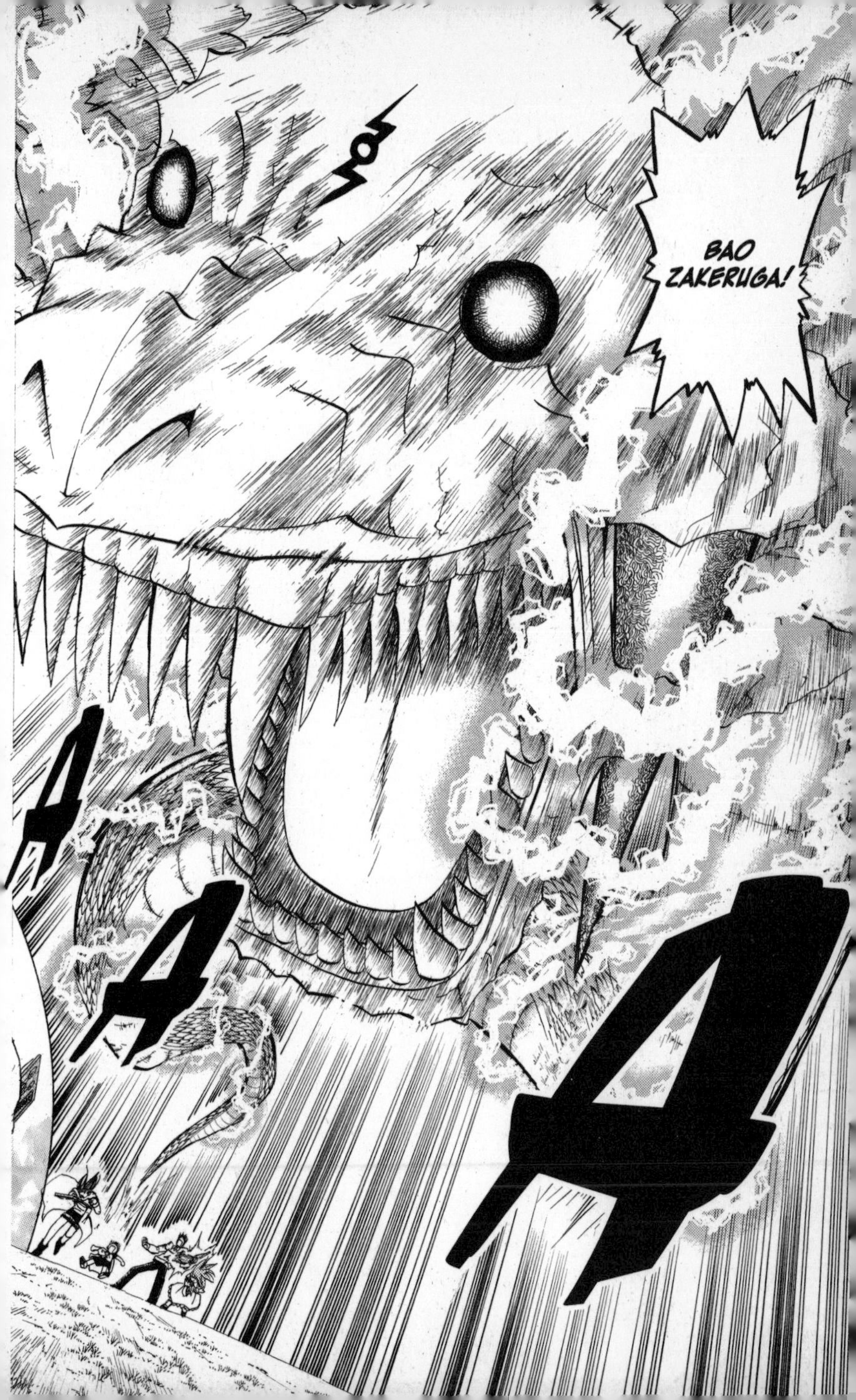
BAO
ZAKERUGA!

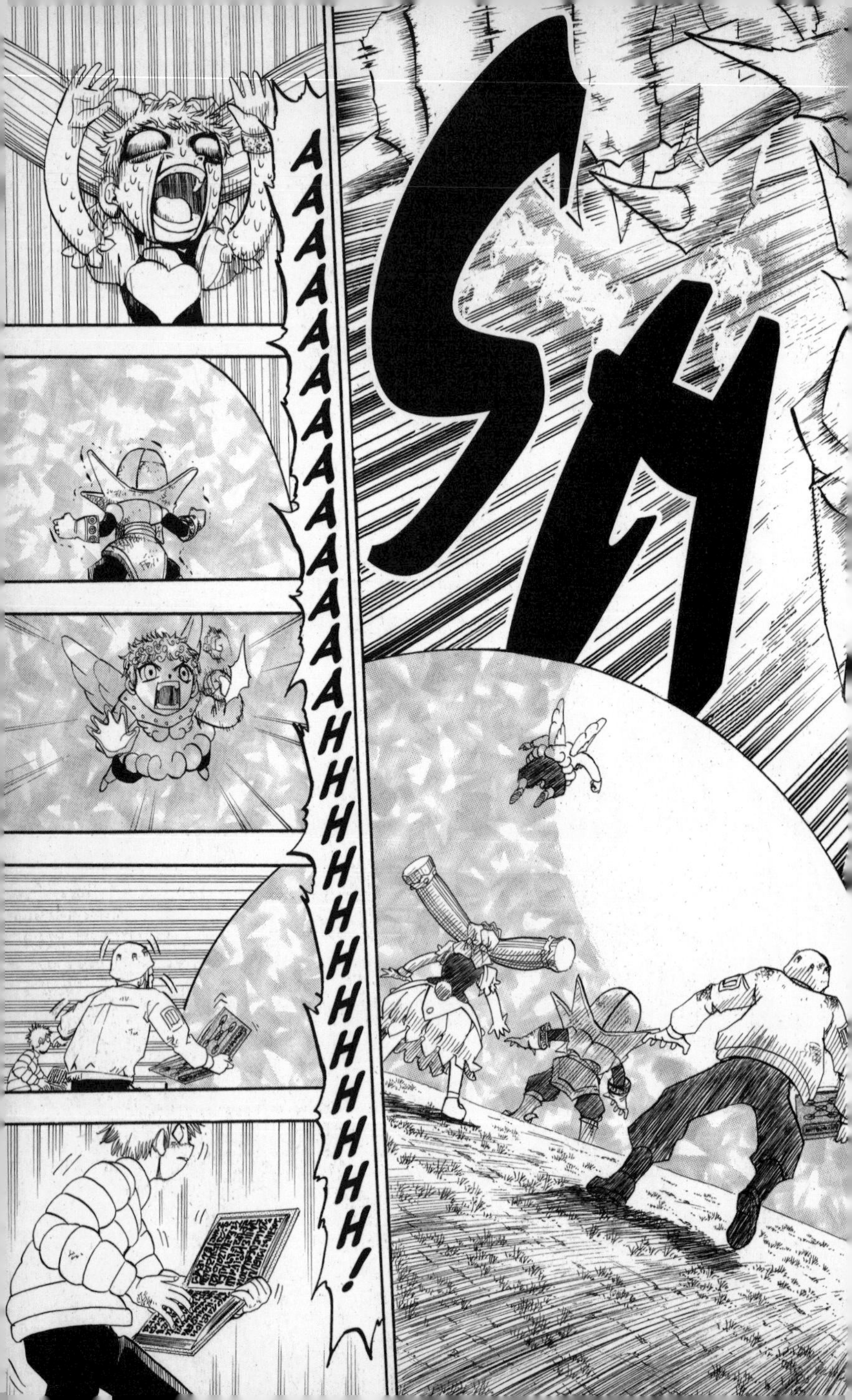
SH
AAAAAAAAAAAAAAAHHHHHHHHHHHHHH!

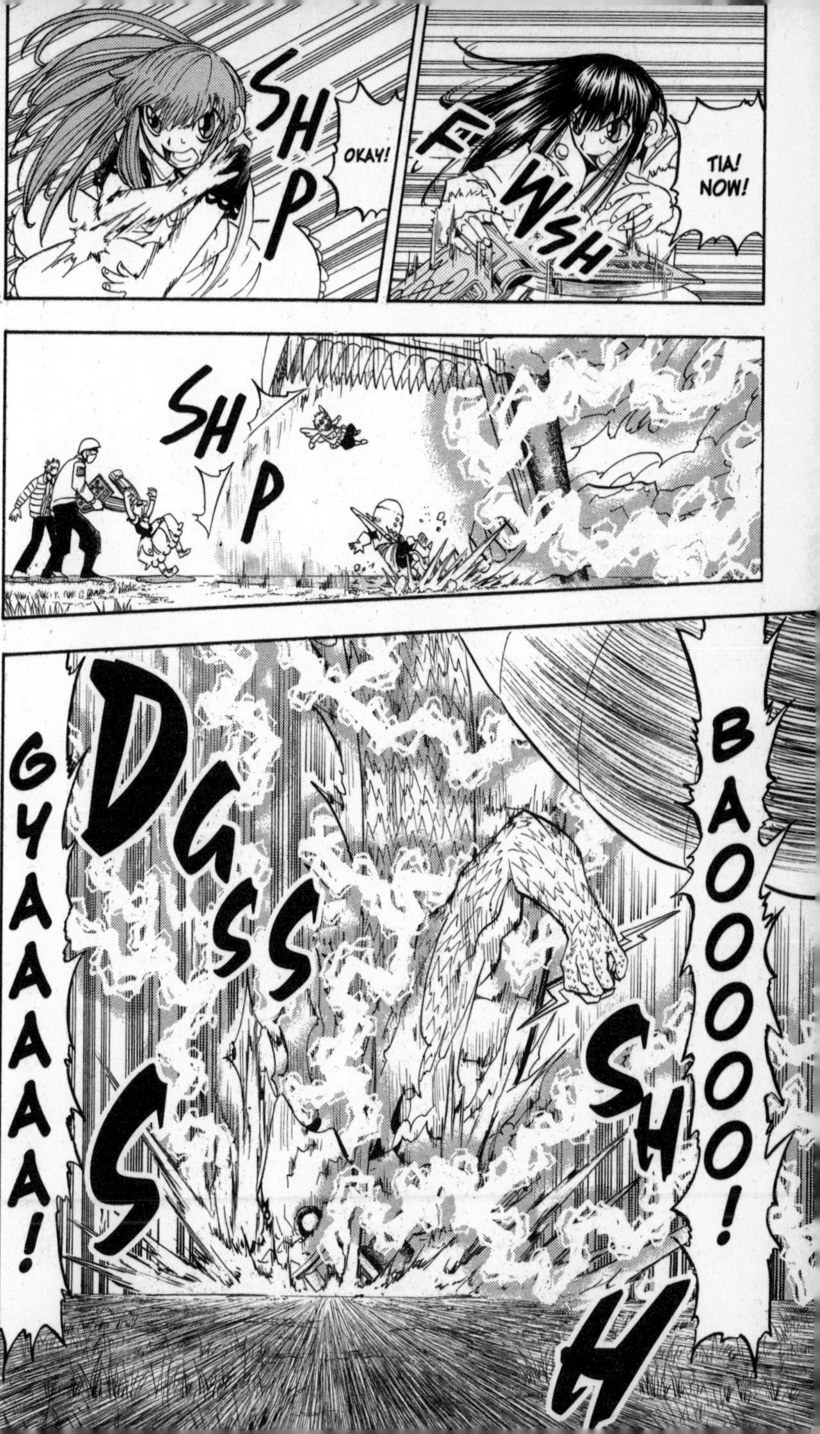
TIA! NOW!
FWSH
OKAY!
SHP
SHP
BAOOOOOO!
SHH
DGSSS
GYAAAAAA!

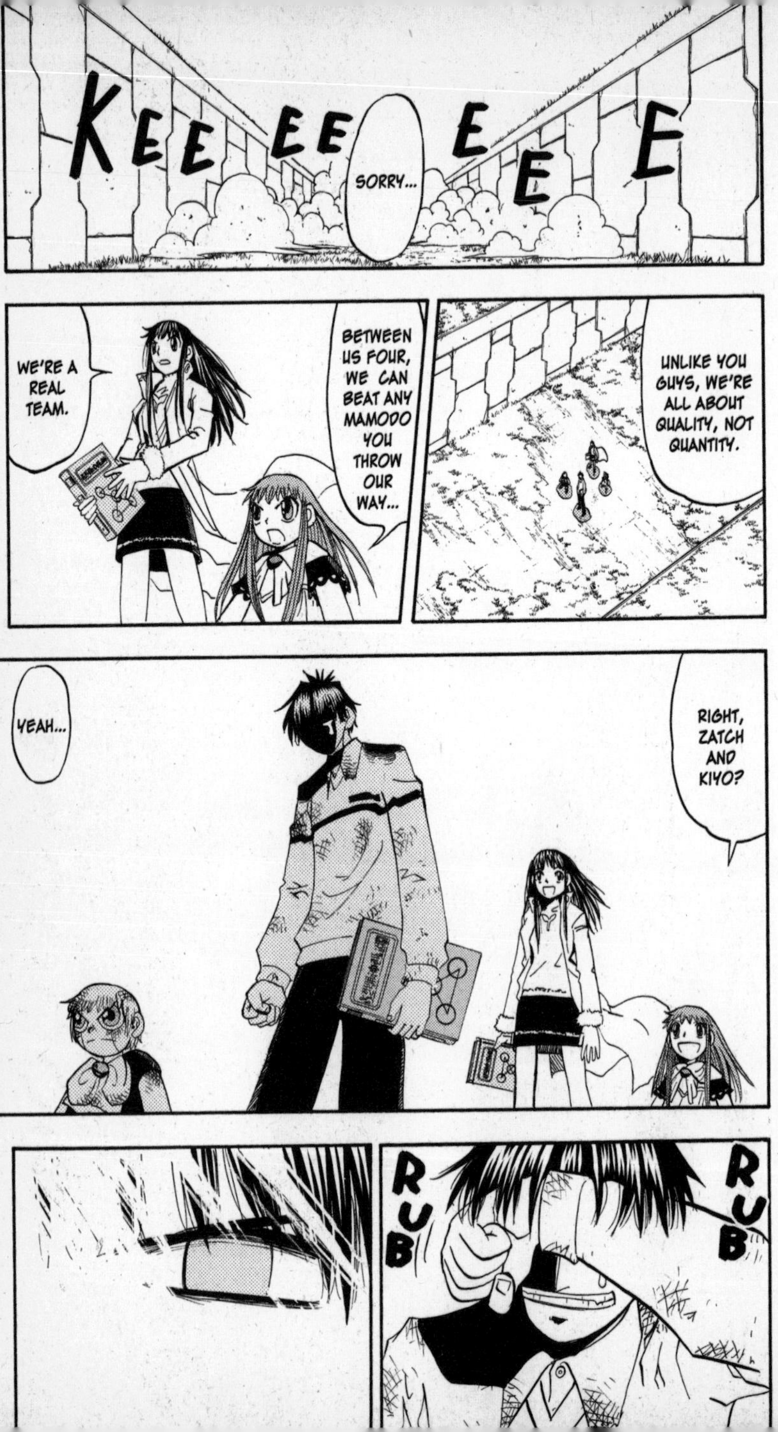
KEEEEEEE
SORRY...
UNLIKE YOU GUYS, WE'RE ALL ABOUT QUALITY, NOT QUANTITY.
BETWEEN US FOUR, WE CAN BEAT ANY MAMODO YOU THROW OUR WAY...
WE'RE A REAL TEAM.
RIGHT, ZATCH AND KIYO?
YEAH...
RUB
RUB

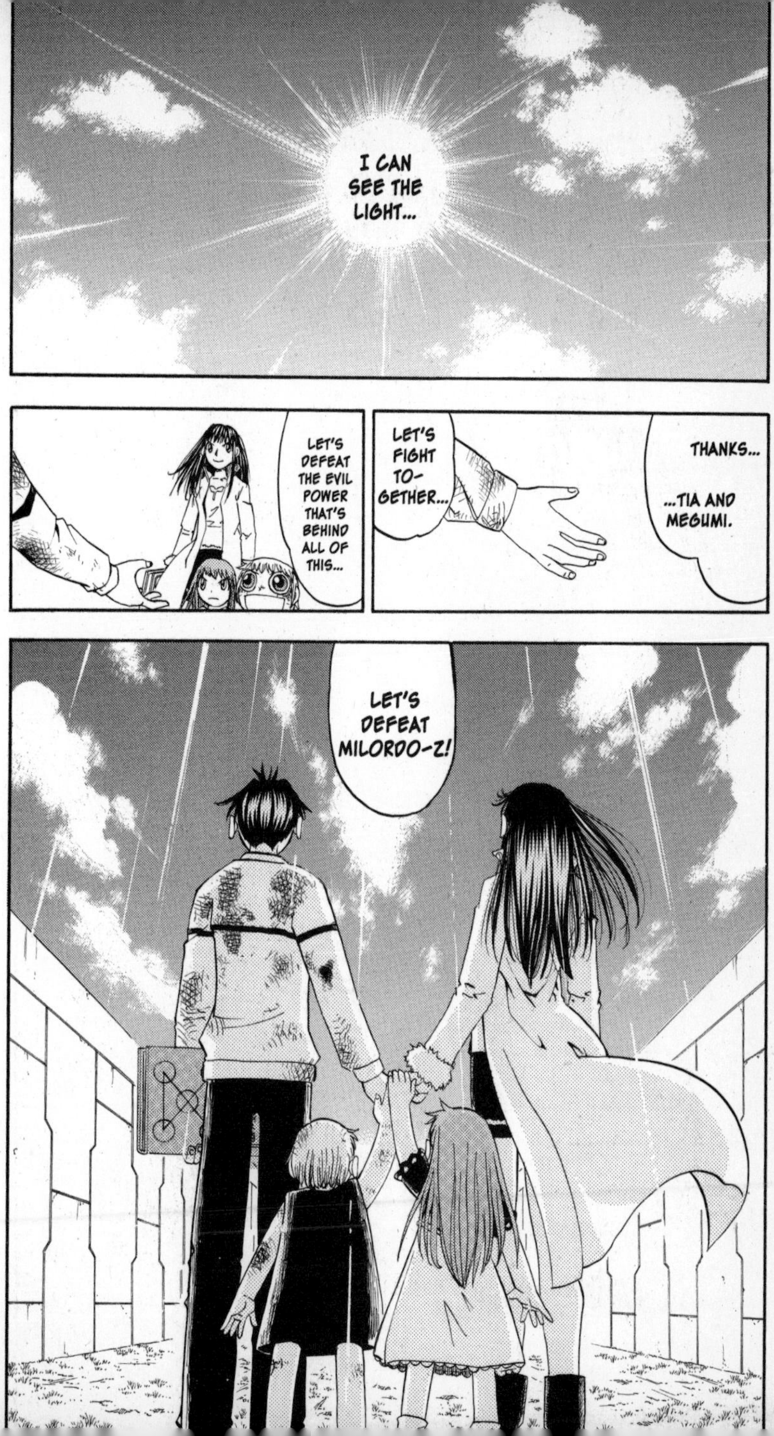

I CAN SEE THE LIGHT...
THANKS...
...TIA AND MEGUMI.
LET'S FIGHT TO-GETHER...
LET'S DEFEAT THE EVIL POWER THAT'S BEHIND ALL OF THIS...
LET'S DEFEAT MILORDO-Z!

LEVEL 109: The Identity of Milordo-Z

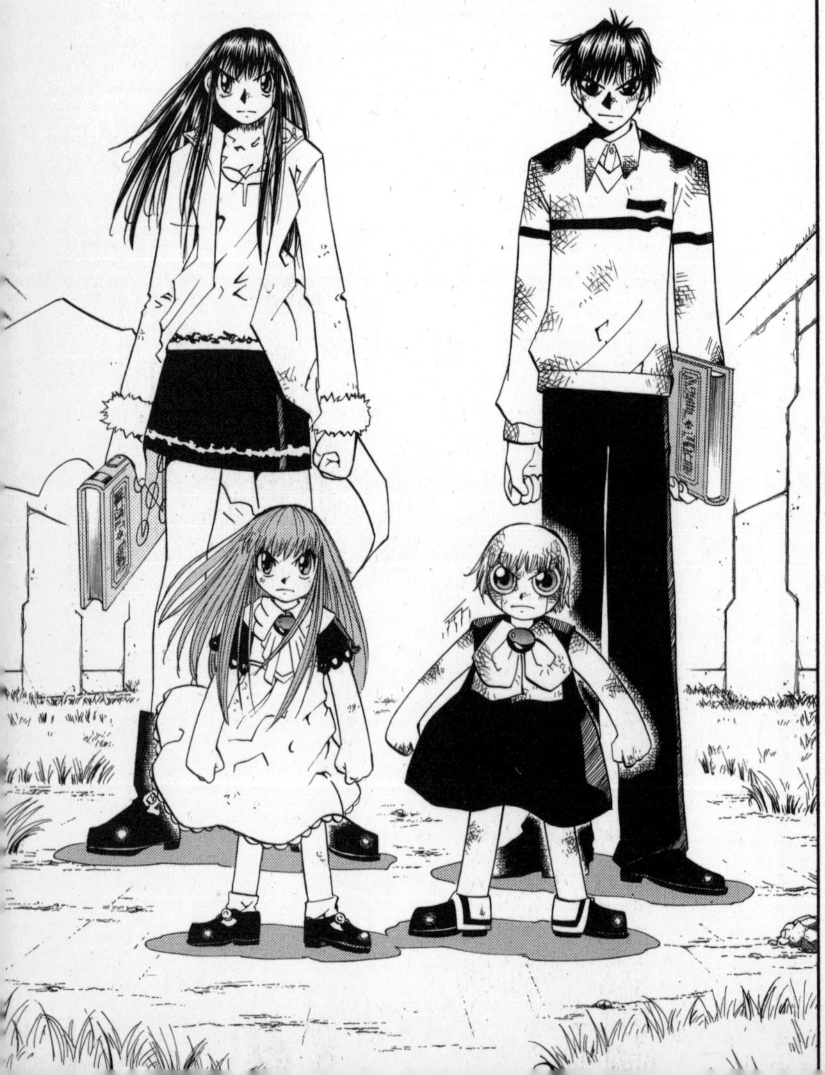

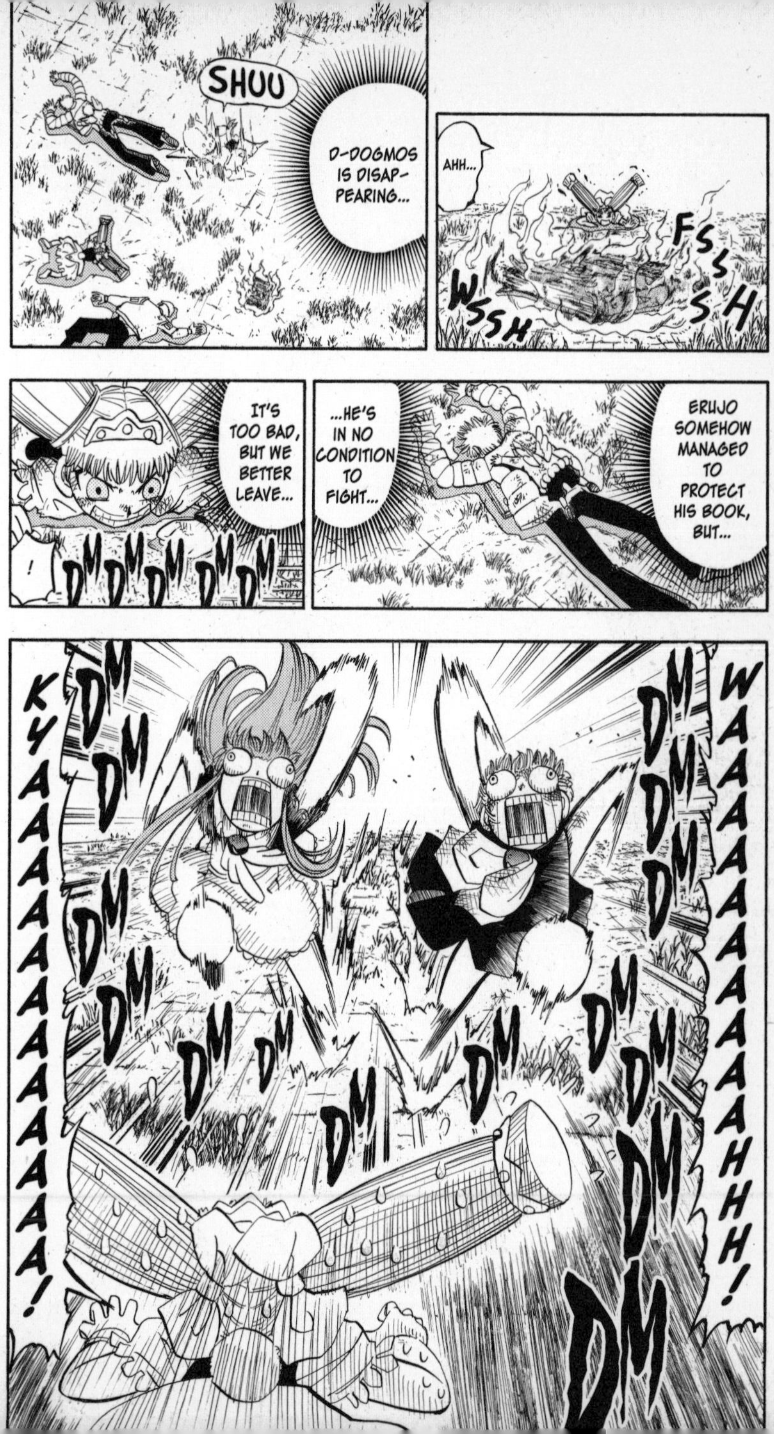
AHH...
FSSSH
WSSH
SHUU
D-DOGMOS IS DISAPPEARING...
ERUJO SOMEHOW MANAGED TO PROTECT HIS BOOK, BUT...
...HE'S IN NO CONDITION TO FIGHT...
IT'S TOO BAD, BUT WE BETTER LEAVE...
!
DM DM DM DM DM
WAAAAAAAAAAHHH!
DM DM DM DM DM DM DM DM
KYAAAAAAAAAAAAAAA!

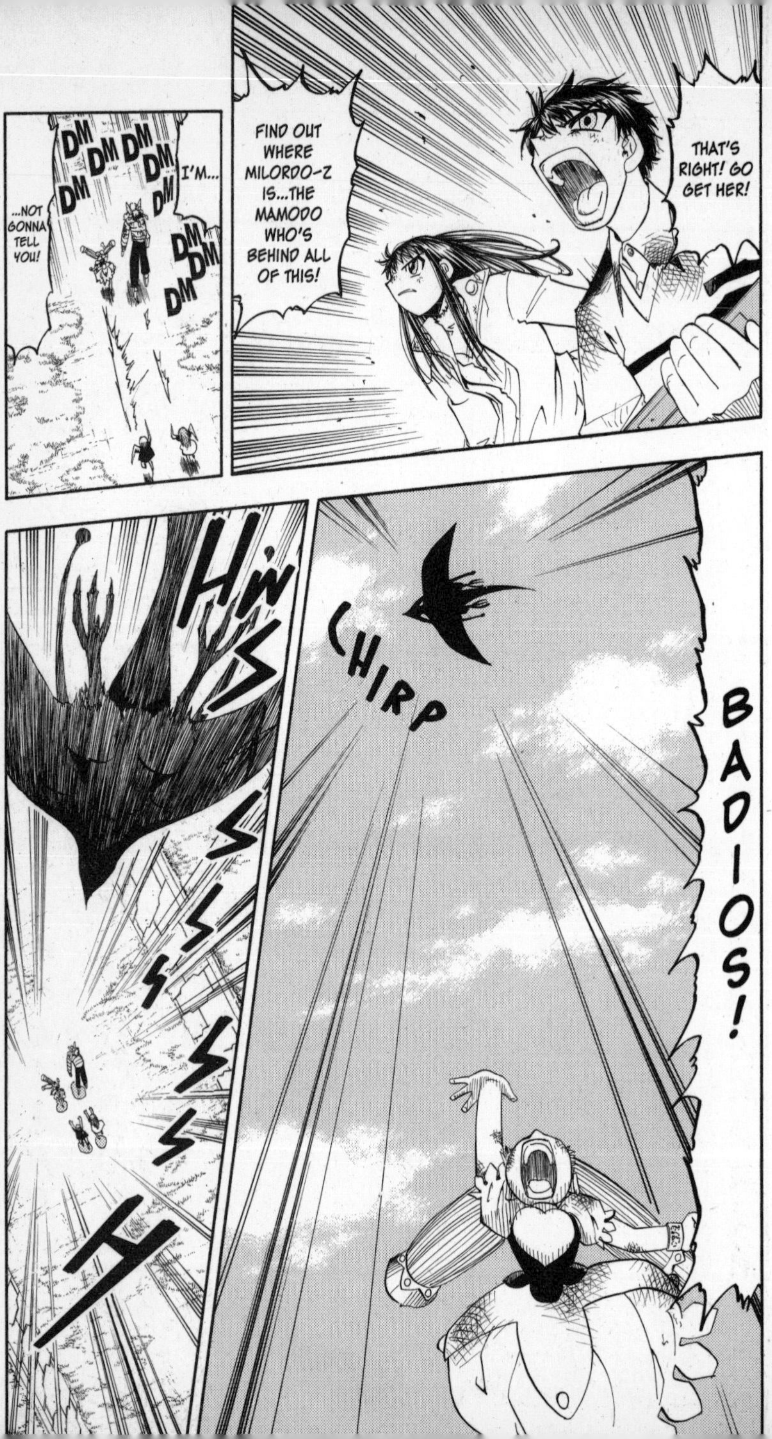
THAT'S RIGHT! GO GET HER!
FIND OUT WHERE MILORDO-Z IS...THE MAMODO WHO'S BEHIND ALL OF THIS!
DM DM DM DM DM DM DM DM DM DM
I'M...
...NOT GONNA TELL YOU!
CHIRP
BADIOS!
HISSSSSSH

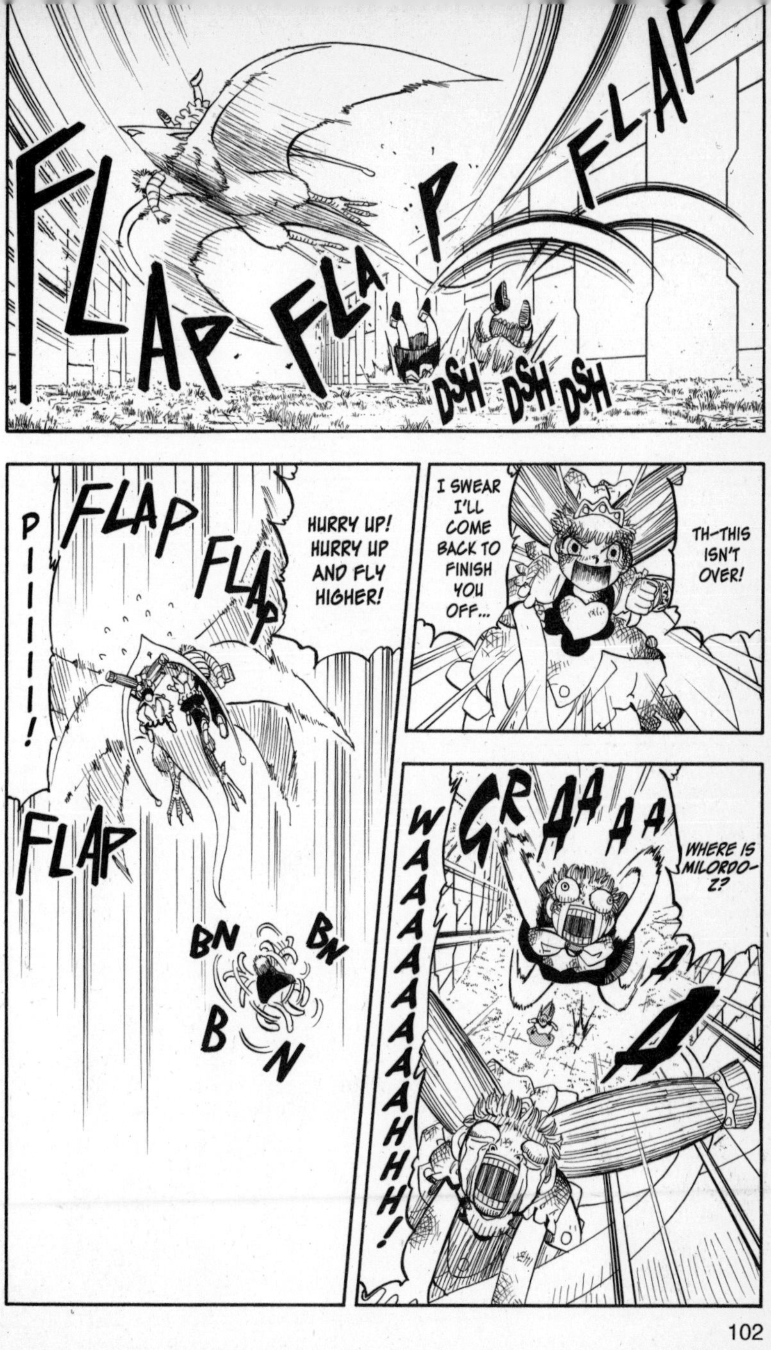
FLAP
FLAP
FLAP
DSH DSH DSH
TH-THIS ISN'T OVER!
I SWEAR I'LL COME BACK TO FINISH YOU OFF...
WHERE IS MILORDO-Z?
GRAAAAAA
WAAAAAAAAAAAAHHHH!
HURRY UP! HURRY UP AND FLY HIGHER!
FLAP
FLAP
P------!
FLAP
BN BN BN

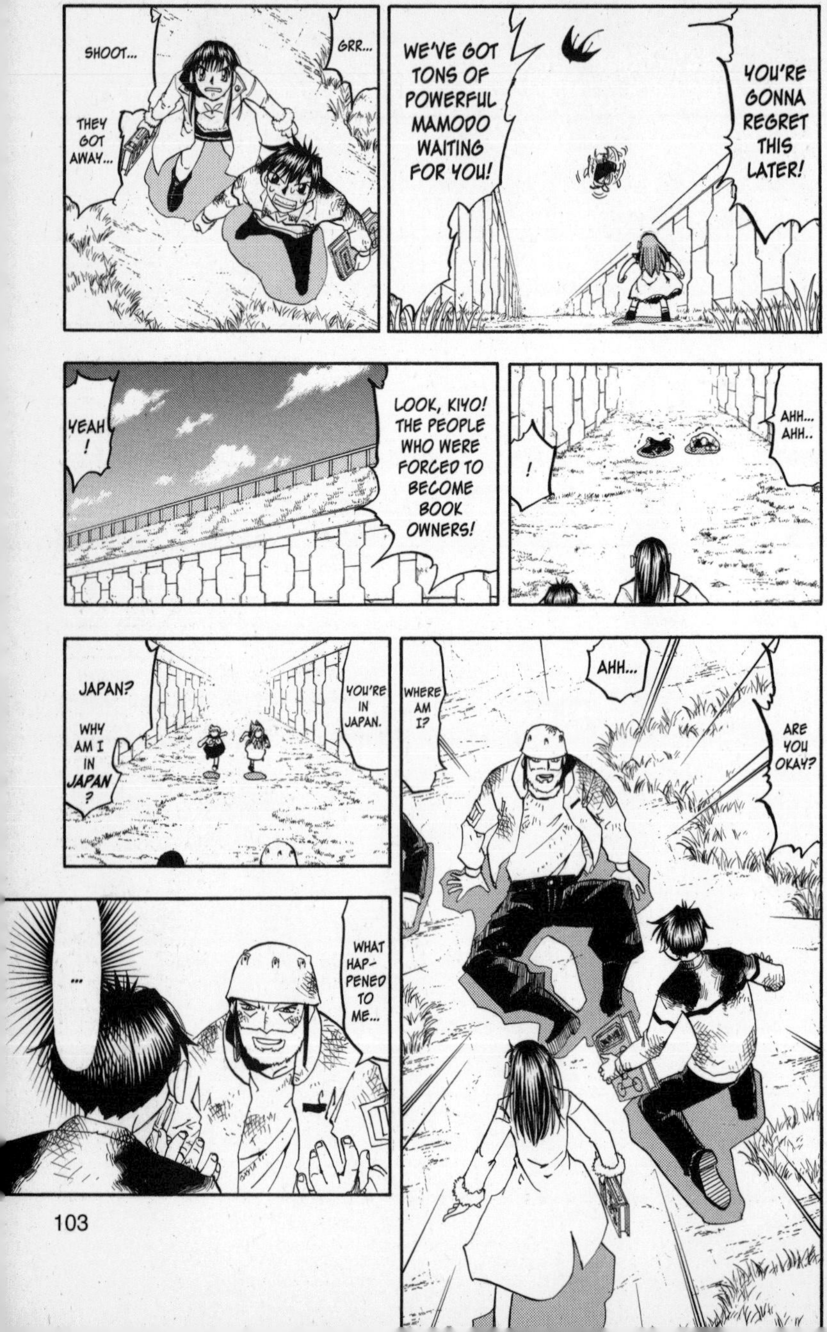

YOU'RE GONNA REGRET THIS LATER!
WE'VE GOT TONS OF POWERFUL MAMODO WAITING FOR YOU!
GRR...
SHOOT...
THEY GOT AWAY...
AHH... AHH..
!
LOOK, KIYO! THE PEOPLE WHO WERE FORCED TO BECOME BOOK OWNERS!
YEAH!
AHH...
ARE YOU OKAY?
WHERE AM I?
YOU'RE IN JAPAN.
JAPAN?
WHY AM I IN *JAPAN*?
WHAT HAP-PENED TO ME...
...

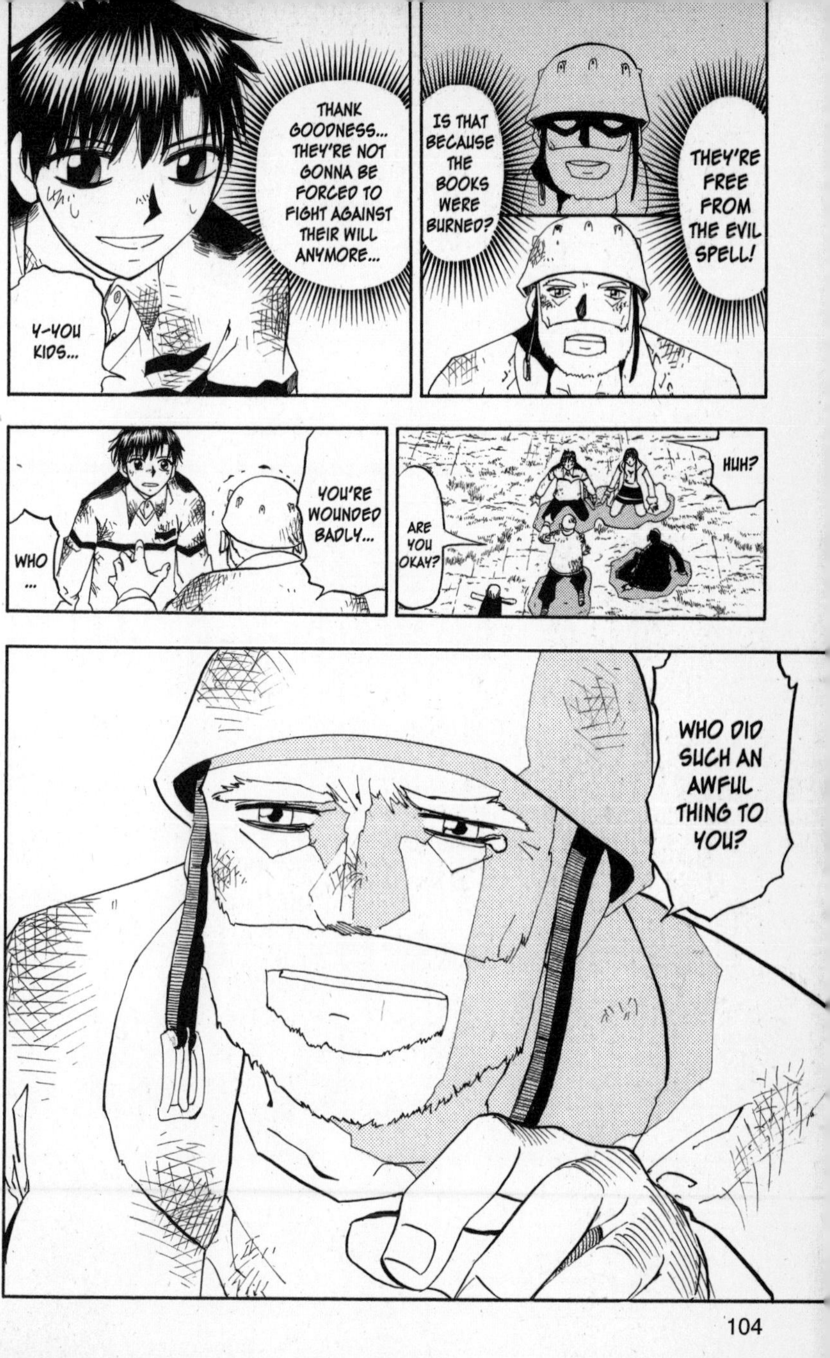
THEY'RE FREE FROM THE EVIL SPELL!
IS THAT BECAUSE THE BOOKS WERE BURNED?
THANK GOODNESS... THEY'RE NOT GONNA BE FORCED TO FIGHT AGAINST THEIR WILL ANYMORE...
Y-YOU KIDS...
HUH?
ARE YOU OKAY?
YOU'RE WOUNDED BADLY...
WHO ...
WHO DID SUCH AN AWFUL THING TO YOU?

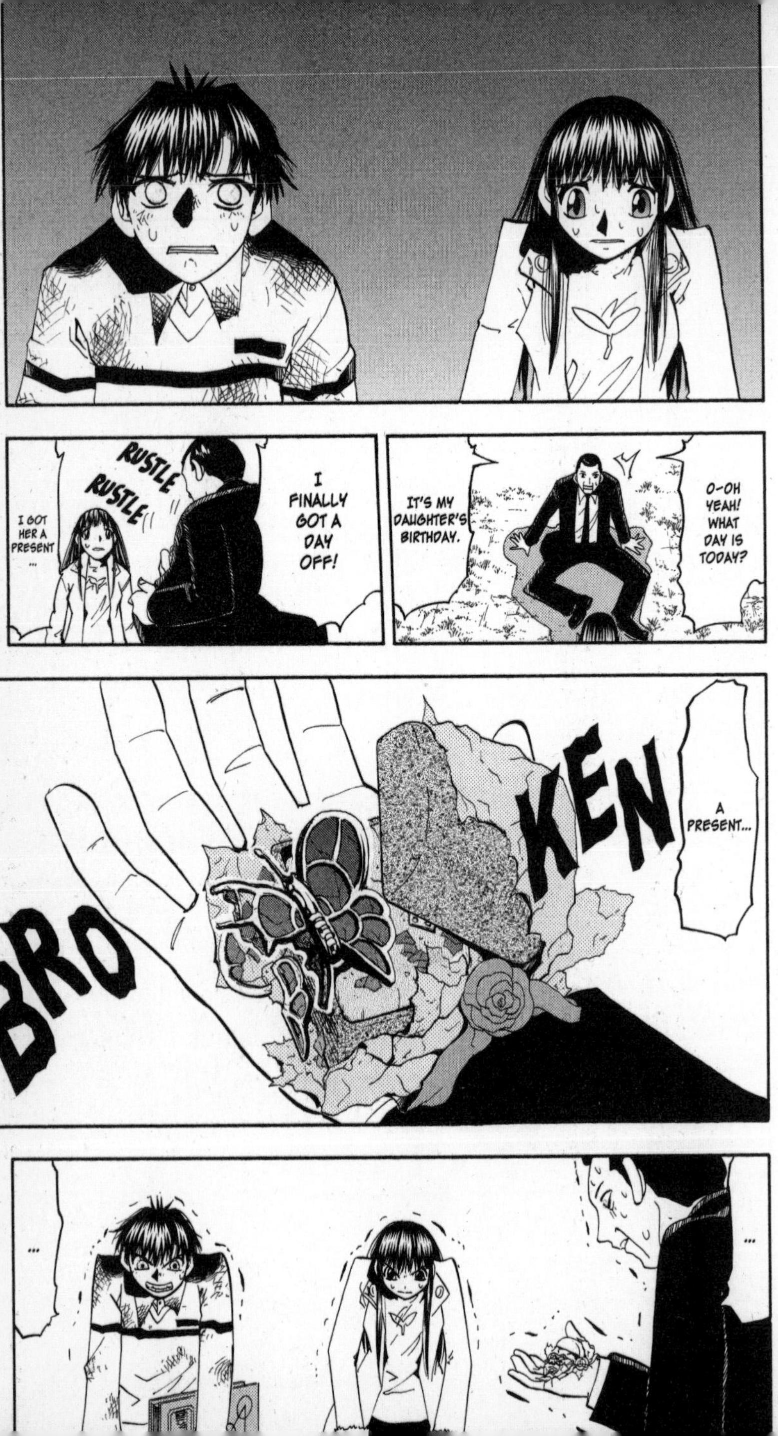
O-OH YEAH! WHAT DAY IS TODAY?
IT'S MY DAUGHTER'S BIRTHDAY.
I FINALLY GOT A DAY OFF!
RUSTLE
RUSTLE
I GOT HER A PRESENT ...
A PRESENT...
BROKEN
...
...

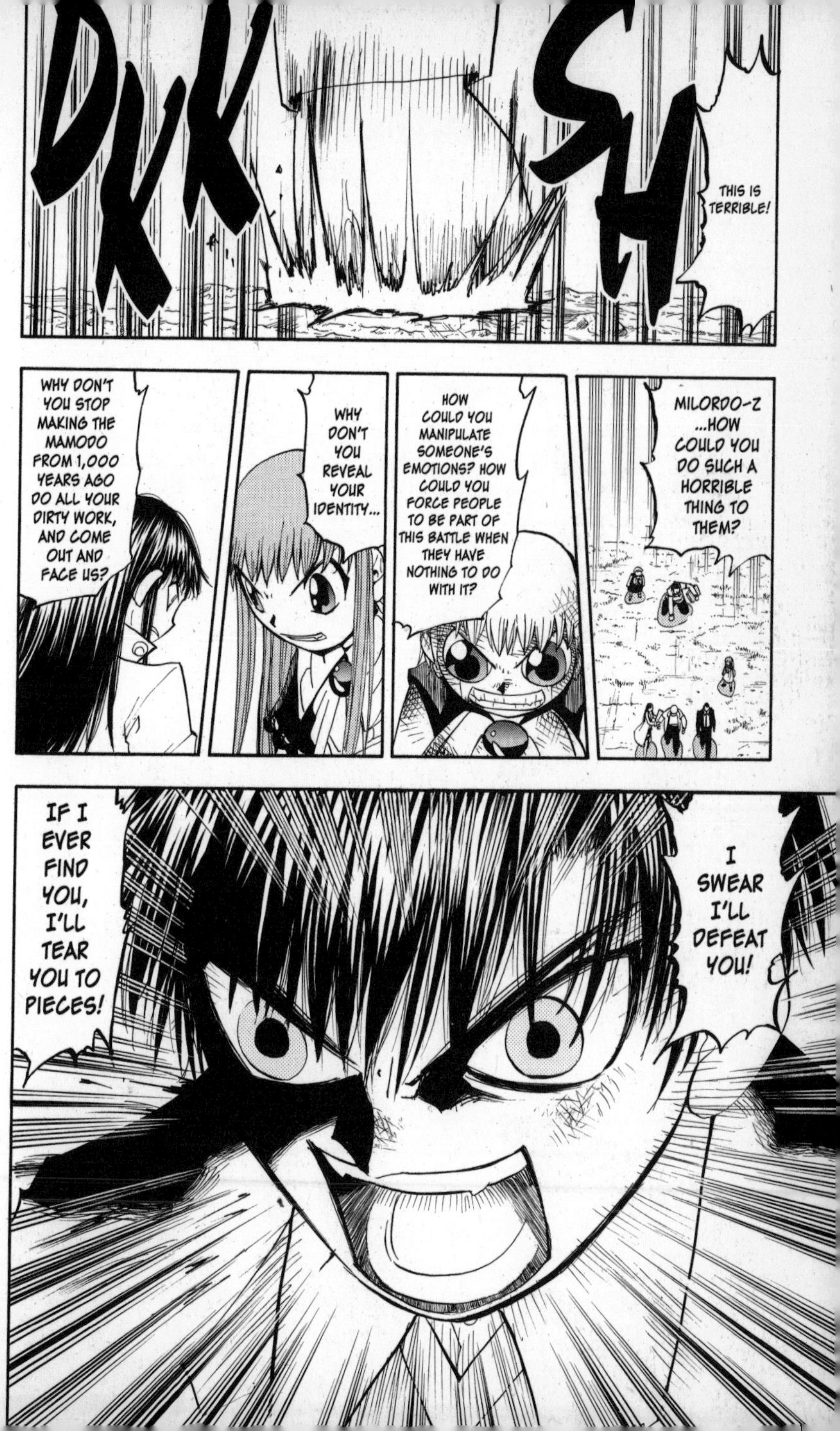

THIS IS TERRIBLE!
DKSH
MILORDO-Z ...HOW COULD YOU DO SUCH A HORRIBLE THING TO THEM?
HOW COULD YOU MANIPULATE SOMEONE'S EMOTIONS? HOW COULD YOU FORCE PEOPLE TO BE PART OF THIS BATTLE WHEN THEY HAVE NOTHING TO DO WITH IT?
WHY DON'T YOU REVEAL YOUR IDENTITY...
WHY DON'T YOU STOP MAKING THE MAMODO FROM 1,000 YEARS AGO DO ALL YOUR DIRTY WORK, AND COME OUT AND FACE US?
I SWEAR I'LL DEFEAT YOU!
IF I EVER FIND YOU, I'LL TEAR YOU TO PIECES!

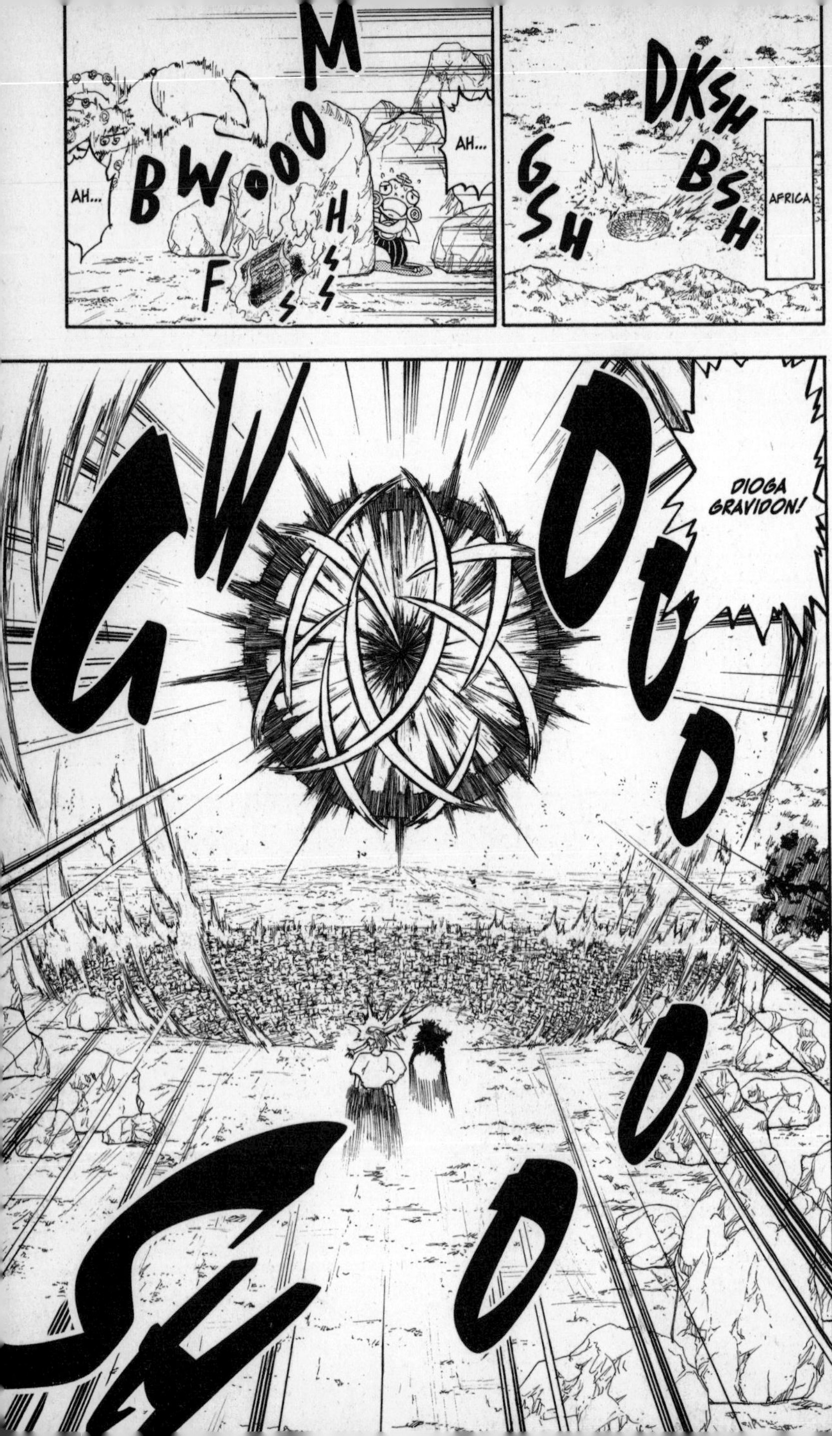
AFRICA
DKSH BSH
GSH
AH...
BWOOOM
AH...
DIOGA GRAVIDON!

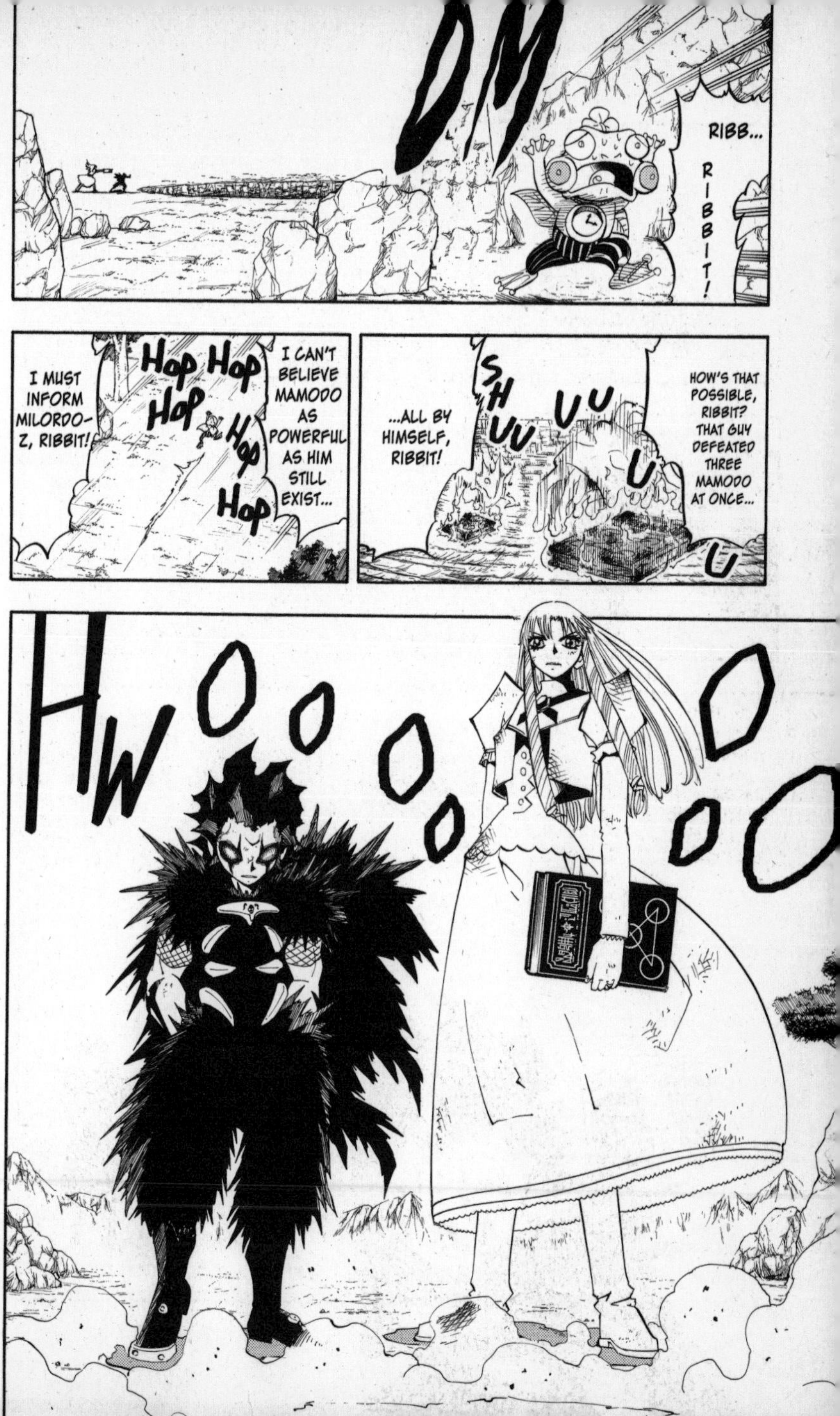
DM
RIBB... RIBBIT!
HOW'S THAT POSSIBLE, RIBBIT? THAT GUY DEFEATED THREE MAMODO AT ONCE...
...ALL BY HIMSELF, RIBBIT!
SHUUUUUU
I CAN'T BELIEVE MAMODO AS POWERFUL AS HIM STILL EXIST...
Hop Hop Hop Hop Hop Hop
I MUST INFORM MILORDO-Z, RIBBIT!
HWOOOOOOOO

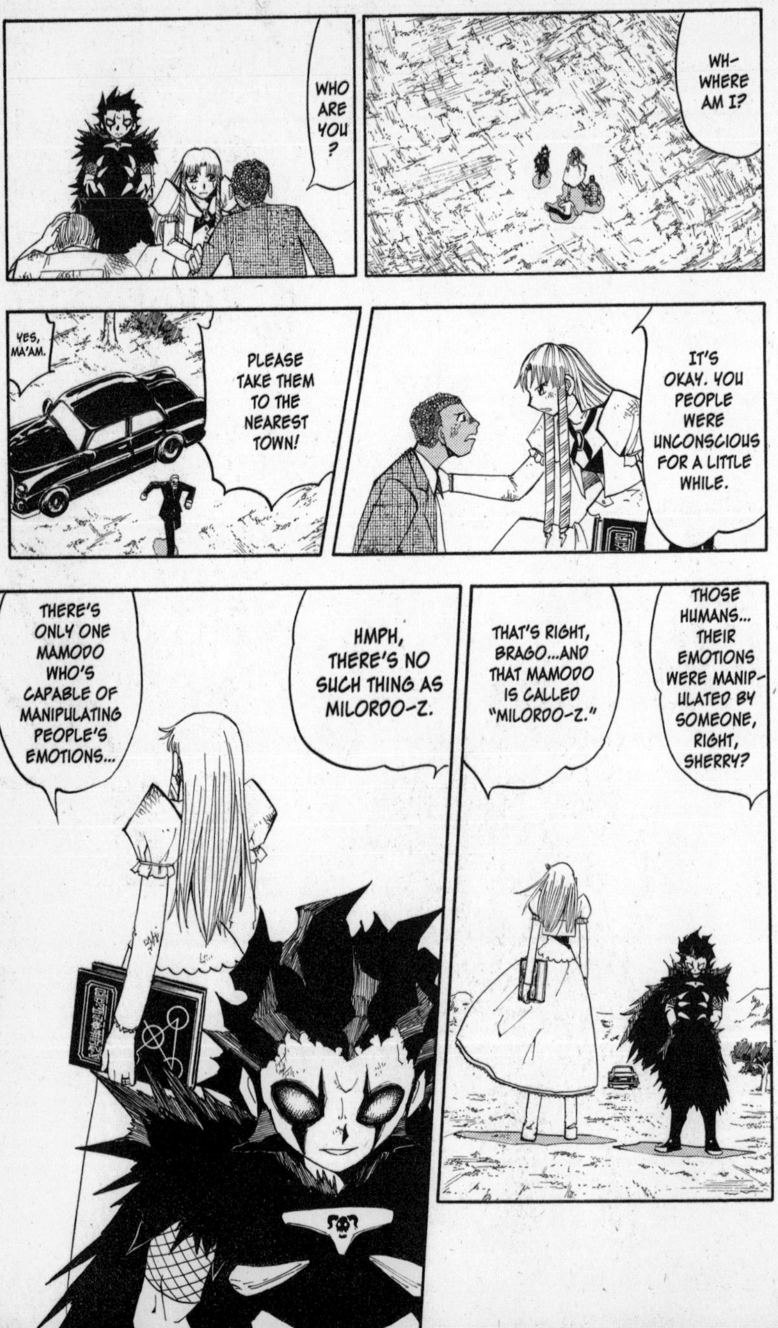
WH- WHERE AM I?
WHO ARE YOU ?
IT'S OKAY. YOU PEOPLE WERE UNCONSCIOUS FOR A LITTLE WHILE.
PLEASE TAKE THEM TO THE NEAREST TOWN!
YES, MA'AM.
THOSE HUMANS... THEIR EMOTIONS WERE MANIPULATED BY SOMEONE, RIGHT, SHERRY?
THAT'S RIGHT, BRAGO...AND THAT MAMODO IS CALLED "MILORDO-Z."
HMPH, THERE'S NO SUCH THING AS MILORDO-Z.
THERE'S ONLY ONE MAMODO WHO'S CAPABLE OF MANIPULATING PEOPLE'S EMOTIONS...

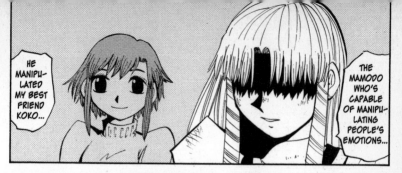

THE MAMODO WHO'S CAPABLE OF MANIPULATING PEOPLE'S EMOTIONS...

HE MANIPULATED MY BEST FRIEND KOKO...

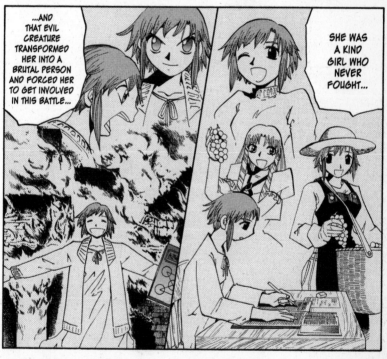

SHE WAS A KIND GIRL WHO NEVER FOUGHT...

...AND THAT EVIL CREATURE TRANSFORMED HER INTO A BRUTAL PERSON AND FORCED HER TO GET INVOLVED IN THIS BATTLE...

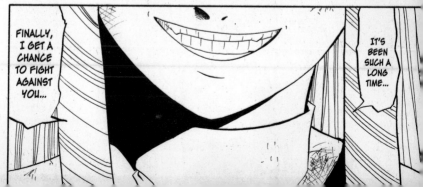

IT'S BEEN SUCH A LONG TIME...

FINALLY, I GET A CHANCE TO FIGHT AGAINST YOU...

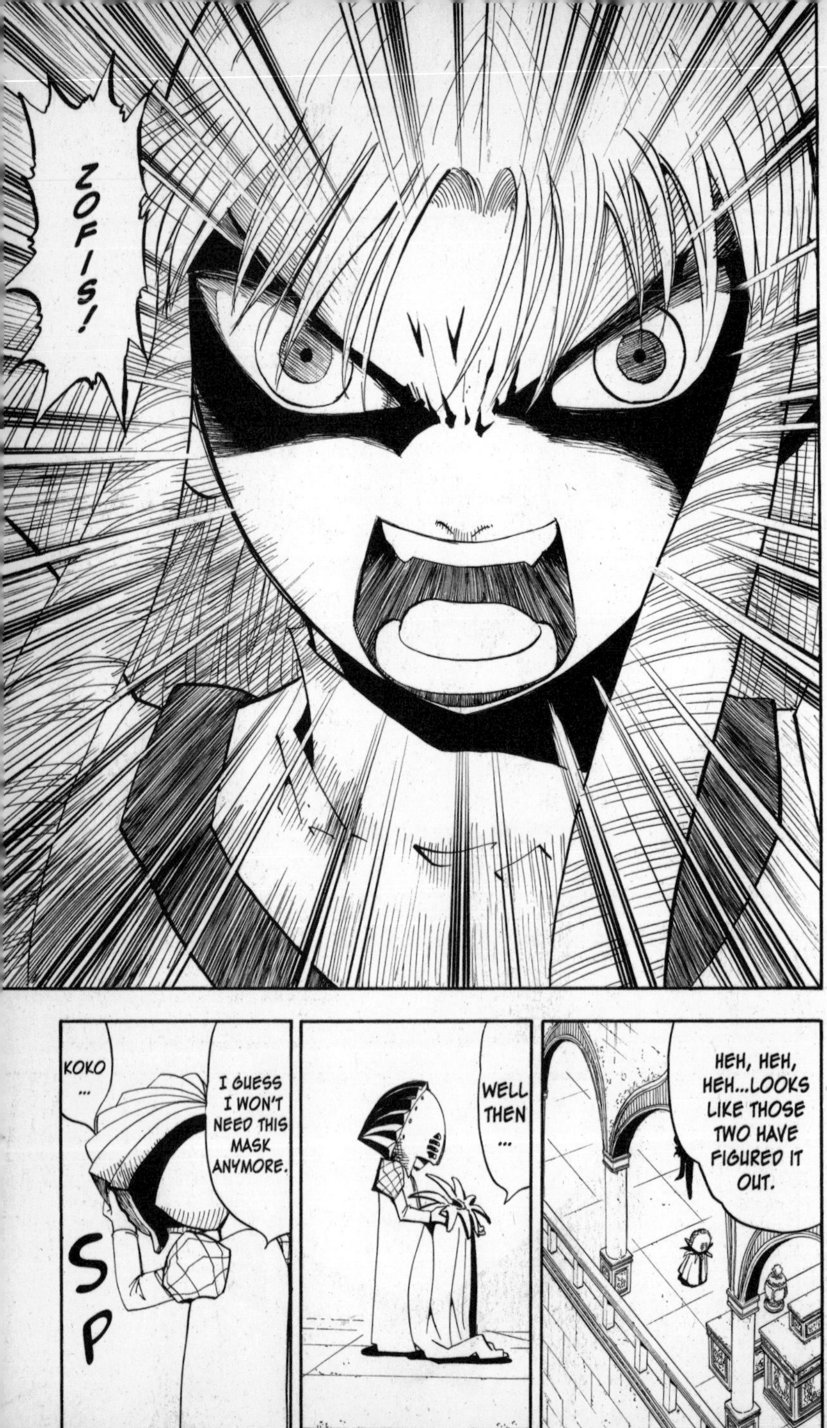
ZOFIS!
HEH, HEH, HEH...LOOKS LIKE THOSE TWO HAVE FIGURED IT OUT.
WELL THEN ...
I GUESS I WON'T NEED THIS MASK ANYMORE.
KOKO ...
SP

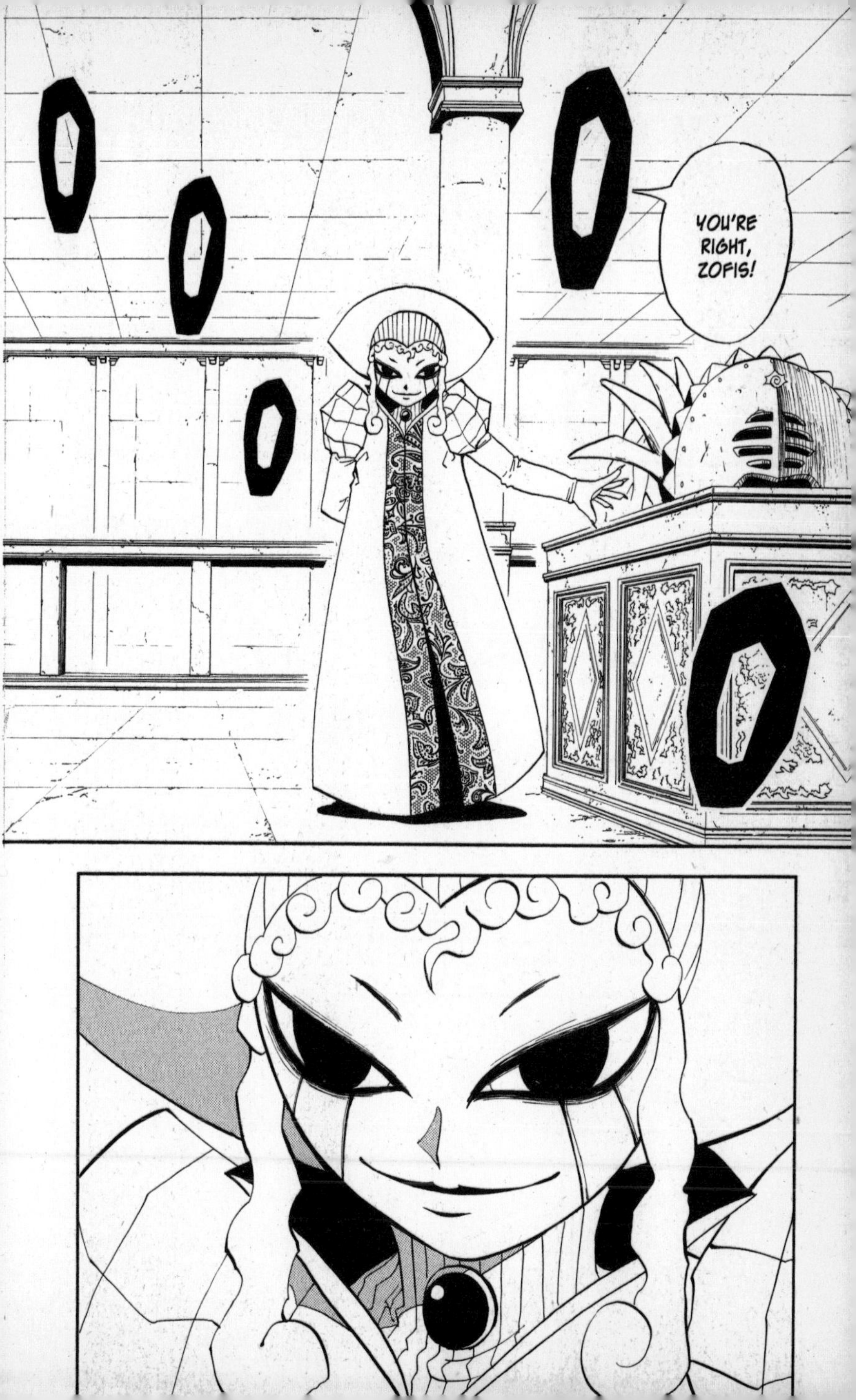
YOU'RE RIGHT, ZOFIS!

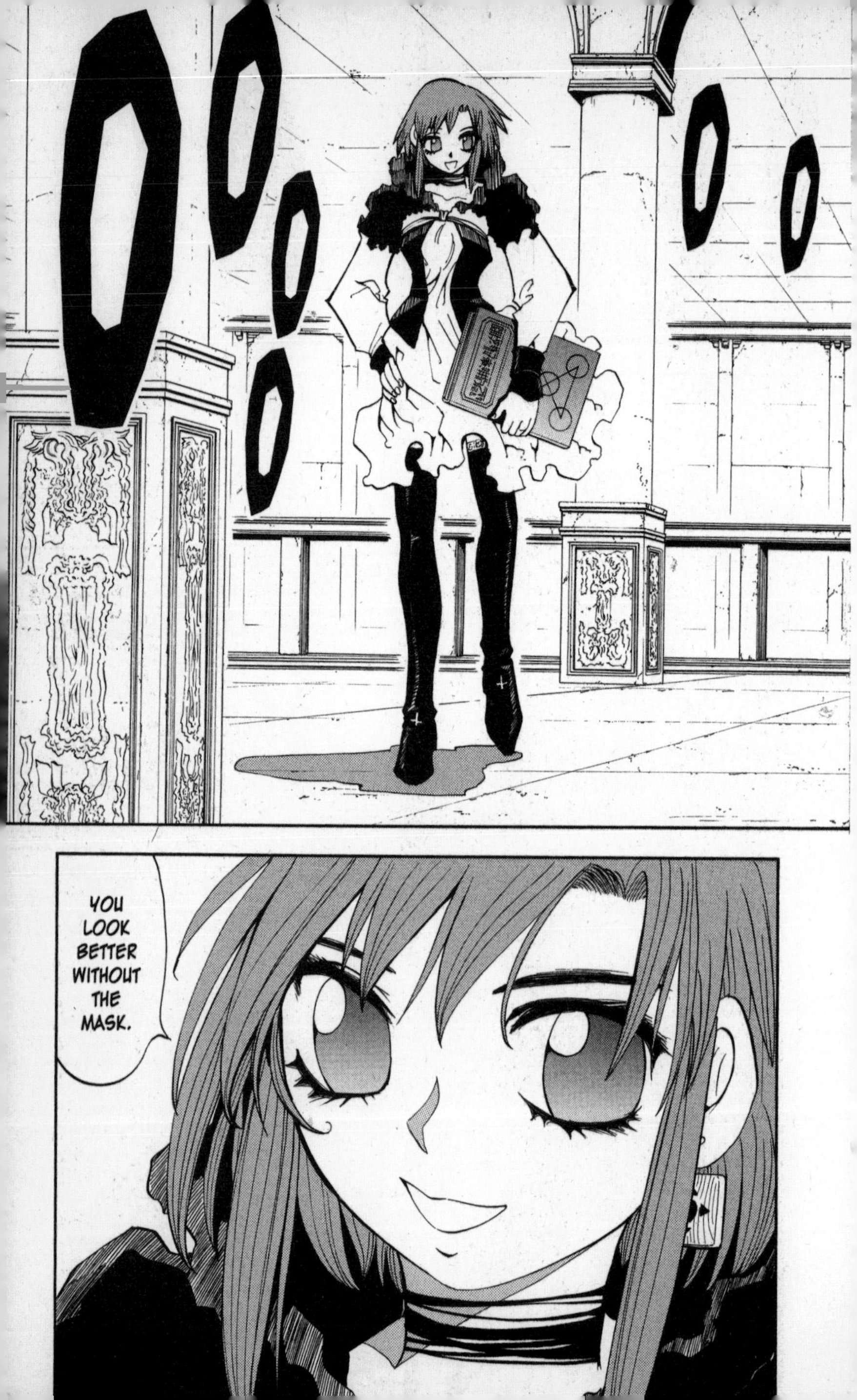
YOU LOOK BETTER WITHOUT THE MASK.

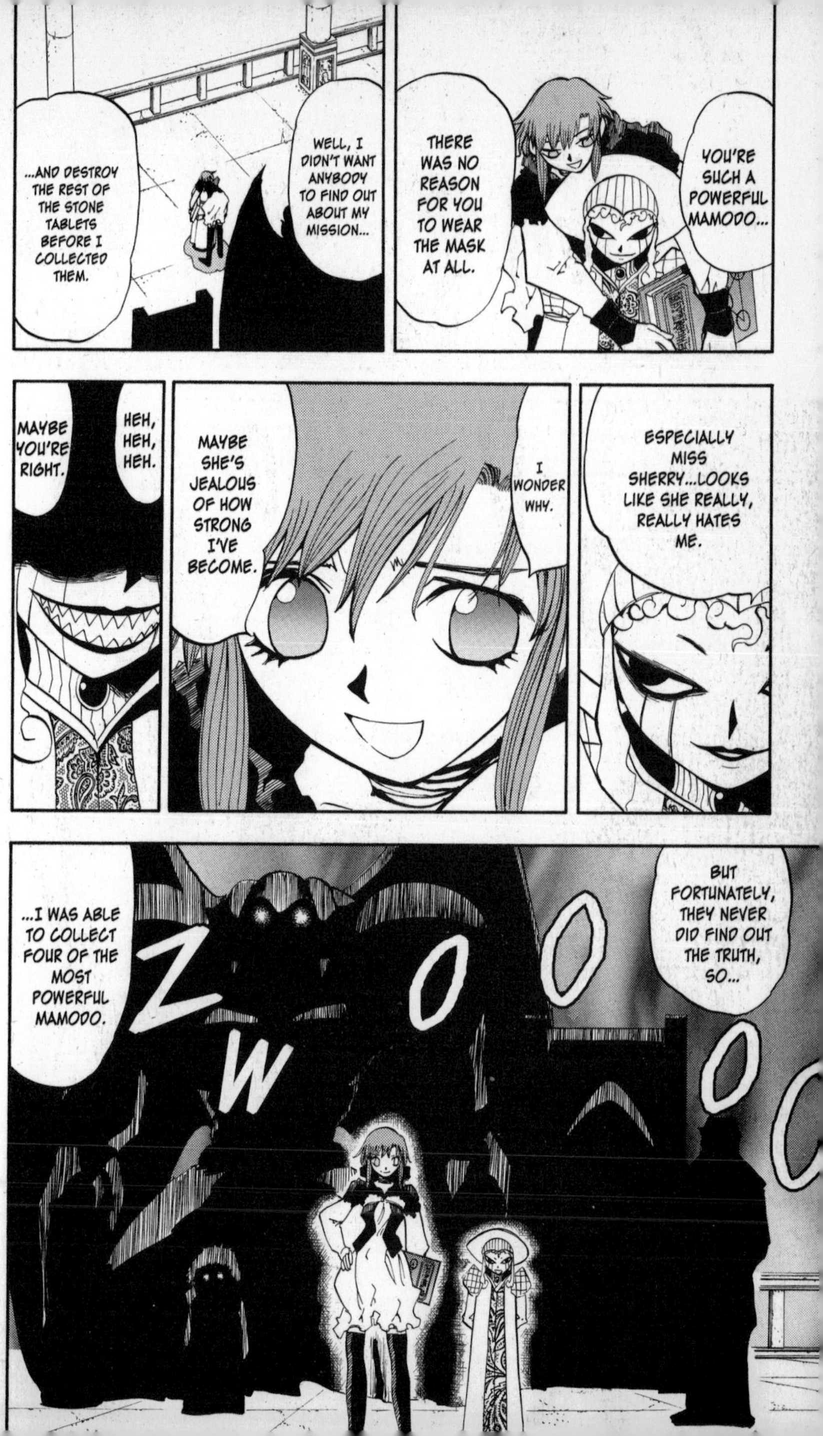
YOU'RE SUCH A POWERFUL MAMODO...
THERE WAS NO REASON FOR YOU TO WEAR THE MASK AT ALL.
WELL, I DIDN'T WANT ANYBODY TO FIND OUT ABOUT MY MISSION...
...AND DESTROY THE REST OF THE STONE TABLETS BEFORE I COLLECTED THEM.
ESPECIALLY MISS SHERRY...LOOKS LIKE SHE REALLY, REALLY HATES ME.
I WONDER WHY.
MAYBE SHE'S JEALOUS OF HOW STRONG I'VE BECOME.
HEH, HEH, HEH.
MAYBE YOU'RE RIGHT.
BUT FORTUNATELY, THEY NEVER DID FIND OUT THE TRUTH, SO...
...I WAS ABLE TO COLLECT FOUR OF THE MOST POWERFUL MAMODO.
ZWOOOOO

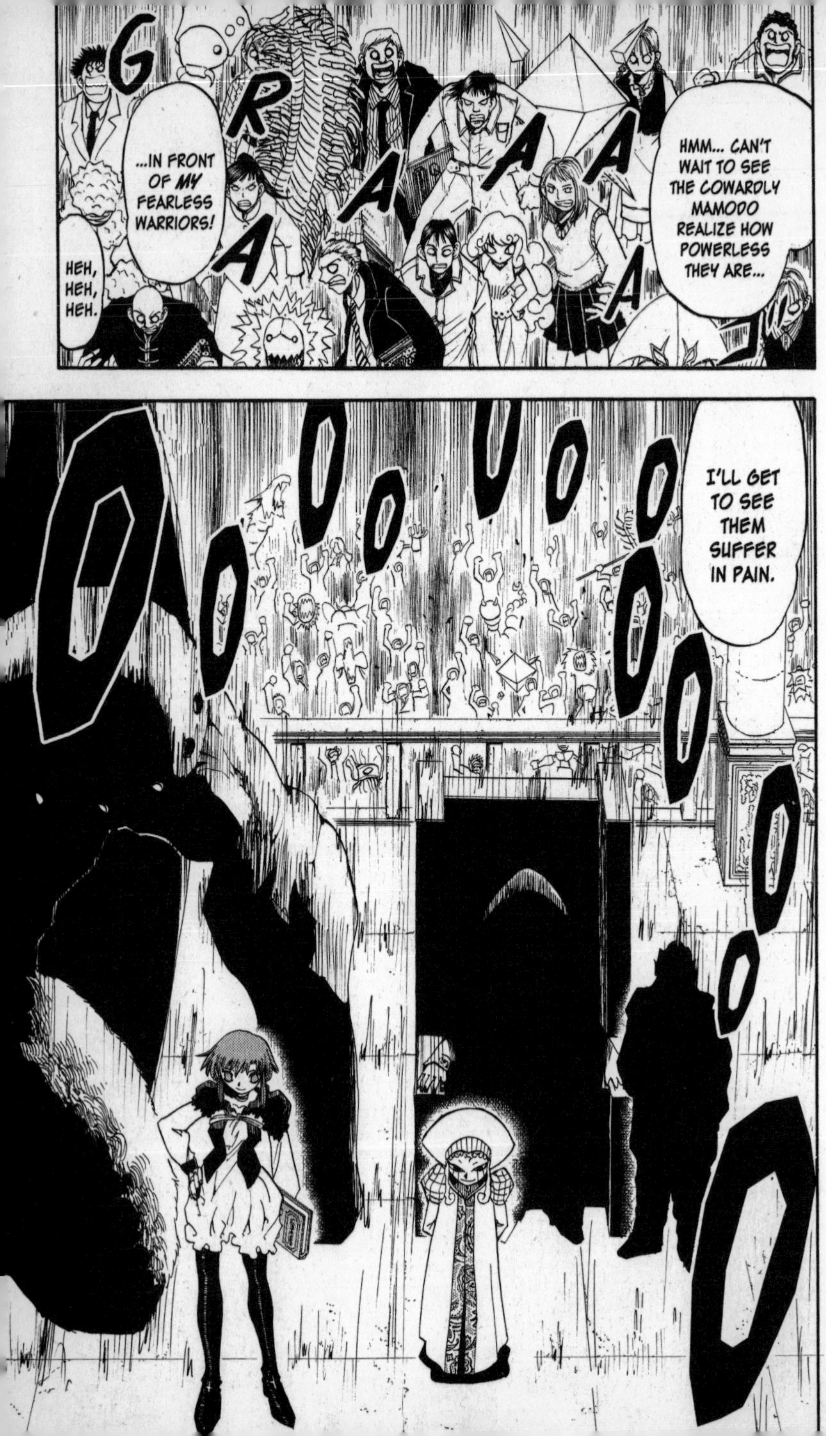
HMM... CAN'T WAIT TO SEE THE COWARDLY MAMODO REALIZE HOW POWERLESS THEY ARE...
...IN FRONT OF MY FEARLESS WARRIORS!
HEH, HEH, HEH.
GRIAAAAAA
I'LL GET TO SEE THEM SUFFER IN PAIN.
OOOOOOOOOOOOOOO

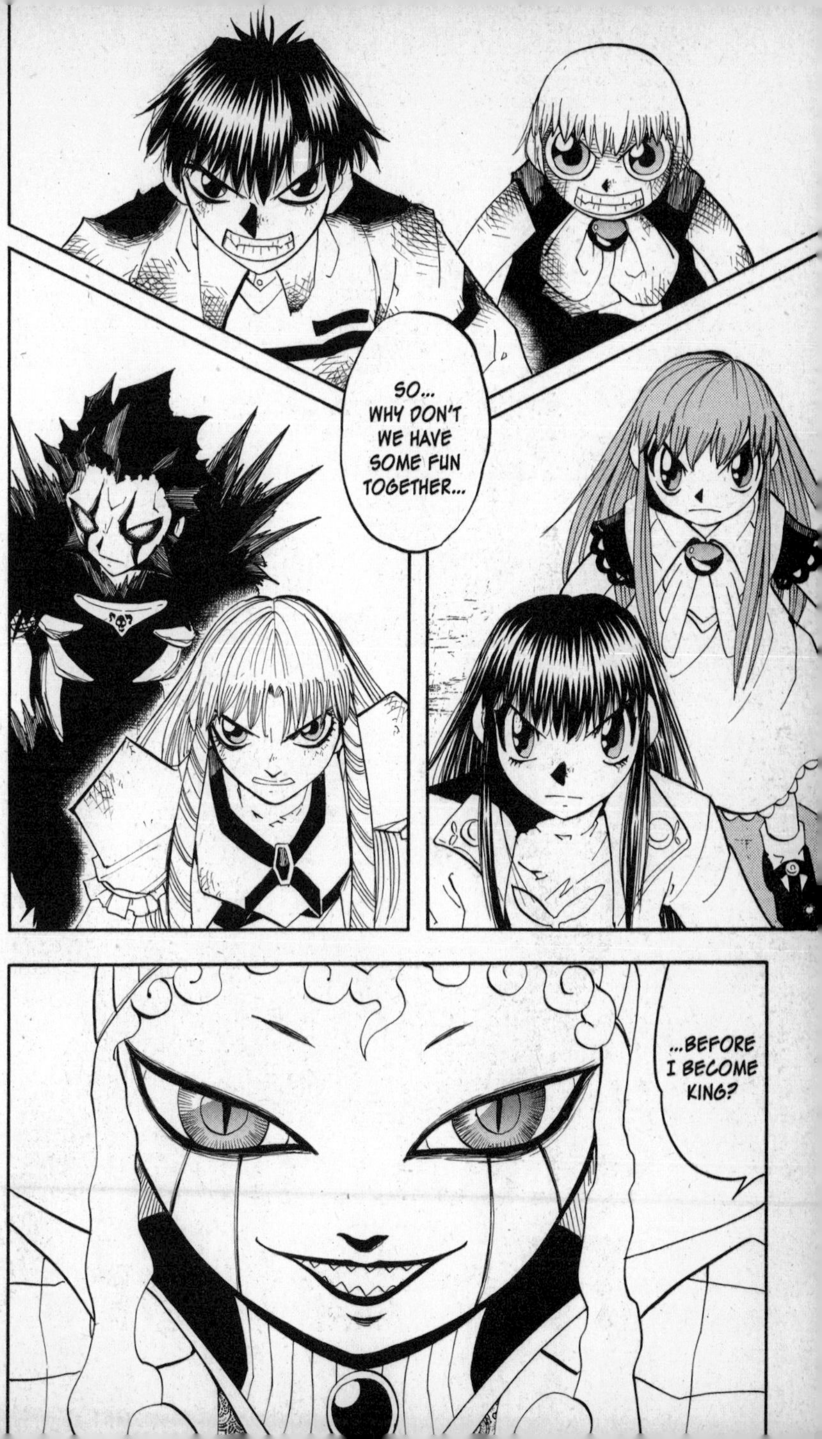
SO... WHY DON'T WE HAVE SOME FUN TOGETHER...
...BEFORE I BECOME KING?

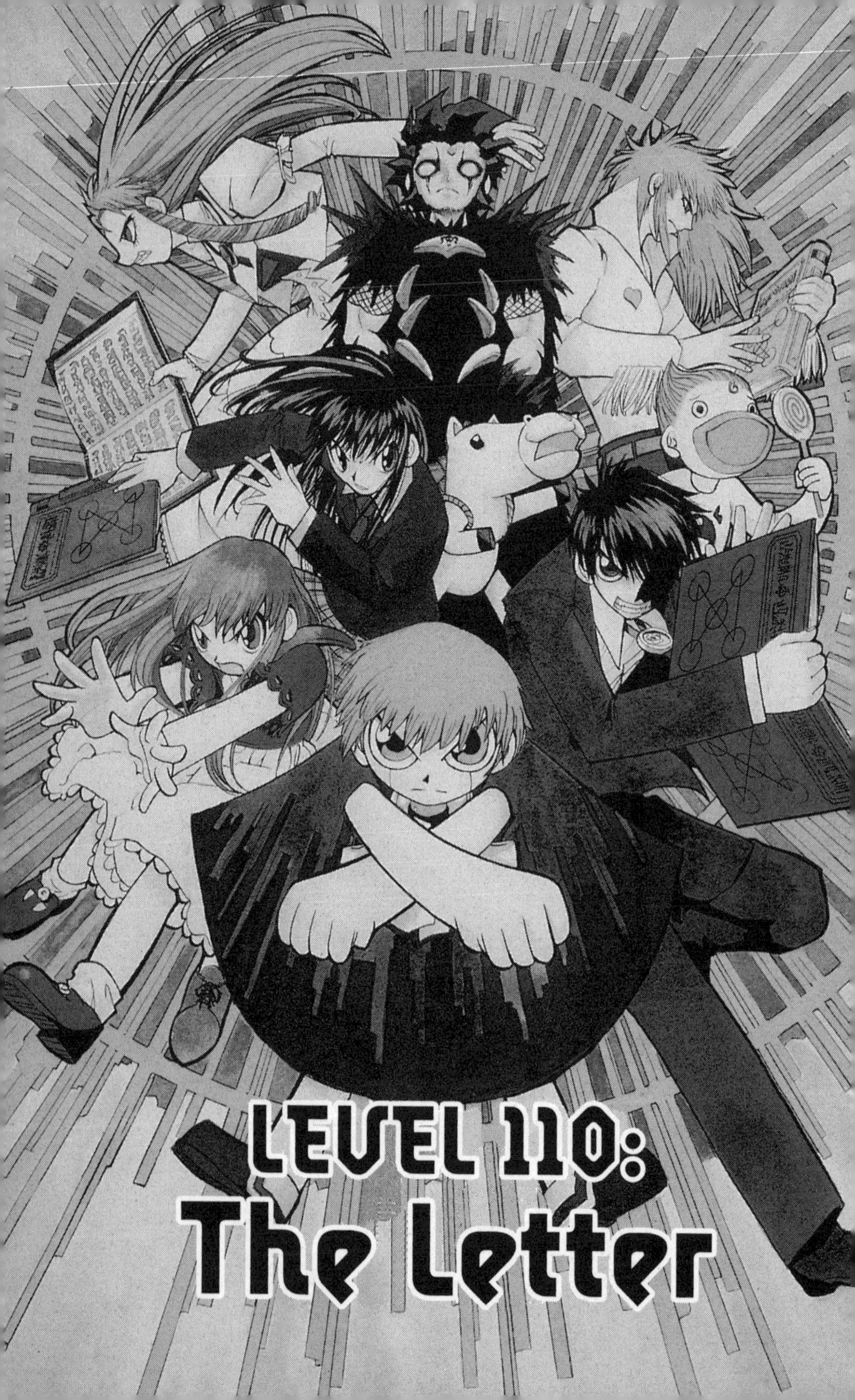

LEVEL 110: The Letter

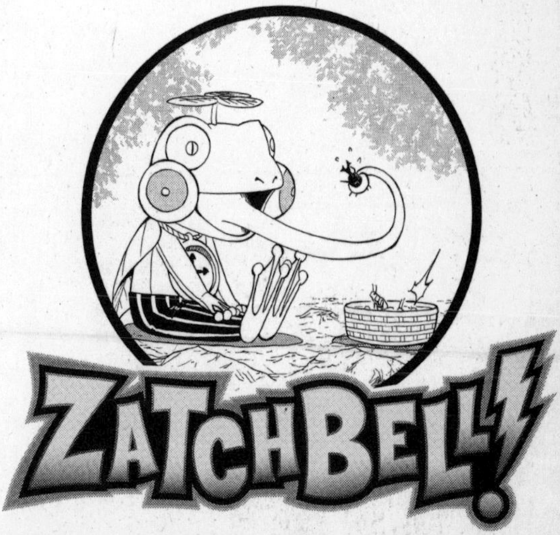
ZATCH BELL!

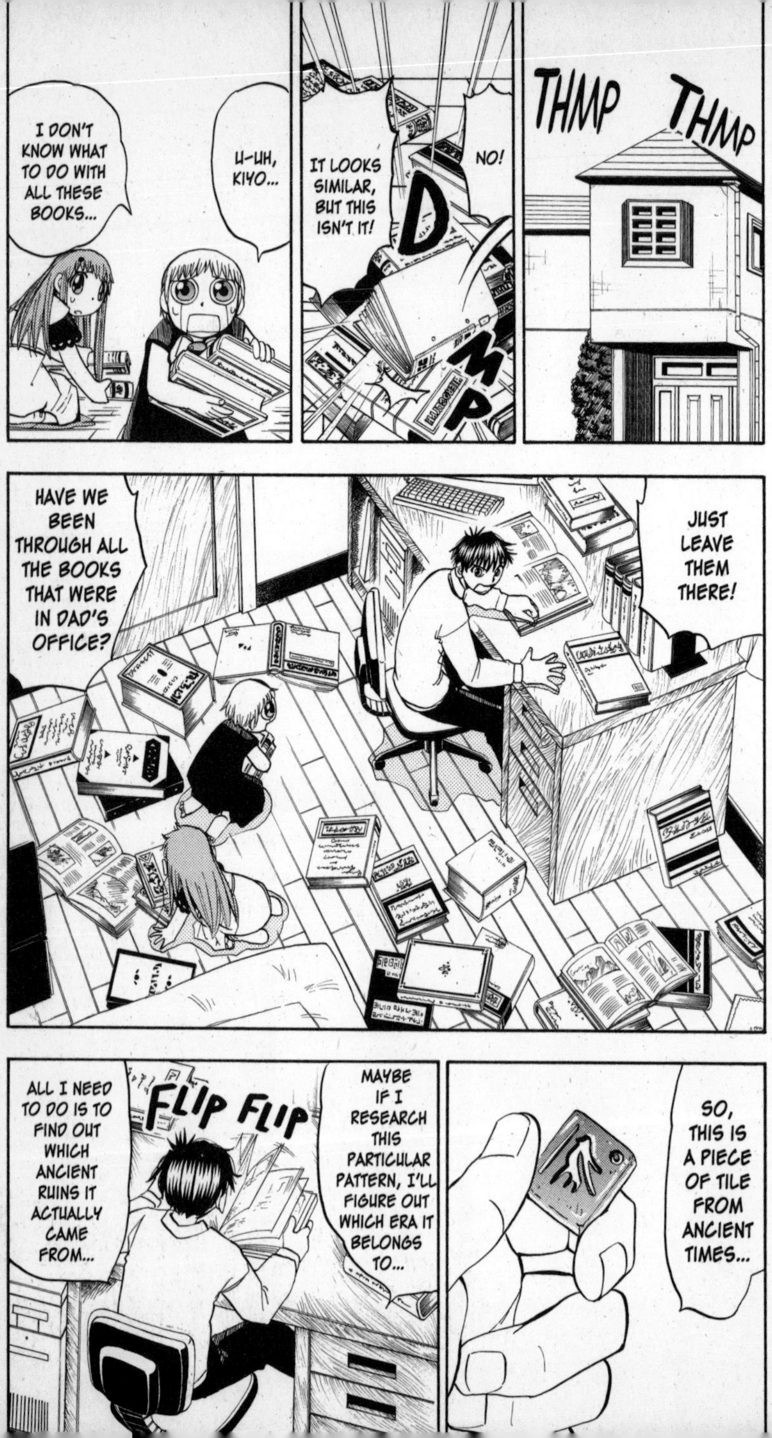
THMP THMP
NO!
IT LOOKS SIMILAR, BUT THIS ISN'T IT!
DMP
U-UH, KIYO...
I DON'T KNOW WHAT TO DO WITH ALL THESE BOOKS...
JUST LEAVE THEM THERE!
HAVE WE BEEN THROUGH ALL THE BOOKS THAT WERE IN DAD'S OFFICE?
SO, THIS IS A PIECE OF TILE FROM ANCIENT TIMES...
MAYBE IF I RESEARCH THIS PARTICULAR PATTERN, I'LL FIGURE OUT WHICH ERA IT BELONGS TO...
FLIP FLIP
ALL I NEED TO DO IS TO FIND OUT WHICH ANCIENT RUINS IT ACTUALLY CAME FROM...

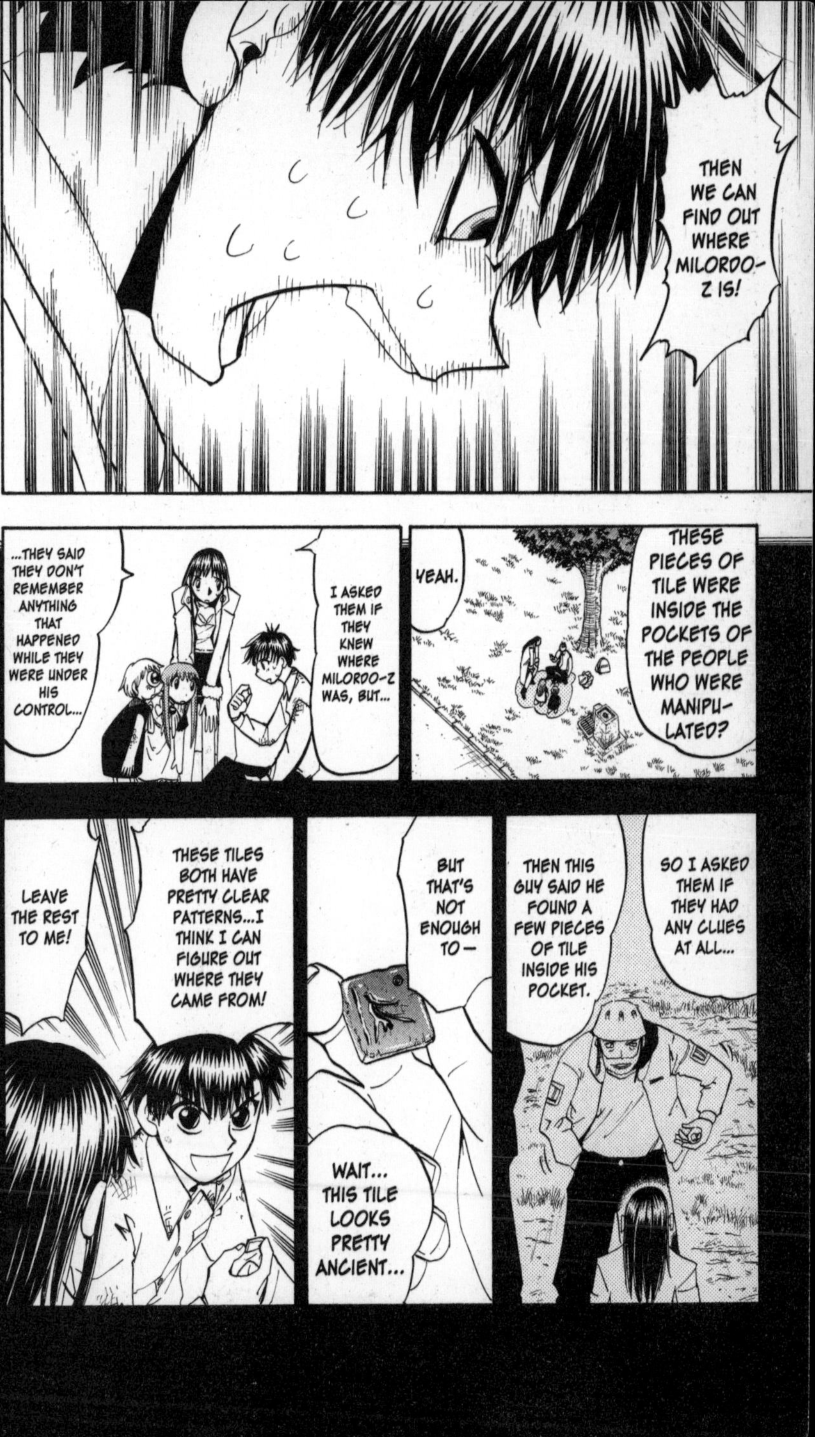
THEN WE CAN FIND OUT WHERE MILORDO-Z IS!
THESE PIECES OF TILE WERE INSIDE THE POCKETS OF THE PEOPLE WHO WERE MANIPULATED?
YEAH.
I ASKED THEM IF THEY KNEW WHERE MILORDO-Z WAS, BUT...
...THEY SAID THEY DON'T REMEMBER ANYTHING THAT HAPPENED WHILE THEY WERE UNDER HIS CONTROL...
SO I ASKED THEM IF THEY HAD ANY CLUES AT ALL...
THEN THIS GUY SAID HE FOUND A FEW PIECES OF TILE INSIDE HIS POCKET.
BUT THAT'S NOT ENOUGH TO—
WAIT... THIS TILE LOOKS PRETTY ANCIENT...
THESE TILES BOTH HAVE PRETTY CLEAR PATTERNS...I THINK I CAN FIGURE OUT WHERE THEY CAME FROM!
LEAVE THE REST TO ME!

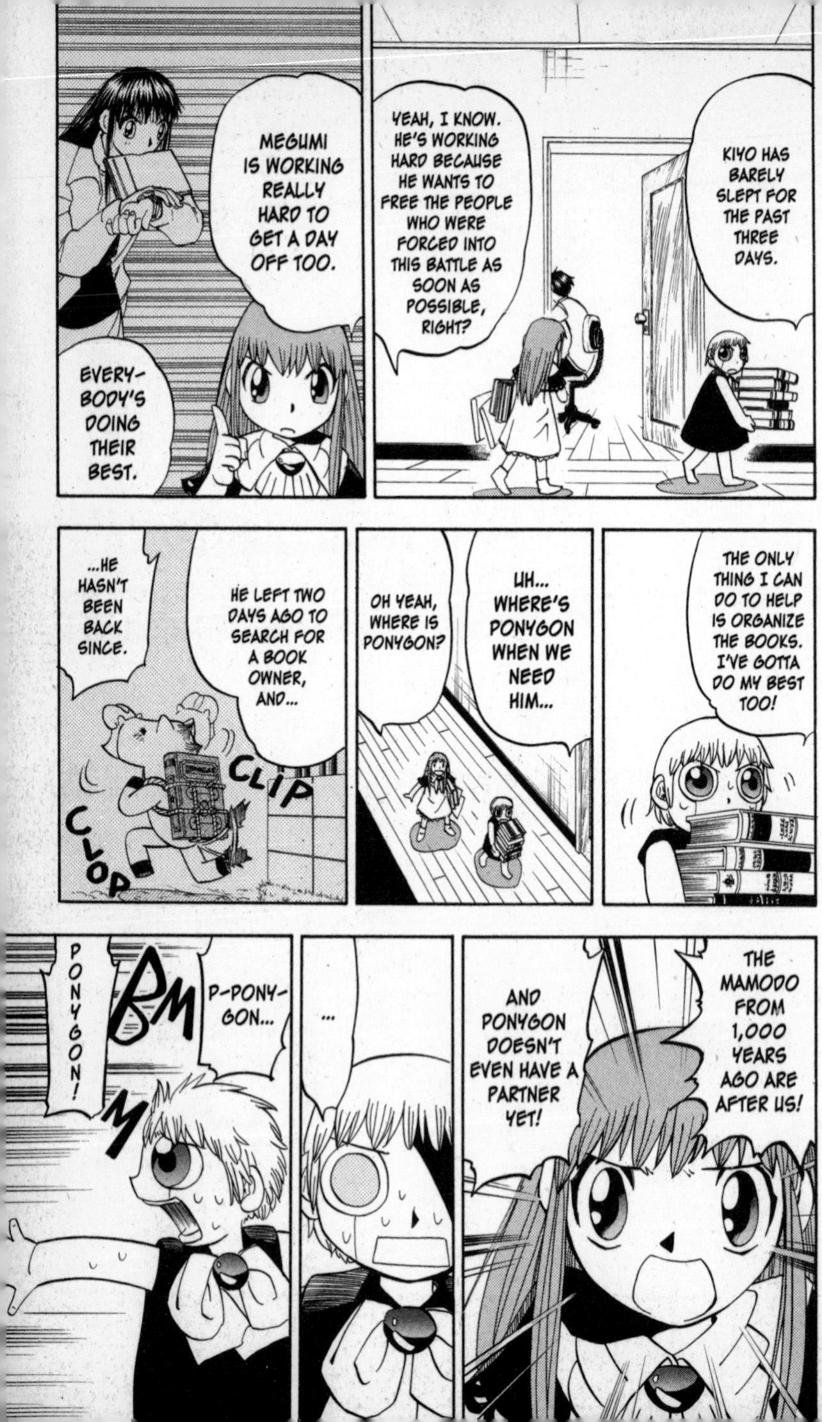
KIYO HAS BARELY SLEPT FOR THE PAST THREE DAYS.
YEAH, I KNOW. HE'S WORKING HARD BECAUSE HE WANTS TO FREE THE PEOPLE WHO WERE FORCED INTO THIS BATTLE AS SOON AS POSSIBLE, RIGHT?
MEGUMI IS WORKING REALLY HARD TO GET A DAY OFF TOO.
EVERYBODY'S DOING THEIR BEST.
THE ONLY THING I CAN DO TO HELP IS ORGANIZE THE BOOKS. I'VE GOTTA DO MY BEST TOO!
UH... WHERE'S PONYGON WHEN WE NEED HIM...
OH YEAH, WHERE IS PONYGON?
HE LEFT TWO DAYS AGO TO SEARCH FOR A BOOK OWNER, AND...
...HE HASN'T BEEN BACK SINCE.
CLIP
CLOP
THE MAMODO FROM 1,000 YEARS AGO ARE AFTER US!
AND PONYGON DOESN'T EVEN HAVE A PARTNER YET!
...
P-PONYGON...
BMM
PONYGON!

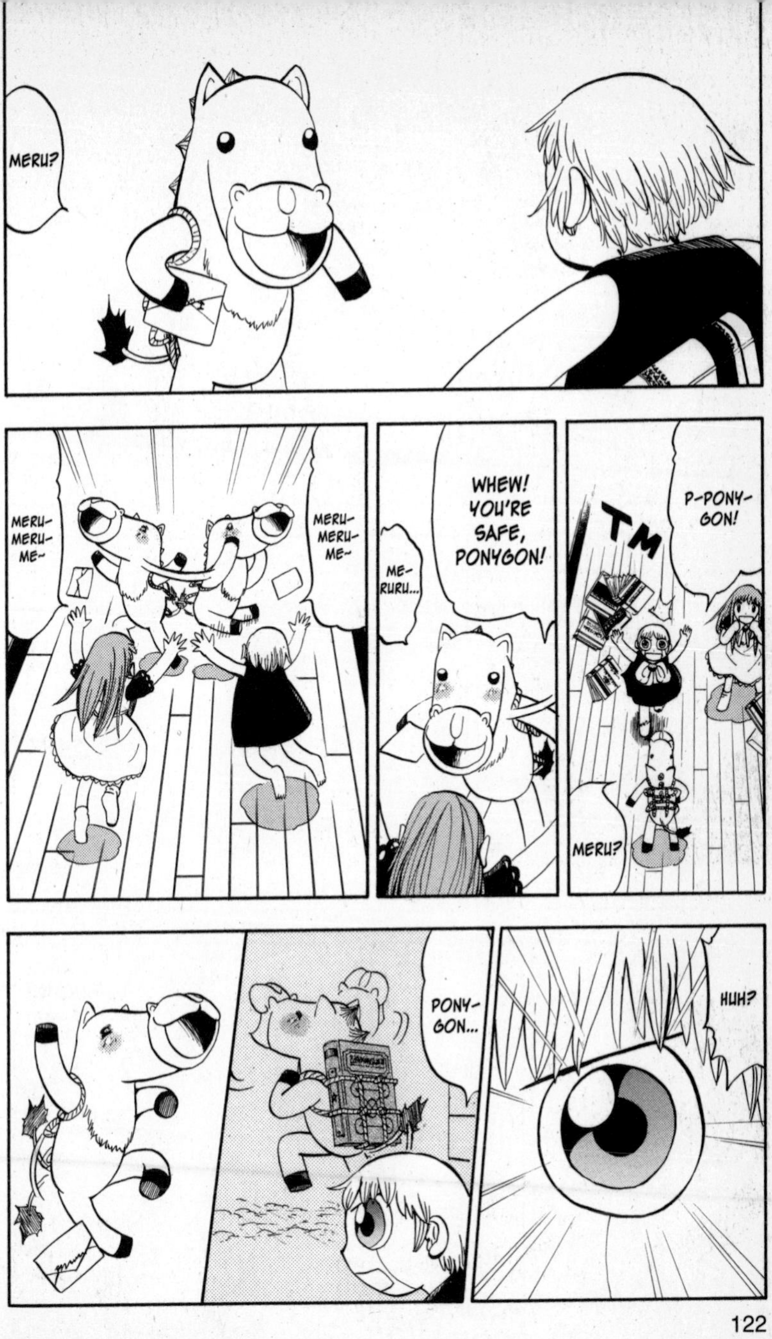
MERU?
P-PONY-GON!
TM
MERU?
WHEW! YOU'RE SAFE, PONYGON!
ME-RURU...
MERU-MERU-ME~
MERU-MERU-ME~
HUH?
PONY-GON...

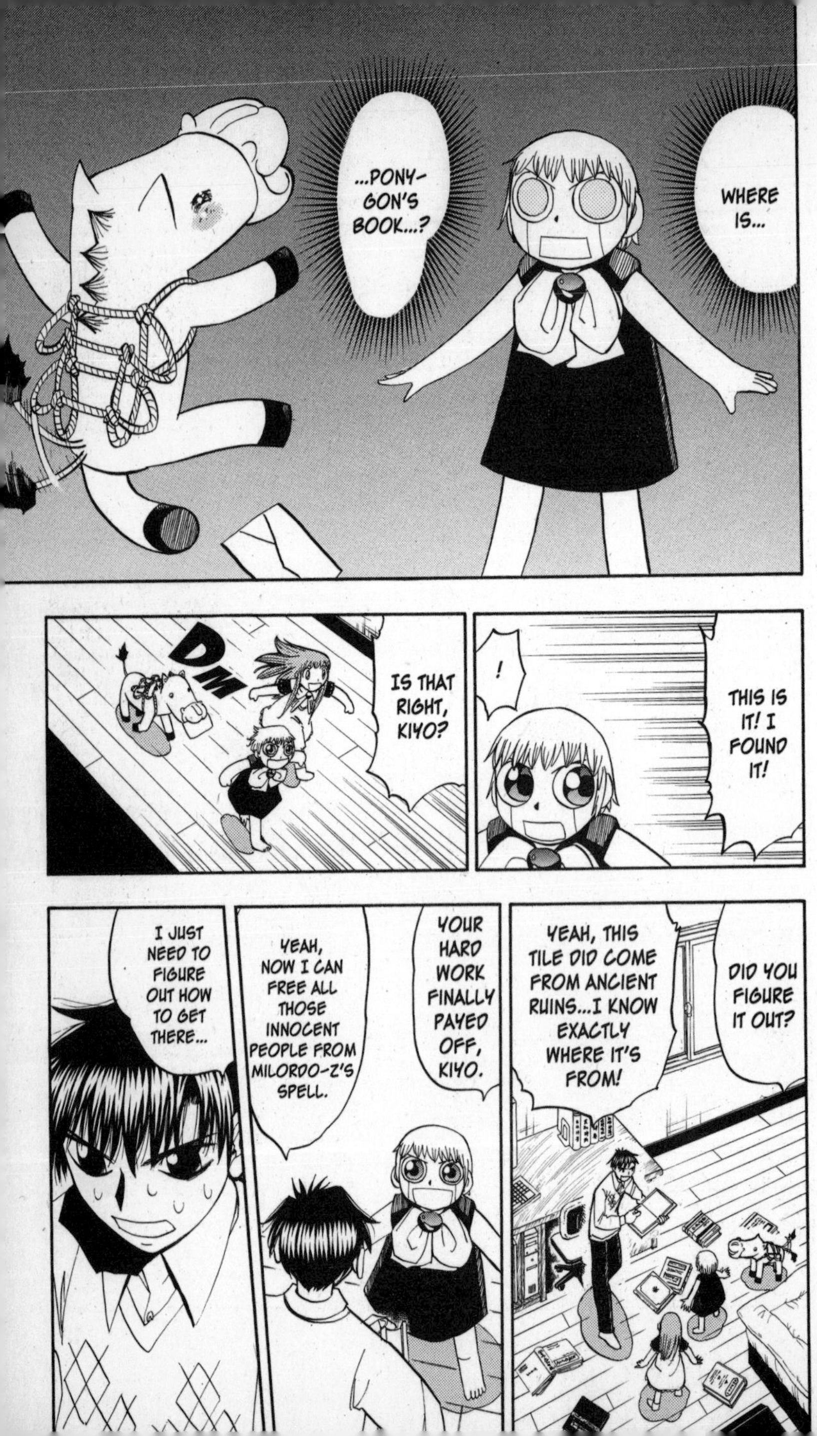
WHERE IS...
...PONY-GON'S BOOK...?
!
THIS IS IT! I FOUND IT!
DM
IS THAT RIGHT, KIYO?
DID YOU FIGURE IT OUT?
YEAH, THIS TILE DID COME FROM ANCIENT RUINS...I KNOW EXACTLY WHERE IT'S FROM!
YOUR HARD WORK FINALLY PAYED OFF, KIYO.
YEAH, NOW I CAN FREE ALL THOSE INNOCENT PEOPLE FROM MILORDO-Z'S SPELL.
I JUST NEED TO FIGURE OUT HOW TO GET THERE...

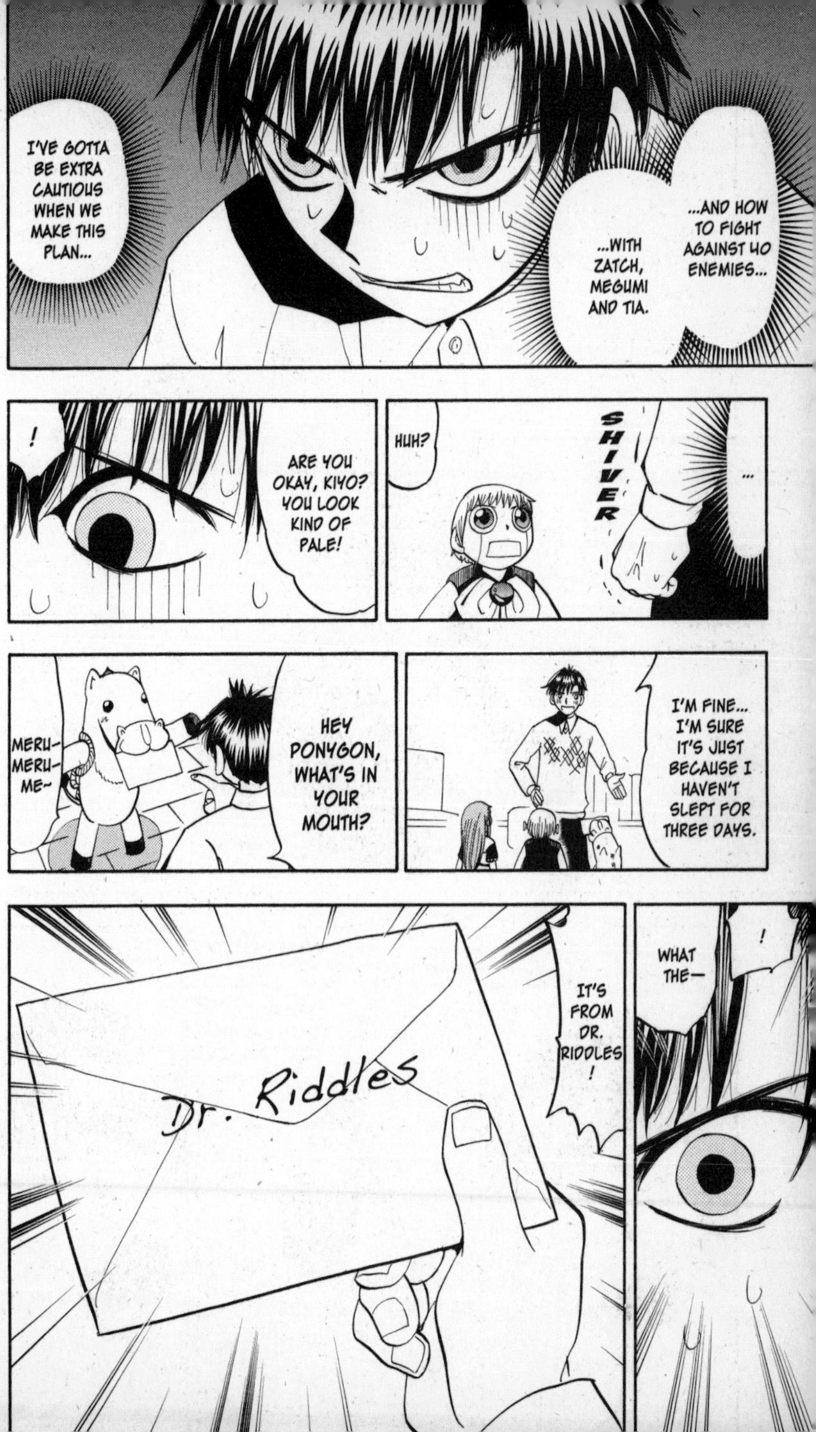
...AND HOW TO FIGHT AGAINST 40 ENEMIES...
...WITH ZATCH, MEGUMI AND TIA.
I'VE GOTTA BE EXTRA CAUTIOUS WHEN WE MAKE THIS PLAN...
...
SHIVER
HUH?
ARE YOU OKAY, KIYO? YOU LOOK KIND OF PALE!
!
I'M FINE... I'M SURE IT'S JUST BECAUSE I HAVEN'T SLEPT FOR THREE DAYS.
HEY PONYGON, WHAT'S IN YOUR MOUTH?
MERU-MERU-ME~
!
WHAT THE—
IT'S FROM DR. RIDDLES!
Dr. Riddles

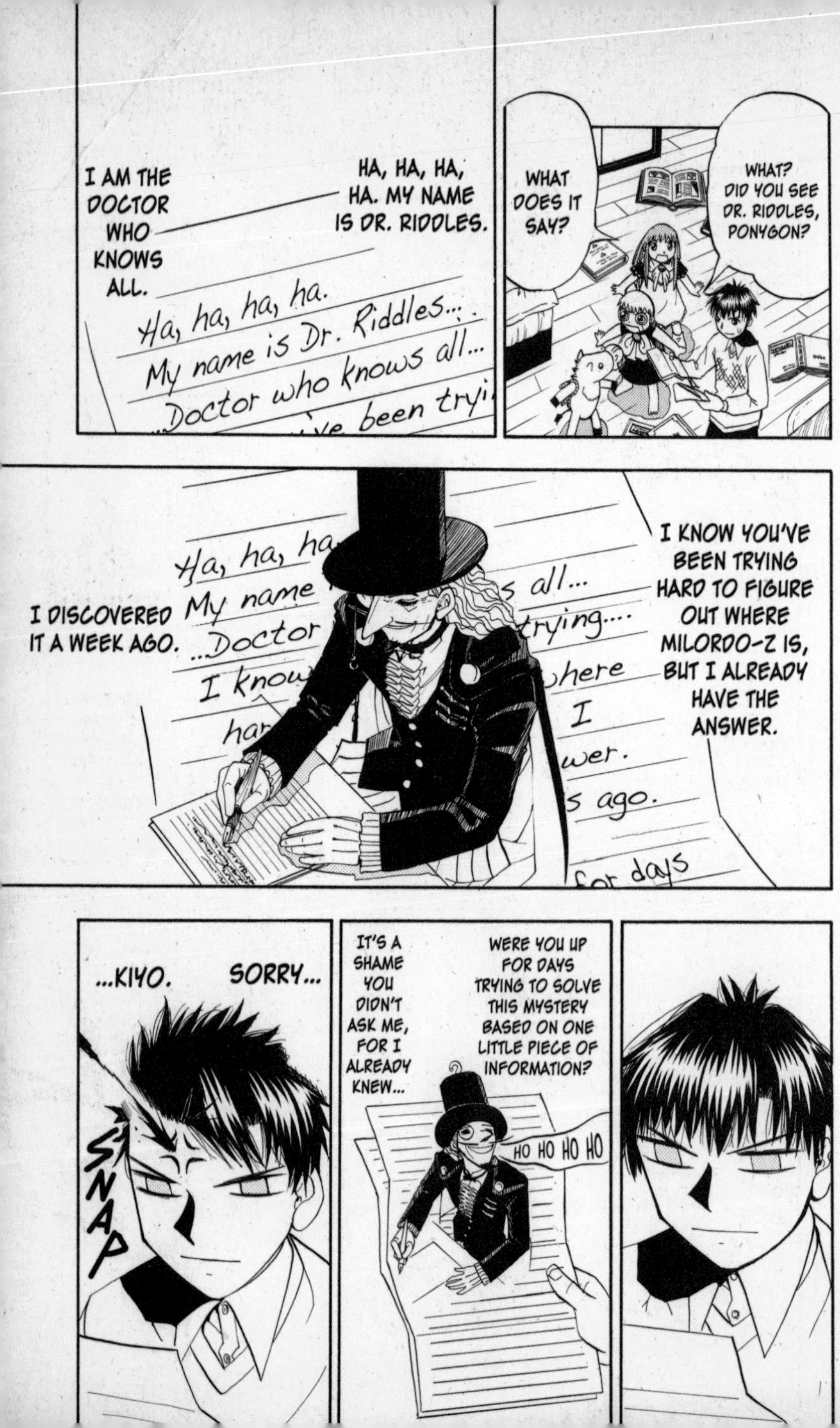
WHAT? DID YOU SEE DR. RIDDLES, PONYGON?
WHAT DOES IT SAY?
HA, HA, HA, HA. MY NAME IS DR. RIDDLES.
I AM THE DOCTOR WHO KNOWS ALL.
Ha, ha, ha, ha.
My name is Dr. Riddles...
Doctor who knows all...
I KNOW YOU'VE BEEN TRYING HARD TO FIGURE OUT WHERE MILORDO-Z IS, BUT I ALREADY HAVE THE ANSWER.
I DISCOVERED IT A WEEK AGO.
WERE YOU UP FOR DAYS TRYING TO SOLVE THIS MYSTERY BASED ON ONE LITTLE PIECE OF INFORMATION?
IT'S A SHAME YOU DIDN'T ASK ME, FOR I ALREADY KNEW...
HO HO HO HO
SORRY...
...KIYO.
SNAP

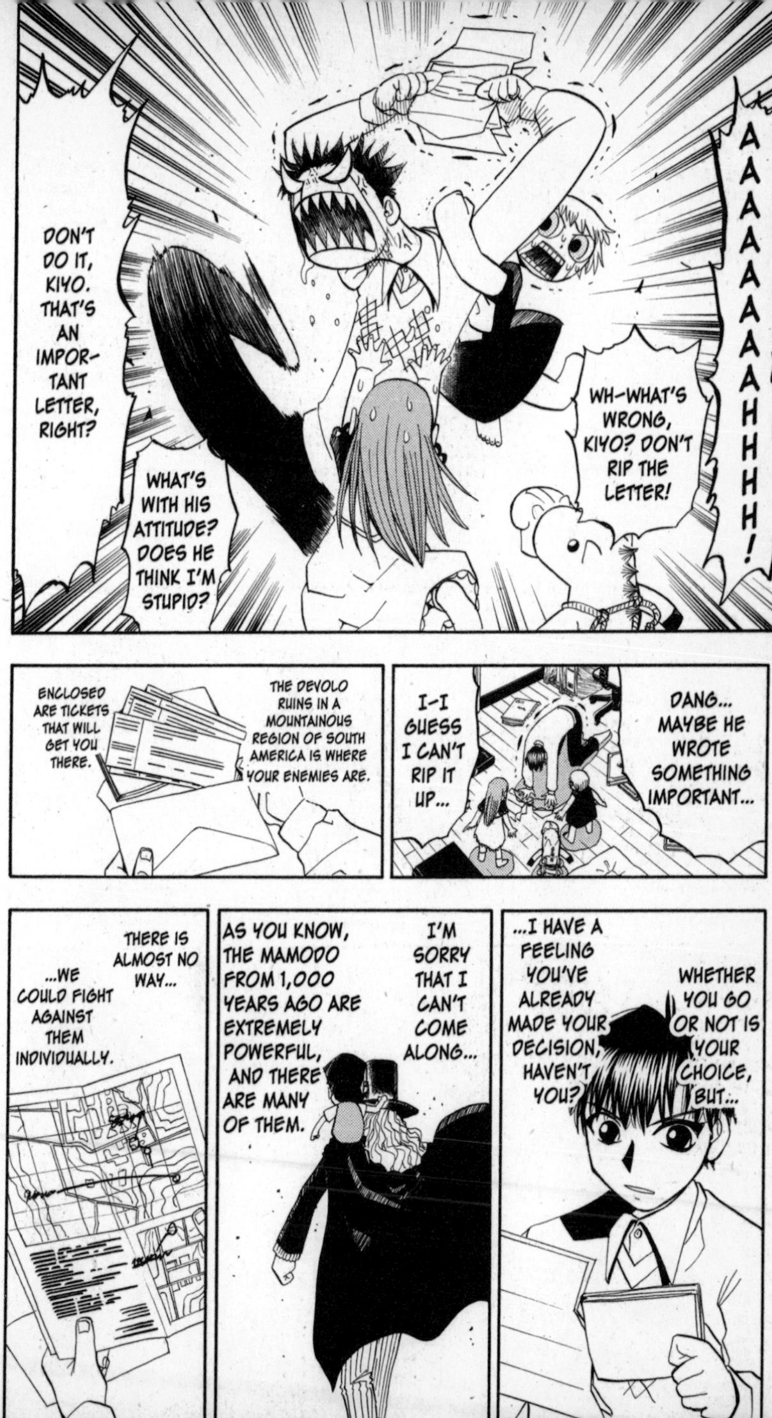
AAAAAAAAHHHH!
WH-WHAT'S WRONG, KIYO? DON'T RIP THE LETTER!
DON'T DO IT, KIYO. THAT'S AN IMPORTANT LETTER, RIGHT?
WHAT'S WITH HIS ATTITUDE? DOES HE THINK I'M STUPID?
DANG... MAYBE HE WROTE SOMETHING IMPORTANT...
I-I GUESS I CAN'T RIP IT UP...
THE DEVOLO RUINS IN A MOUNTAINOUS REGION OF SOUTH AMERICA IS WHERE YOUR ENEMIES ARE.
ENCLOSED ARE TICKETS THAT WILL GET YOU THERE.
WHETHER YOU GO OR NOT IS YOUR CHOICE, BUT...
...I HAVE A FEELING YOU'VE ALREADY MADE YOUR DECISION, HAVEN'T YOU?
I'M SORRY THAT I CAN'T COME ALONG...
AS YOU KNOW, THE MAMODO FROM 1,000 YEARS AGO ARE EXTREMELY POWERFUL, AND THERE ARE MANY OF THEM.
THERE IS ALMOST NO WAY...
...WE COULD FIGHT AGAINST THEM INDIVIDUALLY.

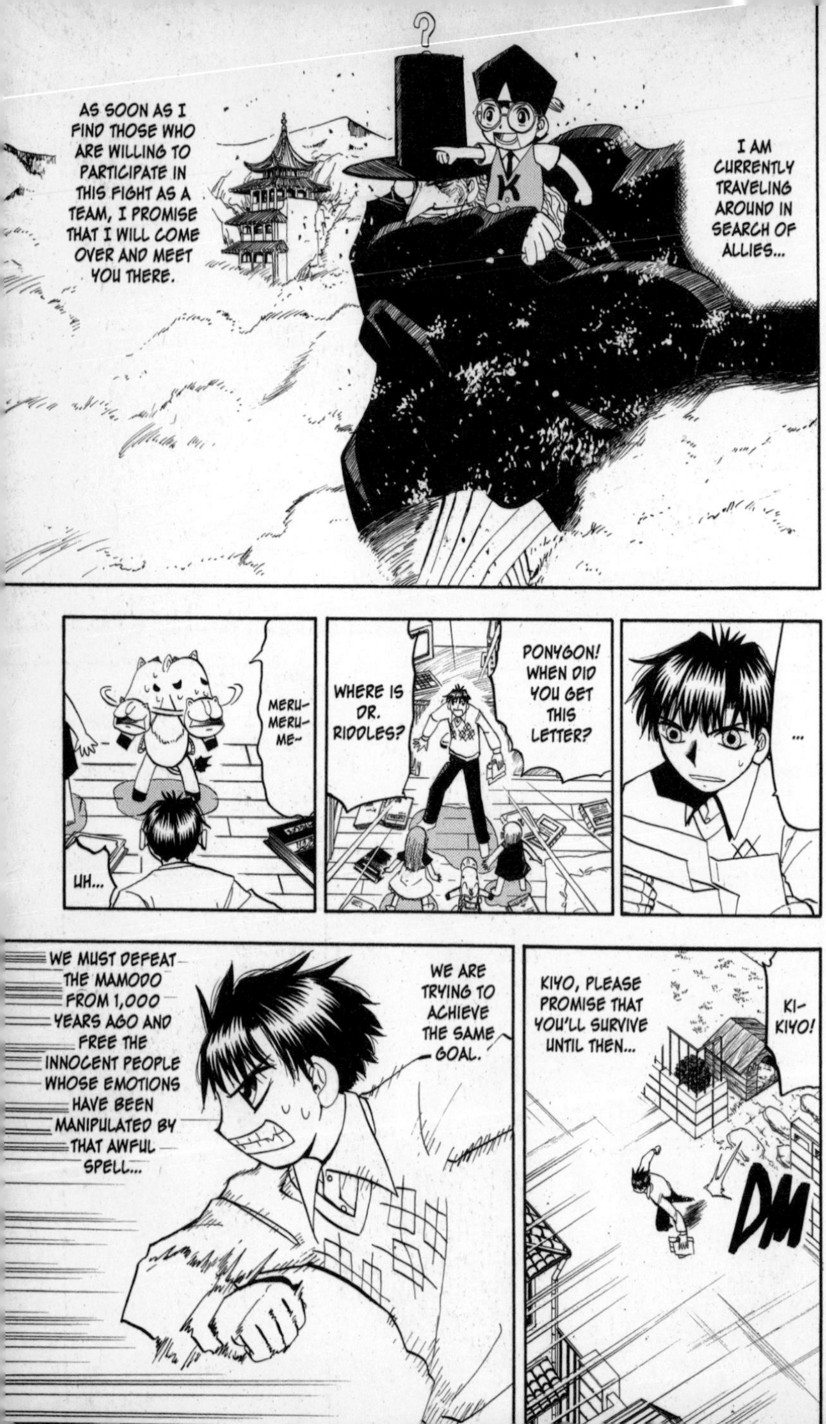
I AM CURRENTLY TRAVELING AROUND IN SEARCH OF ALLIES...
AS SOON AS I FIND THOSE WHO ARE WILLING TO PARTICIPATE IN THIS FIGHT AS A TEAM, I PROMISE THAT I WILL COME OVER AND MEET YOU THERE.
...
PONYGON! WHEN DID YOU GET THIS LETTER?
WHERE IS DR. RIDDLES?
MERU-MERU-ME-
UH...
KI-KIYO!
KIYO, PLEASE PROMISE THAT YOU'LL SURVIVE UNTIL THEN...
DM
WE ARE TRYING TO ACHIEVE THE SAME GOAL.
WE MUST DEFEAT THE MAMODO FROM 1,000 YEARS AGO AND FREE THE INNOCENT PEOPLE WHOSE EMOTIONS HAVE BEEN MANIPULATED BY THAT AWFUL SPELL...

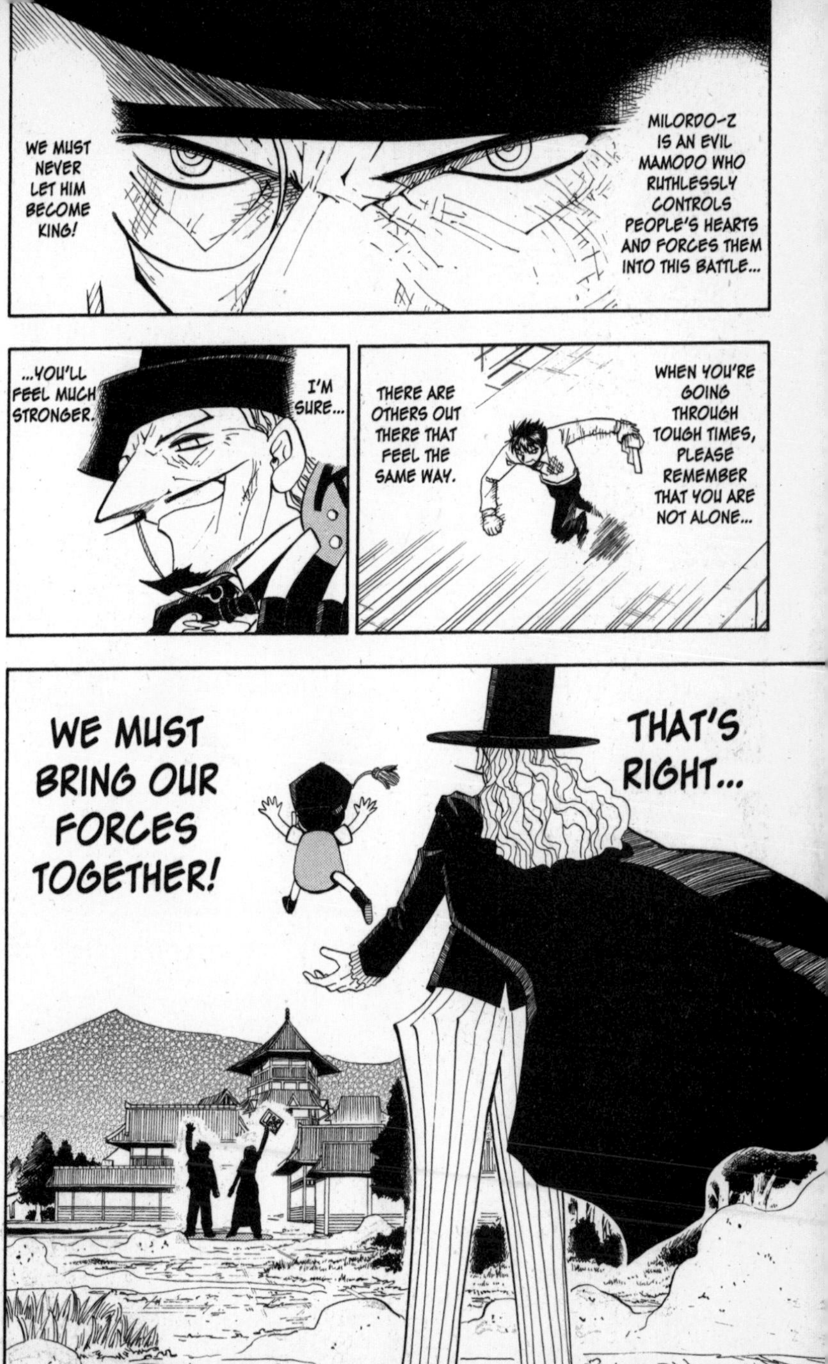
MILORDO-Z IS AN EVIL MAMODO WHO RUTHLESSLY CONTROLS PEOPLE'S HEARTS AND FORCES THEM INTO THIS BATTLE...
WE MUST NEVER LET HIM BECOME KING!
WHEN YOU'RE GOING THROUGH TOUGH TIMES, PLEASE REMEMBER THAT YOU ARE NOT ALONE...
THERE ARE OTHERS OUT THERE THAT FEEL THE SAME WAY.
I'M SURE...
...YOU'LL FEEL MUCH STRONGER.
THAT'S RIGHT...
WE MUST BRING OUR FORCES TOGETHER!

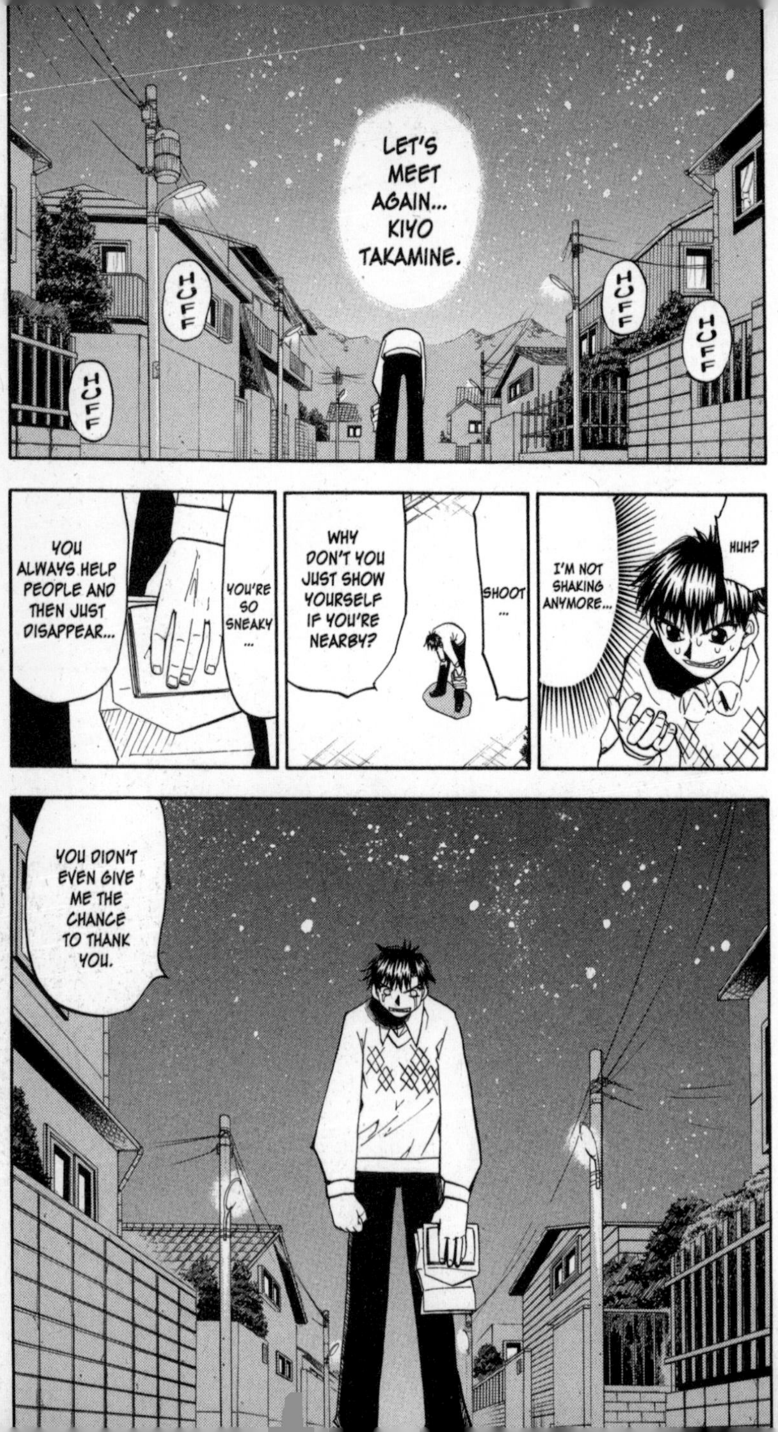
LET'S MEET AGAIN... KIYO TAKAMINE.
HUFF
HUFF
HUFF
HUFF
HUH?
I'M NOT SHAKING ANYMORE...
SHOOT...
WHY DON'T YOU JUST SHOW YOURSELF IF YOU'RE NEARBY?
YOU'RE SO SNEAKY...
YOU ALWAYS HELP PEOPLE AND THEN JUST DISAPPEAR...
YOU DIDN'T EVEN GIVE ME THE CHANCE TO THANK YOU.

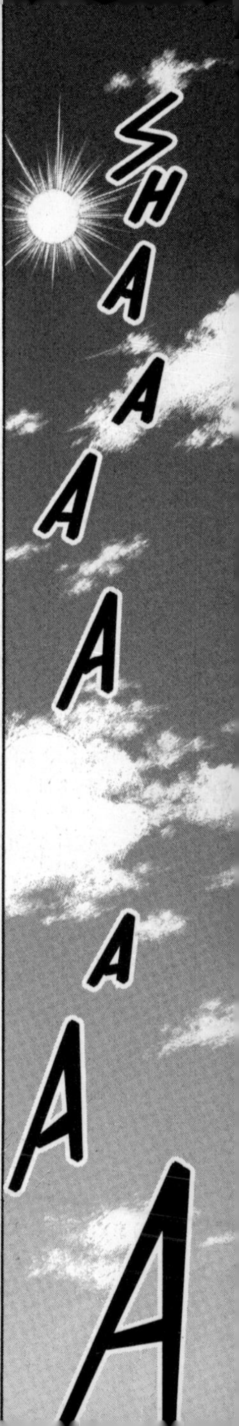
SHAAAAAAA
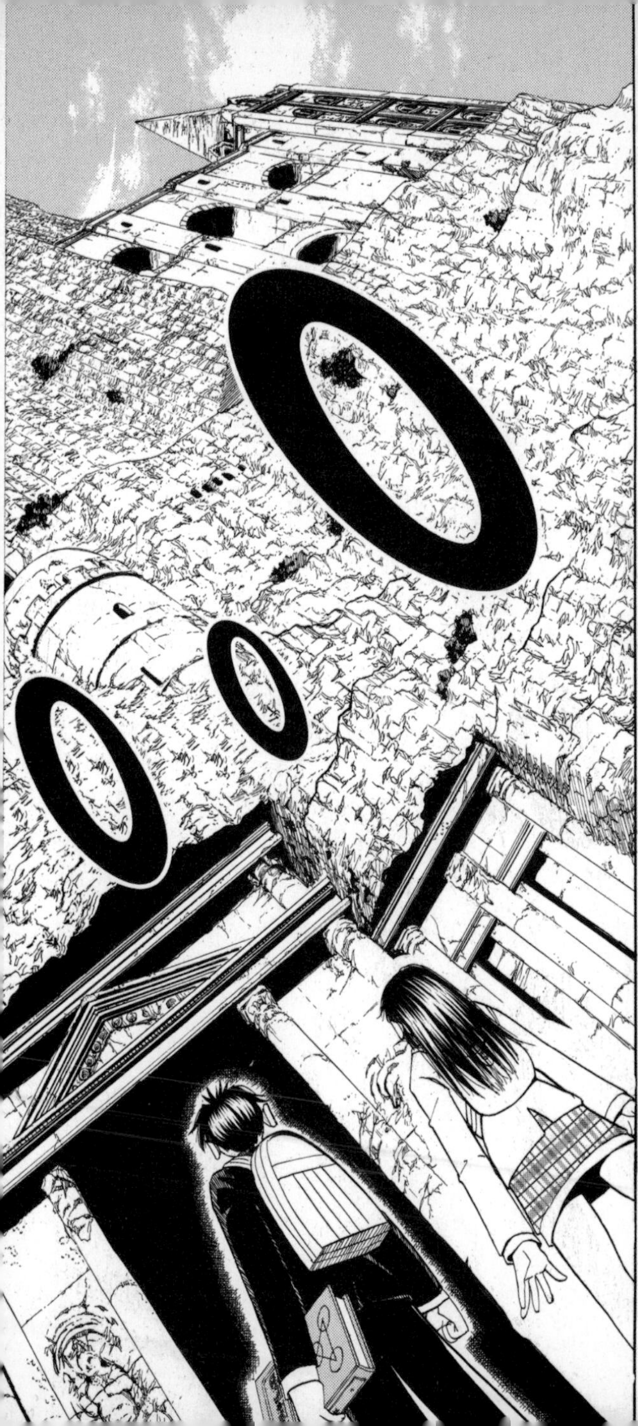
OOO

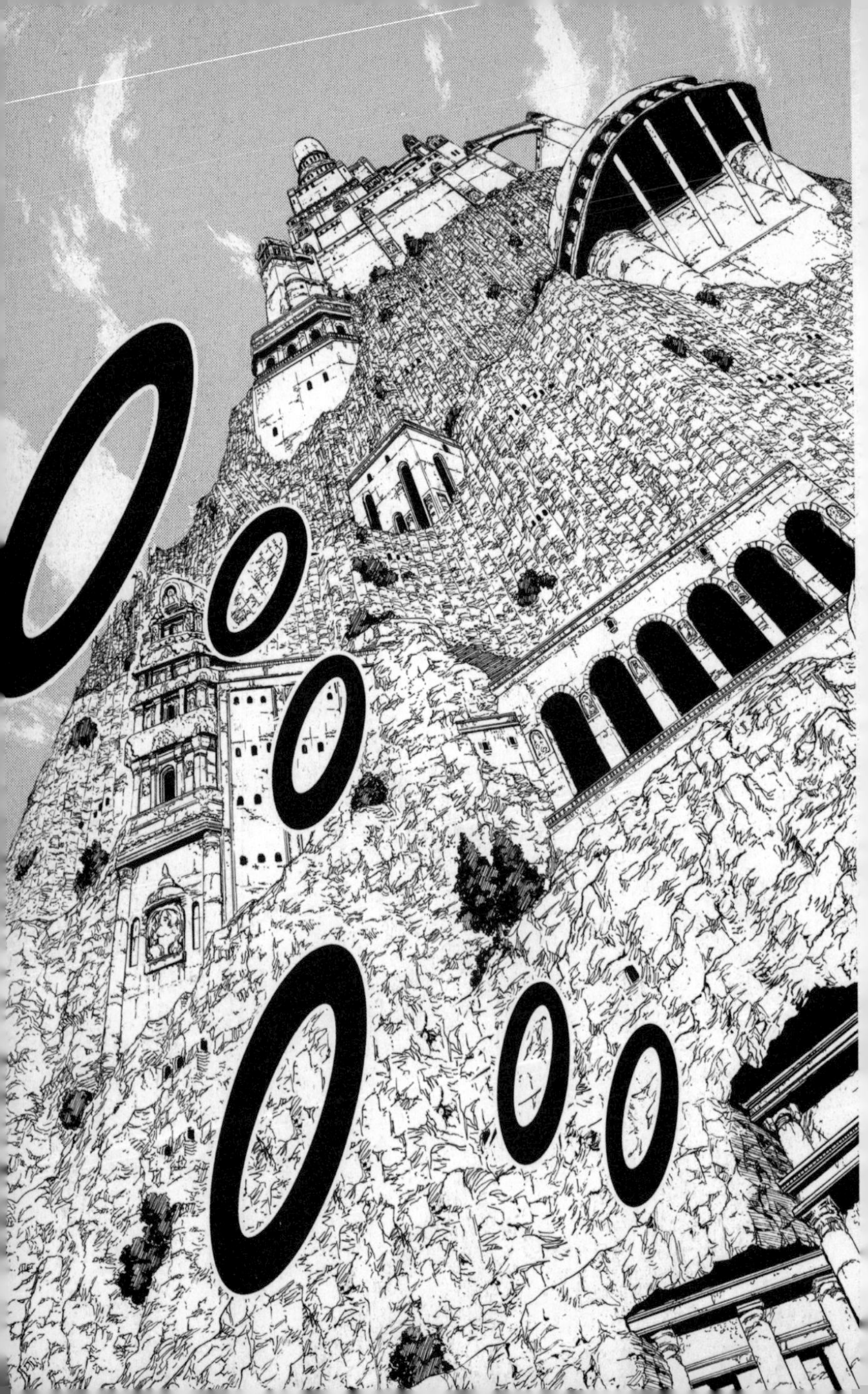
OOOOOO

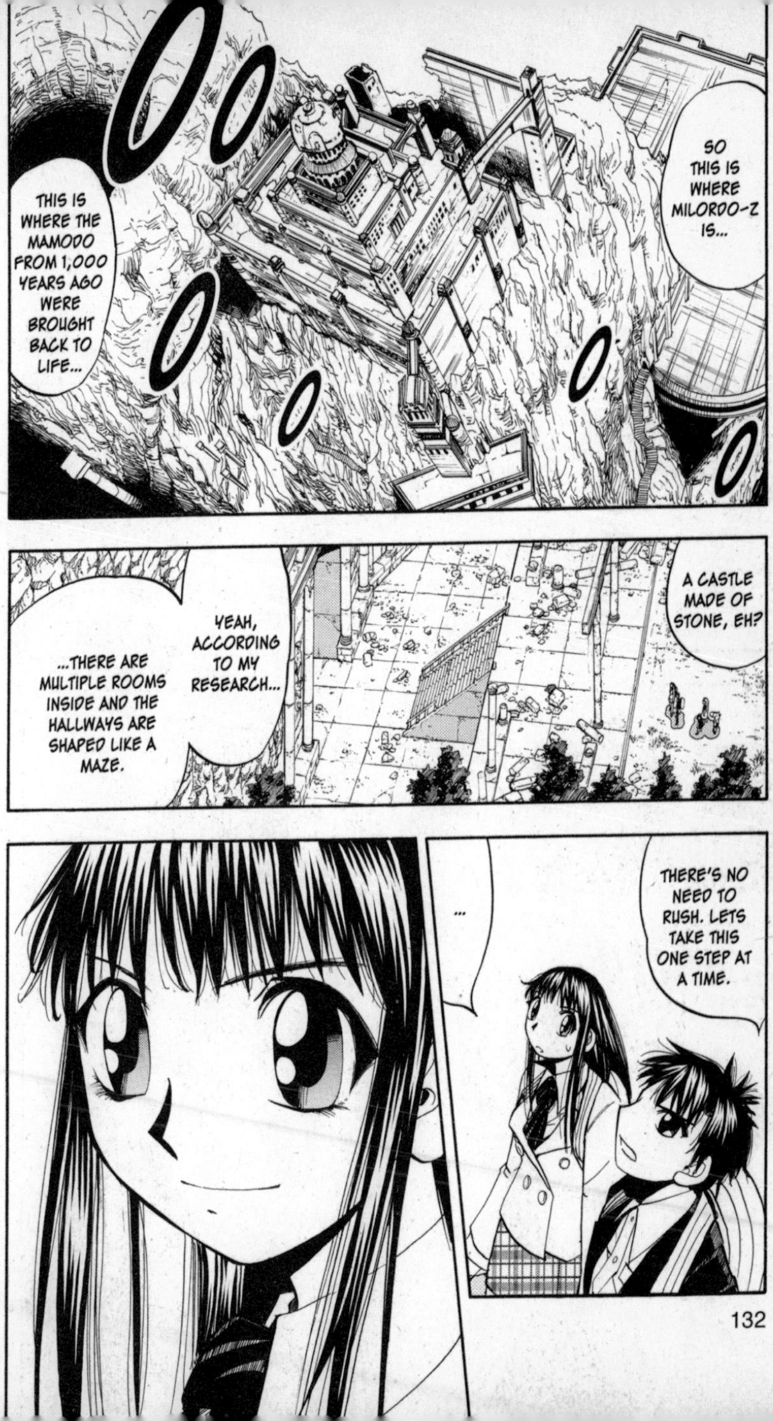
SO THIS IS WHERE MILORDO-Z IS...
THIS IS WHERE THE MAMODO FROM 1,000 YEARS AGO WERE BROUGHT BACK TO LIFE...
A CASTLE MADE OF STONE, EH?
YEAH, ACCORDING TO MY RESEARCH...
...THERE ARE MULTIPLE ROOMS INSIDE AND THE HALLWAYS ARE SHAPED LIKE A MAZE.
THERE'S NO NEED TO RUSH. LETS TAKE THIS ONE STEP AT A TIME.
...

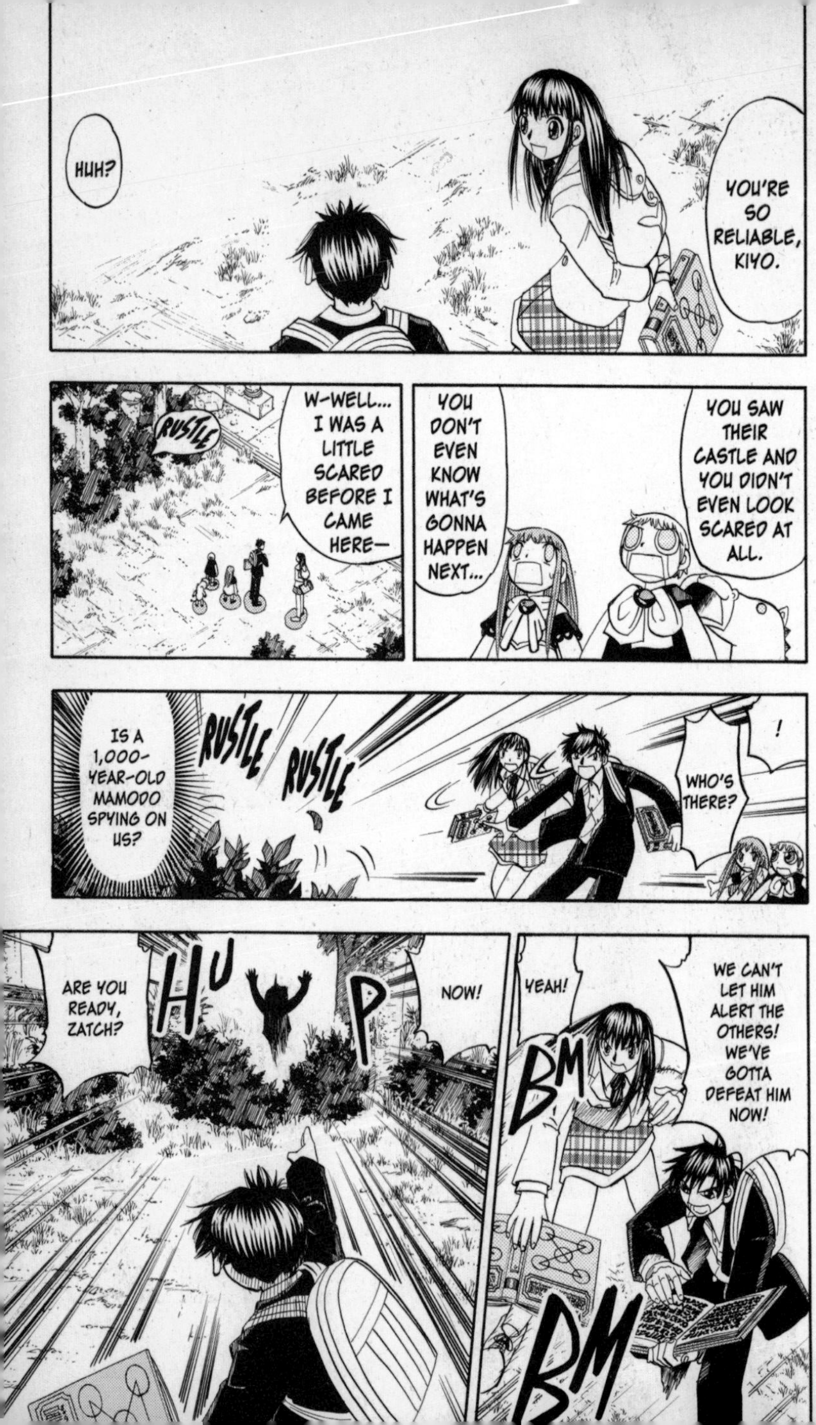
YOU'RE SO RELIABLE, KIYO.
HUH?
YOU SAW THEIR CASTLE AND YOU DIDN'T EVEN LOOK SCARED AT ALL.
YOU DON'T EVEN KNOW WHAT'S GONNA HAPPEN NEXT...
W-WELL... I WAS A LITTLE SCARED BEFORE I CAME HERE—
RUSTLE
!
WHO'S THERE?
RUSTLE
RUSTLE
IS A 1,000-YEAR-OLD MAMODO SPYING ON US?
WE CAN'T LET HIM ALERT THE OTHERS! WE'VE GOTTA DEFEAT HIM NOW!
YEAH!
BM
BM
NOW!
HUP
ARE YOU READY, ZATCH?

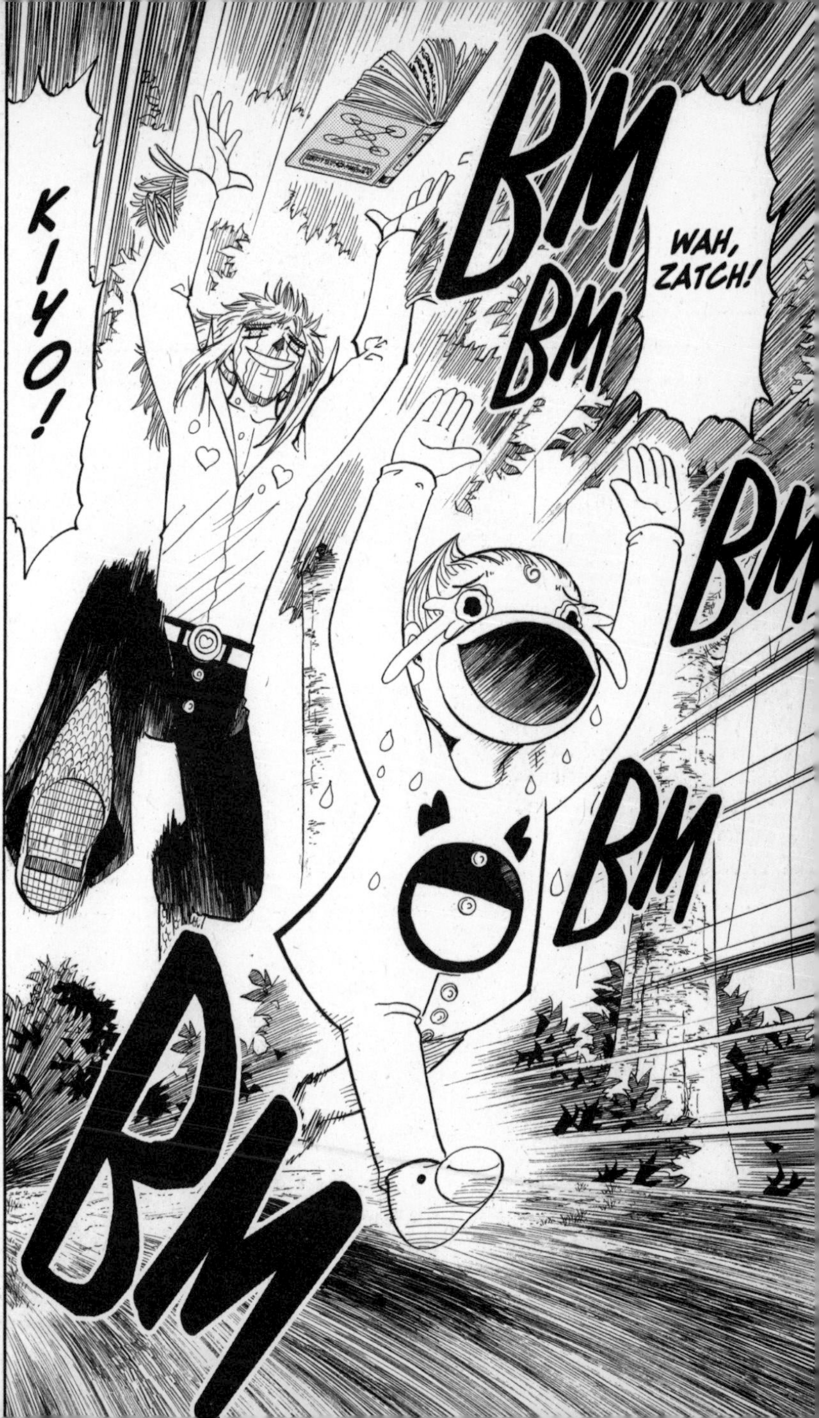
WAH, ZATCH!
BM
BM
BM
BM
BM
KIYO!

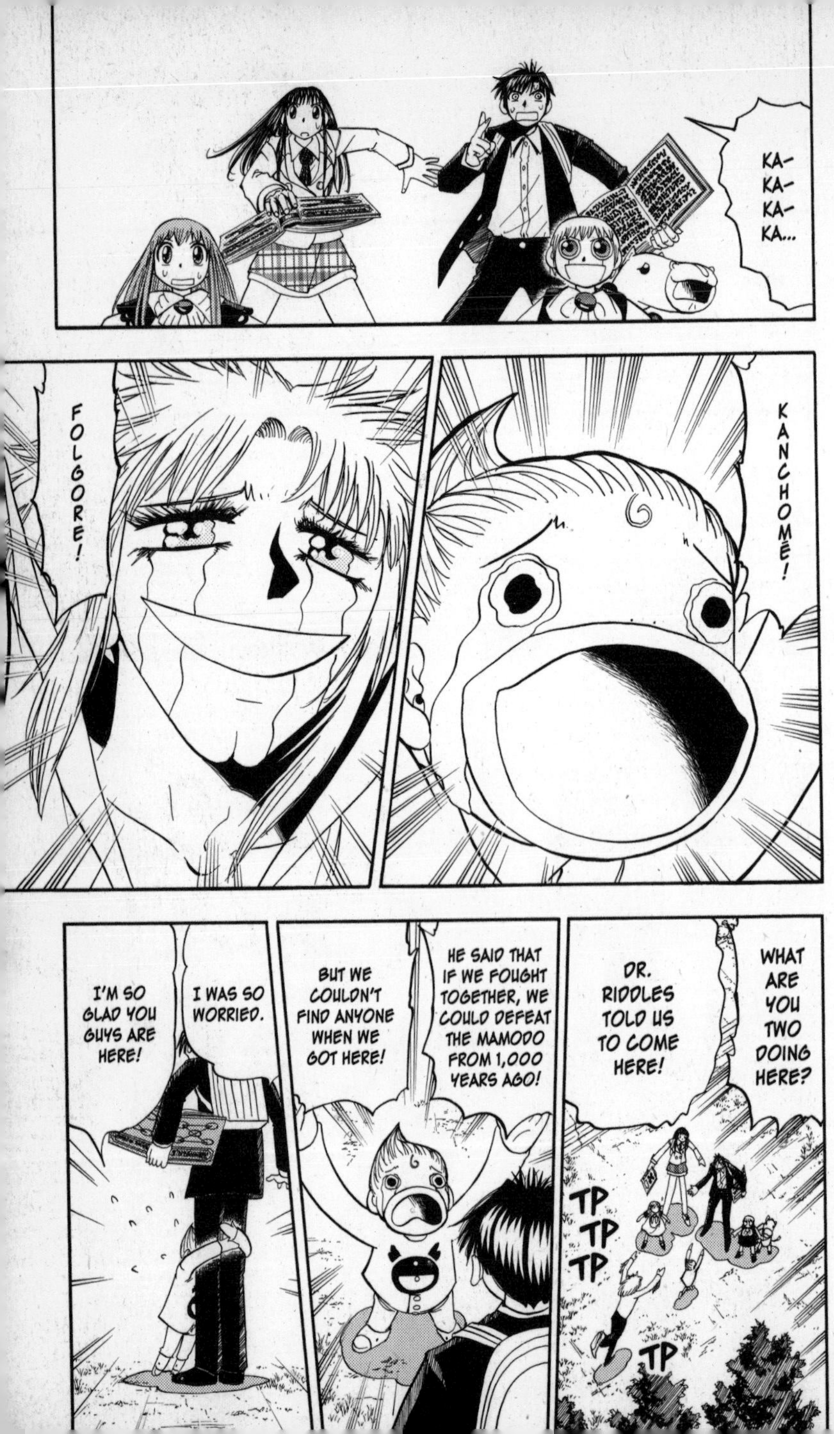
KA-KA-KA-KA...
KANCHOME!
FOLGORE!
WHAT ARE YOU TWO DOING HERE?
DR. RIDDLES TOLD US TO COME HERE!
TP TP TP
TP
HE SAID THAT IF WE FOUGHT TOGETHER, WE COULD DEFEAT THE MAMODO FROM 1,000 YEARS AGO!
BUT WE COULDN'T FIND ANYONE WHEN WE GOT HERE!
I WAS SO WORRIED.
I'M SO GLAD YOU GUYS ARE HERE!

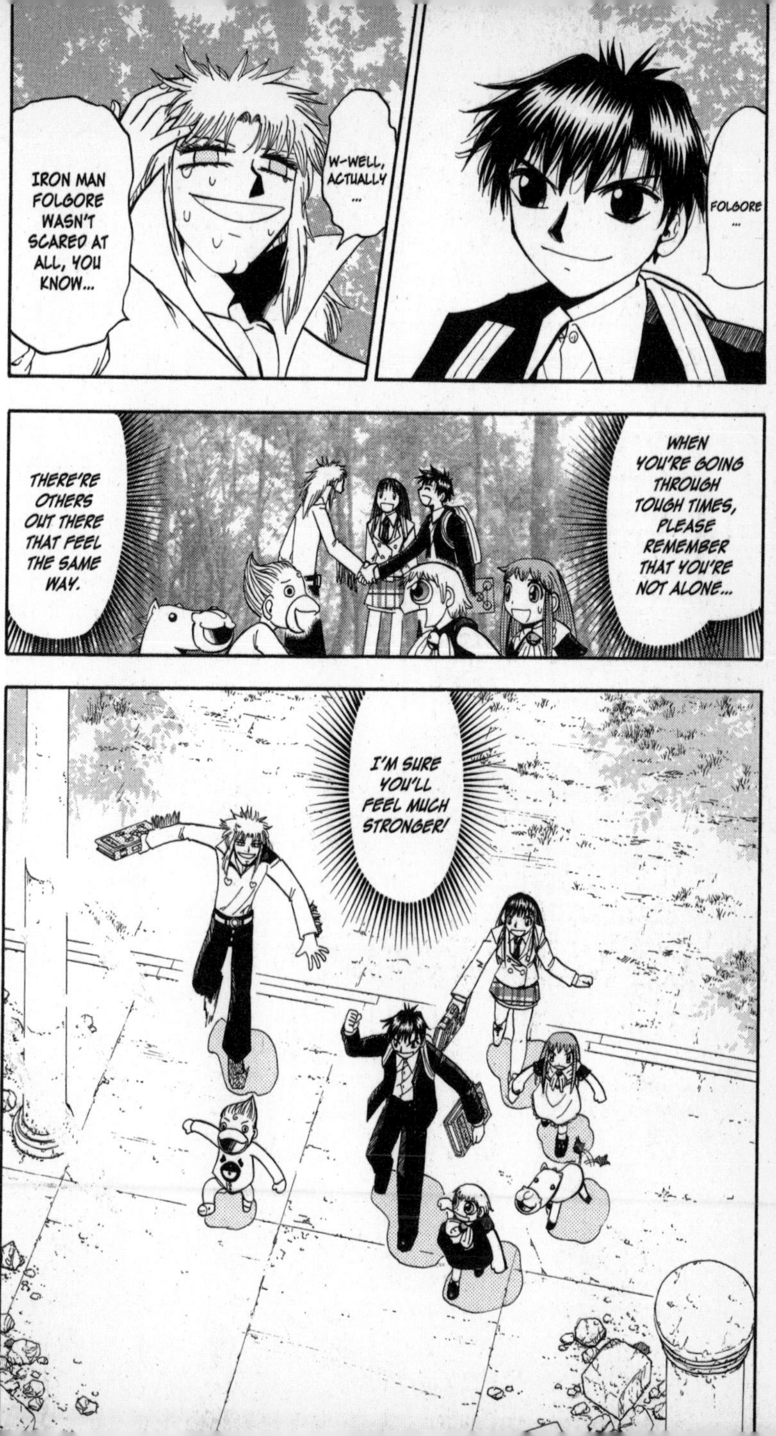
FOLGORE ...
W-WELL, ACTUALLY ...
IRON MAN FOLGORE WASN'T SCARED AT ALL, YOU KNOW...
WHEN YOU'RE GOING THROUGH TOUGH TIMES, PLEASE REMEMBER THAT YOU'RE NOT ALONE...
THERE'RE OTHERS OUT THERE THAT FEEL THE SAME WAY.
I'M SURE YOU'LL FEEL MUCH STRONGER!

LEVEL 111: The Crybaby

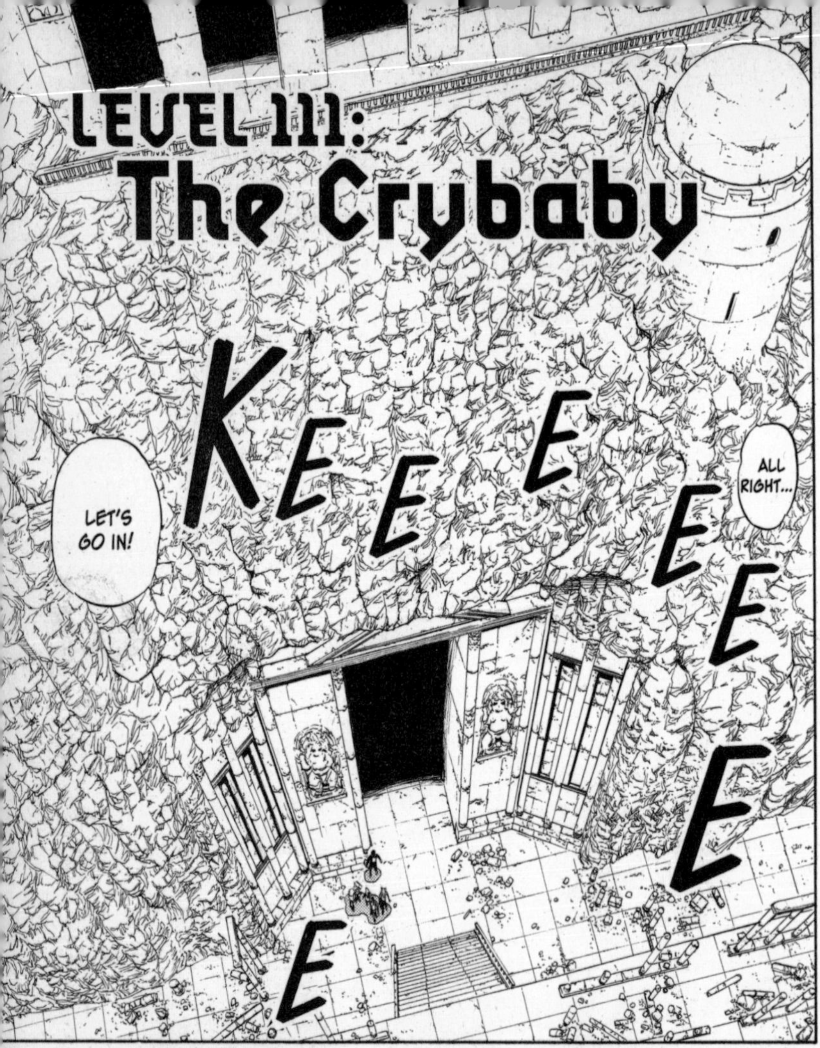
ALL RIGHT...
KEEEEEEE
LET'S GO IN!

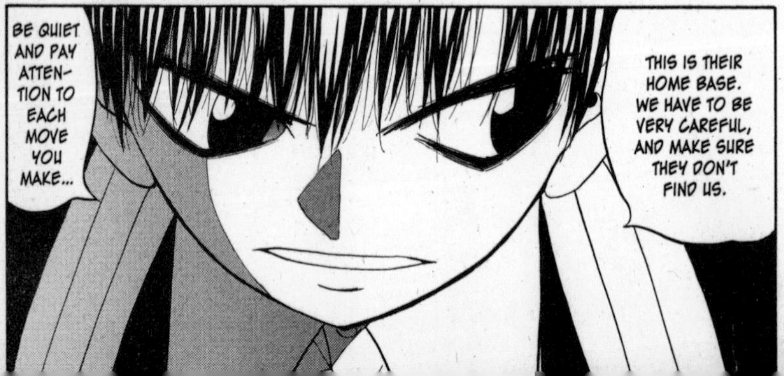
THIS IS THEIR HOME BASE. WE HAVE TO BE VERY CAREFUL, AND MAKE SURE THEY DON'T FIND US.
BE QUIET AND PAY ATTENTION TO EACH MOVE YOU MAKE...

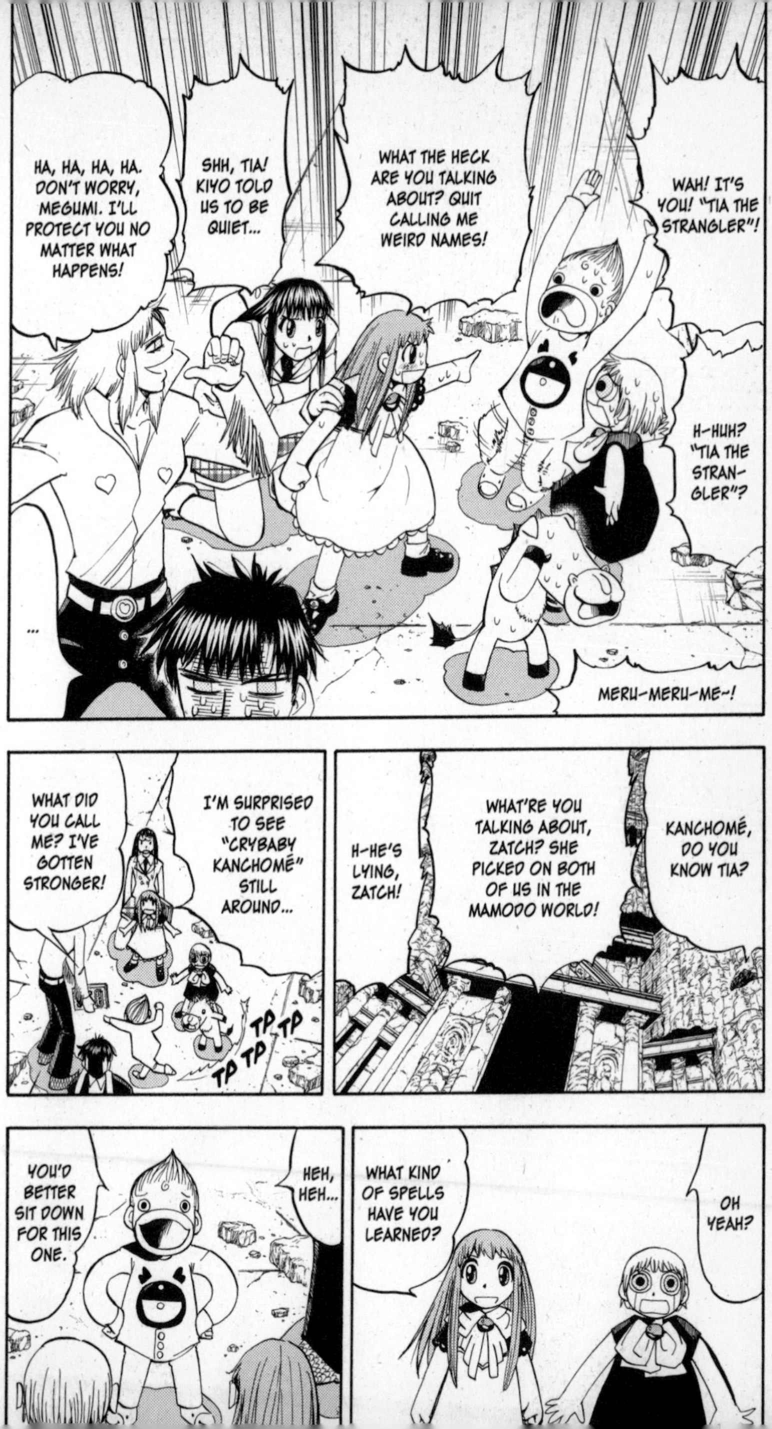
WAH! IT'S YOU! "TIA THE STRANGLER"!
WHAT THE HECK ARE YOU TALKING ABOUT? QUIT CALLING ME WEIRD NAMES!
SHH, TIA! KIYO TOLD US TO BE QUIET...
HA, HA, HA, HA. DON'T WORRY, MEGUMI. I'LL PROTECT YOU NO MATTER WHAT HAPPENS!
H-HUH? "TIA THE STRANGLER"?
MERU-MERU-ME~!
...
KANCHOMÉ, DO YOU KNOW TIA?
WHAT'RE YOU TALKING ABOUT, ZATCH? SHE PICKED ON BOTH OF US IN THE MAMODO WORLD!
H-HE'S LYING, ZATCH!
I'M SURPRISED TO SEE "CRYBABY KANCHOMÉ" STILL AROUND...
WHAT DID YOU CALL ME? I'VE GOTTEN STRONGER!
TP TP TP TP
OH YEAH?
WHAT KIND OF SPELLS HAVE YOU LEARNED?
HEH, HEH...
YOU'D BETTER SIT DOWN FOR THIS ONE.

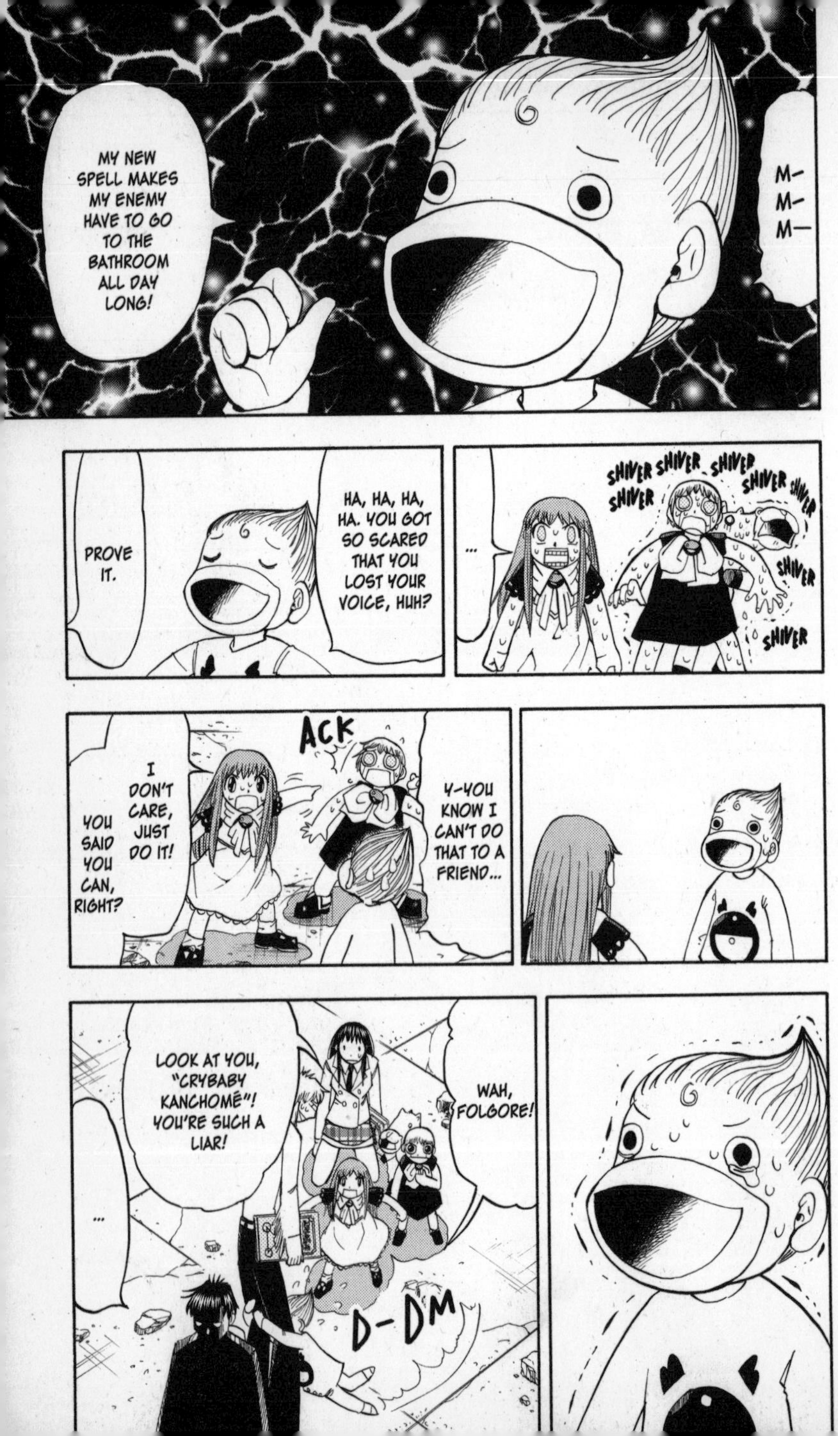
M- M- M—
MY NEW SPELL MAKES MY ENEMY HAVE TO GO TO THE BATHROOM ALL DAY LONG!
...
SHIVER SHIVER SHIVER SHIVER SHIVER SHIVER SHIVER SHIVER
HA, HA, HA, HA. YOU GOT SO SCARED THAT YOU LOST YOUR VOICE, HUH?
PROVE IT.
ACK
Y-YOU KNOW I CAN'T DO THAT TO A FRIEND...
I DON'T CARE, JUST DO IT!
YOU SAID YOU CAN, RIGHT?
WAH, FOLGORE!
LOOK AT YOU, "CRYBABY KANCHOMÉ"! YOU'RE SUCH A LIAR!
...
D-DM

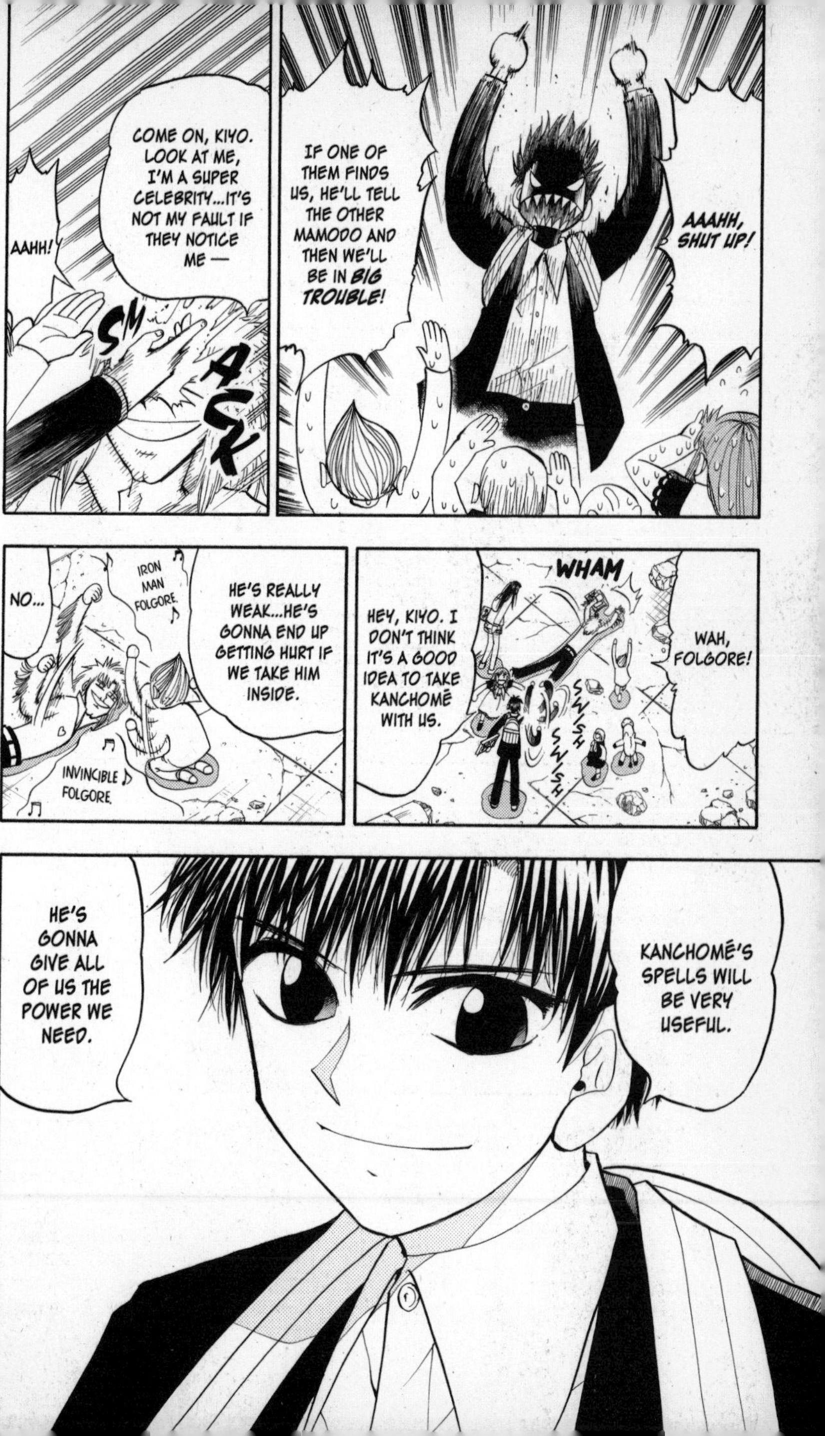
AAAHH, SHUT UP!
IF ONE OF THEM FINDS US, HE'LL TELL THE OTHER MAMODO AND THEN WE'LL BE IN BIG TROUBLE!
COME ON, KIYO. LOOK AT ME, I'M A SUPER CELEBRITY...IT'S NOT MY FAULT IF THEY NOTICE ME —
AAHH!
SMACK
WHAM
WAH, FOLGORE!
HEY, KIYO. I DON'T THINK IT'S A GOOD IDEA TO TAKE KANCHOMÉ WITH US.
SWISH
SWISH
HE'S REALLY WEAK...HE'S GONNA END UP GETTING HURT IF WE TAKE HIM INSIDE.
IRON MAN FOLGORE.
NO...
INVINCIBLE FOLGORE.
KANCHOMÉ'S SPELLS WILL BE VERY USEFUL.
HE'S GONNA GIVE ALL OF US THE POWER WE NEED.

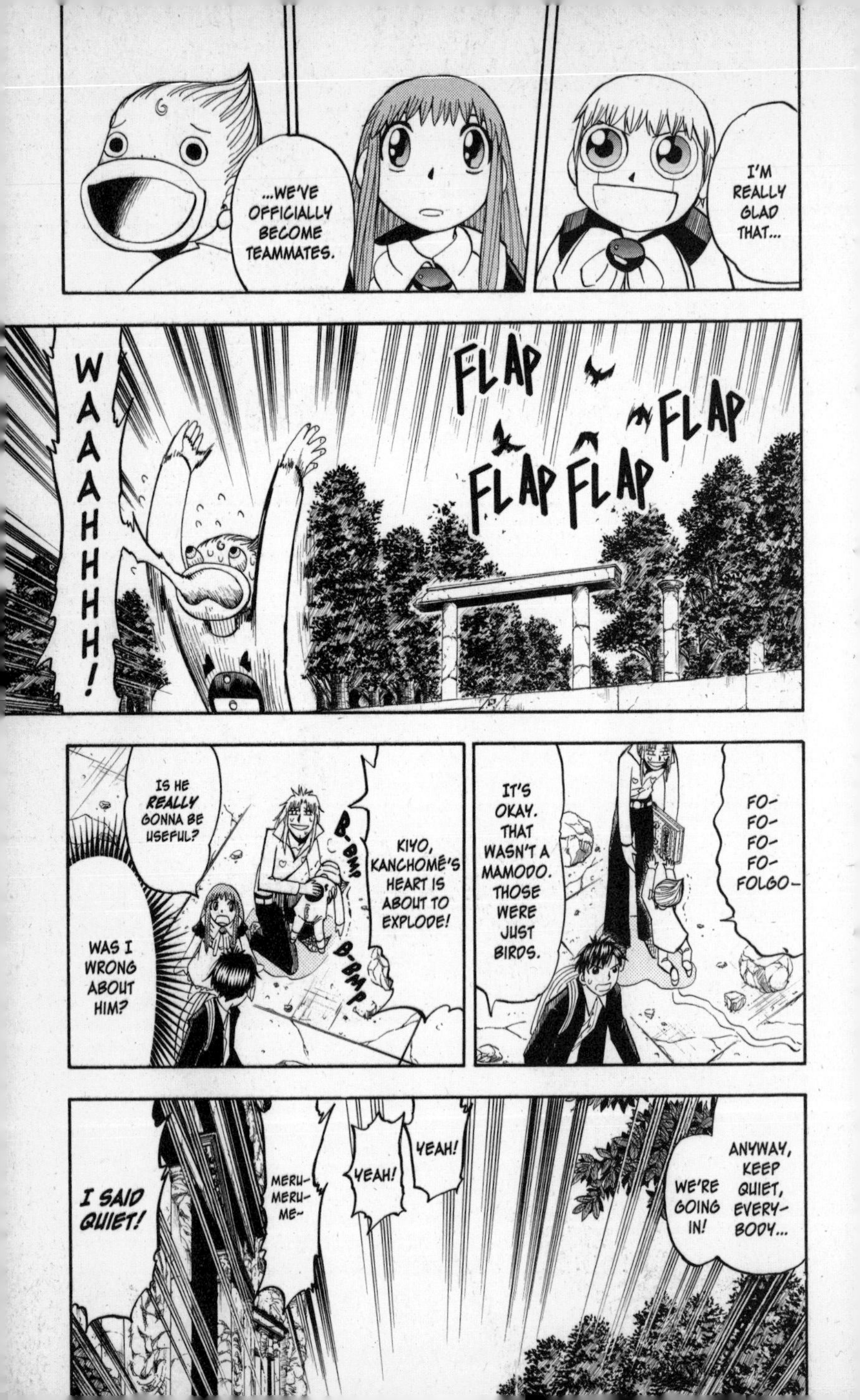
I'M REALLY GLAD THAT...
...WE'VE OFFICIALLY BECOME TEAMMATES.
FLAP
FLAP
FLAP
FLAP
WAAAAHHHHH!
FO-FO-FO-FO-FOLGO-
IT'S OKAY. THAT WASN'T A MAMODO. THOSE WERE JUST BIRDS.
KIYO, KANCHOMÉ'S HEART IS ABOUT TO EXPLODE!
B-BMP
B-BMP
IS HE REALLY GONNA BE USEFUL?
WAS I WRONG ABOUT HIM?
ANYWAY, KEEP QUIET, EVERYBODY...
WE'RE GOING IN!
YEAH!
YEAH!
MERU-MERU-ME~
I SAID QUIET!

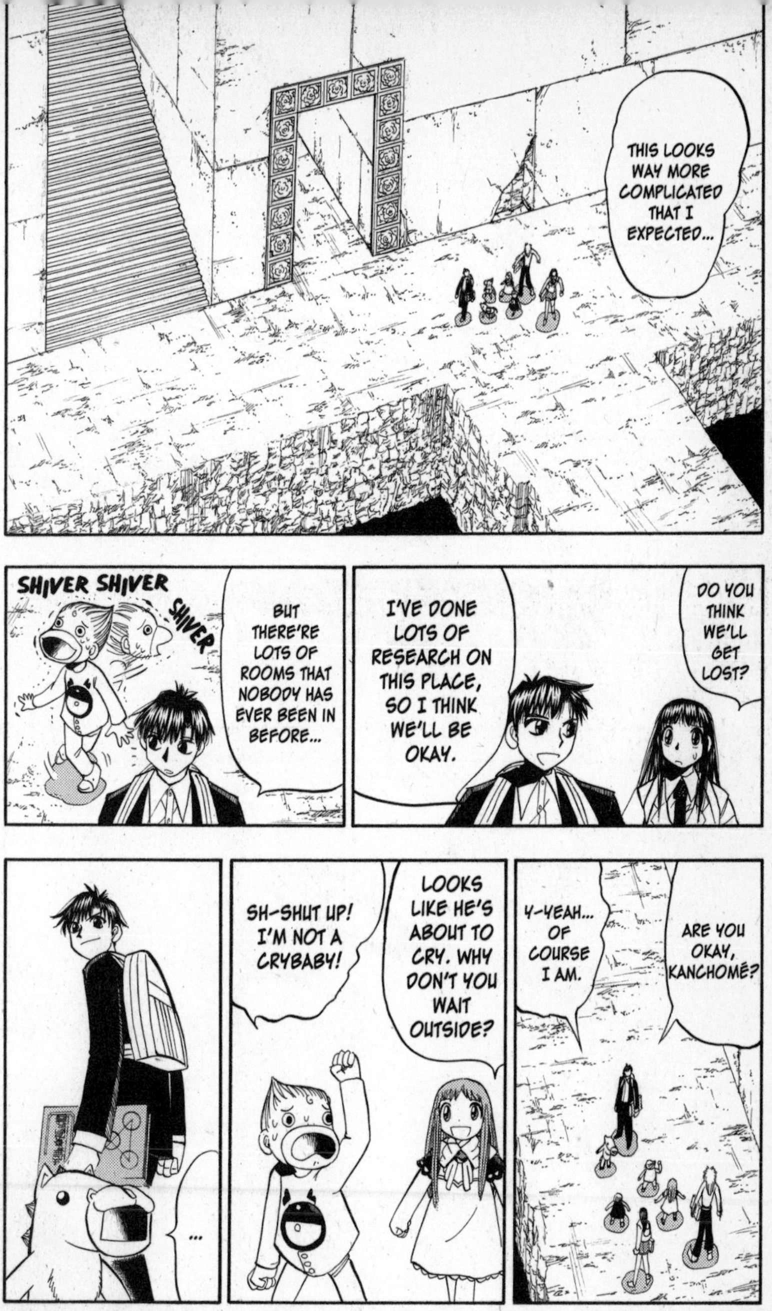
THIS LOOKS WAY MORE COMPLICATED THAT I EXPECTED...
DO YOU THINK WE'LL GET LOST?
I'VE DONE LOTS OF RESEARCH ON THIS PLACE, SO I THINK WE'LL BE OKAY.
BUT THERE'RE LOTS OF ROOMS THAT NOBODY HAS EVER BEEN IN BEFORE...
SHIVER SHIVER
SHIVER
ARE YOU OKAY, KANCHOMÉ?
Y-YEAH... OF COURSE I AM.
LOOKS LIKE HE'S ABOUT TO CRY. WHY DON'T YOU WAIT OUTSIDE?
SH-SHUT UP! I'M NOT A CRYBABY!
...

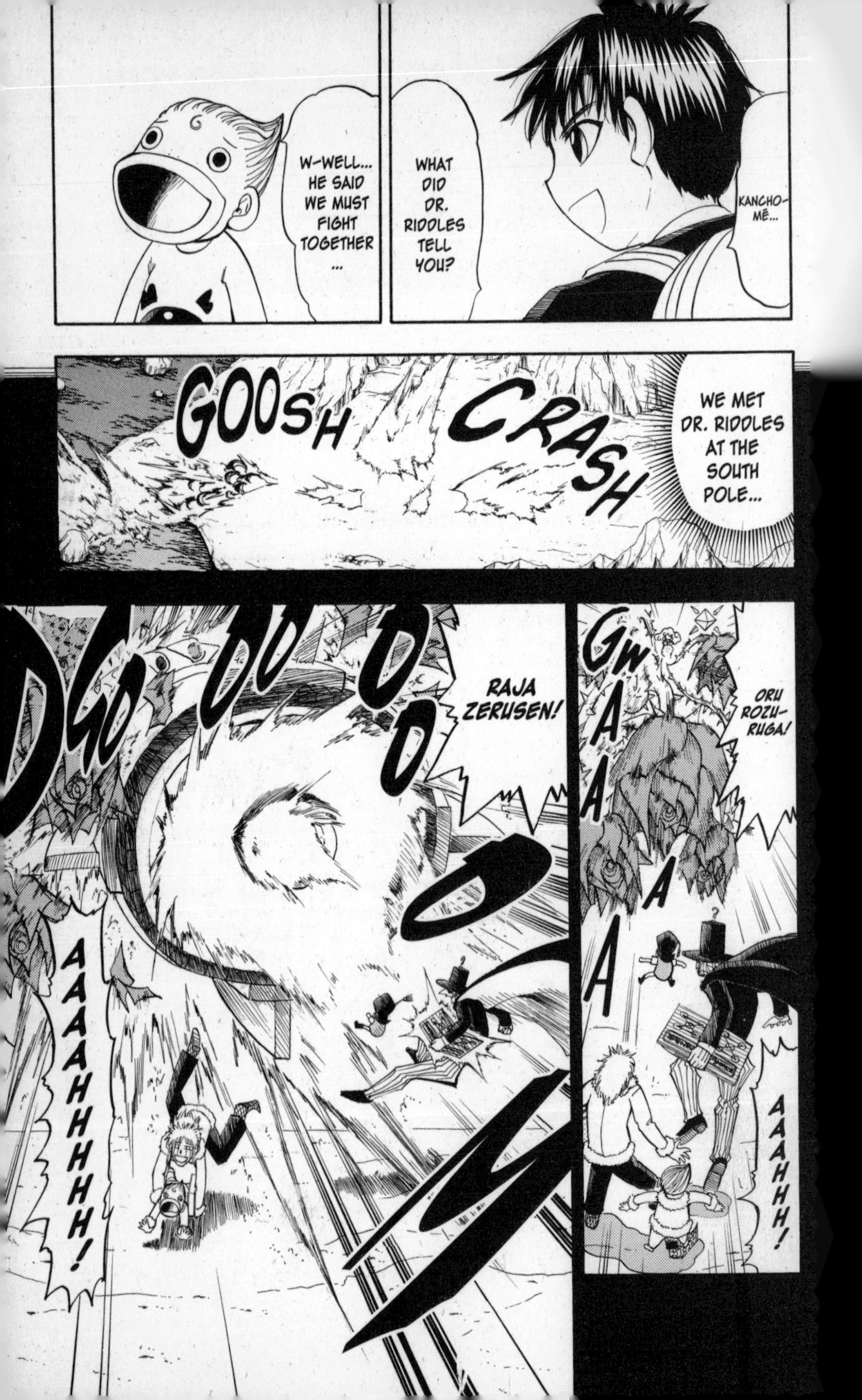
KANCHOMÉ...
WHAT DID DR. RIDDLES TELL YOU?
W-WELL... HE SAID WE MUST FIGHT TOGETHER...
WE MET DR. RIDDLES AT THE SOUTH POLE...
CRASH
GOOSH
ORU ROZURUGA!
GWAAAAAA
AAAHHH!
RAJA ZERUSEN!
DOOOOOOOM
AAAAAHHHHHH!

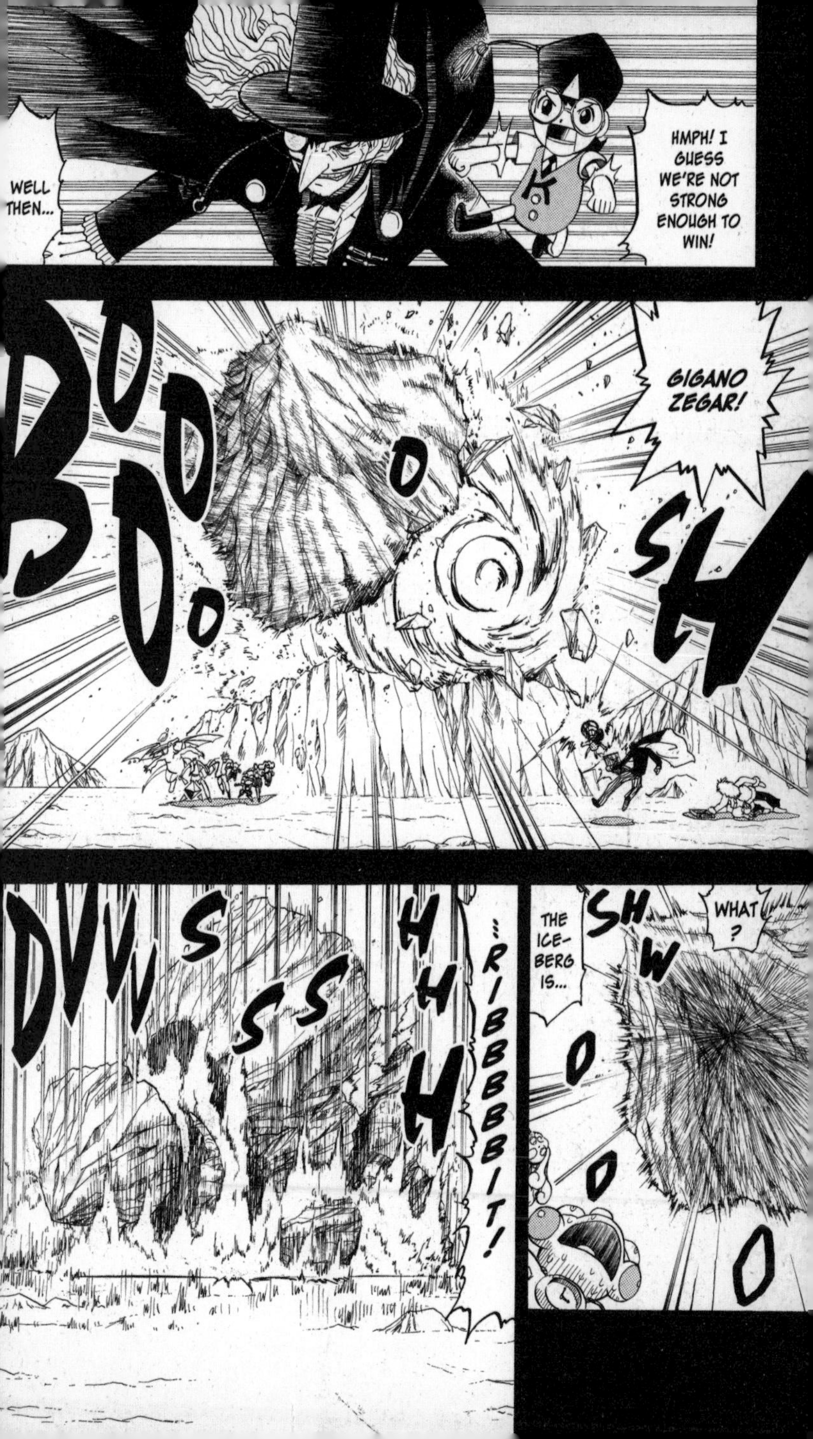
HMPH! I GUESS WE'RE NOT STRONG ENOUGH TO WIN!
WELL THEN...
GIGANO ZEGAR!
SH
WHAT?
THE ICEBERG IS...
SHWOOOO
RIBBBBBIT!
DVVSSSHHHH

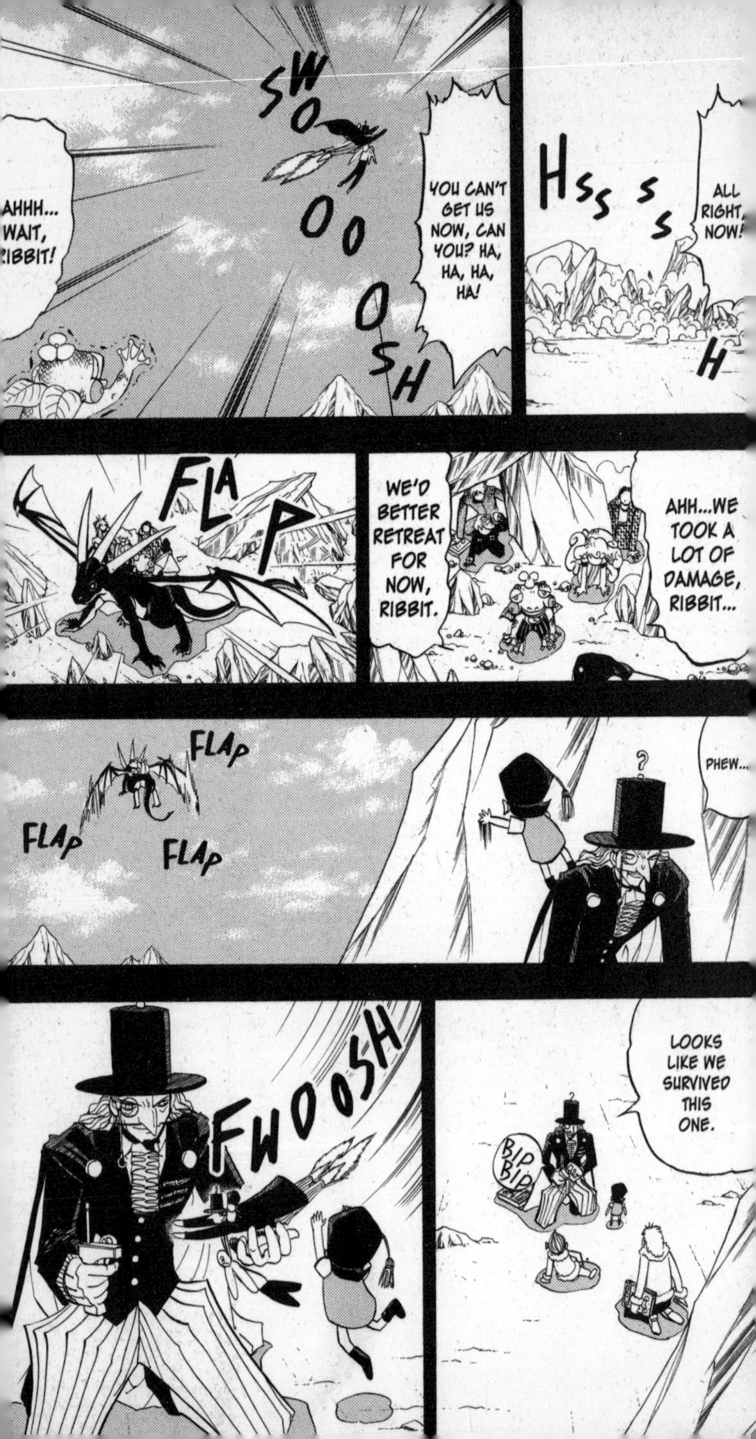
ALL RIGHT, NOW!
HSSSSH
YOU CAN'T GET US NOW, CAN YOU? HA, HA, HA, HA!
SWOOOOSH
AHHH... WAIT, IBBIT!
AHH...WE TOOK A LOT OF DAMAGE, RIBBIT...
WE'D BETTER RETREAT FOR NOW, RIBBIT.
FLAP
PHEW...
?
FLAP
FLAP
FLAP
LOOKS LIKE WE SURVIVED THIS ONE.
BIP BIP
FWOOSH

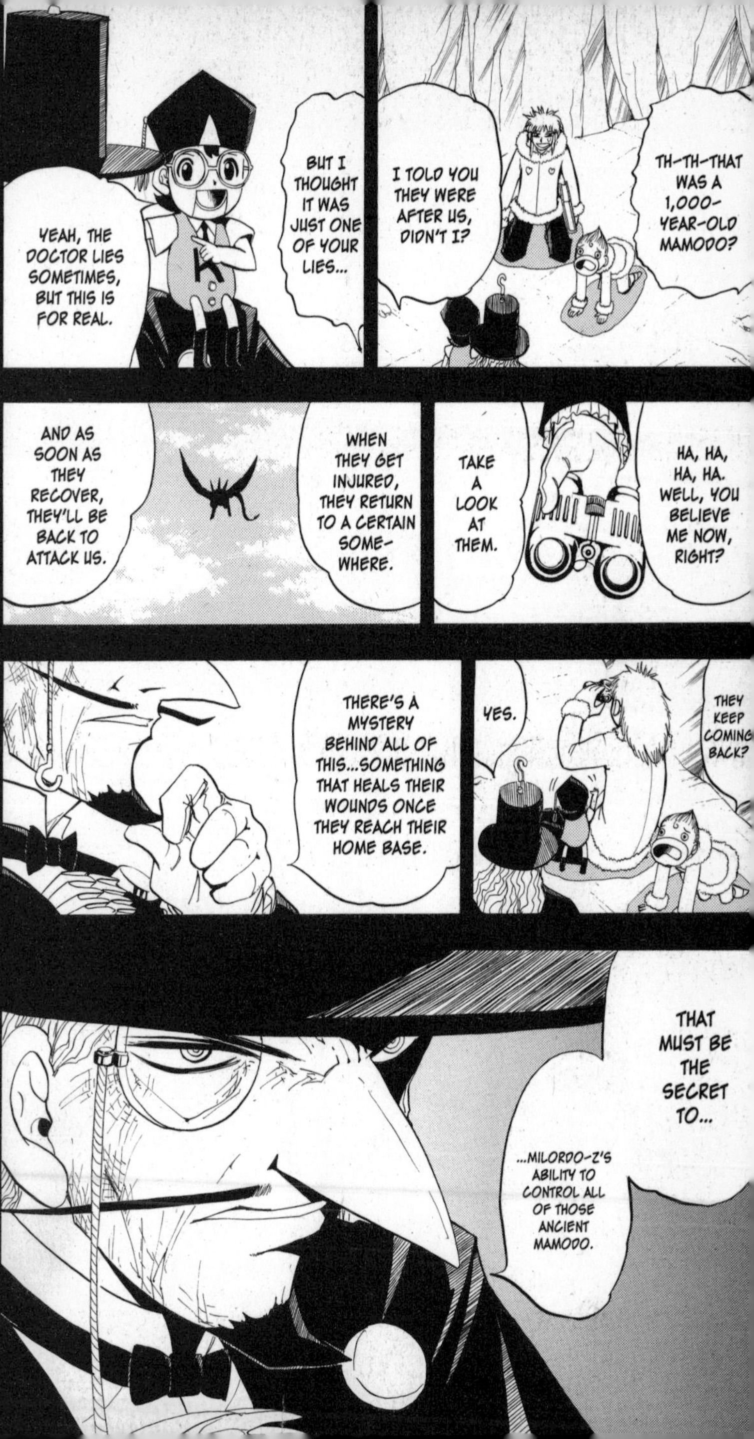
TH-TH-THAT WAS A 1,000-YEAR-OLD MAMODO?
I TOLD YOU THEY WERE AFTER US, DIDN'T I?
BUT I THOUGHT IT WAS JUST ONE OF YOUR LIES...
YEAH, THE DOCTOR LIES SOMETIMES, BUT THIS IS FOR REAL.
HA, HA, HA, HA. WELL, YOU BELIEVE ME NOW, RIGHT?
TAKE A LOOK AT THEM.
WHEN THEY GET INJURED, THEY RETURN TO A CERTAIN SOME-WHERE.
AND AS SOON AS THEY RECOVER, THEY'LL BE BACK TO ATTACK US.
THEY KEEP COMING BACK?
YES.
THERE'S A MYSTERY BEHIND ALL OF THIS...SOMETHING THAT HEALS THEIR WOUNDS ONCE THEY REACH THEIR HOME BASE.
THAT MUST BE THE SECRET TO...
...MILORDO-Z'S ABILITY TO CONTROL ALL OF THOSE ANCIENT MAMODO.

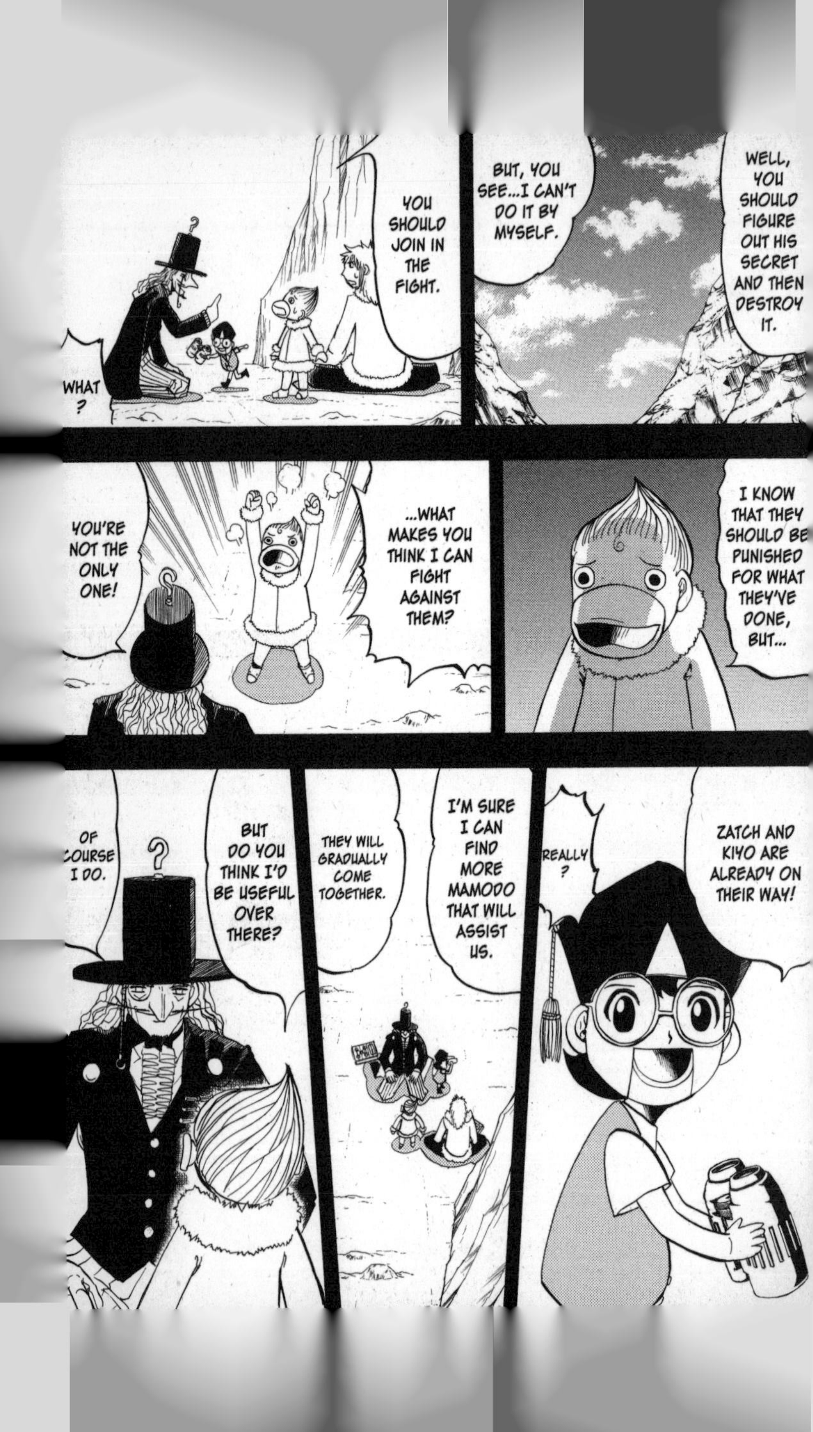
WELL, YOU SHOULD FIGURE OUT HIS SECRET AND THEN DESTROY IT.
BUT, YOU SEE...I CAN'T DO IT BY MYSELF.
YOU SHOULD JOIN IN THE FIGHT.
WHAT ?
I KNOW THAT THEY SHOULD BE PUNISHED FOR WHAT THEY'VE DONE, BUT...
...WHAT MAKES YOU THINK I CAN FIGHT AGAINST THEM?
YOU'RE NOT THE ONLY ONE!
ZATCH AND KIYO ARE ALREADY ON THEIR WAY!
REALLY ?
I'M SURE I CAN FIND MORE MAMODO THAT WILL ASSIST US.
THEY WILL GRADUALLY COME TOGETHER.
BUT DO YOU THINK I'D BE USEFUL OVER THERE?
OF COURSE I DO.

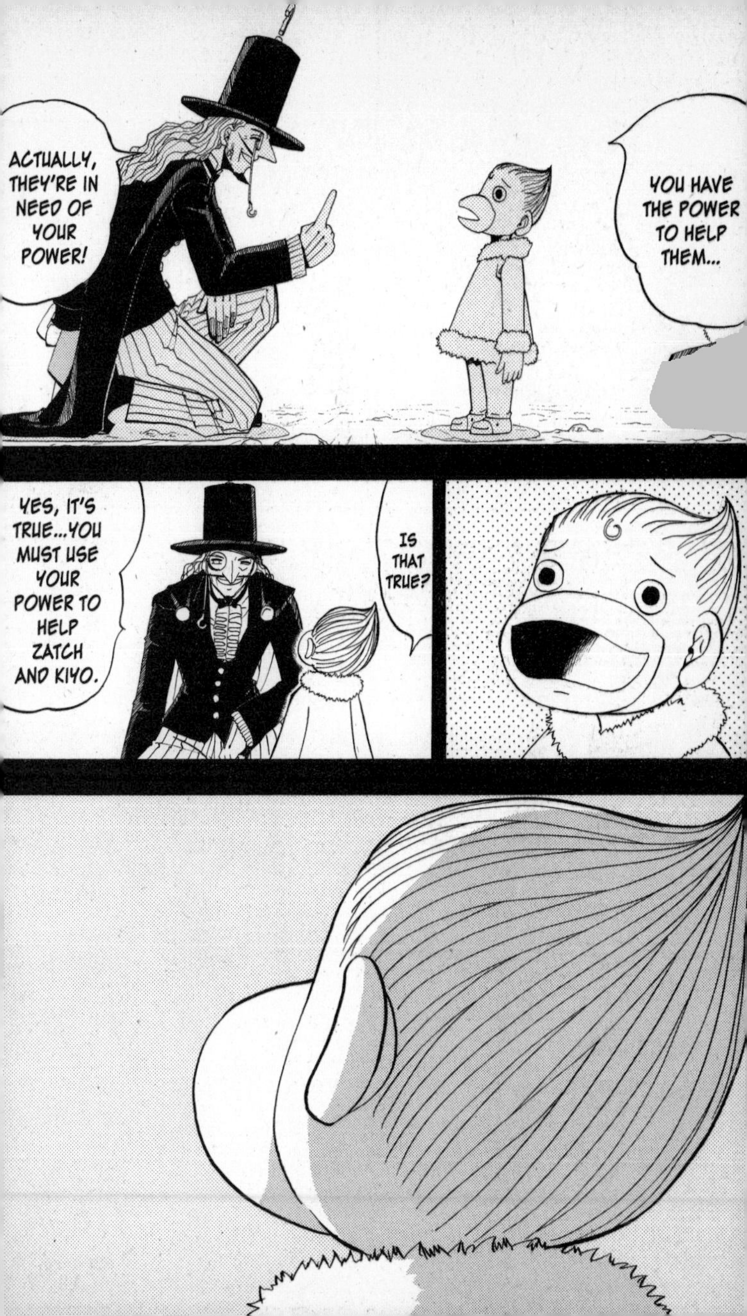
YOU HAVE THE POWER TO HELP THEM...
ACTUALLY, THEY'RE IN NEED OF YOUR POWER!
IS THAT TRUE?
YES, IT'S TRUE...YOU MUST USE YOUR POWER TO HELP ZATCH AND KIYO.

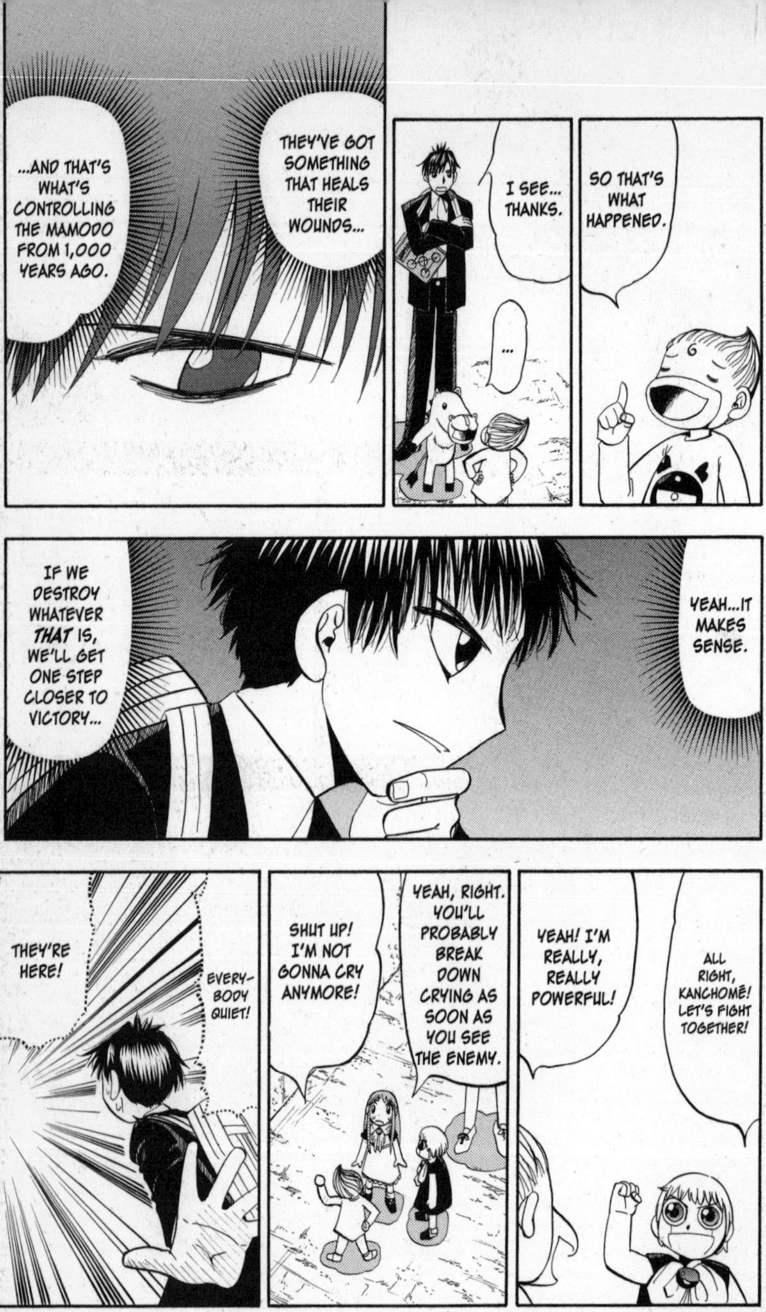
SO THAT'S WHAT HAPPENED.
I SEE... THANKS.
...
THEY'VE GOT SOMETHING THAT HEALS THEIR WOUNDS...
...AND THAT'S WHAT'S CONTROLLING THE MAMODO FROM 1,000 YEARS AGO.
YEAH...IT MAKES SENSE.
IF WE DESTROY WHATEVER *THAT* IS, WE'LL GET ONE STEP CLOSER TO VICTORY...
ALL RIGHT, KANCHOMÉ! LET'S FIGHT TOGETHER!
YEAH! I'M REALLY, REALLY POWERFUL!
YEAH, RIGHT. YOU'LL PROBABLY BREAK DOWN CRYING AS SOON AS YOU SEE THE ENEMY.
SHUT UP! I'M NOT GONNA CRY ANYMORE!
EVERY-BODY QUIET!
THEY'RE HERE!

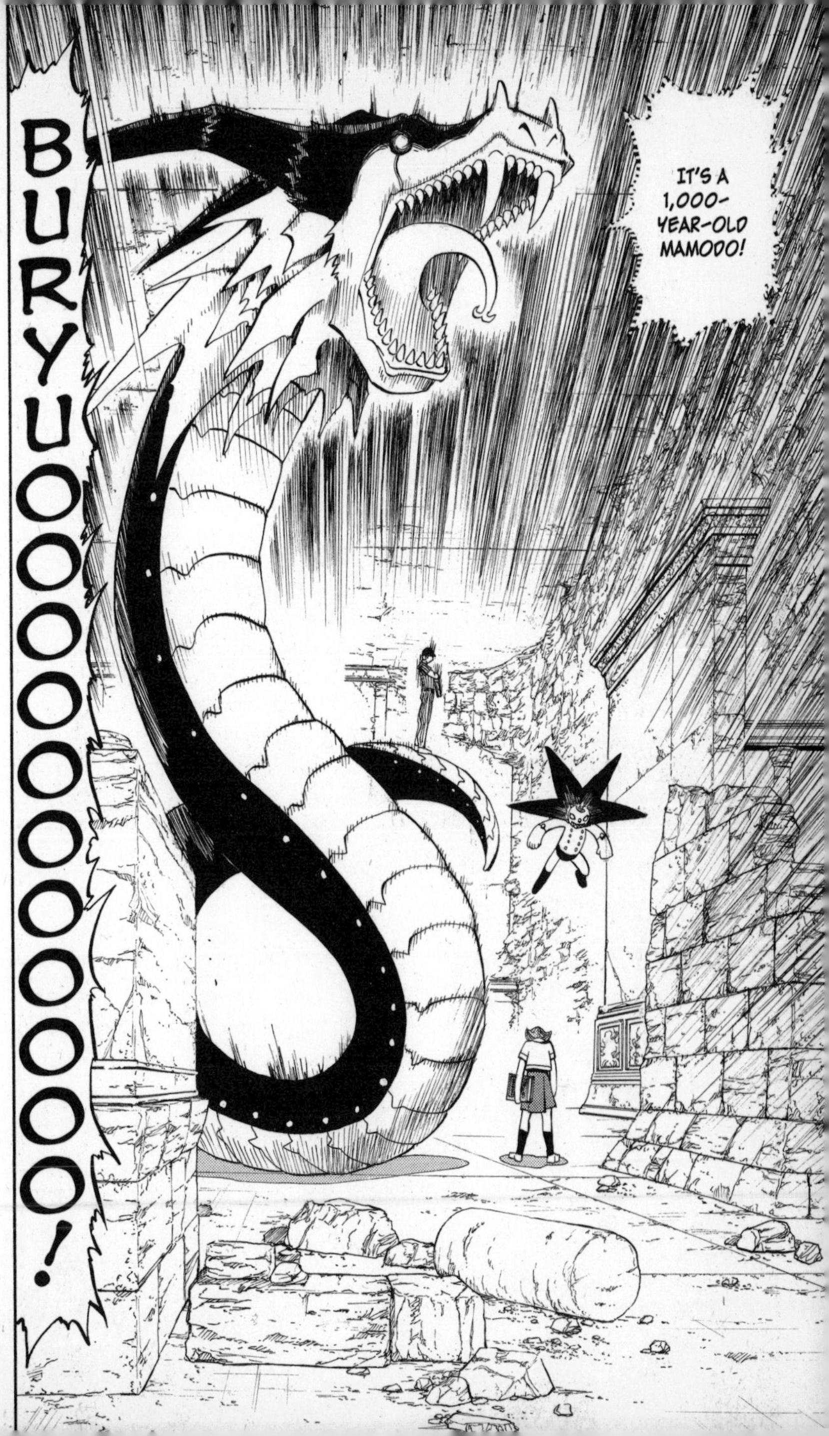
IT'S A 1,000-YEAR-OLD MAMODO!
BURYUOOOOOOOOOOO!

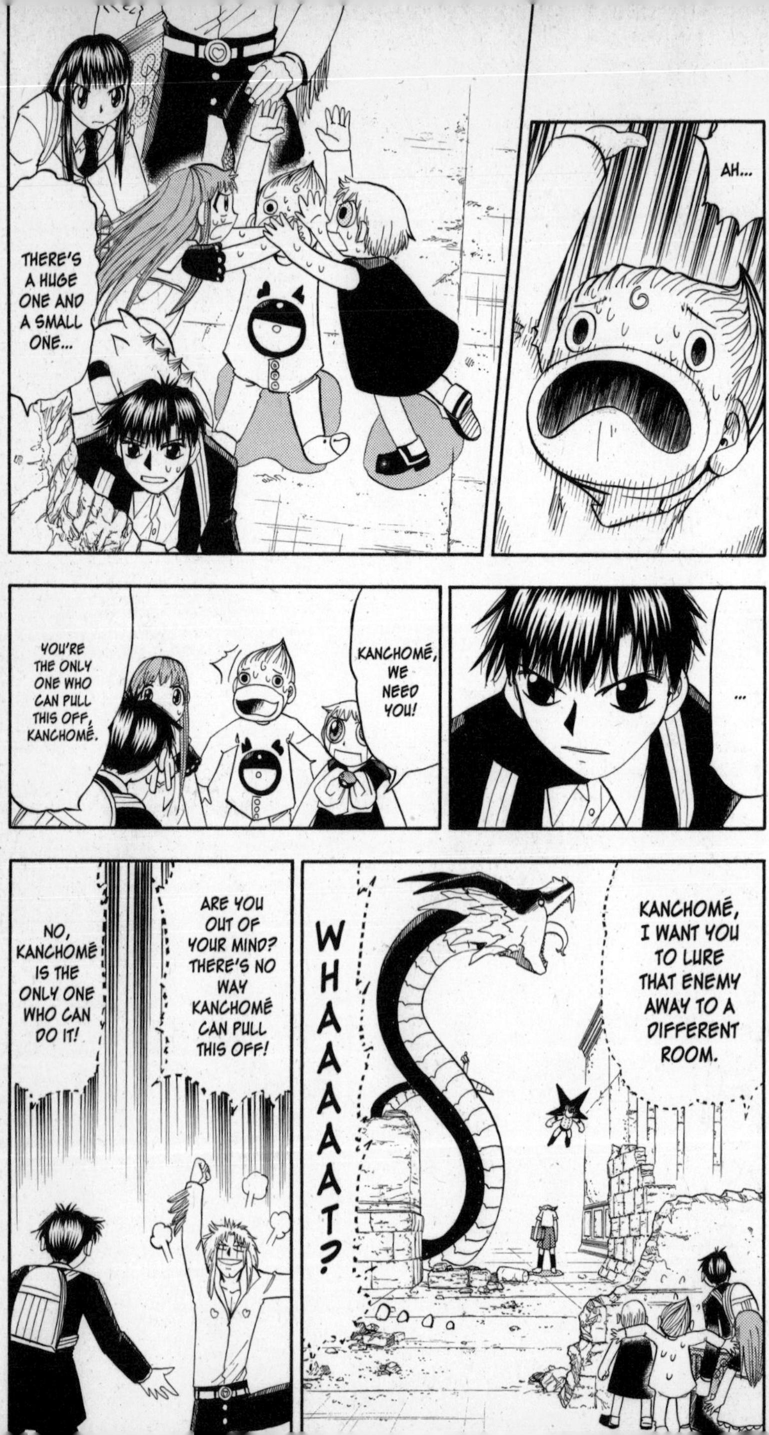
AH...
THERE'S A HUGE ONE AND A SMALL ONE...
...
KANCHOMÉ, WE NEED YOU!
YOU'RE THE ONLY ONE WHO CAN PULL THIS OFF, KANCHOMÉ.
KANCHOMÉ, I WANT YOU TO LURE THAT ENEMY AWAY TO A DIFFERENT ROOM.
WHAAAAAT?
ARE YOU OUT OF YOUR MIND? THERE'S NO WAY KANCHOMÉ CAN PULL THIS OFF!
NO, KANCHOMÉ IS THE ONLY ONE WHO CAN DO IT!

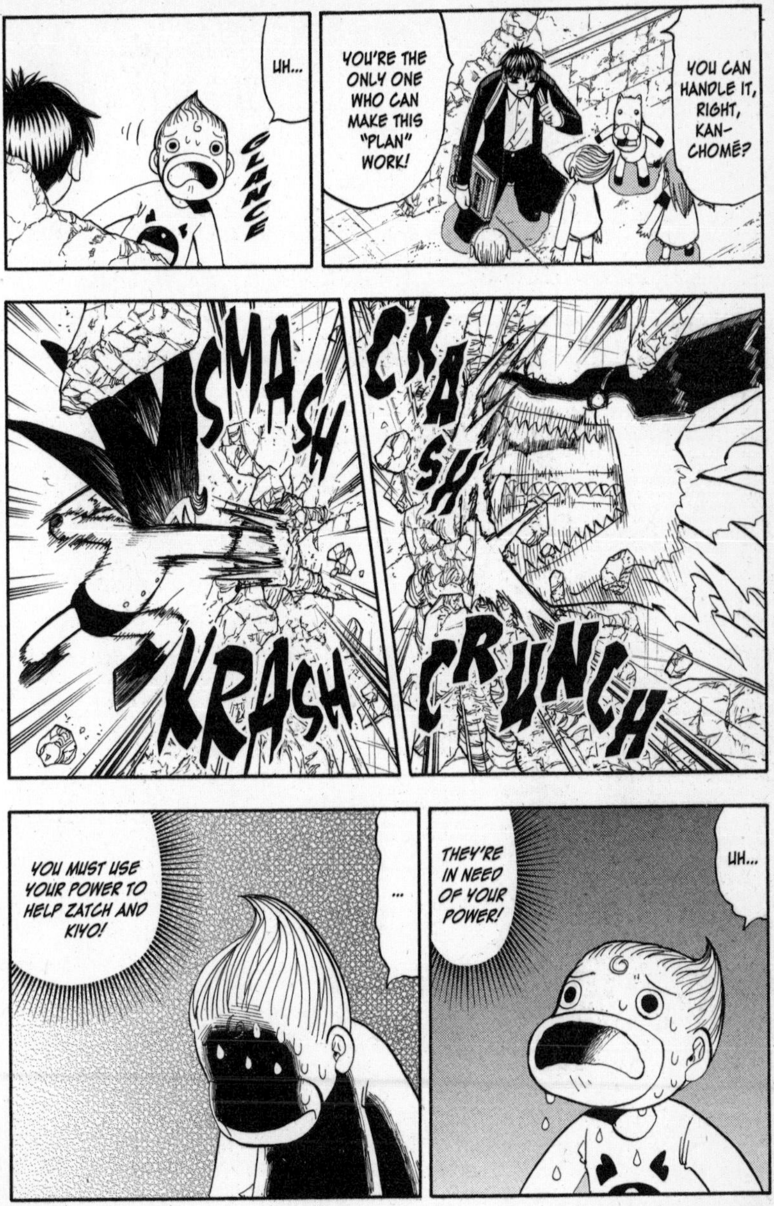
YOU CAN HANDLE IT, RIGHT, KAN-CHOMÉ?
YOU'RE THE ONLY ONE WHO CAN MAKE THIS "PLAN" WORK!
UH...
GLANCE
CRASH
CRUNCH
SMASH
KRASH
UH...
THEY'RE IN NEED OF YOUR POWER!
...
YOU MUST USE YOUR POWER TO HELP ZATCH AND KIYO!

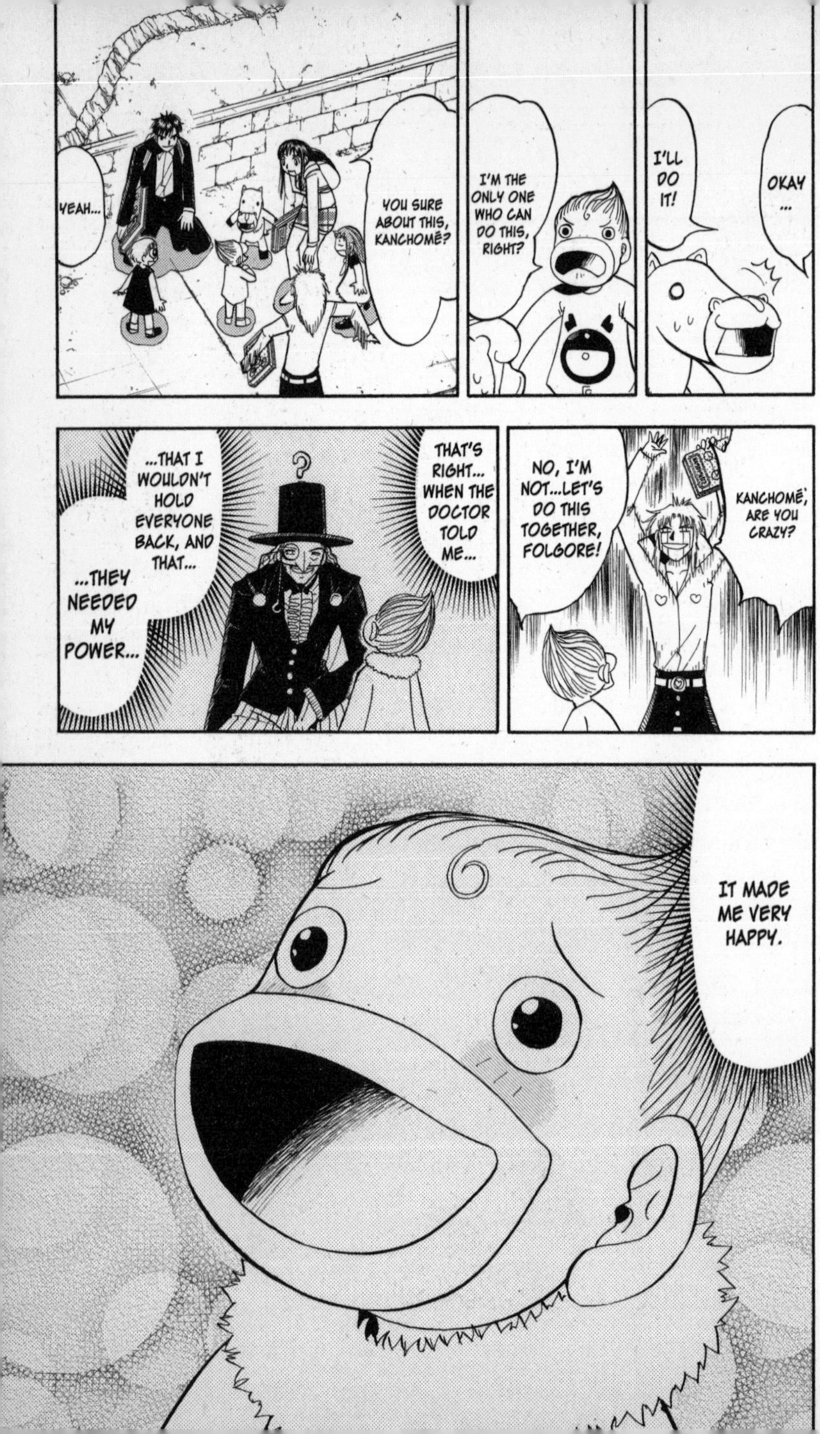
OKAY ...
I'LL DO IT!
I'M THE ONLY ONE WHO CAN DO THIS, RIGHT?
YOU SURE ABOUT THIS, KANCHOMĒ?
YEAH...
KANCHOMĒ, ARE YOU CRAZY?
NO, I'M NOT...LET'S DO THIS TOGETHER, FOLGORE!
THAT'S RIGHT... WHEN THE DOCTOR TOLD ME...
...THAT I WOULDN'T HOLD EVERYONE BACK, AND THAT...
...THEY NEEDED MY POWER...
IT MADE ME VERY HAPPY.

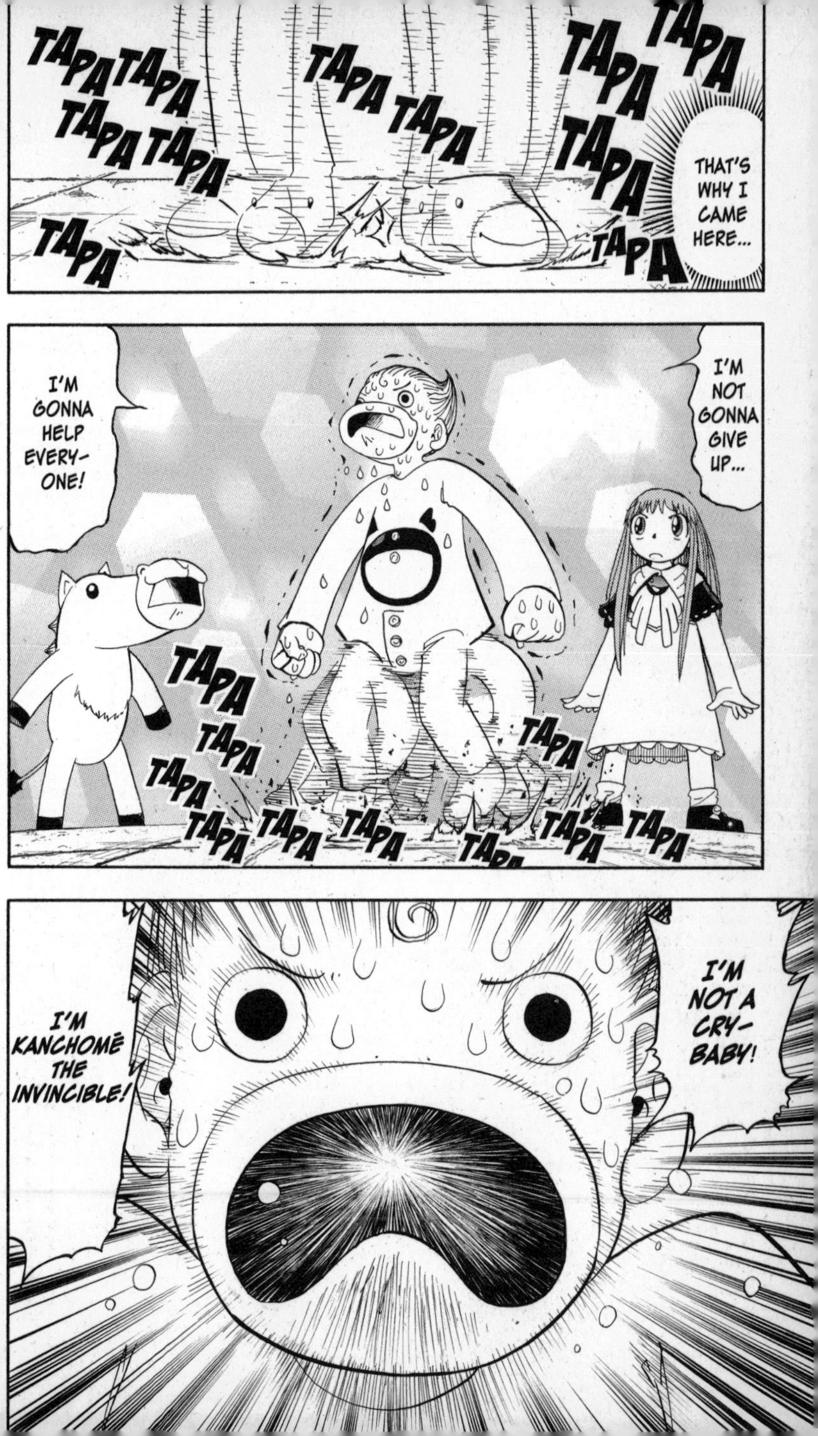
THAT'S WHY I CAME HERE...
TAPA TAPA TAPA TAPA TAPA
TAPA TAPA TAPA TAPA TAPA TAPA TAPA
I'M NOT GONNA GIVE UP...
I'M GONNA HELP EVERY-ONE!
TAPA TAPA TAPA TAPA TAPA TAPA TAPA TAPA TAPA TAPA
I'M NOT A CRY-BABY!
I'M KANCHOMÉ THE INVINCIBLE!

LEVEL 112: Kanchomé's Power

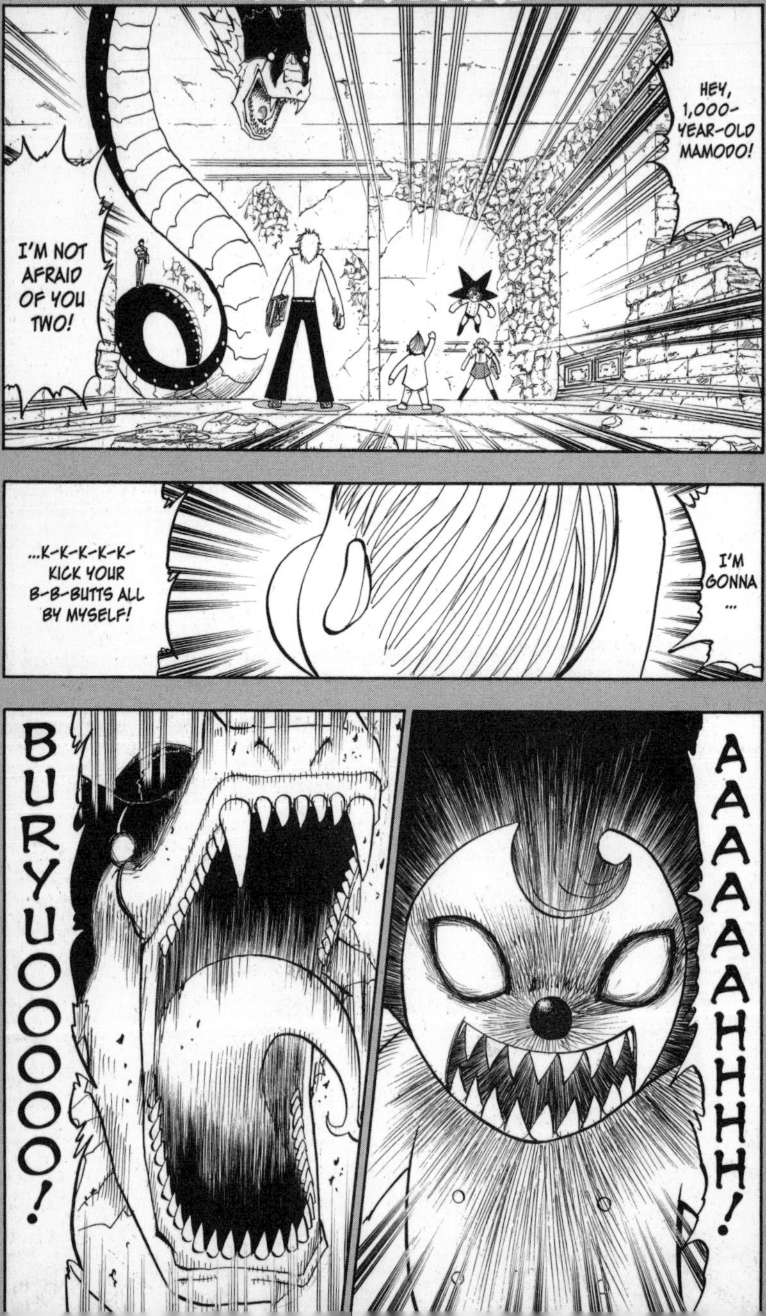
HEY, 1,000-YEAR-OLD MAMODO!
I'M NOT AFRAID OF YOU TWO!
I'M GONNA...
...K-K-K-K-K-KICK YOUR B-B-BUTTS ALL BY MYSELF!
AAAAAAHHHH!
BURYUOOOOO!

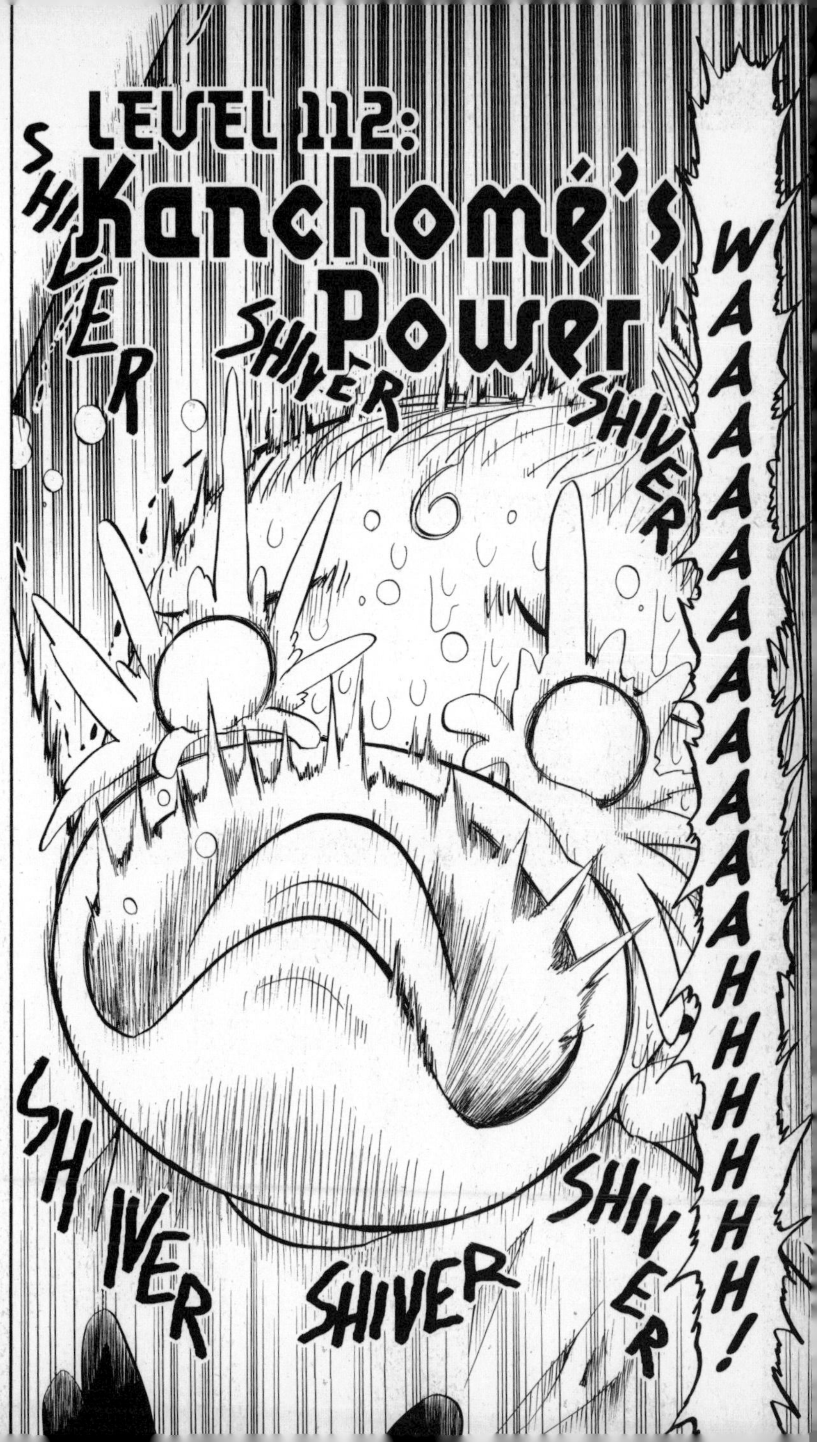
LEVEL 112:
Kanchomé's Power
WAAAAAAAAAAAAAHHHHHHHH!
SHIVER
SHIVER
SHIVER
SHIVER
SHIVER
SHIVER
SHIVER

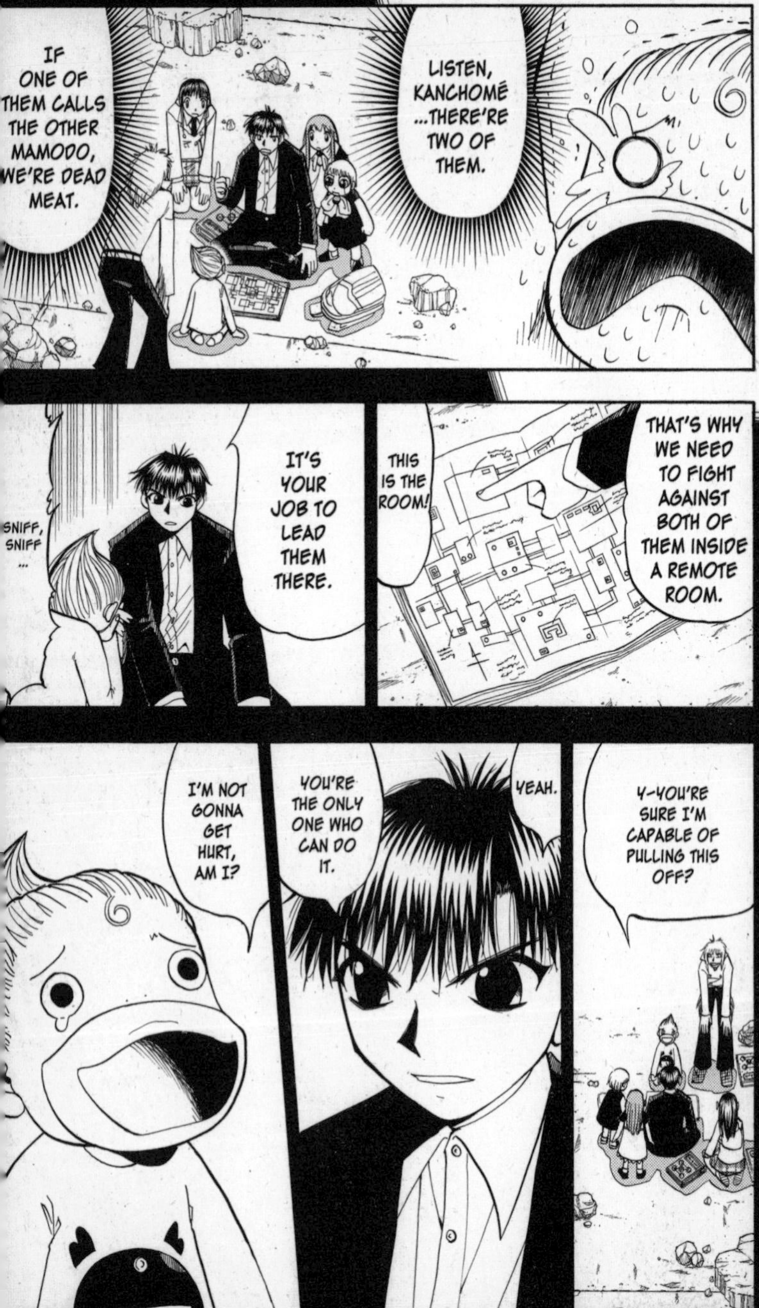
LISTEN, KANCHOMÉ ...THERE'RE TWO OF THEM.
IF ONE OF THEM CALLS THE OTHER MAMODO, WE'RE DEAD MEAT.
THAT'S WHY WE NEED TO FIGHT AGAINST BOTH OF THEM INSIDE A REMOTE ROOM.
THIS IS THE ROOM!
IT'S YOUR JOB TO LEAD THEM THERE.
SNIFF, SNIFF ...
Y-YOU'RE SURE I'M CAPABLE OF PULLING THIS OFF?
YEAH.
YOU'RE THE ONLY ONE WHO CAN DO IT.
I'M NOT GONNA GET HURT, AM I?

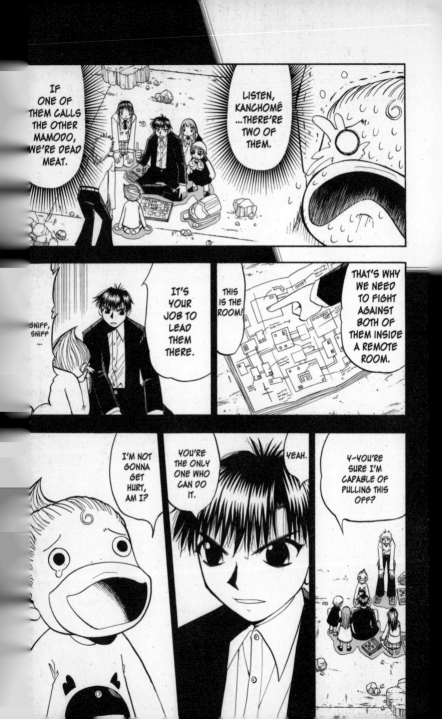

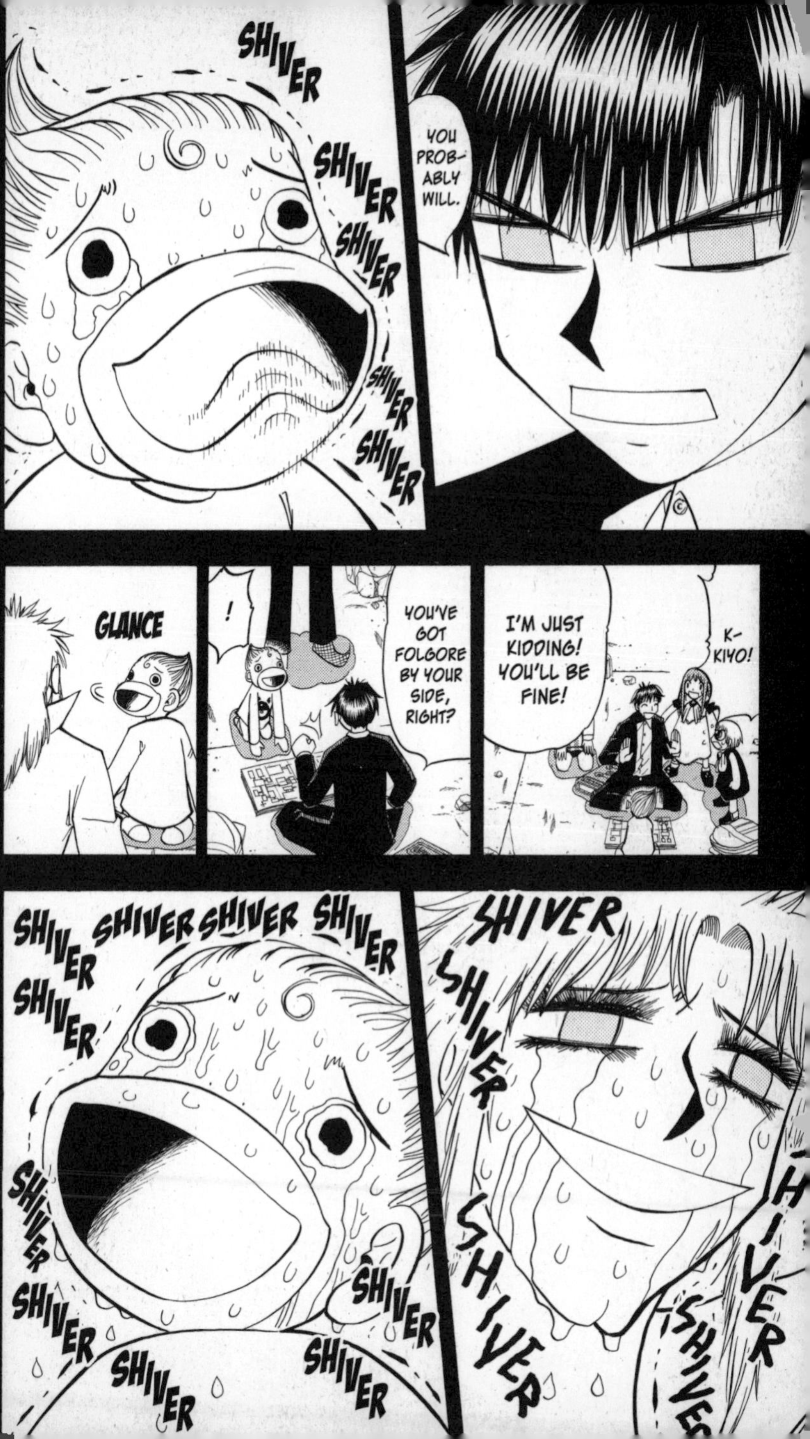
YOU PROBABLY WILL.
SHIVER
SHIVER
SHIVER
SHIVER
SHIVER
K-KIYO!
I'M JUST KIDDING! YOU'LL BE FINE!
YOU'VE GOT FOLGORE BY YOUR SIDE, RIGHT?
!
GLANCE
SHIVER
SHIVER
SHIVER
SHIVER
SHIVER
SHIVER
SHIVER
SHIVER
SHIVER
SHIVER
SHIVER
SHIVER
SHIVER

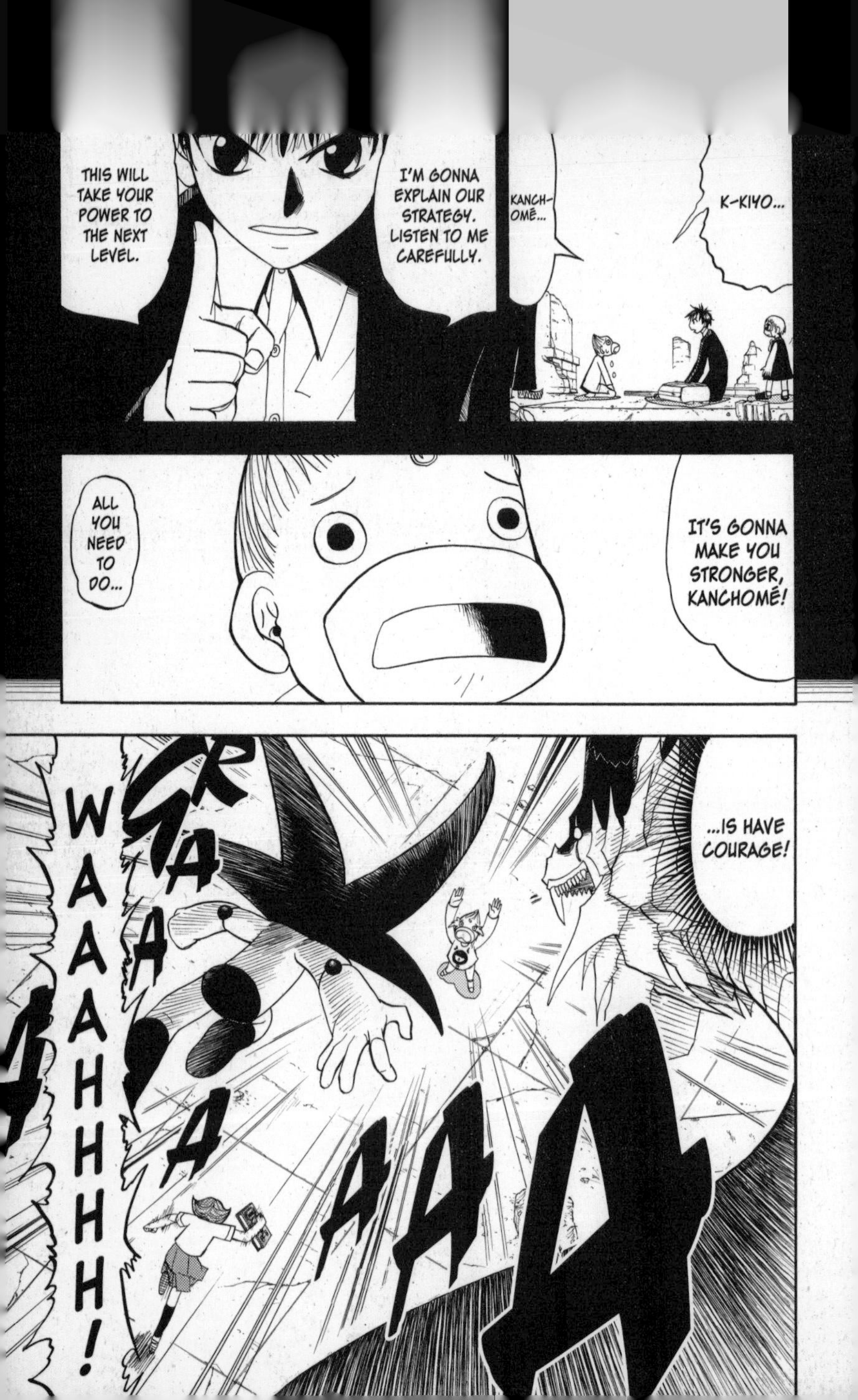
K-KIYO...
KANCH-OMÉ...
I'M GONNA EXPLAIN OUR STRATEGY. LISTEN TO ME CAREFULLY.
THIS WILL TAKE YOUR POWER TO THE NEXT LEVEL.
IT'S GONNA MAKE YOU STRONGER, KANCHOMÉ!
ALL YOU NEED TO DO...
...IS HAVE COURAGE!
WAAAAHHHH!

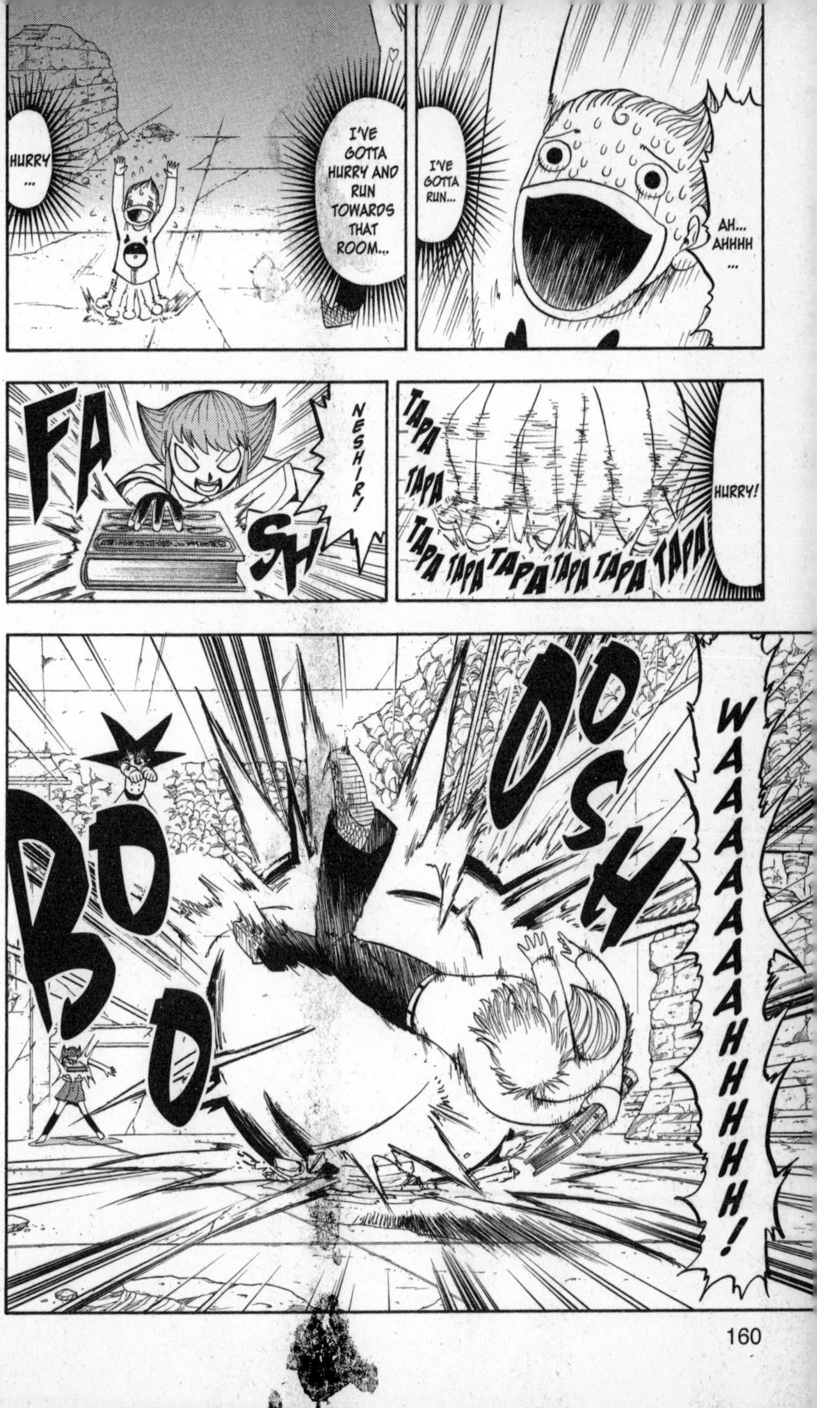
AH... AHHHH ...
I'VE GOTTA RUN...
I'VE GOTTA HURRY AND RUN TOWARDS THAT ROOM...
HURRY ...
HURRY!
TAPA TAPA TAPA TAPA TAPA TAPA TAPA TAPA
NESHIR!
FASH
WAAAAAAAAHHHHHH!
DOSH
BOO

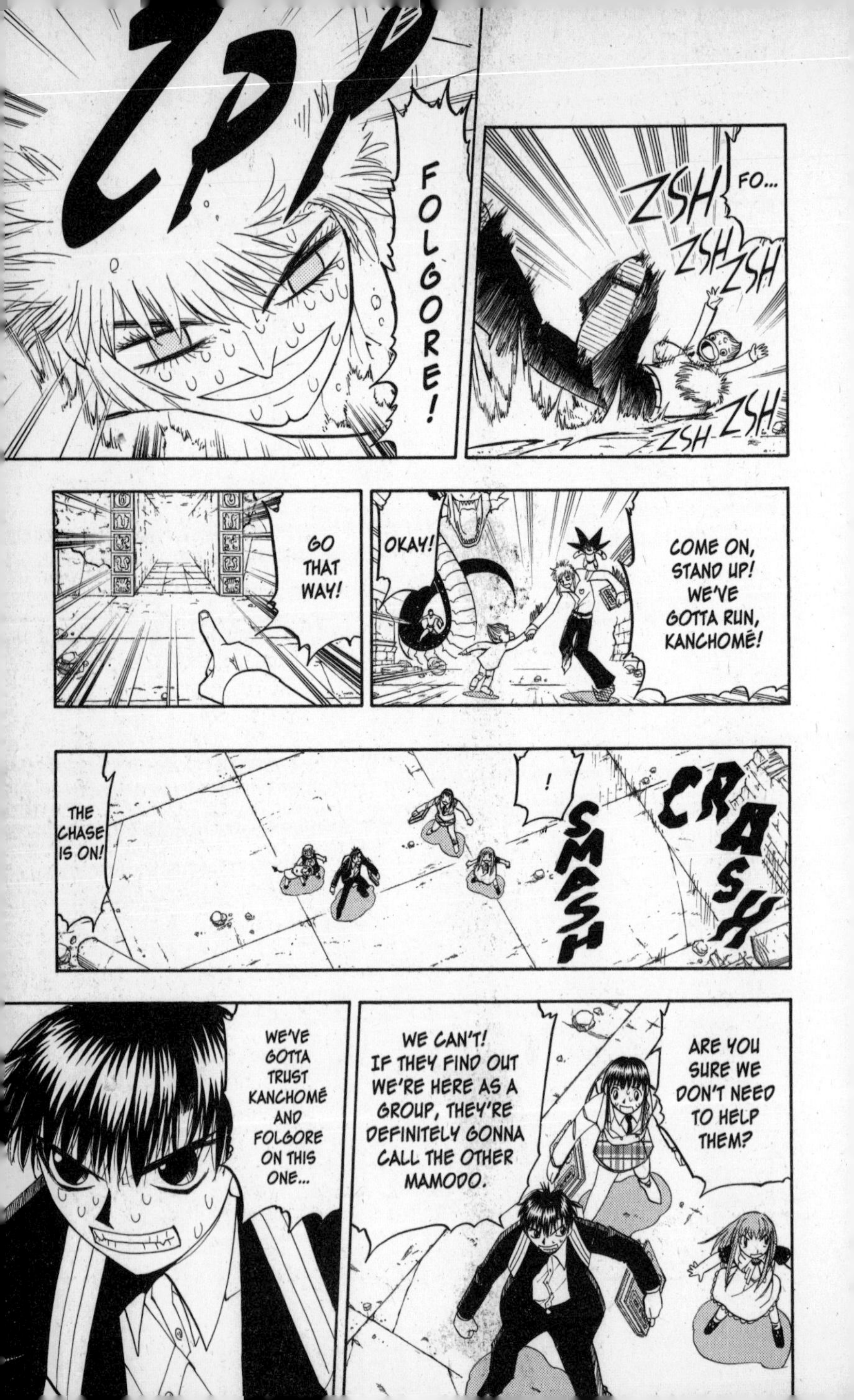
ZSH
FO...
ZSH ZSH
ZSH ZSH
ZAP
FOLGORE!
COME ON, STAND UP! WE'VE GOTTA RUN, KANCHOMÉ!
OKAY!
GO THAT WAY!
!
CRASH
SMASH
THE CHASE IS ON!
ARE YOU SURE WE DON'T NEED TO HELP THEM?
WE CAN'T! IF THEY FIND OUT WE'RE HERE AS A GROUP, THEY'RE DEFINITELY GONNA CALL THE OTHER MAMODO.
WE'VE GOTTA TRUST KANCHOMÉ AND FOLGORE ON THIS ONE...

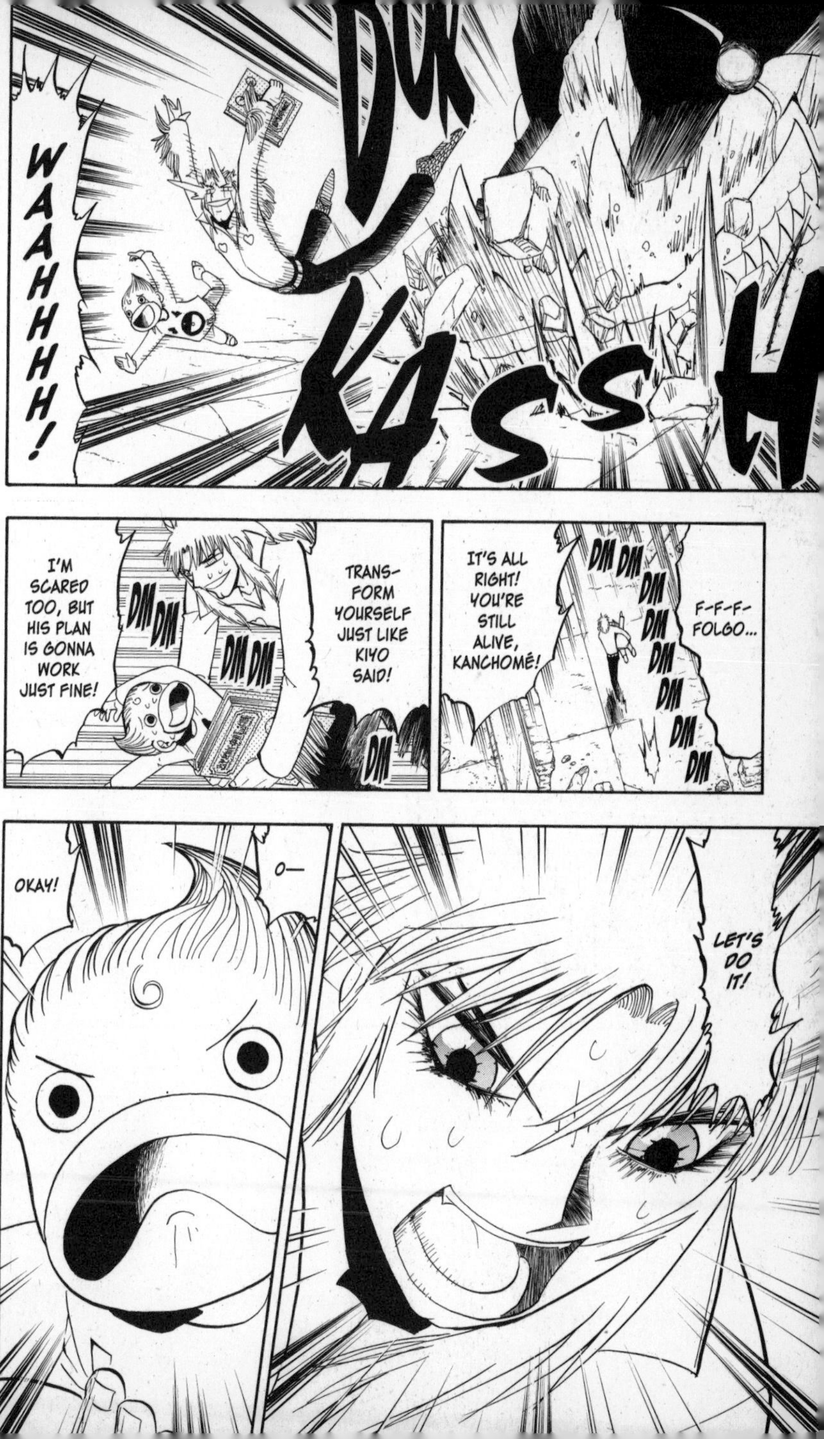
KASSH
WAAHHHHH!
F-F-F-FOLGO...
IT'S ALL RIGHT! YOU'RE STILL ALIVE, KANCHOMÉ!
DM DM DM DM DM DM DM DM DM
TRANS-FORM YOURSELF JUST LIKE KIYO SAID!
DM DM DM DM DM
I'M SCARED TOO, BUT HIS PLAN IS GONNA WORK JUST FINE!
LET'S DO IT!
O—
OKAY!

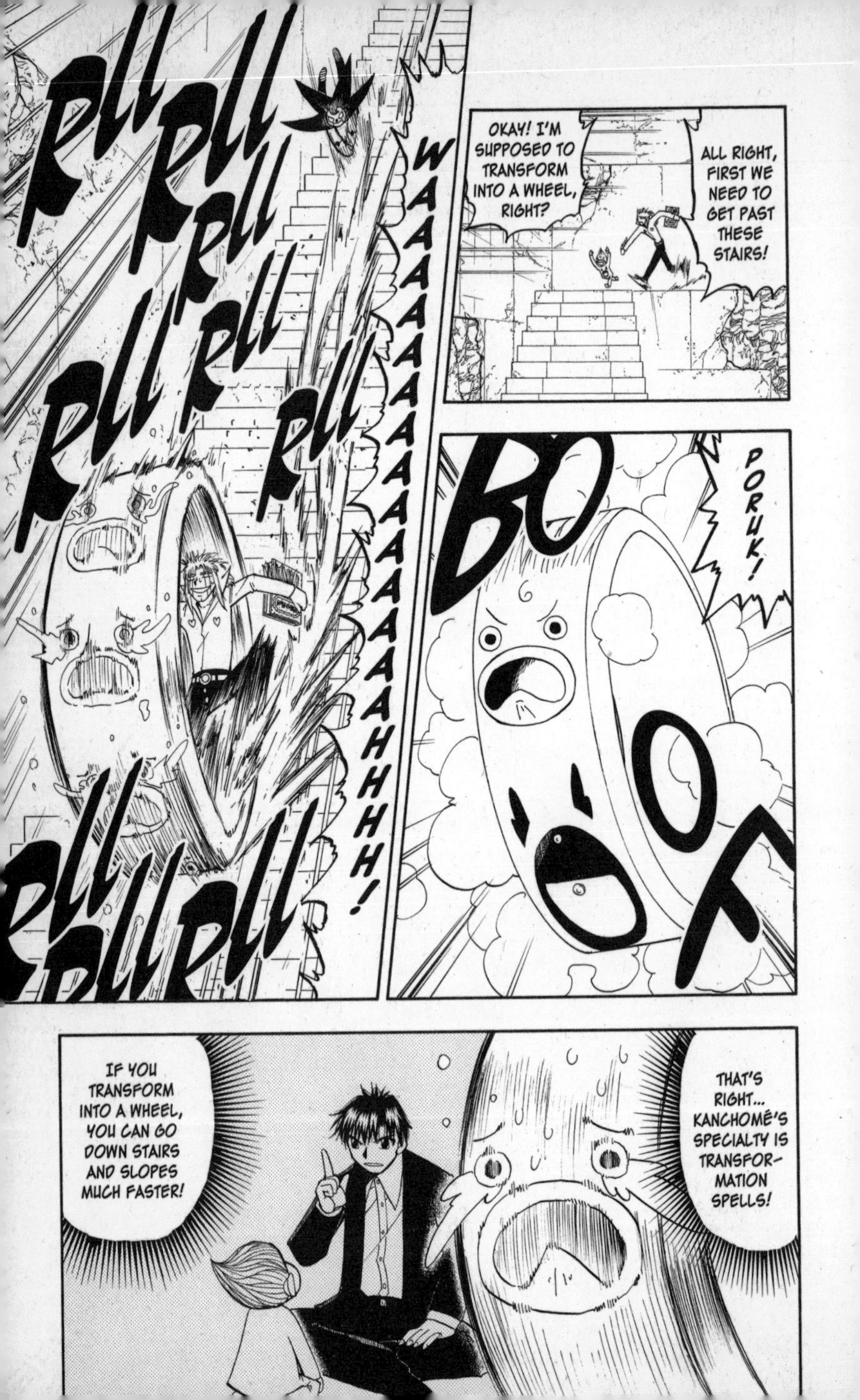
ALL RIGHT, FIRST WE NEED TO GET PAST THESE STAIRS!
OKAY! I'M SUPPOSED TO TRANSFORM INTO A WHEEL, RIGHT?
PORUK!
BOOF
RLL RLL RLL RLL RLL RLL RLL
WAAAAAAAAAAAAAAHHHHH!
RLL RLL RLL
THAT'S RIGHT... KANCHOMÉ'S SPECIALTY IS TRANSFORMATION SPELLS!
IF YOU TRANSFORM INTO A WHEEL, YOU CAN GO DOWN STAIRS AND SLOPES MUCH FASTER!

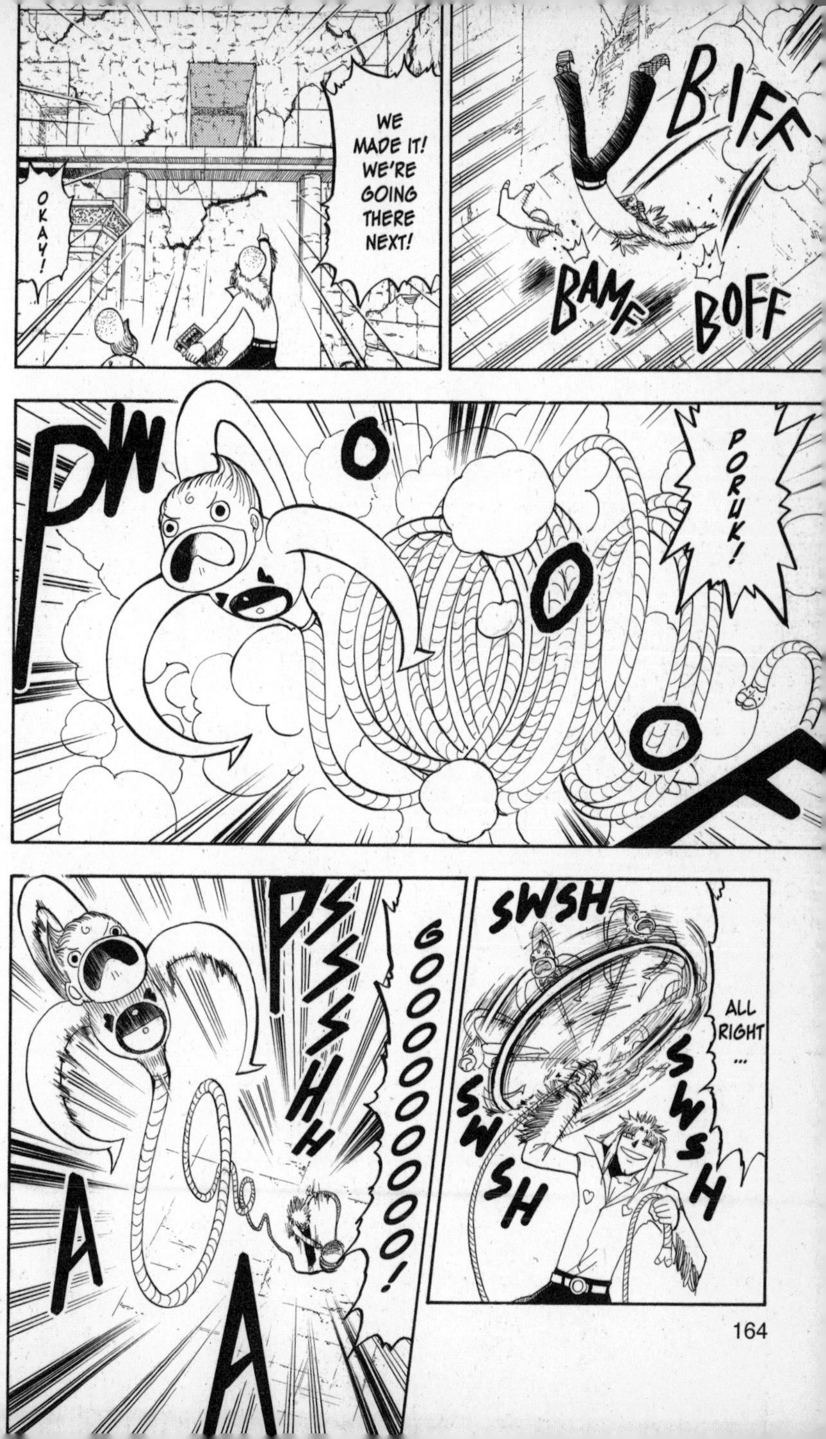

BIFF
BAMF
BOFF
WE MADE IT! WE'RE GOING THERE NEXT!
OKAY!
PORUK!
PWOOOF
SWSH
ALL RIGHT ...
SWSH
SWSH
PSSHHH
GOOOOOOOOOO!
AA

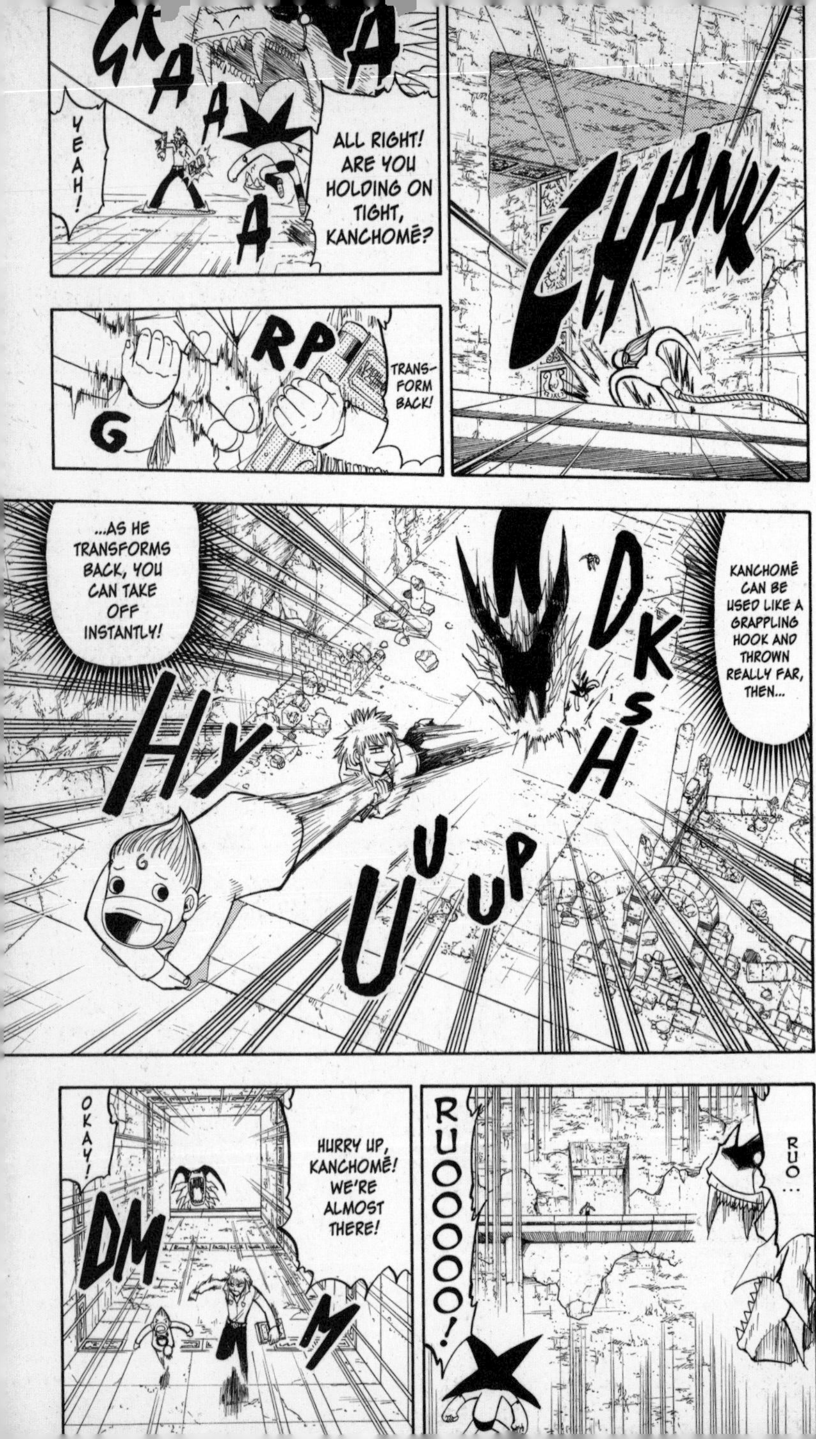
CHANK
ALL RIGHT! ARE YOU HOLDING ON TIGHT, KANCHOMĒ?
YEAH!
GRAAAA
TRANS-FORM BACK!
GRPI
KANCHOMĒ CAN BE USED LIKE A GRAPPLING HOOK AND THROWN REALLY FAR, THEN...
DKSH
...AS HE TRANSFORMS BACK, YOU CAN TAKE OFF INSTANTLY!
HYUUUP
RUO...
RUOOOOOO!
HURRY UP, KANCHOMĒ! WE'RE ALMOST THERE!
OKAY!
DMM

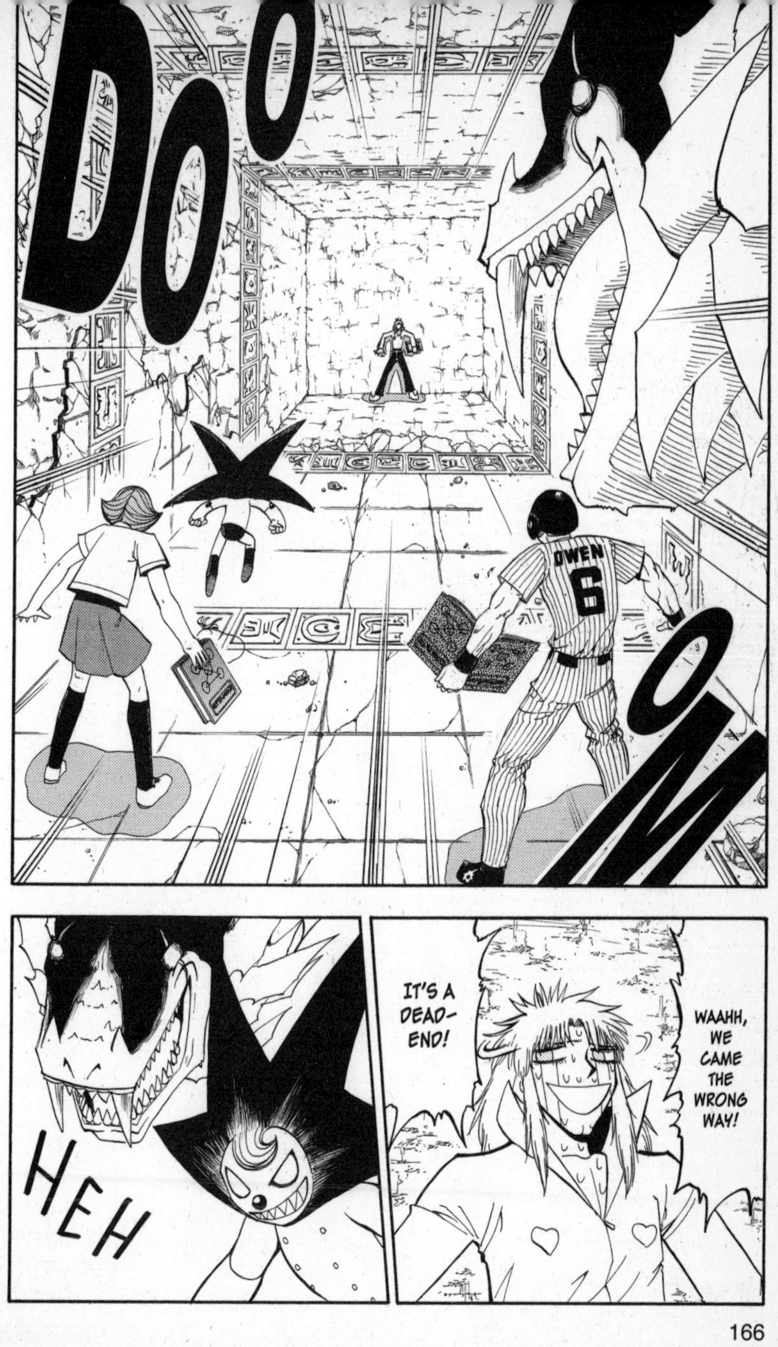
DOOOOM
OWEN
6
WAAHH, WE CAME THE WRONG WAY!
IT'S A DEAD-END!
HEH

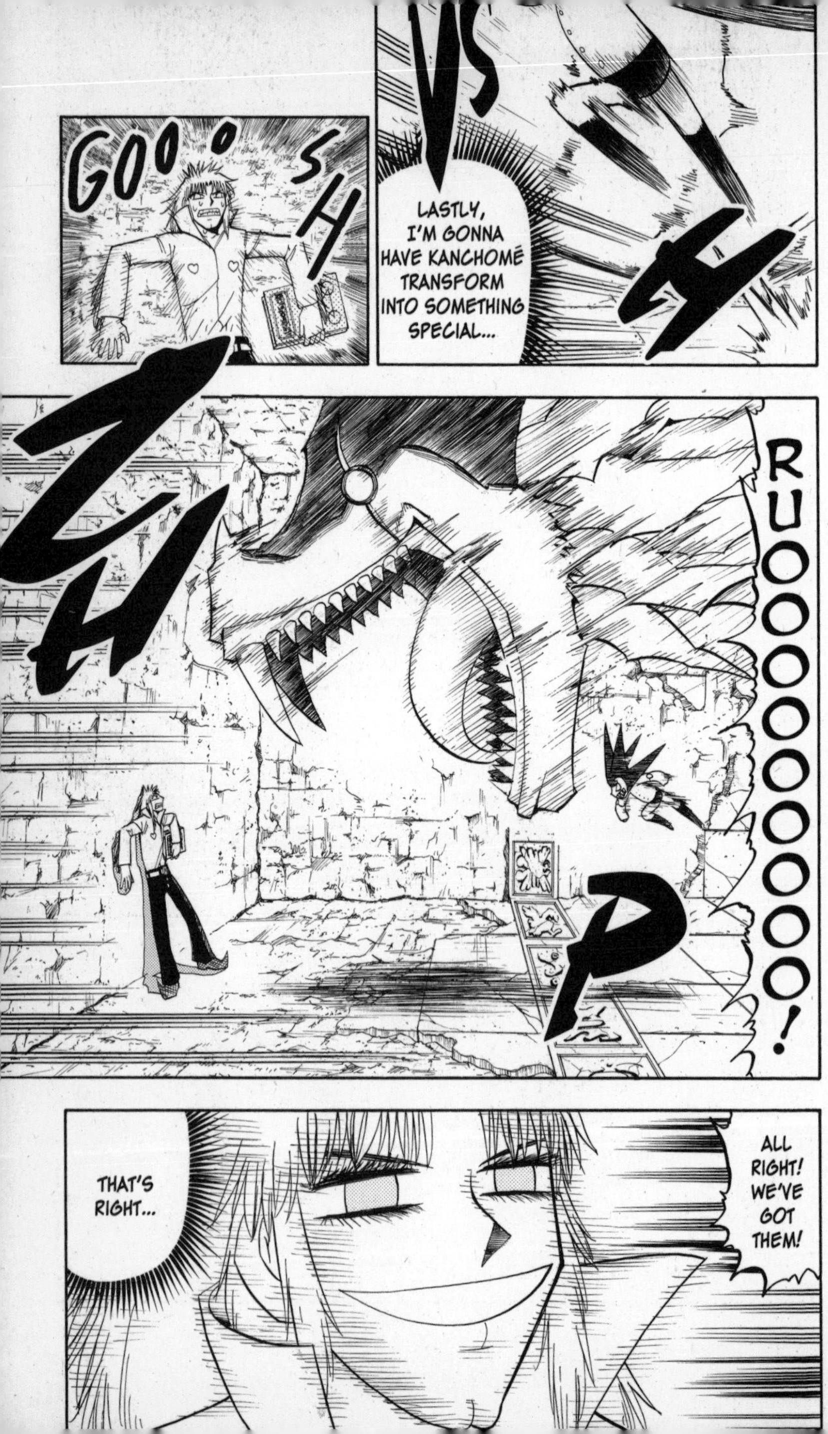
VSH
LASTLY, I'M GONNA HAVE KANCHOMÉ TRANSFORM INTO SOMETHING SPECIAL...
GOOOSH
RUOOOOOOOOOOOOOO!
ALL RIGHT! WE'VE GOT THEM!
THAT'S RIGHT...

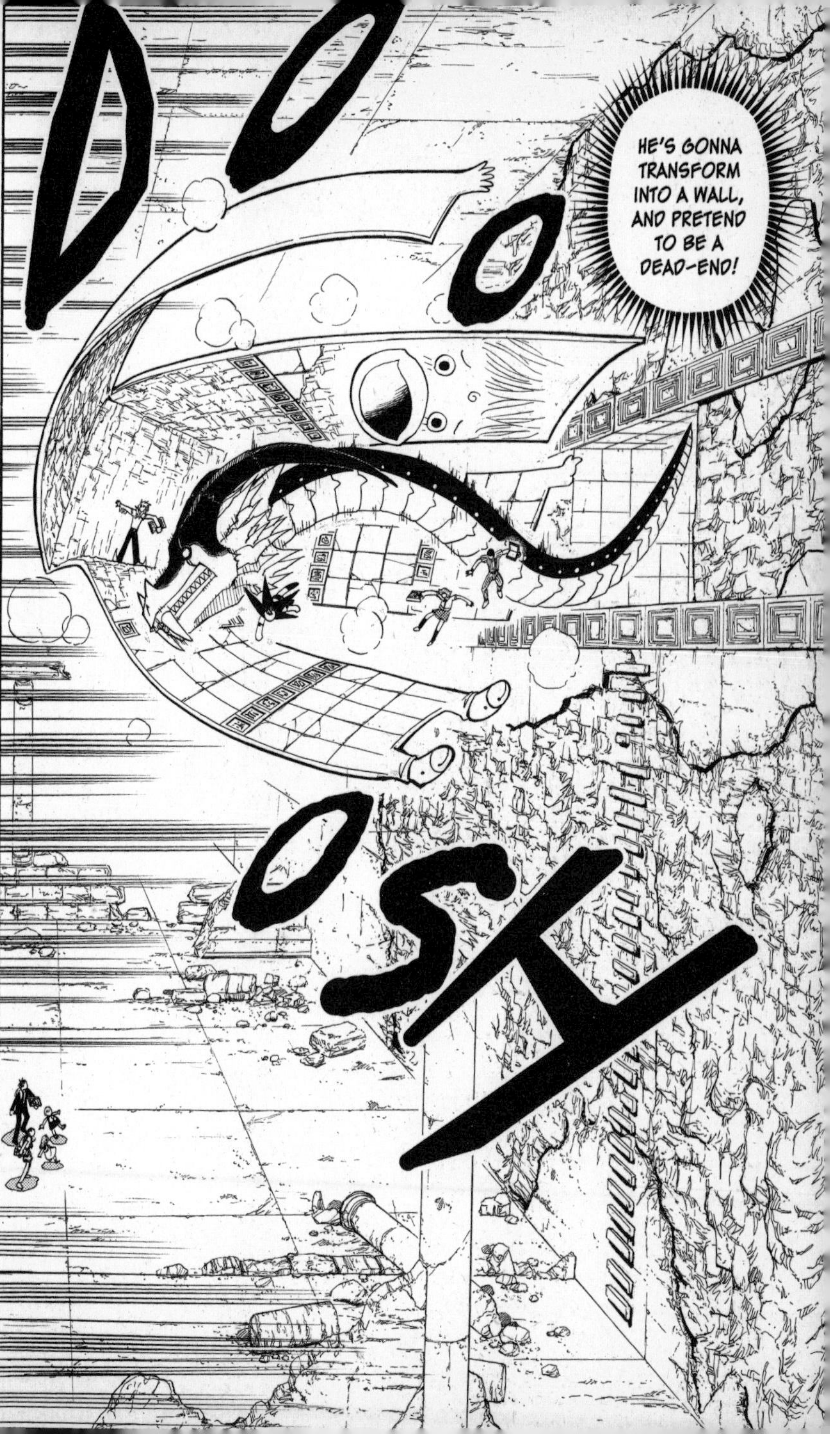
HE'S GONNA TRANSFORM INTO A WALL, AND PRETEND TO BE A DEAD-END!
DOOOSH

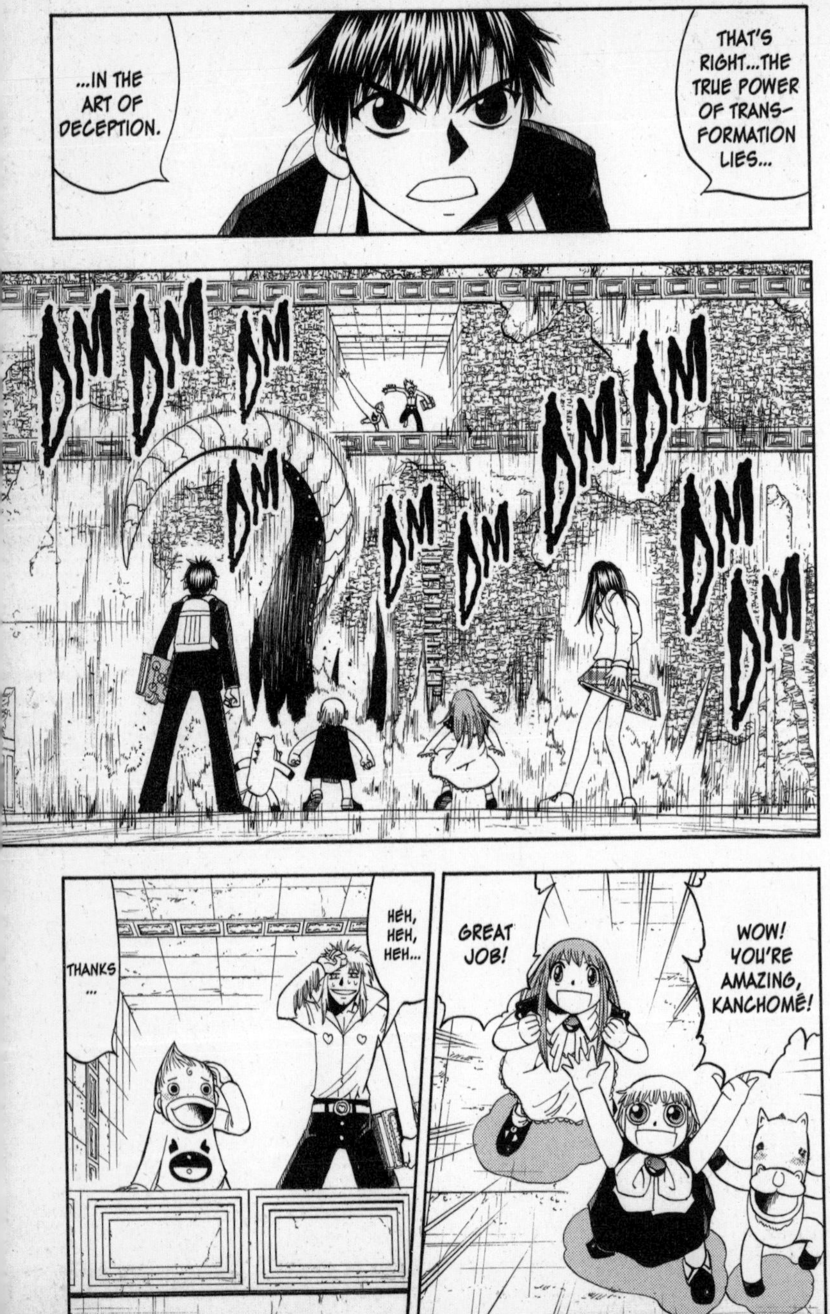
THAT'S RIGHT...THE TRUE POWER OF TRANS-FORMATION LIES...
...IN THE ART OF DECEPTION.
DM DM DM DM DM DM
DM DM DM DM DM DM DM
WOW! YOU'RE AMAZING, KANCHOMÉ!
GREAT JOB!
HEH, HEH, HEH...
THANKS ...

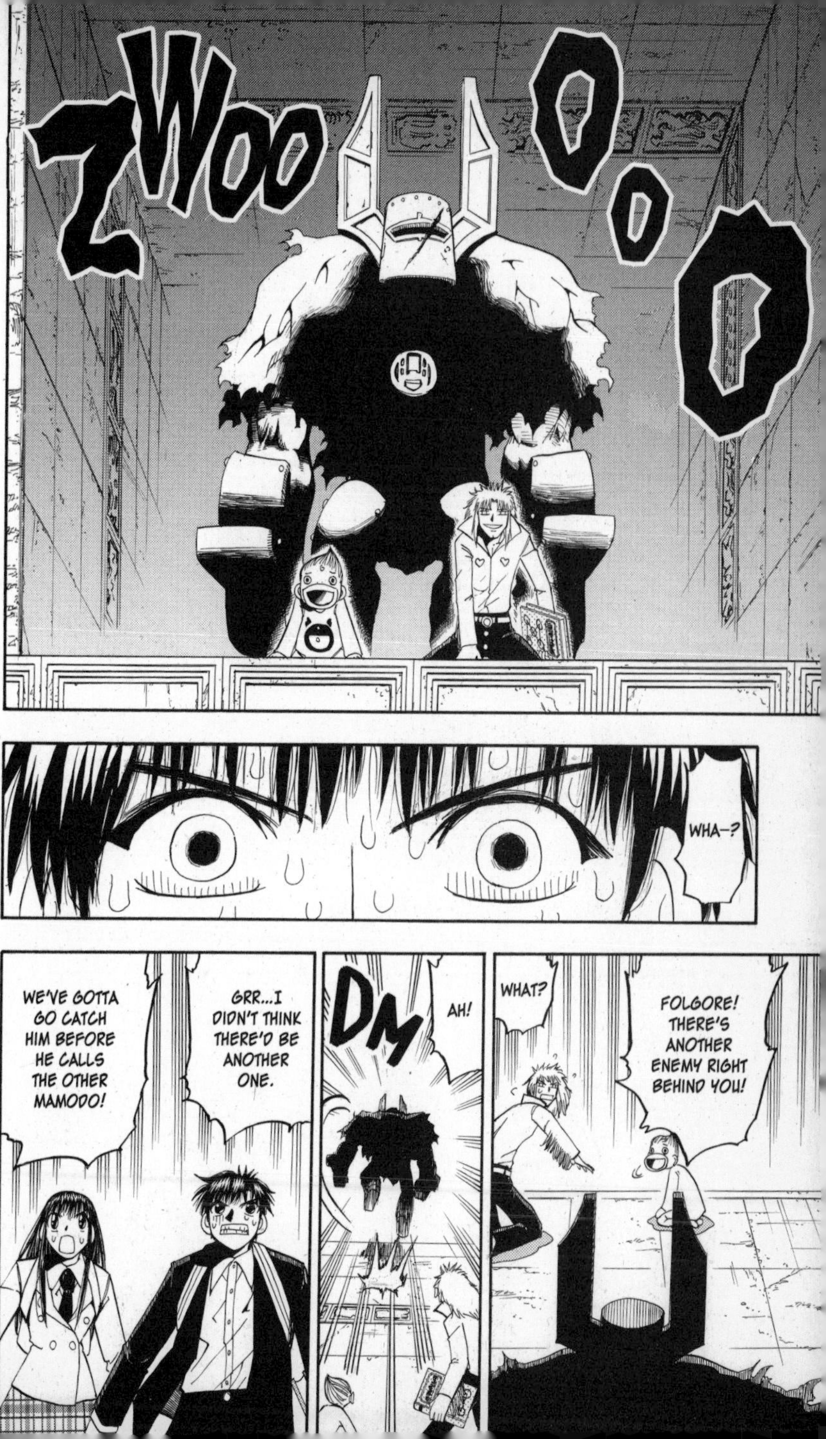
ZWOOOOP
WHA-?
FOLGORE! THERE'S ANOTHER ENEMY RIGHT BEHIND YOU!
WHAT?
AH!
DM
GRR...I DIDN'T THINK THERE'D BE ANOTHER ONE.
WE'VE GOTTA GO CATCH HIM BEFORE HE CALLS THE OTHER MAMODO!

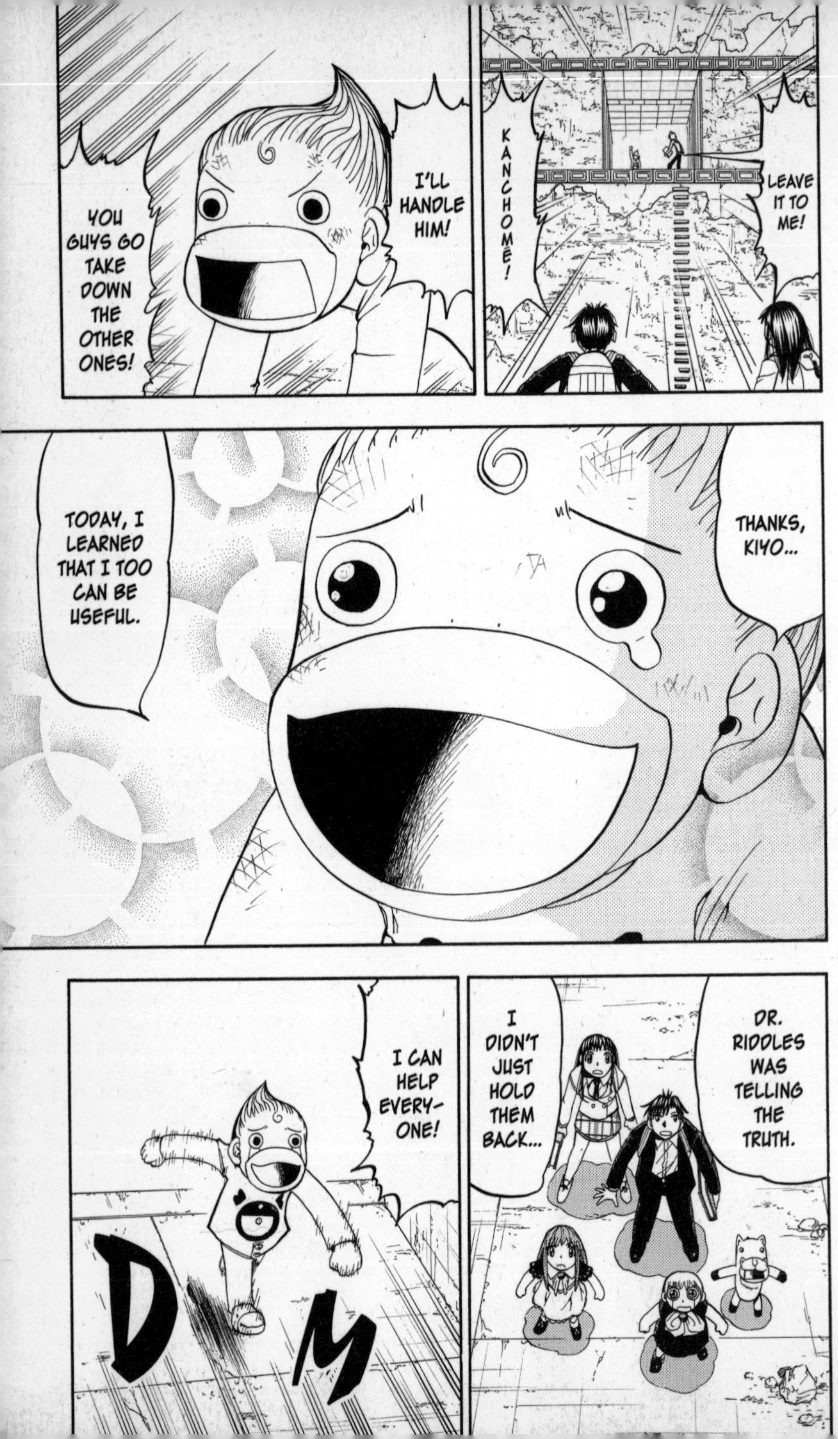
LEAVE IT TO ME!
KANCHOMÉ!
I'LL HANDLE HIM!
YOU GUYS GO TAKE DOWN THE OTHER ONES!
THANKS, KIYO...
TODAY, I LEARNED THAT I TOO CAN BE USEFUL.
DR. RIDDLES WAS TELLING THE TRUTH.
I DIDN'T JUST HOLD THEM BACK...
I CAN HELP EVERY-ONE!
D M

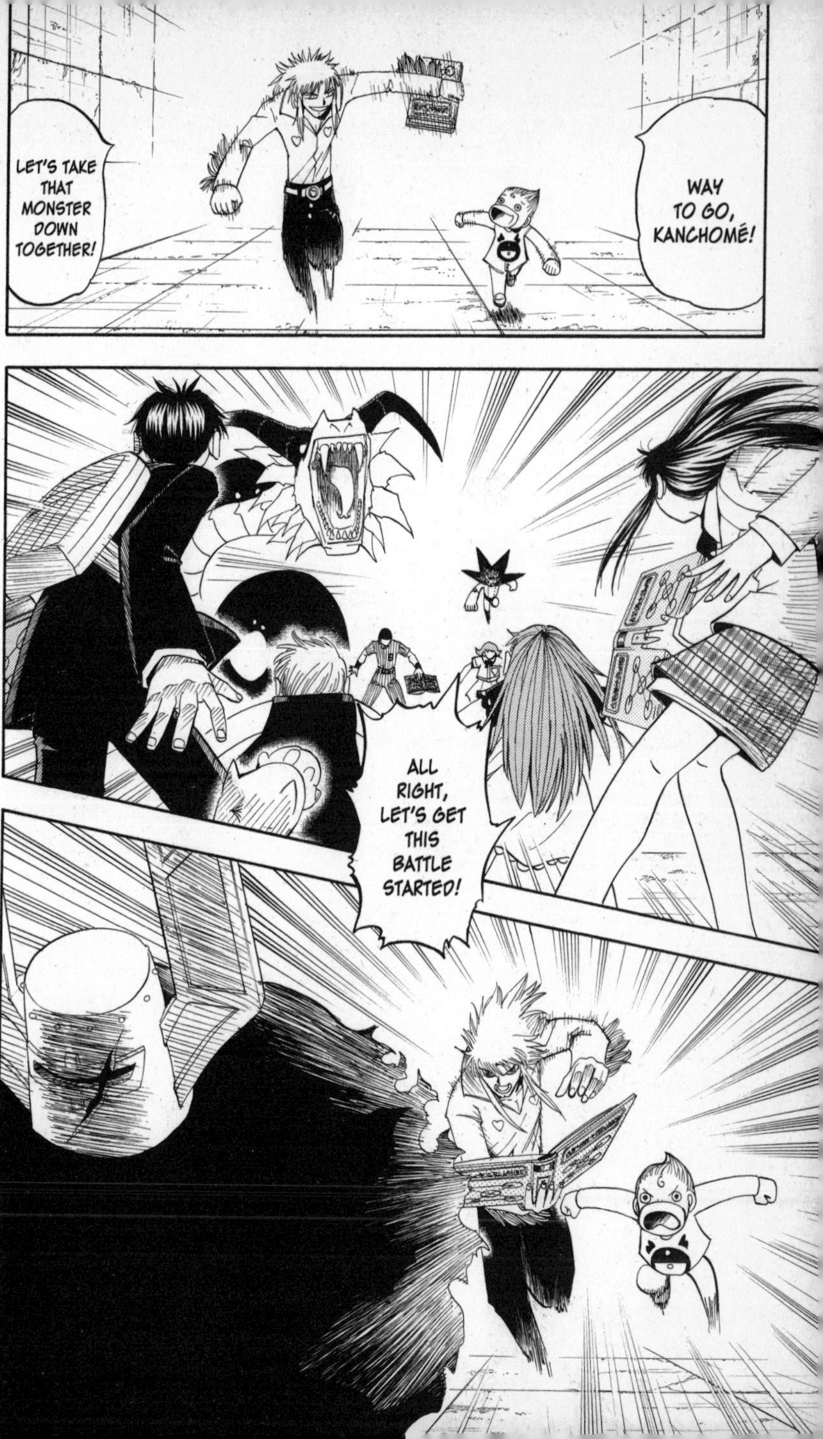
WAY TO GO, KANCHOMÉ!
LET'S TAKE THAT MONSTER DOWN TOGETHER!
ALL RIGHT, LET'S GET THIS BATTLE STARTED!

LEVEL 113: The Battery

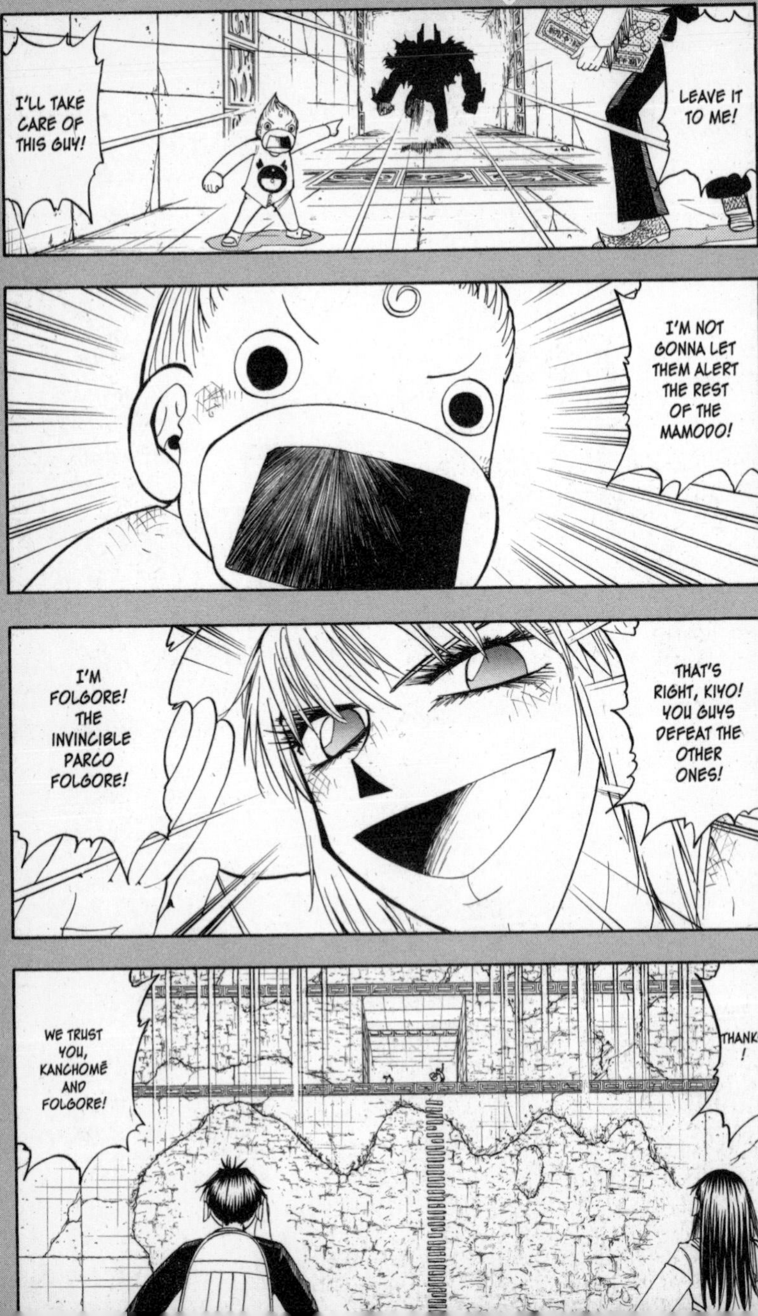

LEAVE IT TO ME!
I'LL TAKE CARE OF THIS GUY!
I'M NOT GONNA LET THEM ALERT THE REST OF THE MAMODO!
THAT'S RIGHT, KIYO! YOU GUYS DEFEAT THE OTHER ONES!
I'M FOLGORE! THE INVINCIBLE PARCO FOLGORE!
THANKS!
WE TRUST YOU, KANCHOMĒ AND FOLGORE!

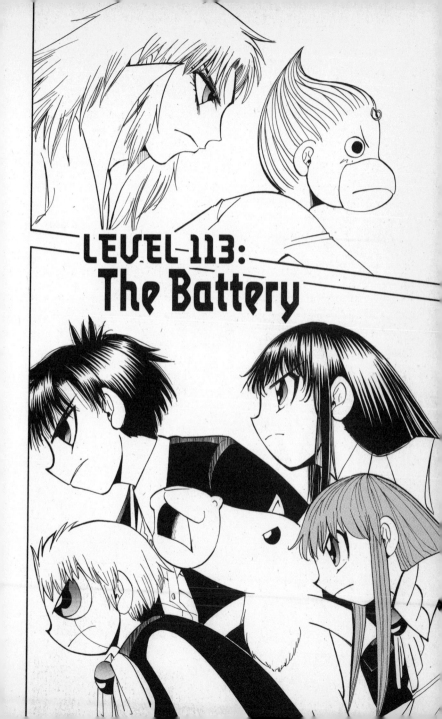

LEVEL 113:
The Battery

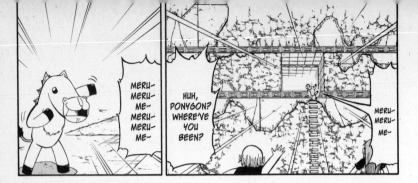

HUH, PONYGON? WHERE'VE YOU BEEN?
MERU-MERU-ME~
MERU-MERU-ME~ MERU-MERU-ME~
YOU WANNA HELP KANCHOMÉ?
GO FOR IT!
MERU-MERU-ME~!
BU...
BURYUOOOOO!
GYAAAA
!
OH NO!
I HAVEN'T SEALED OFF THE HALLWAY WITH A ZAKER YET!
IF THEY GET OUT, OUR PLAN WILL BE RUINED...

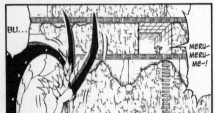

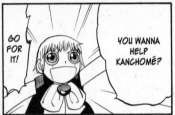

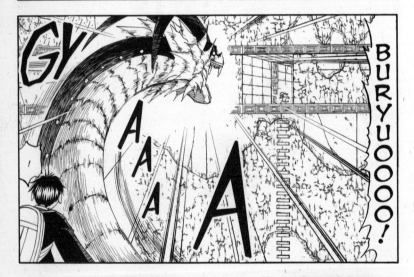

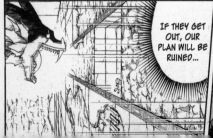

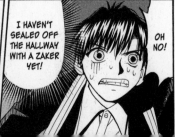

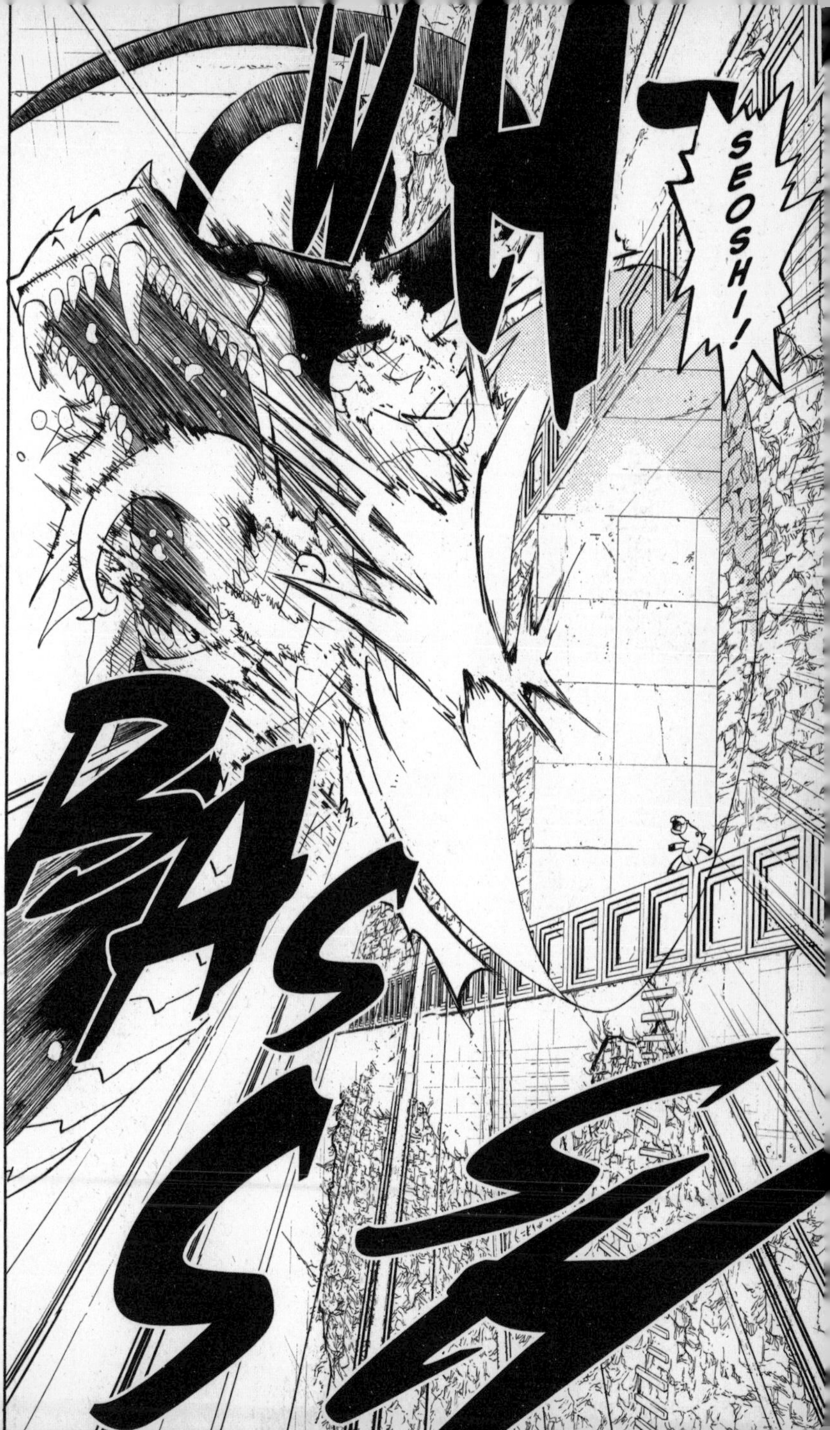
SEOSHI!

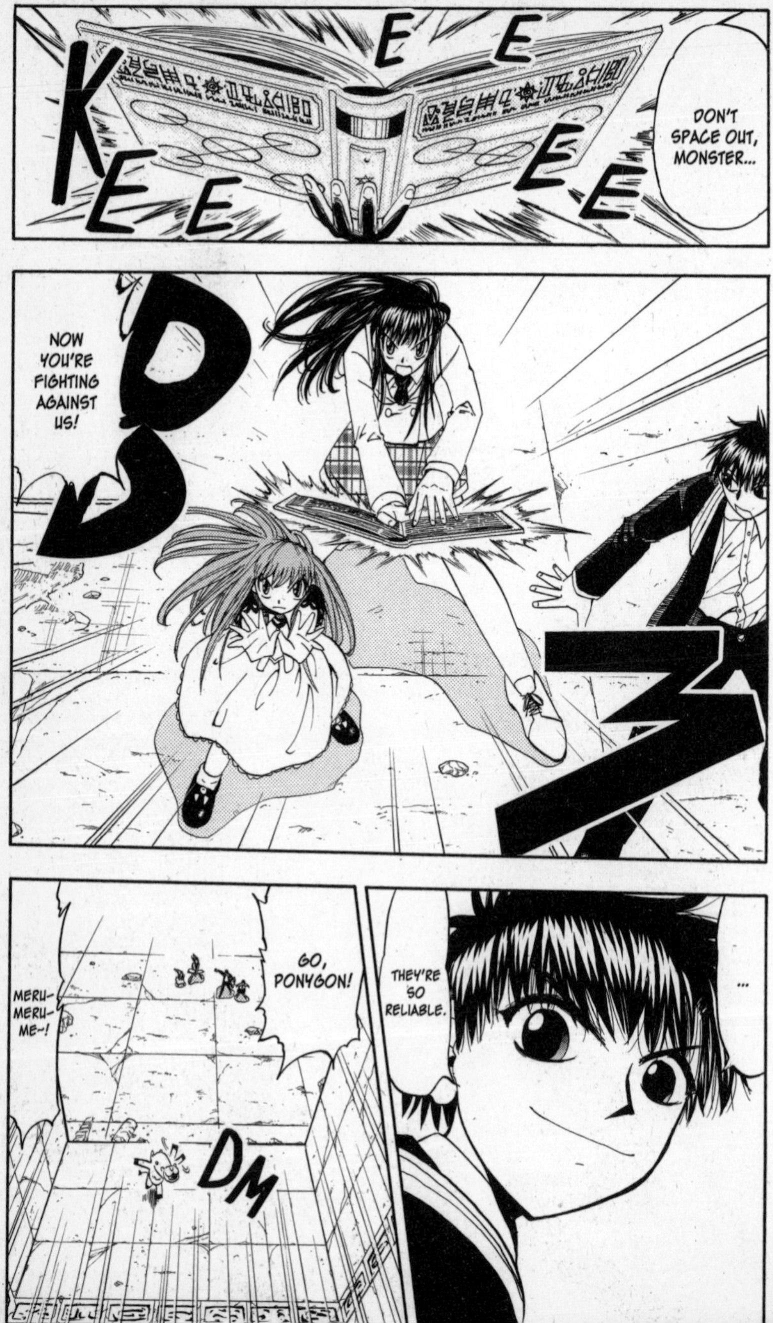
DON'T SPACE OUT, MONSTER...
KEEEEEE
NOW YOU'RE FIGHTING AGAINST US!
DZ
...
THEY'RE SO RELIABLE.
GO, PONYGON!
MERU-MERU-ME~!
DM

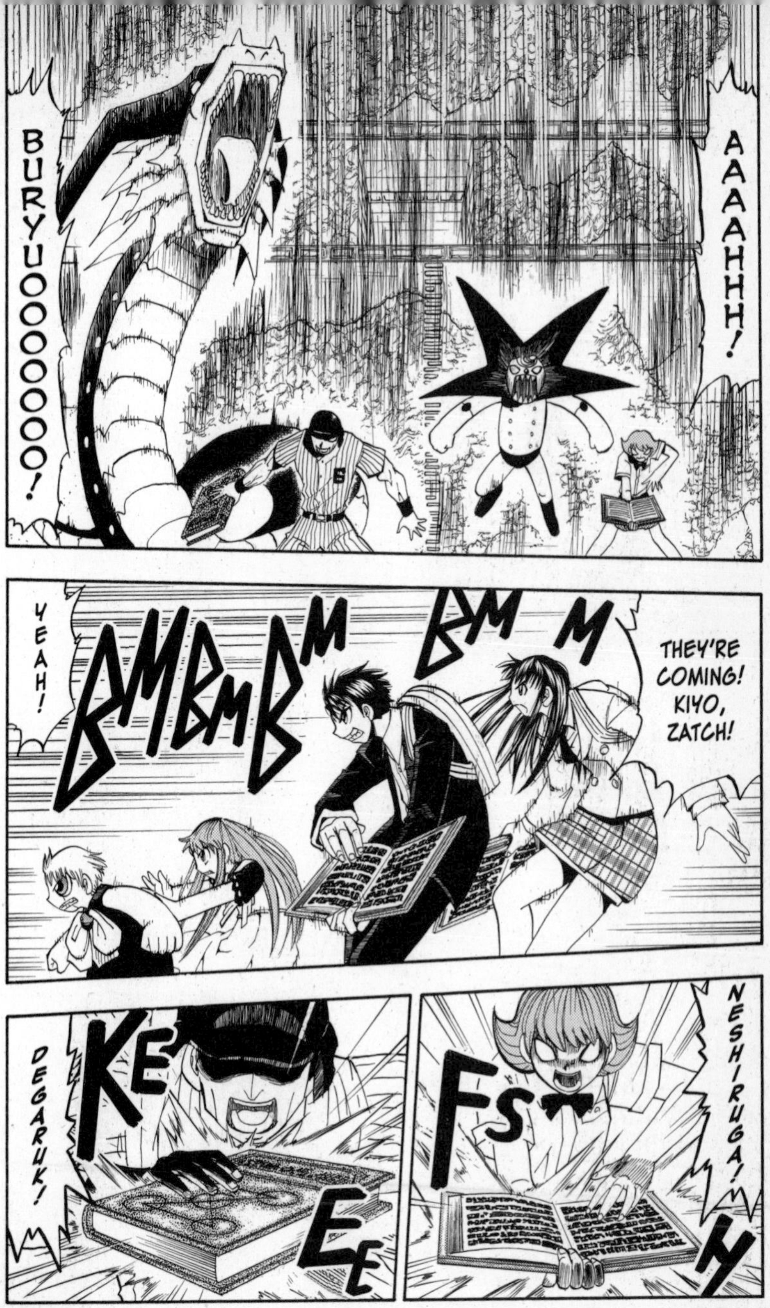
AAAAHHH!
BURYUOOOOOOOO!
THEY'RE COMING! KIYO, ZATCH!
YEAH!
NESHIRUGA!
DEGARUK!

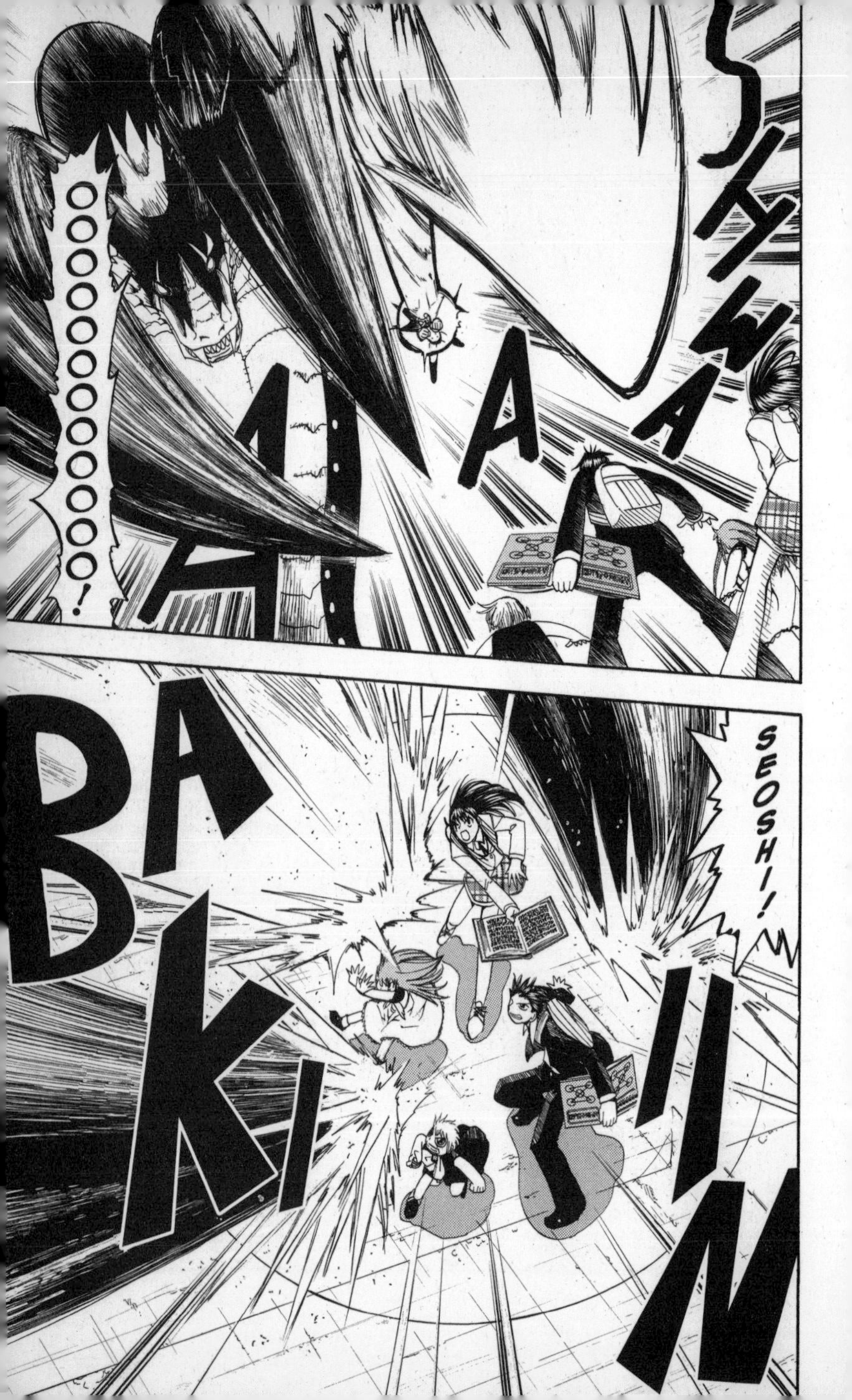
SHWAAA
OOOOOOOOOOOO!
SEOSHI!
BAKIIN

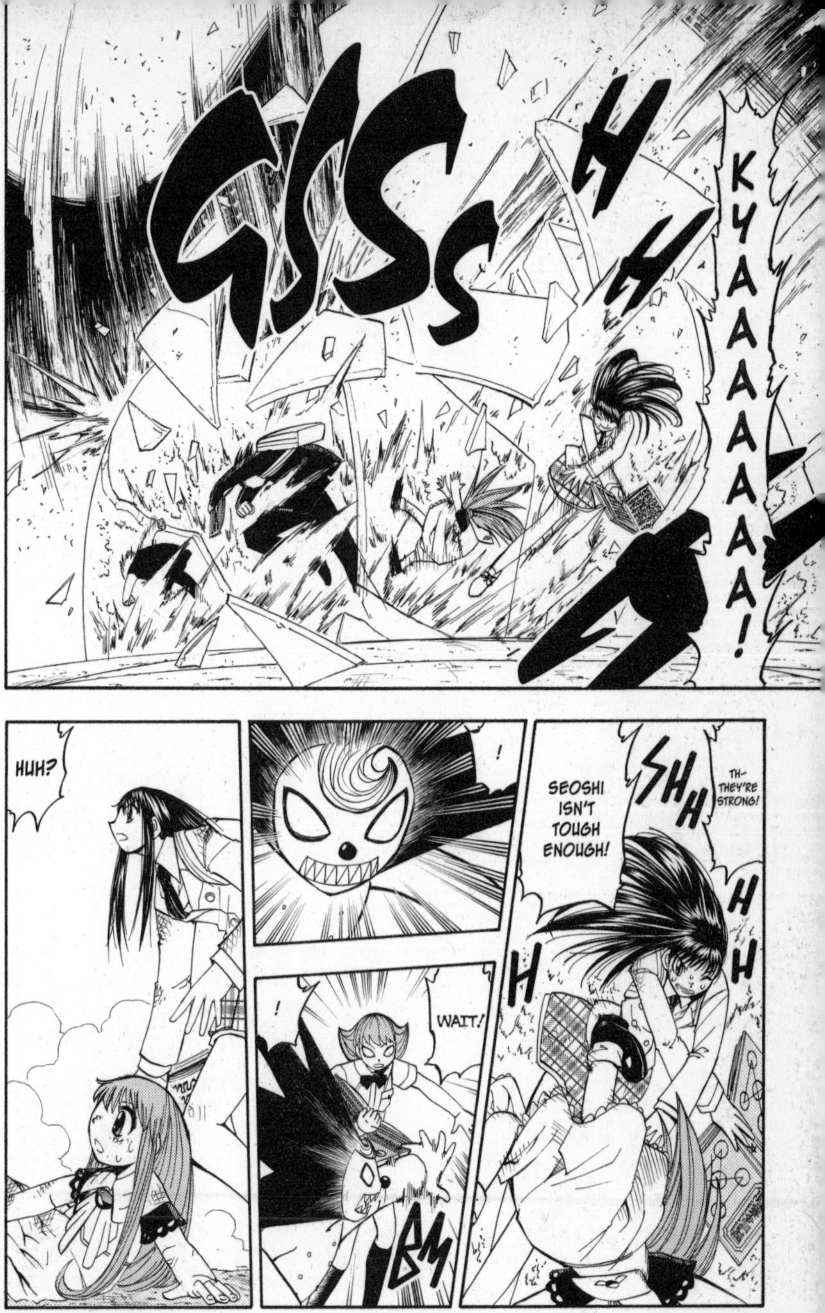
KYAAAAAAAA!
GSSSHH
TH-THEY'RE STRONG!
SHH
SEOSHI ISN'T TOUGH ENOUGH!
HHH
!
!
WAIT!
BM
HUH?

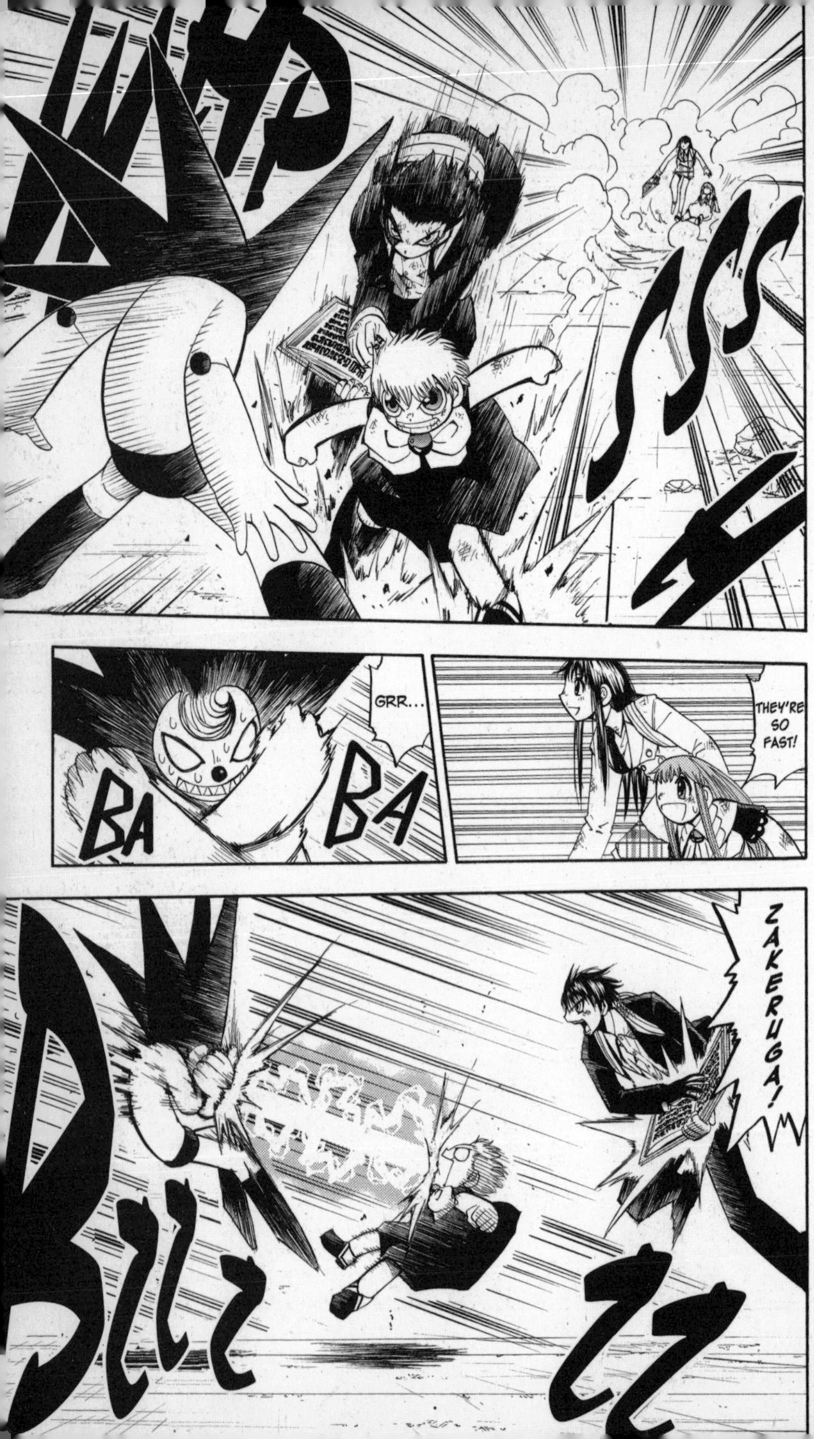
SSSH
WHP
THEY'RE SO FAST!
GRR...
BA
BA
ZAKERUGA!

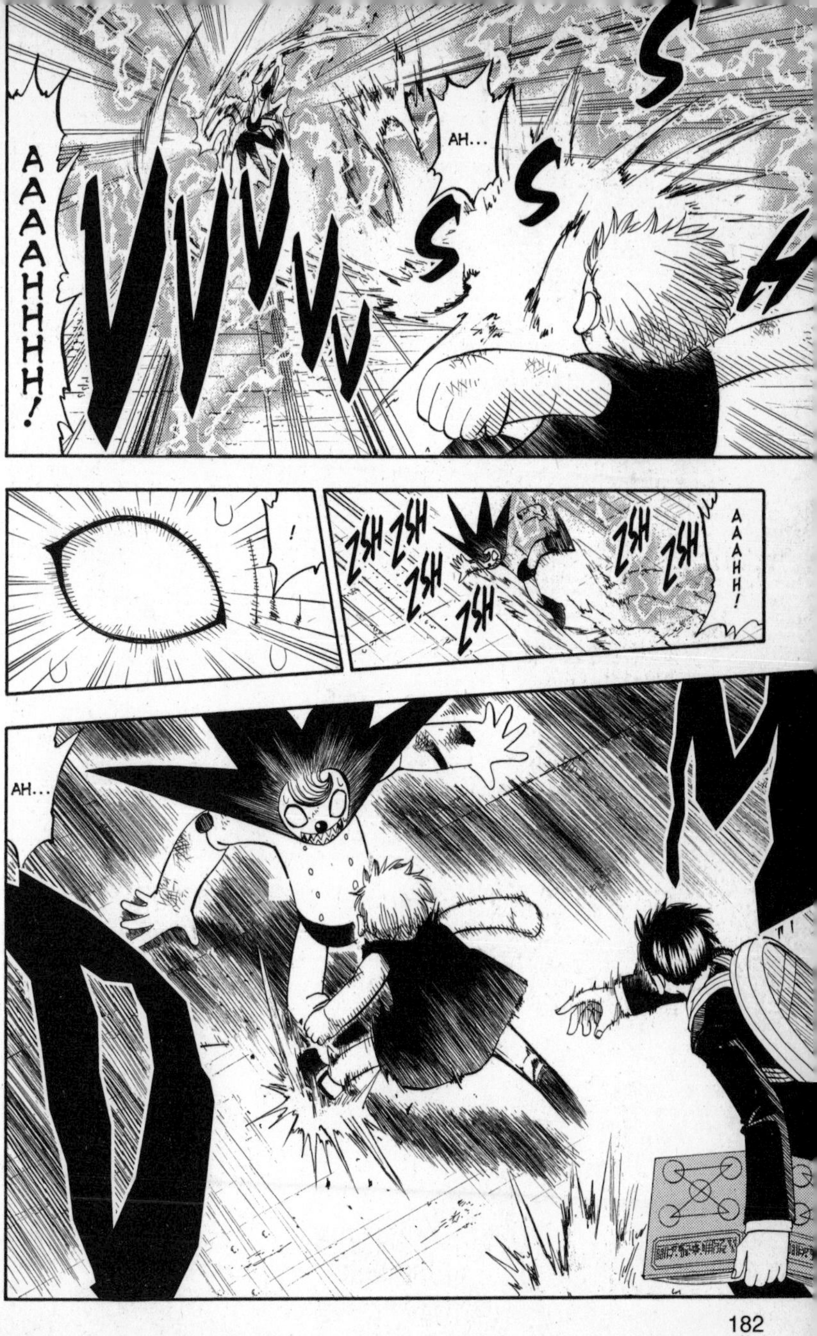
SSSH
AH...
VVVVV
AAAAHHHH!
AAAHH!
ZSH ZSH ZSH ZSH ZSH ZSH
!
M
AH...
D

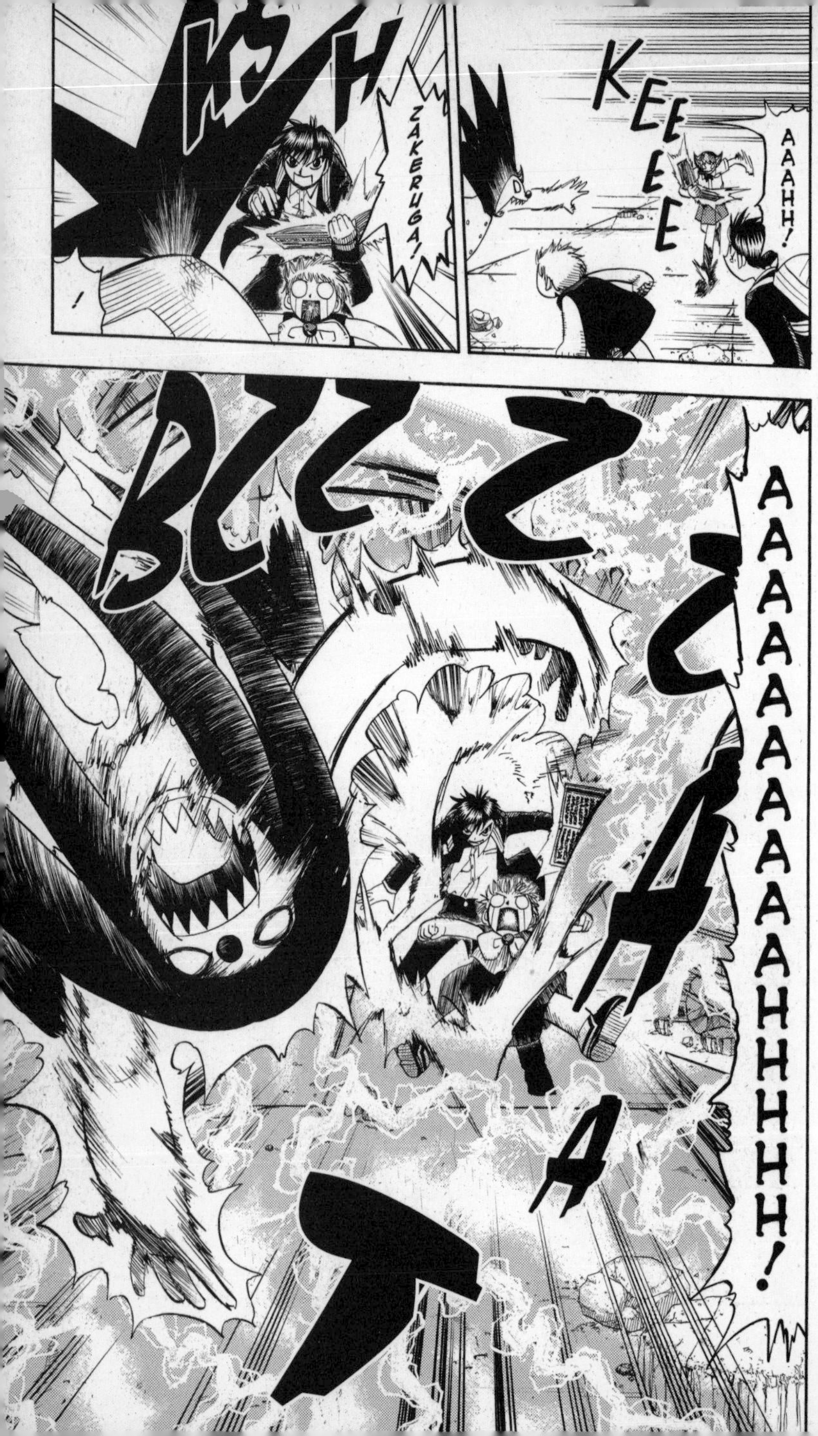
KEEEEE
AAAAHH!
KSH
ZAKERUGA!
!
BZZZZAAT
AAAAAAAAAAAHHHHH!

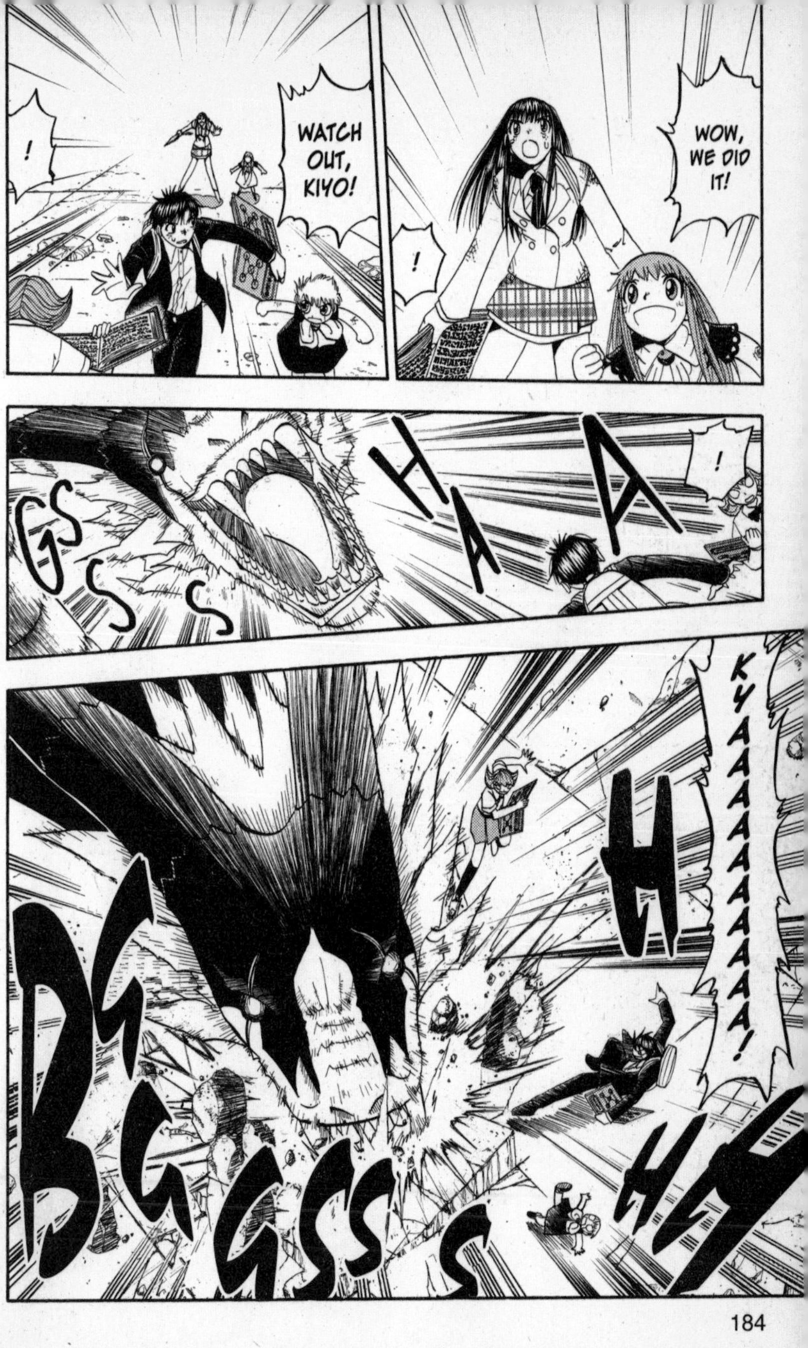
!
WOW, WE DID IT!
WATCH OUT, KIYO!
!
!
HA
GSSS
KYAAAAAAAAAA!
H
BGGSSSHH

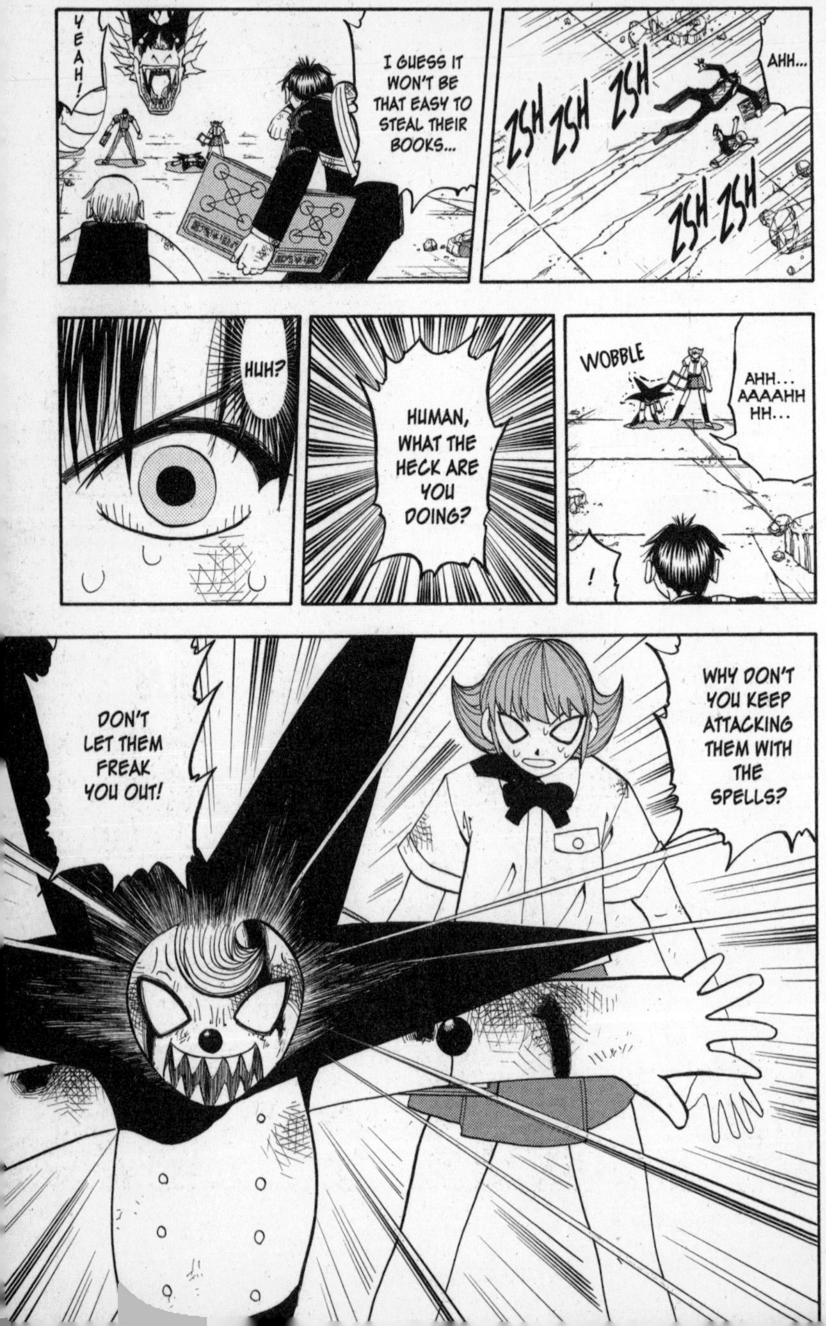
AHH...
ZSH ZSH ZSH
ZSH ZSH
I GUESS IT WON'T BE THAT EASY TO STEAL THEIR BOOKS...
YEAH!
AHH... AAAAAHH HH...
WOBBLE
!
HUMAN, WHAT THE HECK ARE YOU DOING?
HUH?
WHY DON'T YOU KEEP ATTACKING THEM WITH THE SPELLS?
DON'T LET THEM FREAK YOU OUT!

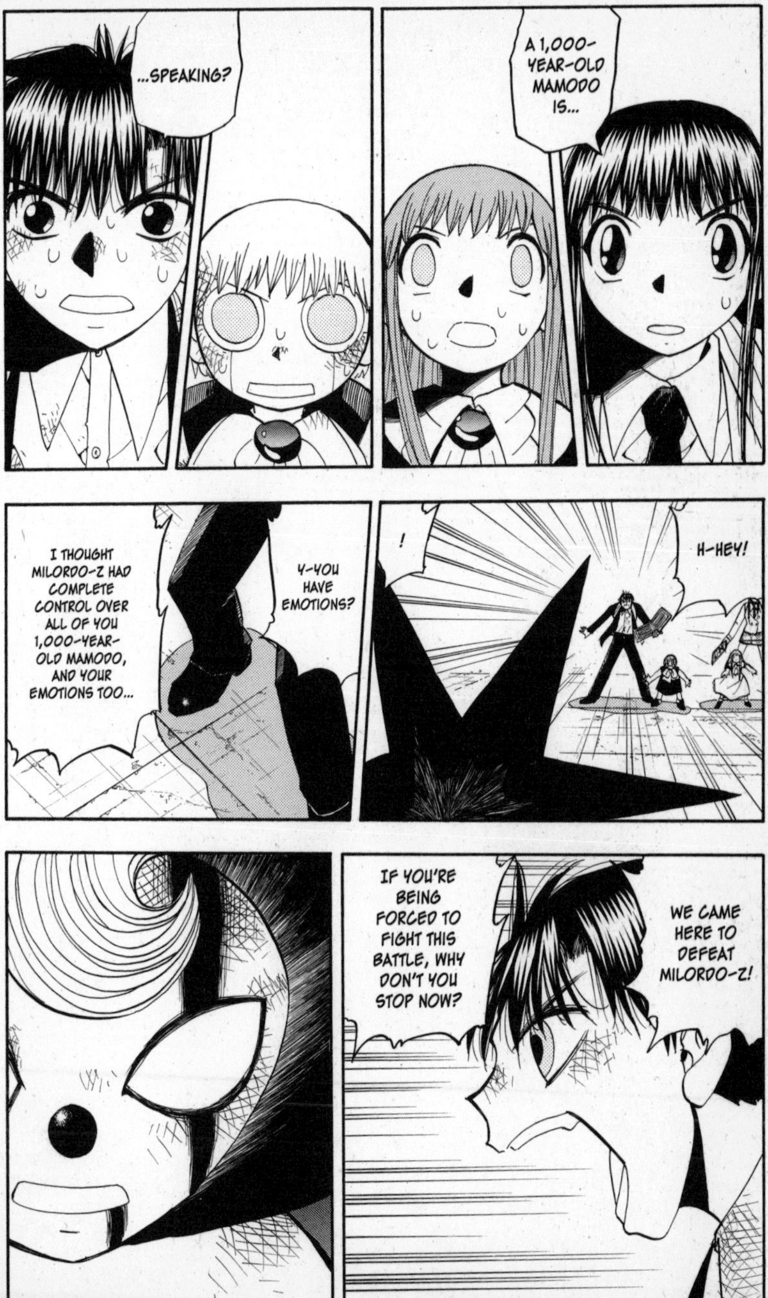
A 1,000-YEAR-OLD MAMODO IS...
...SPEAKING?
H-HEY!
!
Y-YOU HAVE EMOTIONS?
I THOUGHT MILORDO-Z HAD COMPLETE CONTROL OVER ALL OF YOU 1,000-YEAR-OLD MAMODO, AND YOUR EMOTIONS TOO...
WE CAME HERE TO DEFEAT MILORDO-Z!
IF YOU'RE BEING FORCED TO FIGHT THIS BATTLE, WHY DON'T YOU STOP NOW?

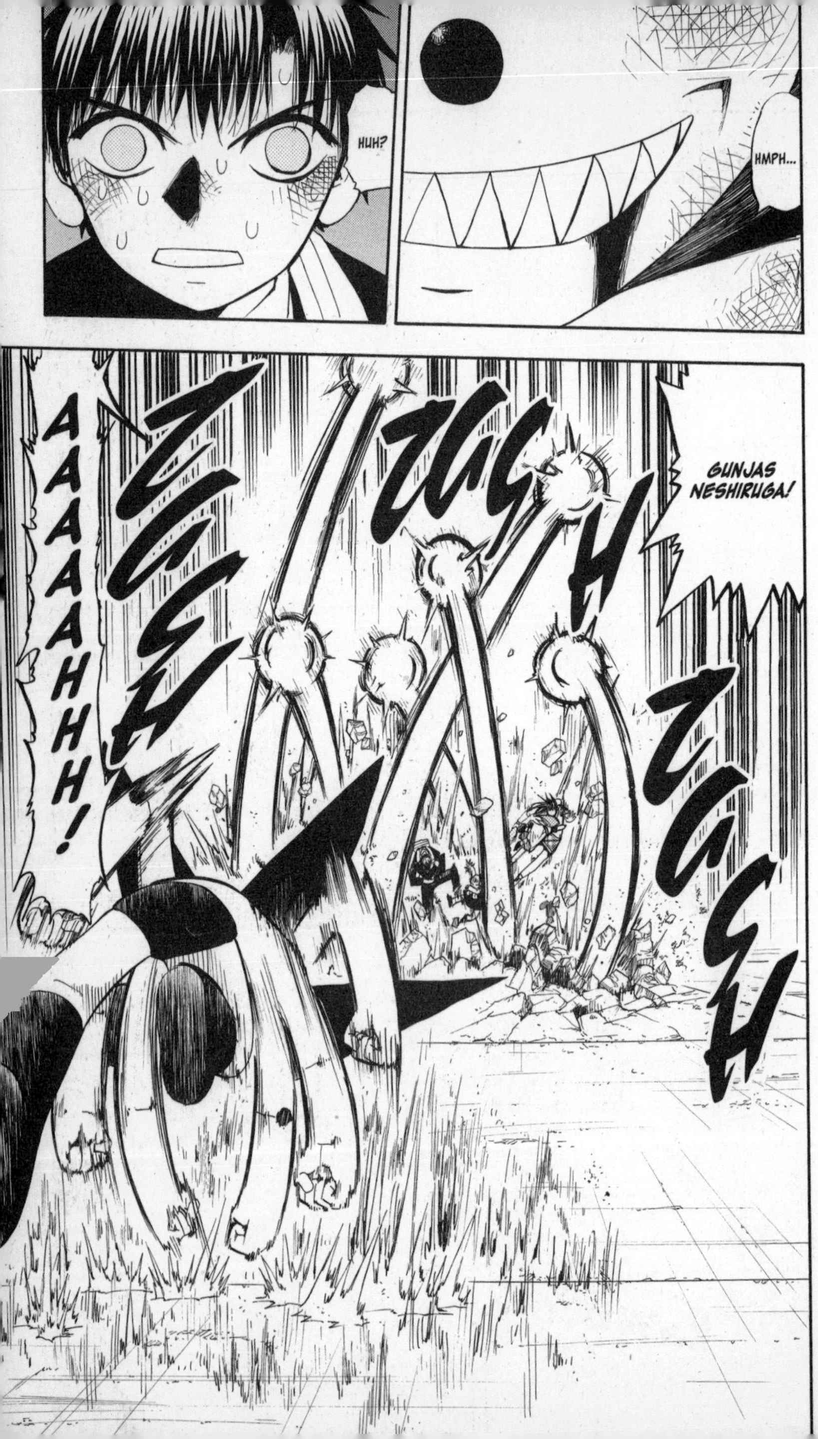
HMPH...
HUH?
GUNJAS NESHIRUGA!
AAAAAHHH!

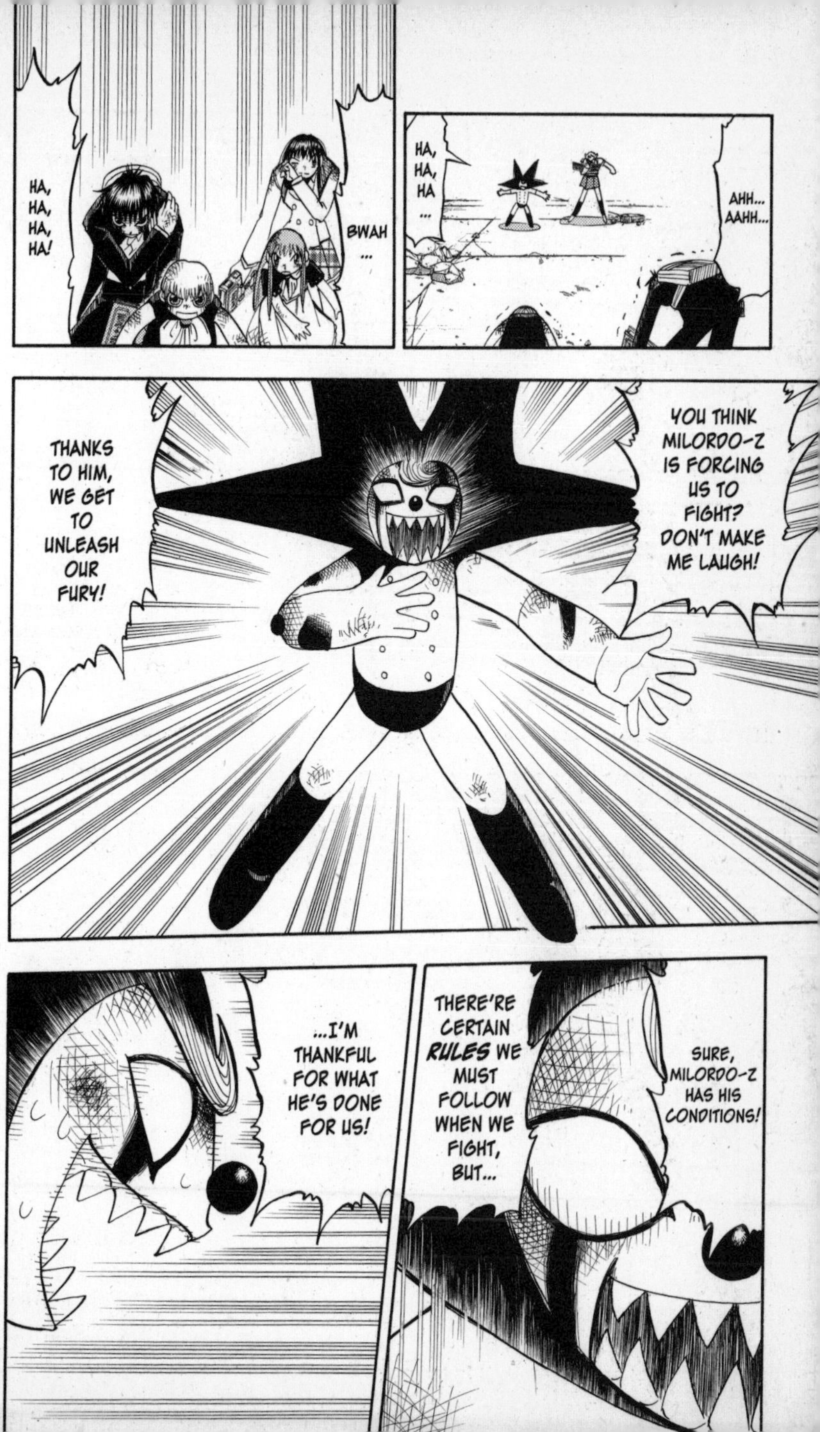
AHH... AAHH...
HA, HA, HA ...
BWAH ...
HA, HA, HA, HA!
YOU THINK MILORDO-Z IS FORCING US TO FIGHT? DON'T MAKE ME LAUGH!
THANKS TO HIM, WE GET TO UNLEASH OUR FURY!
SURE, MILORDO-Z HAS HIS CONDITIONS!
THERE'RE CERTAIN **RULES** WE MUST FOLLOW WHEN WE FIGHT, BUT...
...I'M THANKFUL FOR WHAT HE'S DONE FOR US!

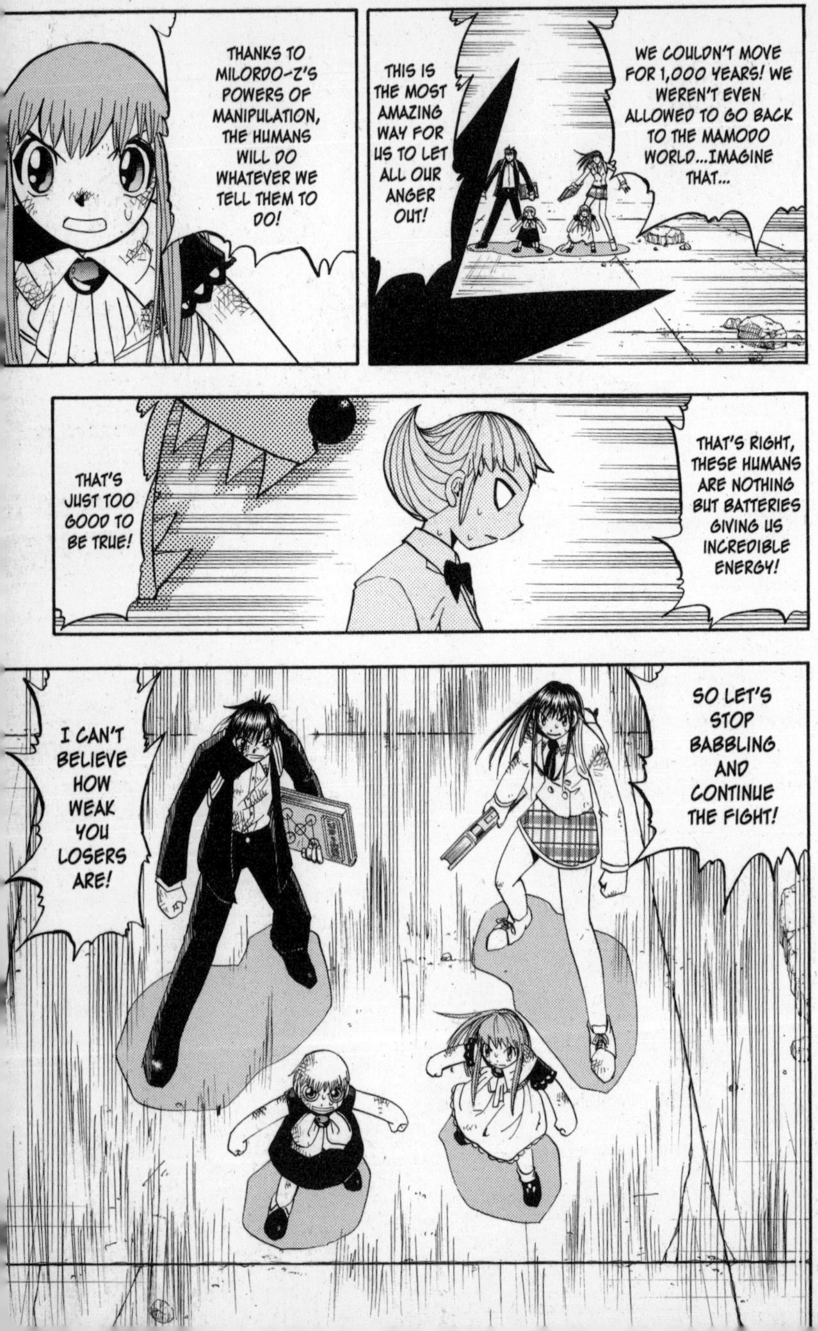
WE COULDN'T MOVE FOR 1,000 YEARS! WE WEREN'T EVEN ALLOWED TO GO BACK TO THE MAMODO WORLD...IMAGINE THAT...
THIS IS THE MOST AMAZING WAY FOR US TO LET ALL OUR ANGER OUT!
THANKS TO MILORDO-Z'S POWERS OF MANIPULATION, THE HUMANS WILL DO WHATEVER WE TELL THEM TO DO!
THAT'S RIGHT, THESE HUMANS ARE NOTHING BUT BATTERIES GIVING US INCREDIBLE ENERGY!
THAT'S JUST TOO GOOD TO BE TRUE!
SO LET'S STOP BABBLING AND CONTINUE THE FIGHT!
I CAN'T BELIEVE HOW WEAK YOU LOSERS ARE!

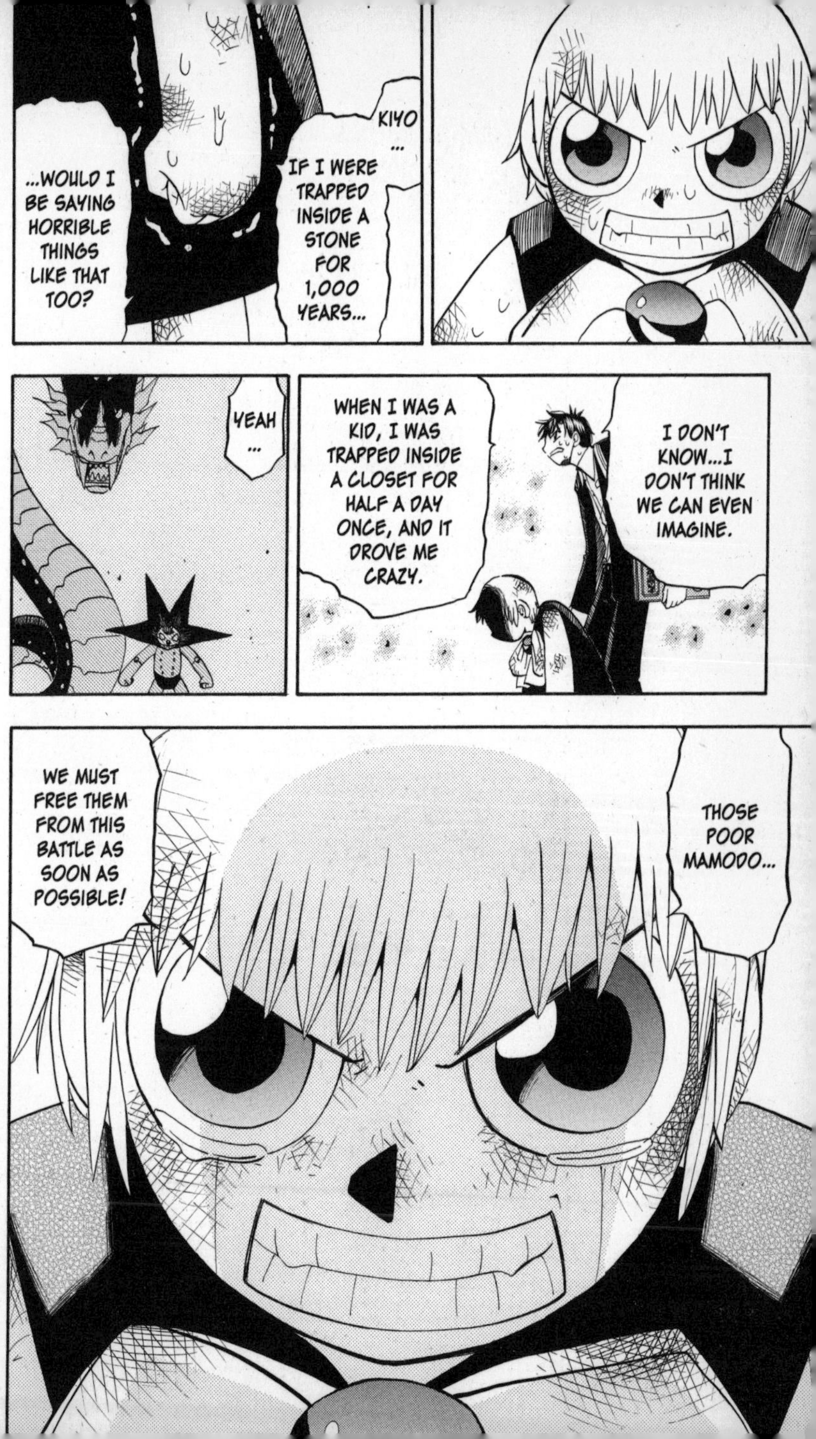
KIYO ...
IF I WERE TRAPPED INSIDE A STONE FOR 1,000 YEARS...
...WOULD I BE SAYING HORRIBLE THINGS LIKE THAT TOO?
I DON'T KNOW...I DON'T THINK WE CAN EVEN IMAGINE.
WHEN I WAS A KID, I WAS TRAPPED INSIDE A CLOSET FOR HALF A DAY ONCE, AND IT DROVE ME CRAZY.
YEAH ...
THOSE POOR MAMODO...
WE MUST FREE THEM FROM THIS BATTLE AS SOON AS POSSIBLE!

TO BE CONTINUED!

ZATCH & SUZY

BY MAKOTO RAIKU

HEY, ZATCH. WHERE'RE YOU GOING?
I'M GOING OUT.
CAN I COME WITH YOU?
NO, YOU HAVE TO STAY HERE.
OKAY, I'LL STAY HERE BY MYSELF.
VWOO
VWOO
HAVE FUN!
CHIRP CHIRP CHIRP
...
WHAT A WEIRD DREAM...

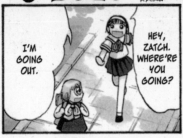

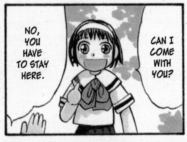

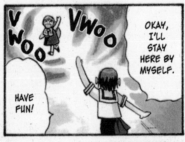

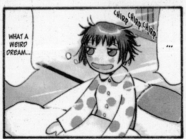

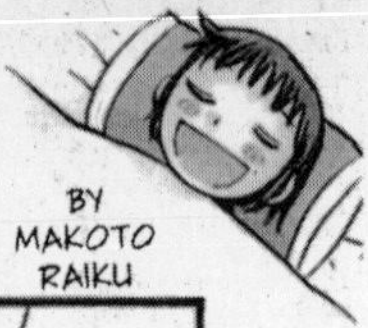

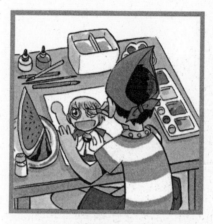

MAKOTO RAIKU

I used to be in the Boy Scouts.
Every summer, I remember how fun
it was to go camping.

…Yeah, I just remember that it was
fun. That's all.

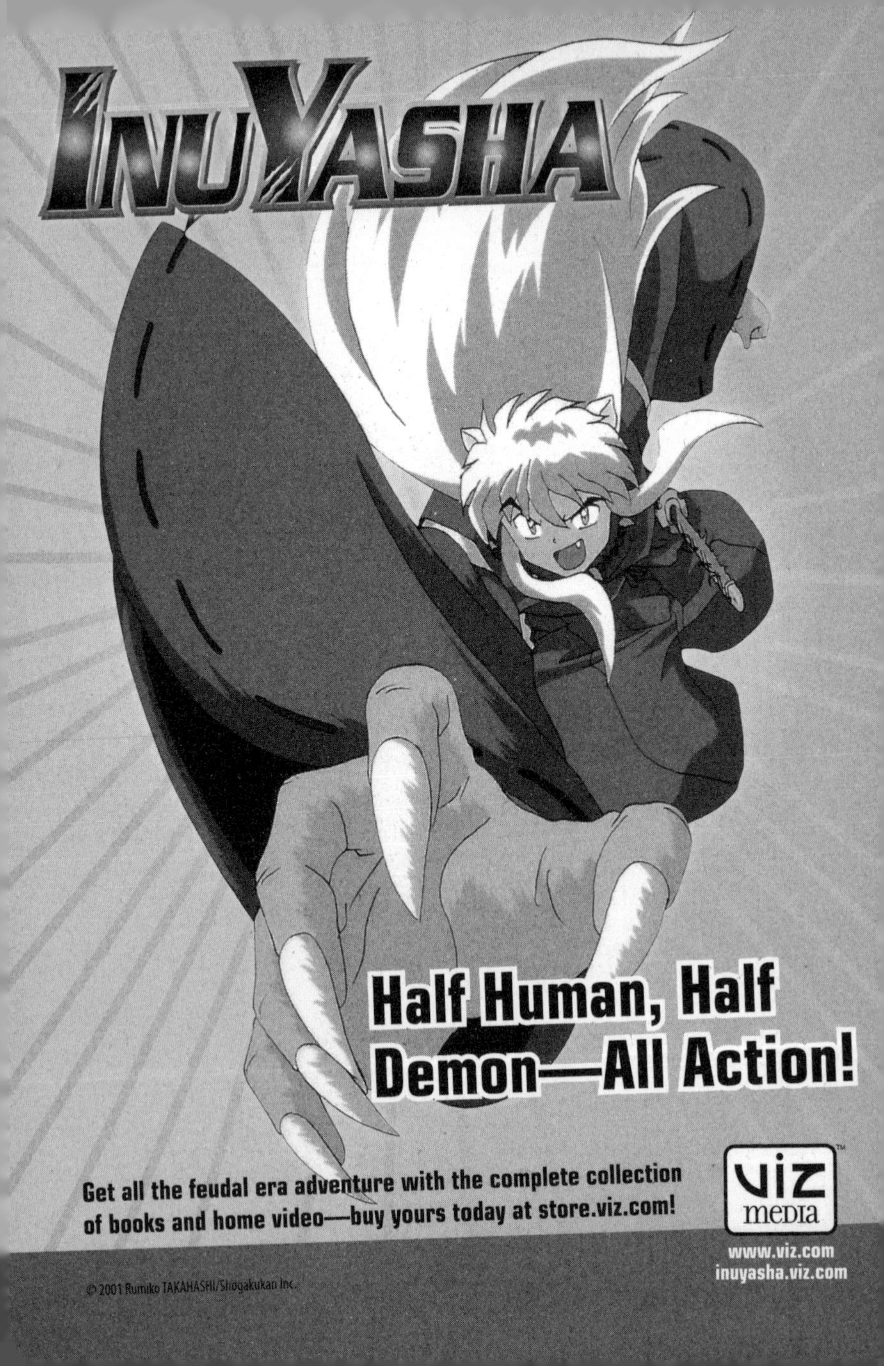
InuYasha
Half Human, Half Demon—All Action!
Get all the feudal era adventure with the complete collection of books and home video—buy yours today at store.viz.com!
viz media
www.viz.com
inuyasha.viz.com
© 2001 Rumiko TAKAHASHI/Shogakukan Inc.

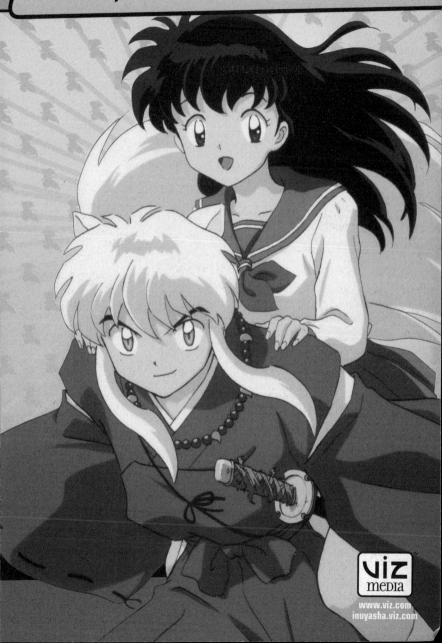

INU YASHA

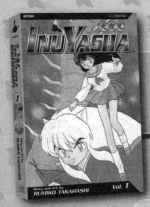

Read the action from the start with the original manga series

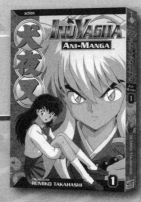

Full color adaptation of the popular TV series

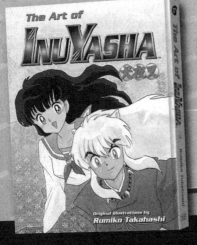

Art book with cel art, paintings, character profiles and more

TV SERIES & MOVIES ON DVD!

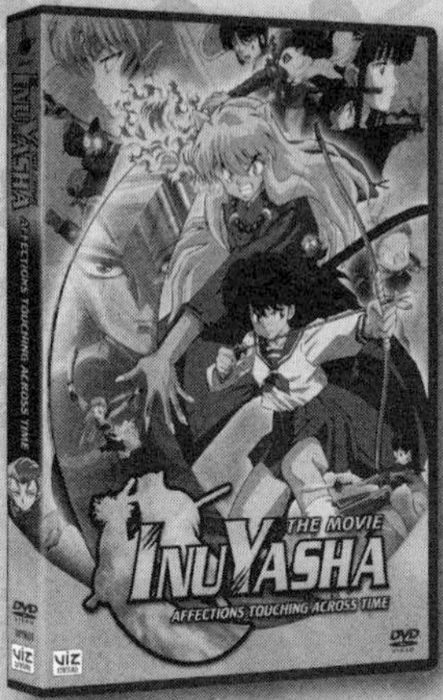
INUYASHA
AFFECTIONS TOUCHING ACROSS TIME
THE MOVIE
INUYASHA
AFFECTIONS TOUCHING ACROSS TIME
DVD
VIZ

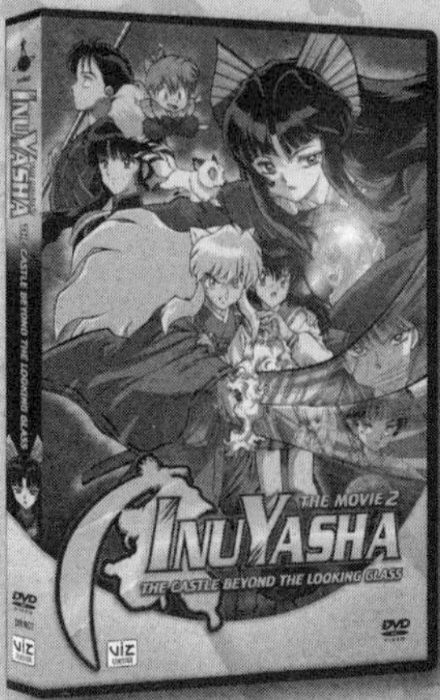
INUYASHA
THE CASTLE BEYOND THE LOOKING GLASS
THE MOVIE 2
INUYASHA
THE CASTLE BEYOND THE LOOKING GLASS
DVD
VIZ

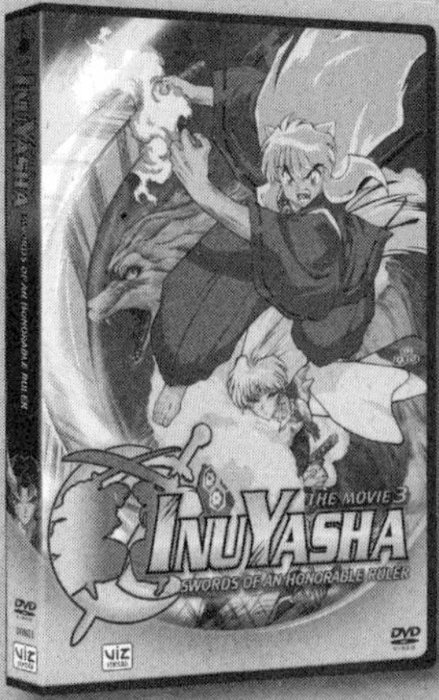
INUYASHA
SWORDS OF AN HONORABLE RULER
THE MOVIE 3
INUYASHA
SWORDS OF AN HONORABLE RULER
DVD
VIZ

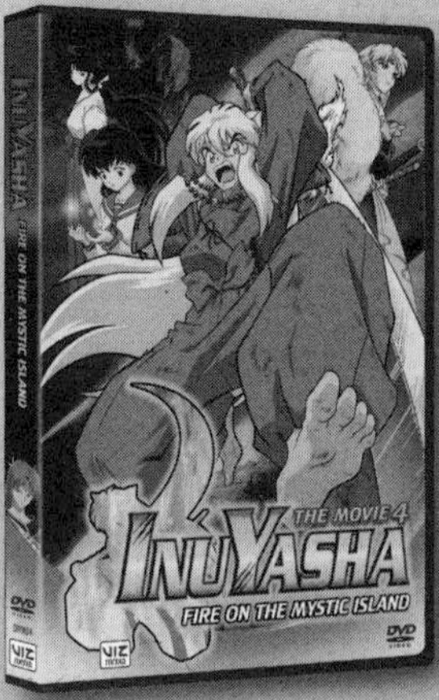
INUYASHA
FIRE ON THE MYSTIC ISLAND
THE MOVIE 4
INUYASHA
FIRE ON THE MYSTIC ISLAND
DVD
VIZ

See more of the action in Inuyasha full-length movies

VIZ MEDIA™

www.viz.com
inuyasha.viz.com

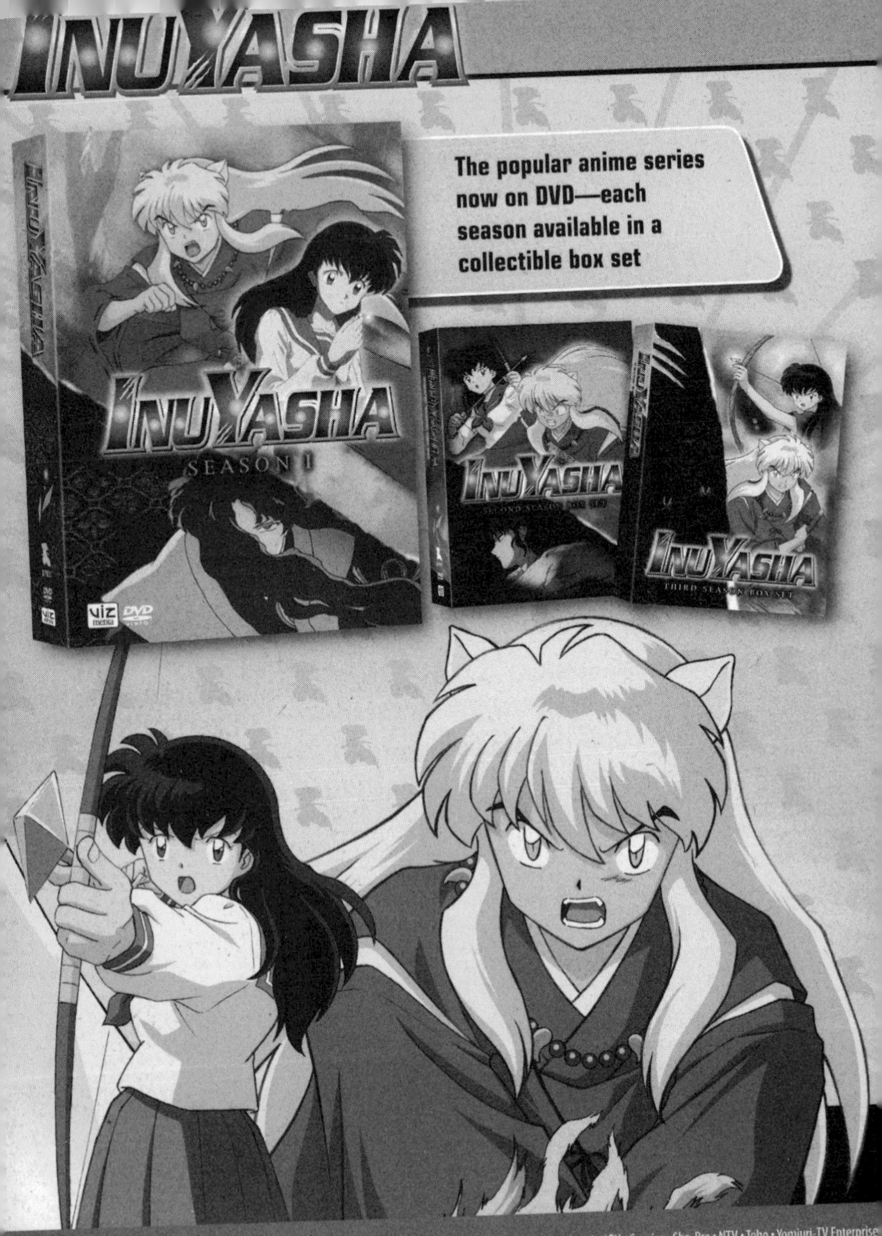
INUYASHA
The popular anime series now on DVD—each season available in a collectible box set
INUYASHA SEASON 1
INUYASHA
INUYASHA THIRD SEASON BOX SET

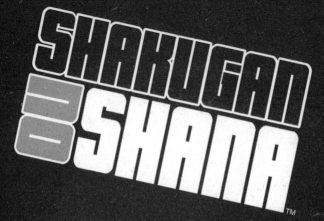
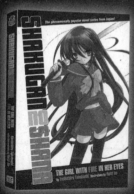
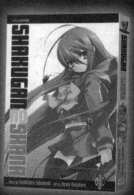

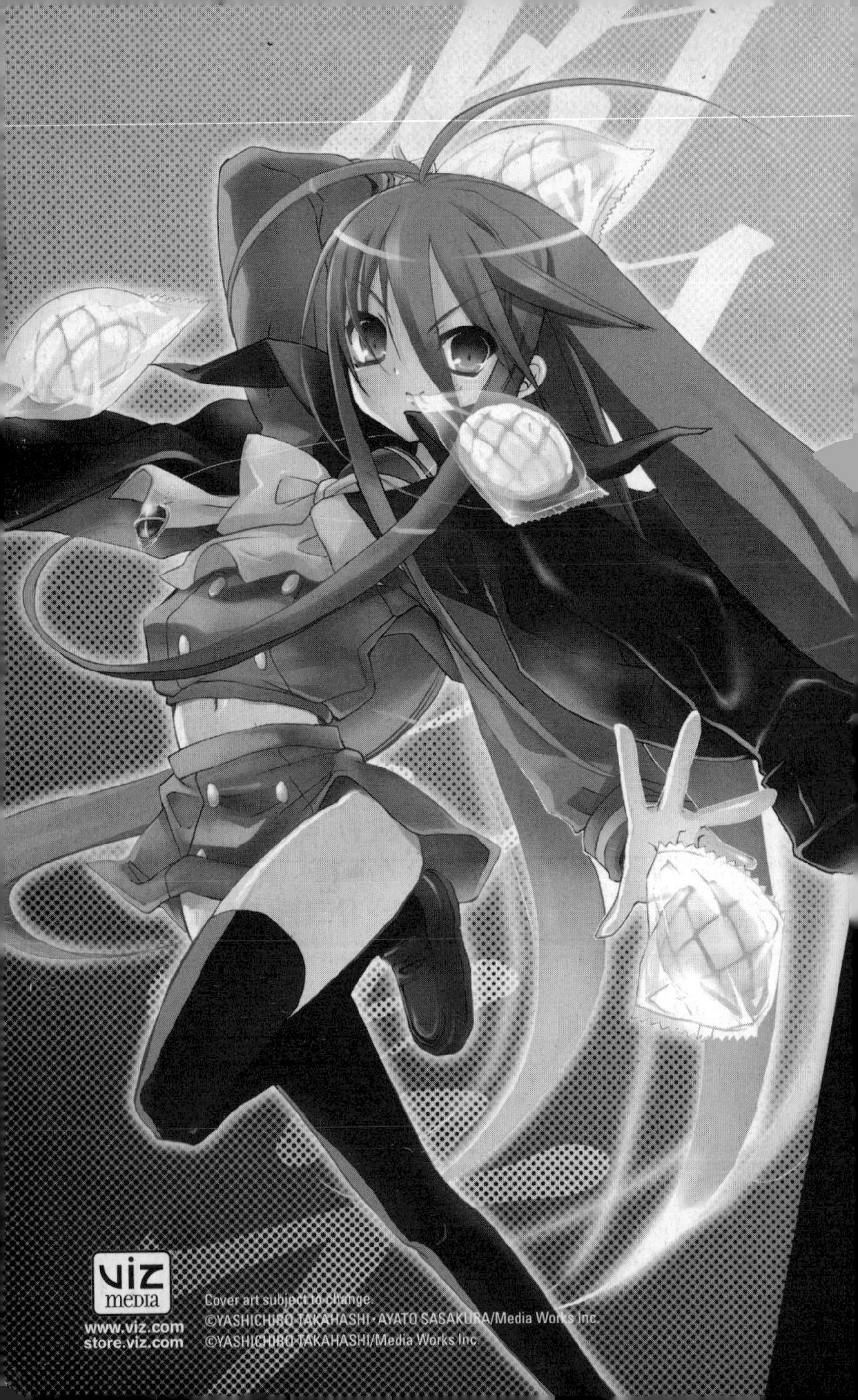

LOVE MA

LET US KNOW WHAT YOU THINK!

OUR MANGA SURVEY IS NOW AVAILABLE ONLINE. PLEASE VISIT: VIZ.COM/MANGASURVEY

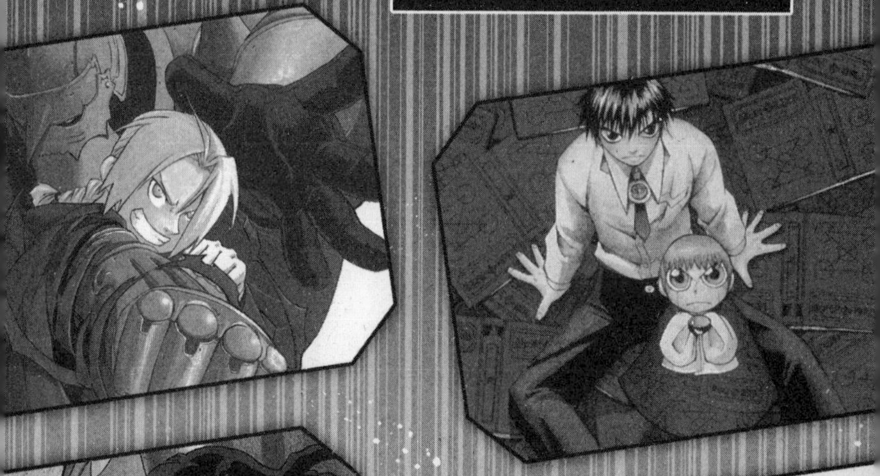

HELP US MAKE THE MANGA YOU LOVE BETTER!

viz media

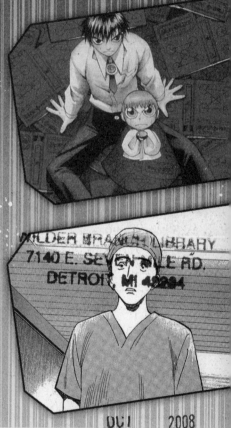